THE OVERLOOK MARTIAL ARTS READER

VOLUME 2

EDITED BY
JOHN DONOHUE

The themes, ideas, and images generated by the martial arts have found their way in myriad forms into the minds of millions of westerners over the past few decades—from the films of Bruce Lee and Jackie Chan to the traditions of Asian meditation and exercise. At the same time that a wide spectrum of people have a passing familiarity with the martial arts, the topic is also one that is subject to wide misunderstanding and misinterpretation. *The Overlook Martial Arts Reader* is an in-depth anthology and analysis of the fundamental writings—both ancient and modern—that demonstrates exactly why the martial arts exert such a powerful hold on the western imagination.

John Donohue, a world-renowned scholar in the Asian martial arts, and a black belt in both Karate and Karatedo, provides penetrating and insightful analysis on the selections he has gathered for this volume—the core writings that martial arts masters regard as the backbone and underpinning of their training and technique. With highlights ranging from Lao Tzu on the Taoist principles of striving for the "natural" to Musashi's classic writings on swordsmanship and discipline in the heat of attack; from Issai Chozan on the pinnacle of martial skill development to modern masters and apprentices such as Dave Lowry, G. Cameron Hurst, Mark Salzman, Herman Kauz, and Nicklaus Suino, *The Overlook Martial Arts Reader* is the one book absolutely every serious student of the martial arts and Asian culture must have.

THE

OVERLOOK
MARTIAL ARTS
READER

VOLUME 2

THE

OVERLOOK
MARTIAL ARTS
READER

VOLUME 2

EDITED BY

JOHN DONOHUE

THE OVERLOOK PRESS
WOODSTOCK & NEW YORK

To Kimura Hiroaki Sensei
He keeps my feet on the path

First published in the United States in 2004 by
The Overlook Press, Peter Mayer Publishers, Inc.
Woodstock & New York

WOODSTOCK:
One Overlook Drive
Woodstock, NY 12498
www.overlookpress.com
[for individual orders, bulk and special sales, contact our Woodstock office]

NEW YORK:
141 Wooster Street
New York, NY 10012

∞ The paper used in this book meets the requirements for paper
permanence as described in the ANSI Z39.48-1992 standard.

Cataloging-in-Publication Data is available from the Library of Congress

Page 351 constitutes an extension of the copyright page.

Book design and type formatting by Bernard Schleifer
Manufactured in the United States of America
FIRST EDITION
ISBN 1-58567-463-X
10 9 8 7 6 5 4 3 2 1

CONTENTS

III Travelers – Analysis and Inspiration   125

ACKNOWLEDGMENTS

MARTIAL ARTISTS CAN BE A TOUGH BUNCH, but I have also found that they are unstintingly generous with their knowledge. The process of putting together selections for this reader has only reinforced my conviction in this regard. Special thanks go to Mike DeMarco, editor in chief of *The Journal of Asian Martial Arts*, Diane Skoss of Koryu Books, and Cynthia Kim of Turtle Press. I should also acknowledge the generosity of John Weatherhill, Inc, and Shambhala Publications. Donald Levine, Cappy Hurst, Dave Jones, and Doug Wile, fine scholars all, were kind enough to let me use their work. And James Grady generously provided his valuable insight into martial fiction.

Perceptive readers may notice the striking absence of some material that should have been included in this work. The one disappointment in this process was in having the Japanese copyright holder of the English language translation of the writings of some important modern artists refuse to grant reprint permission. It is a shame that the generosity of spirit in the arts they focus on has not found a place in their business philosophy.

But all in all, I am grateful to the many different individuals and organizations who were kind enough to grant me their permission to use their work. Thanks go as well to my editor at Overlook, David Mulrooney, who has been supportive and helpful in the process of putting the reader together.

Finally, I must once more express the debt I owe to my wife and children. They not only tolerate the distractions and moods of a writer, they make it possible for me to try in some small way to create the linkage between *bun* and *bu*, the ways of the pen and those of sword.

EDITOR'S INTRODUCTION

L AOZI MAY HAVE COMMENTED on the fact that the way that can be spoken of is not the way, but we in the West seem bent on trying anyway. And, as someone reared in the West who has also been shaped by the martial traditions of the East, I will say in my editorial defense that there is a hoary tradition among the *samurai* regarding *bunbu ryodo*—the unity of learning and martial pursuits. I hope this reader can be accepted in the same spirit.

For purposes of this work, I have focused on arts with an East Asian origin. All areas of the world have martial traditions, but the unique systems of East Asia are worthy of our particular attention. This is because they are so well developed and effective (the product of highly sophisticated and venerable societies) and because their exotic provenance, their blend of philosophy and physicality, has engaged the Western imagination.

Although their origins are in Asia, the popularity of the martial arts has spread worldwide. People respond to their beauty and elegance, as well as the efficacy of techniques. Sophisticated philosophies accompany the arts. And, in a time of increasing alienation, a focus on immediate gratification and a stress on the "new", pursuit of the martial arts is revealed as distinctly contrarian—an activity that celebrates tradition, fidelity to principle, social obligation, self-reflection, and the formative effects of hard won, painstaking advancement.

There are, it seems, no shortage of books on the Asian martial arts. The reasons for this are varied, but there is no doubt that it is a subject worthy of considerable treatment

What sorts of materials could be contained in a work such as this?

When we examine the many martial arts forms in the world, their technical complexity alone would suggest that a considerable body of literature was needed. And certainly many of the early writings on martial arts in the West were often "how-to" manuals breathlessly revealing the fighting secrets of the mysterious East. This tradition continues today, although with considerably improved sophistication and accuracy. But these are not the sorts of texts that prove of interest to the general public. Besides, martial arts manuals are much like written instructions on how to ride a bicycle—they tend to make more sense after you've experienced the thing being written about. So I have not included selections from any of the many fine manuals currently available in this reader.

When we note the rich cultural and intellectual heritage of the Asian environment in which the martial arts were formed, another layer of complexity is added that invites extended interpretation and comment. Certainly the philosophical aspects of these Asian traditions have proven of interest to people in the West. Meditation, intrinsic energy, the pursuit of a Way—all are topics that are familiar to many people today. While Western understanding is conditioned by many factors—after all, few of us are experts in Asian culture and philosophy or fluent in their languages, and people tend to see in the exotic exactly what they want to see anyway—an appreciation of the cultural and ideological dimensions of the martial arts piques peoples' interest.

Part of what this reader is designed to do it to provide a very rudimentary exposure to some of the essential ideas and texts that have influenced the martial arts. There is nothing very mysterious about the selections—Laozi, Konfuzi, Xunzi, Zen commentaries, etc.—but there is nothing like reading the fundamental texts, particularly since their influence echoes throughout the selections that follow.

I have also taken pains to present some of the best and most accessible scholarly work on martial arts. It has been particularly gratifying to see the increase of serious attention being paid to these systems as cultural and historical phenomena, and to benefit from the research and insight of trained professionals who not only have competence in the complex histories and ideologies that have shaped the martial arts, but who are quite often practitioners as well. This creates a fertile synthesis between personal experience and objective analysis. Their activities have helped to lay to rest various myths, inaccuracies and stereotypes and simultaneously deepen our appreciation of the topic.

Millions of people in the contemporary world find these arts intrinsically fascinating, and we have witnessed significant martial arts presence in mass media and entertainment. You don't have to be a student struggling to achieve a black belt or a seeker interested in mysticism to be struck by the sheer excitement and beauty of a martial arts performance, or respond to the drama of the action.

People of all types seem interested in reading about this fascinating topic. I have included chapters that attempt to reflect these varied interests and to show how the martial arts have become incorporated into the human process of defining the self and explaining our world.

Finally, I should note that any compilation of this type has its limitations, generated by circumstance, the availability of material, as well as the igno-rance or prejudice of the editor. This work is no exception. I have been read-ing and writing about the martial arts for almost twenty years, however, and I wanted to be able to present some of what I have found helpful as I have made my way along this path. I would hope that readers who find that the samples I have provided are intriguing will follow up by fully reading the works from which they are excerpted. Without exception, they are worthy of attention.

It is assumed that many readers of this book will be martial artists them-selves with some familiarity with evolution of these arts and their significant features. For those without this background, this initial sketch may help.

China is the point of origin for the first formal East Asian "martial arts." The development of sophisticated weapons and the practice of warfare is a hallmark of complex societies, and the state developed early in China. With it came various systems of weapons use, as well as unarmed forms of fight-ing increasingly associated with non-military segments of society, such as peasants and monks.

There are any number of weapons systems currently practiced in China or by people influenced by the Chinese tradition: a variety of swords, halberds, staffs, and other weapons are used in arts like modern *wushu* or as adjuncts to the various boxing methods that have been popularized in the West as "kung-fu." The flowing forms of *taiji*, rooted in fighting arts but often prac-ticed today for therapeutic purpose, are also popular around the world.

China also spawned several sophisticated philosophical traditions that helped effect the way people trained in martial arts: Daoism, Confucianism, and, after its entry to China from India, Buddhism. One of the most impor-tant features that differentiates Asian martial arts from those of other parts of the world is the degree to which philosophy has permeated theory and practice in East Asia.

The concept of the "Way" as a path of training and cultivation that leads to a type of wisdom or enlightenment infuses many martial arts systems. Daoism focused on achieving a naturalness that would permit the adept to harness the intrinsic energy of nature; Confucianism stressed the role of learning and refinement in cultivating the "superior man," and Buddhism, particularly Zen, focused on experience as a method for attaining enlight-enment. These systems, freely adopted and adapted, served to provide mar-tial arts practice with a rationale that transcended a concern with mere fight-ing skills.

East Asian society is also one focused on the importance of proper rela-tionships between individuals in society. The social universe was conceived of as a hierarchical one, with clear delineations of juniors and seniors, and well-developed ideas regarding etiquette and behavior related to status.

Combined with a Confucian reverence for elders and for teachers, the social norms that evolved are reflected in the outlook and organization of the Asian martial arts.

Both the technology martial technology and ideologies of China spread to its East Asian neighbors. Countries like Korea developed martial systems with unique stylistic differences, but was heavily influenced by China and Japan. Developing a complex society considerably later than China, Japan looked to its massive neighbor to the east for inspiration in many areas. Daoism, Confucianism, and Buddhism were adopted in Japan, and mixed with the unique strains of Shinto, the indigenous religion. At the same time, the Japanese developed fighting systems of their own that used unique weapons and techniques, but incorporated the ideologies that had been infused into mainland martial arts. The warrior class of feudal Japan, the *samurai,* dominated the political and intellectual life of the country for centuries. They refined and promulgated literally hundreds of schools of armed combat using weapons like swords, spears, and staffs. Adjunct arts of unarmed combat were also developed, and have been modified into modern sports and systems of self defense. These arts—such as *judo, karate, sumo,* and *aikido*—are widely known today all over the world

In many ways, the organization, philosophy and symbolism of these modern Japanese arts have shaped the organization and practice of martial arts around the world. The use of colored belts for rank, standardized syllabi for training and grading, the ritualized etiquette, and the modification of technique for safe practice and sport application are things that have been pioneered by the Japanese. In addition, the exposure of Western servicemen to training in these arts during the occupation of Japan after World War II (as well as similar experiences in Korea, learning that country's variant of karate) could be considered one of the prime reasons that these arts became so popular in the West.

These arts were originally introduced to the West as a blend of the practical and the mystical—fearsome fighting techniques that harnessed some occult power. Growing familiarity with the details of the arts revealed them in time to be sophisticated, but not miraculous. Yet the philosophies associated with them also proved attractive at a time when the idea of a "counterculture" was emerging. What the staid warriors of old Japan, pledged to die in the service of their lords, would have thought about this trend is amusing to contemplate, but the fact that these arts involved meditation, alternative philosophies, and the potential for altered states certainly enhanced their cachet in the West.

Finally, the arts have been embraced by entertainment vehicles as well. Books, television, and movies often incorporate martial arts techniques/themes. People like Bruce Lee, Chuck Norris, Jackie Chan, and Jet Li have worked to keep a version of martial arts activity (often highly stylized and shaped by the dictates of entertainment, not tradition) in the public eye. Schools of unarmed systems abound in the West—kung-fu, *quan-fa*, *taiji, karate, taekwondo, judo, jujutsu, aikido*—and it is even possible to find places where individuals train in the use of the samurai sword and other exotic weapons.

So these arts are simultaneously exotic and familiar for us. Products of another time and culture, they have been imported into our lives (with varying interpretations) and serve many purposes. Martial arts can be studied for fitness or self-defense. The competitive can study systems that could take them to the Olympics. Seekers after "something else" can find styles that emphasize mind/body integration and things of the spirit. And, in the process, they all find that the experience is one that can become a valued form, not only of self-expression, but of self-discovery and self definition.

For all these reasons—the intrinsic interest of other cultures and history, the varying uses they can be put to, and the record of human experience they encompass— the martial arts are a fascinating and complex topic. It is hoped that this reader can help in shedding some faint light on the terrain of the martial path and the experiences of those who had traveled along it.

I. PATHWAYS

INTRODUCTION

ONE OF THE CENTRAL ELEMENTS that distinguishes Asian martial systems from physcial activities with a martial inspiration or origin in other world areas is the degree to which the underlying theory of the martial arts has been permeated by philosophical systems. It can be plausibly argued that the rational influence of Western science has largely bled its martial systems of any reliance on philsophical components, while East Asia has proceeded along a somewhat different trajectory. Although all fighters are concerned with efficacy, it cannot be denied that much of the underlying theory of Asian martial systems is expressed in a philosophical idiom, although we find variation in emphasis during different historical periods and in different countries. As we will see in later sections, martial arts have been interpreted and reinterpreted in varying ways to serve the needs of people during different times.

This does not, however, mean that the traditional ideas that serve as justification for or as an explanation of, the martial arts do not bear careful investigation. The basic tenets of these systems can, for instance, be deepened by an of understanding traditional sources and explanations. And these philosophies can in some way explain the enduring hold of the martial arts on the human imagination. For many people today, martial arts practice can be understood as having a significance that that transcend the mere physical. In fact, this is often the attraction of these arts for many people: the integration of the overtly phsyical with the spiritual, creating demanding disciplines that also contain within them something transcendent.

East Asia has spawned a host of complex, sophisticated and beautiful ideological systems that have been intertwined with the practice of the martial arts. What follows are a few excerpts from seminal classic sources in the East Asian tradition designed to provide the reader with an exposure to the cultural/philosophical perspectives that have influenced generations of martial artists. While this introductory session cannot do full justice to these philosophies—mystics and scholars have been attempting to do just that for thousands of years—it can provide the reader with an exposure to some of the thinking and reflection that has been most influential in helping to shape the martial arts. The reader will note many themes orignially explored here that are replicated in selections in Sections II and III, a testament to the enduring influence of these ideas on martial artists in many times and places.

1. LAOZI

Daoism (Taoism) is an ancient Chinese philosophy that has had tremendous influence on Chinese thought, coloring even the ideas of China's other dominant philosophical systems, Confucianism and Buddhism. While little specific detail is known of Laozi, his brief (a little over 5,000 words) yet seminal work has been perpetuated, interpreted, and reinterpreted over the centuries. In many subtle ways, it still engages the folk imagination of the Chinese people today, while its more diffuse and philosophical interpretation has proven of interest to people all over the world.

This "classic" Daoist philosophy emphasizes the need to align oneself with the fundamental order inherent in the universe. It is, in fact, Daoism which has, in part, given martial artists the idea of a "Way" to be followed. While later "religious" Daoism evolved into a popular folk tradition in China that featured many magical elements and an interest in alchemy, in its original form Daoism speaks to the human search for meaning, exhibits a conviction that such meaning and order exists, and stresses that concentrated thought and right action can lead the individual to harmony with the universe. Daoism often stresses the need for flexibility, or "naturalness," and celebrates the inherent strength in things that appear weak. In this aspect, it has been quite easily incorporated into the thought systems of various Chinese hard and soft style boxing systems, and can also be glimpsed in the ideas behind Japanese systems like jujutsu, judo, and aikido.

Therefore the Tao te Ching *(as it is most widely known in the West) serves to establish various enduring themes in Asian philosophy that are of importance to martial arts. Daoist philosophy reflects an awareness of duality: hard and soft, dark and light, male and female are but some of the binary phenomena that make up the natural world. Daoism posits a dynamic nature to the universe, where the need for flexibility and adaptation are paramount. Daoist thought also reveals an emphasis on breath control, a common theme in yogic and some Buddhist systems that has been transmitted to the martial arts as well. Above all, Daoism stresses the seeming contradiction between appearance and reality, and the celebration of the natural way as the path to enlightenment. The confusing and often contradictory statements in the work seek to both highlight the fact that things are not always as they seem and to inculcate a sense of questioning on the part of the reader. The desire to develop a type of instinctual perception, a visceral grasp of reality, is something that would be taken up centuries later in the school of Buddhism that would be popularly known as Zen. In the following selection, the martial artist should note the enduring admonition that weapons are instruments of ill-omen and that the true seeker's emphasis should be one focused on self-cultivation and humility.*

From the *Tao te Ching*

PART I.

Ch. 1.

1. The Tao that can be trodden is not the enduring and unchanging Tao. The name that can be named is not the enduring and unchanging name.

2. (Conceived of as) having no name, it is the Originator of heaven and earth; (conceived of as) having a name, it is the Mother of all things.

3. Always without desire we must be found, If its deep mystery we would sound; But if desire always within us be, Its outer fringe is all that we shall see.

4. Under these two aspects, it is really the same ; but as development takes place, it receives the different names. Together we call them the Mystery. Where the Mystery is the deepest is the gate of all that is subtle and wonderful.

2.

1. All in the world know the beauty of the beautiful, and in doing this they have (the idea of) what ugliness is ; they all know the skill of the skilful, and in doing this they have (the idea of) what the want of skill is.

2. So it is that existence and non-existence give birth the one to (the idea of) the other; that difficulty and ease produce the one (the idea of) the other; that length and shortness fashion out the one the figure of the other; that (the ideas of) height and lowness arise from the contrast of the one with the other; that the musical notes and tones become harmonious through the relation of one with another; and that being before and behind give the idea of one following another.

3. Therefore the sage manages affairs without doing anything, and conveys his instructions without the use of speech.

4. All things spring up, and there is not one which declines to show itself; they grow, and there is no claim made for their ownership ; they go through their processes, and there is no expecta-tion (of a reward for the results). The work is accomplished, and there is no resting in it (as an achievement).
    The work is done, but how no one can see; It is this that makes the power not cease to be.

11. The thirty spokes unite in the one nave; but it is on the empty space (for the axle), that the use of the wheel depends. Clay is fashioned into vessels; but it is on their empty hollowness, that their use depends. The door and windows are cut out (from the walls) to form an apartment; but it is on the empty space (within), that its use depends. Therefore, what has a (positive) existence serves for profitable adaptation, and what has not that for (actual) usefulness.

21. The grandest forms of active force
From Tao come, their only source.
Who can of Tao the nature tell ?
Our sight it flies, our touch as well.
Eluding sight, eluding touch,
The forms of things all in it crouch;
Eluding touch, eluding sight,
There are their semblances, all right.
Profound it is, dark and obscure;
Things' essences all there endure.
Those essences the truth enfold
Of what, when seen, shall then be told.
Now it is so; 'twas so of old.
Its name—what passes not away ;
So, in their beautiful array,
Things form and never know decay. How know I that it is so with all the beauties of existing things ? By this (nature of the Tao).

31.

1. Now arms, however beautiful, are instruments of evil omen, hateful, it may be said, to all creatures. Therefore they who have the Tao do not like to employ them.

2. The superior man ordinarily considers the left hand the most honourable place, but in time of war the right hand. Those sharp weapons are instru-ments of evil omen, and not the instruments of the superior man;— he uses them only on the compulsion of necessity. Calm and repose are what he prizes ; victory (by force of arms) is to him undesirable. To consider this desirable would be to delight in the slaughter of men ; and he who delights in the slaughter of men cannot get his will in the kingdom.

3. On occasions of festivity to be on the left hand is the prized position; on occasions of mourning, the right hand. The second in command of the army has his place on the left; the general commanding in chief has his on the right;—his place, that is, is assigned to him as in the rites of mourning. He who has killed multitudes of men should weep for them with the bitterest grief; and the victor in battle has his place (rightly) according to those rites.

34.

1. All-pervading is the Great Tao! It may be found on the left hand and on the right.

2. All things depend on it for their production, which it gives to them, not one refusing obedience to it. When its work is accomplished, it does not claim the name of having done it. It clothes all things as with a garment, and makes no assumption of being their lord;—it may be named in the smallest things. All things return (to their root and disappear), and do not know that it is it which presides over their doing so;—it may be named in the greatest things.

3. Hence the sage is able (in the same way) to accomplish his great achievements. It is through his not making himself great that he can accomplish them.

48.

1. He who devotes himself to learning (seeks) from day to day to increase (his knowledge); he who devotes himself to the Tao (seeks) from day to day to diminish (his doing).

2. He diminishes it and again diminishes it, till he arrives at doing nothing (on purpose). Having arrived at this point of non-action, there is nothing which he does not do.

3. He who gets as his own all under heaven does so by giving himself no trouble (with that end). If one take trouble (with that end), he is not equal to getting as his own all under heaven.

53.

1. If I were suddenly to become known, and (put into a position to) conduct (a government) according to the Great Tao, what I should be most afraid of would be a boastful display.

2. The great Tao (or way) is very level and easy; but people love the by-ways.

3. Their court(-yards and buildings) shall be well kept, but their fields shall be ill-cultivated, and their granaries very empty. They shall wear elegant and ornamented robes, carry a sharp sword at their girdle, pamper themselves in eating and drinking, and have a superabundance of property and wealth;—such (princes) may be called robbers and boasters. This is contrary to the Tao surely!

55.

1. He who has in himself abundantly the attributes (of the Tao) is like an infant. Poisonous insects will not sting him; fierce beasts will not seize him; birds of prey will not strike him.

2. (The infant's) bones are weak and its sinews soft, but yet its grasp is firm. It knows not yet the union of male and female, and yet its virile member may be excited;—showing the perfection of its physical essence. All day long it will cry without its throat becoming hoarse;—showing the harmony (in its constitution).

3. To him by whom this harmony is known, (The secret of) the unchanging (Tao) is shown, And in the knowledge wisdom finds its throne. All life-increasing arts to evil turn; Where the mind makes the vital breath to burn, (False) is the strength, (and o'er it we should mourn.)

4. When things have become strong, they (then) become old, which may be said to be contrary to the Tao. Whatever is contrary to the Tao soon ends.

76.

1. Man at his birth is supple and weak; at his death, firm and strong. (So it is with) all things. Trees and plants, in their early growth, are soft and brittle ; at their death, dry and withered.

2. Thus it is that firmness and strength are the concomitants of death; softness and weakness, the concomitants of life.

3. Hence he who (relies on) the strength of his forces does not conquer; and a tree which is strong will fill the out-stretched arms, (and thereby invites the feller.)

4. Therefore the place of what is firm and strong is below, and that of what is soft and weak is above.

78.

1. There is nothing in the world more soft and weak than water, and yet for attacking things that are firm and strong there is nothing that can take precedence of it;—for there is nothing {so effectual) for which it can be changed.

2. Every one in the world knows that the soft overcomes the hard, and the weak the strong, but no one is able to carry it out in practice.

3. Therefore a sage has said,
"He who accepts his state's reproach, Is hailed therefore its altars' lord; To him who bears men's direful woes They all the name of King accord."

4. Words that are strictly true seem to be paradoxical.

2. KONGFUZI

Confucius (K'ung-fu-tzu or Kongfuzi) is universally recognized as the Chinese *philosopher. He lived at about the same time as Laozi. His family name was Kong and he was honored with the title Grand Master Kong (Kongfuzi), which is where the Western name Confucius came from. His life, which stretched from 551-479 B.C., was distinguished not just by his ideas, but by his devotion to teaching.*

Confucian philosophy has decisively shaped the social and philosophical underpinnings of all East Asian civilizations. It is, in fact, difficult to think of the social systems and ideologies of East Asia without reference to Confucian principles. Confucian scholarship influenced the administrative mechanism of Chinese dynasties until the modern era—a unique experience where philosophers and scholars played an integral part in the political life of empire. Confucian principles were the organizing template used in Feudal Japan as well.

The commentary on Confucius is vast, but the central texts attributed to him are few. His teachings are often brief and epigrammatic. Although a modern reader may find this thinker somewhat pedantic (and obviously dated in terms of the male chauvinism he exhibits), there are broad themes in Confucian thought that are worth our attention, particularly as we seek to understand the martial arts.

The selections below underscore a few central Confucian principles: the emphasis on personal refinement and learning, individual rectitude as the basis for all social systems, and a stress on the fact that human beings exist within a social nexus, not as isolated actors, and should therefore demonstrate respect for others. While Confucius' understanding of the human world was one that was highly stratified and hierarchical, a product of his age, he is at base a thinker intent on explicating a system for orderly behavior and stressing the important role of self-control and self-development in society. While the ideal Confucian is the scholar-official, not the warrior, the traditional Confucian precepts that value self-discipline and cultivation in the service of something larger than the self are concepts that should be very familiar to martial artists.

From THE GREAT LEARNING

1. What the *Great Learning* teaches is—to illustrate illustrious virtue; to renovate the people; and to rest in the highest excellence.

2. The point where to rest being known, the object of pursuit is then determined; and that being determined, a calm unperturbedness maybe attained to. To that calmness there will succeed a tranquil repose. In that repose there may be careful deliberation and that deliberation will be followed by the attainment of the desired end.

3. Things have their root and their branches. Affairs have their end and their beginning. To know what is first and what is last will lead near to what is taught in the *Great Learning*.

4. The ancients who wished to illustrate illustrious virtue throughout the kingdom, first ordered well their own States. Wishing to order well their States, they first regulated their families. Wishing to regulate their families, they first cultivated their persons, they rectified their hearts. Wishing to rectify their hearts, they first sought to be sincere in their thoughts. Wishing to be sincere in their thoughts, they first extended to the utmost their knowledge. Such extensions of knowledge lay in the investigation of things.

5. Things being investigated, knowledge became complete. Their knowledge being complete, their thoughts were sincere. Their thoughts being sincere, their hearts were then rectified. Their hearts being rectified, their persons were cultivated. Their persons being cultivated, their families were regulated. Their families being regulated, their States were rightly governed. Their States being rightly governed, the whole kingdom was made tranquil and happy.

6. From the Son of Heaven down to the mass of people, all must consider the cultivation of the person the root of everything besides.

7. It cannot be, when the root is neglected, that what should spring from it will be well ordered. It never has been the case that what was of great importance has been slightly cared for, and at the same time, that what was of slight importance has been greatly cared for.

From THE DOCTRINE OF THE MEAN

Chapter I.

1. What Heaven has conferred is called the *Nature*; and accordance with this nature is called the *Path of duty*; the regulation of this path is called *Instruction*.

2. The path may not be left for an instant. If it could be left, it would not be the path. On this account, the superior man does not wait till he sees things to be cautious, nor till he hears things to be apprehensive.

3. There is nothing more visible than what is secret, and nothing more manifest than what is minute. Therefore the superior man is watchful over himself, when he is alone.

4. While there are no stirrings of pleasure, anger, sorrow, or joy, the mind may be said to be in a state of *Equilibrium*. When these feelings have not been stirred, and they act in their due degree, there ensues what may be called the state of *Harmony*. This *Equilibrium* is the great root from which grow all the human actings in the world, and this *Harmony* is the universal path which they all should pursue.

5. Let the states of equilibrium and harmony exist in perfection, and a happy order will prevail throughout heaven and earth, and all things will be nourished and flourish.

Chapter XIV.
6. The Master said, "In archery we have something like the way of the superior man. When the archer misses the center of the target, he turns round and seeks for the cause of failure in himself."

Chapter XX.
8. The duties of universal obligation are five, and the virtues wherewith they are practiced are three. The duties are those between sovereign and minister, between father and son, between husband and wife, between elder brother and younger, and those belonging to the intercourse of friends. Those five are the duties of universal obligation. Knowledge, magnanimity and energy, these three are the virtues universally binding. And the means by which they carry the duties into practice is singleness.

3. XUNZI

Xunzi (Hsun Tzu in the selection, also rendered Sun tzu in some translations) is often characterized as a naturalistic Confucian. Unlike Mencius, another prominent Confucian who believed that human nature was essentially good, Xunzi believed that the fundamentally evil aspect of human nature could best be controlled and changed through rules and law. He was active during the years that stretched from 298 to 238 B.C. While stressing the classic Confucian values, Xunzi was deeply interested in the application of this philosophy to the practical needs of governance, which included the use of force. Indeed, his works show a clever strategic thinker who has thought long and hard on the effective use of military force and who has specific ideas about the justification for and implications of military action.

China, possessed of a long and complex history that exhibits brilliant cultural achievements, has also not escaped from the effects of the darker side of human nature. As such, its history is also one of armies and battle, atrocity, and of the violent overthrow of dynasties. As a result, we see a paradoxical situation in China: it has served as an important source of martial arts systems while simultaneously echoing Laozi's caution on the use of military force. There is, after all, a Chinese saying to the effect that in the same way you don't waste good iron to make a nail, you don't waste a good man by making him a soldier.

But the practical realities of Chinese social and political life were such that thinkers such as Xunzi were impelled to think about how best to attempt to harness military action and serve a greater good. The section below demonstrates the sophistication of Asian strategic thinking as it relates to conflict. Xunzi was, in fact, the pre-eminent military theorist in China and Japan until the modern era. A careful reading can see how aspects of his strategy influenced the thinking modern strategists such as Mao Zedong and Ho Chi Minh, demonstrating the continual relevance of his insights.

DEBATING MILITARY AFFAIRS

The lord of Lin-wu and Hsun Tzu were debating military affairs in the presence of King Hsiao-ch'eng of Chao. "May I ask what are the most essential points to be observed in taking up arms?" inquired the king.

The lord of Lin-wu replied, "Above, utilize the most season-able times of heaven; below, take advantage of the most profitable aspects of the earth. Observe the movements of your enemy, set out after he does, but get there before him. This is the essential point in the art of using arms!"

"Not so!" objected Hsun Tzu. "From what I have heard of the way of the ancients, the basis of all aggressive warfare and military undertaking lies in the unification of the people. If the bow and arrow are not properly adjusted, even the famous archer Yi could not hit the mark. If the six horses of the team are not properly trained, even the famous carriage driver Tsao-fu could not go far. If the officers and people are not devoted to their leaders, even the sages T'ang or Wu could not win victory. The one who is good at winning the support of his people is the one who will be good at using arms. Therefore what is really essential in military undertakings is to be good at winning the support of the people."

"I disagree," said the lord of Lin-wu. "In using arms, one should place the highest value upon advantageous circumstances, and should move by stealth and deception. He who is good at using arms moves suddenly and secretly, and no one knows from whence he comes. Sun Wu and Wu Chi employed this method and there was no one in the world who could stand up against them. Why is it necessary to win the support of the people?"

"You do not understand," said Hsun Tzu. "What I am speaking about are the soldiers of a benevolent man, the intentions of a true king. You speak of the value of plots and advantageous circumstances, of moving by sudden attack and stealth—but these are matters appropriate only to one of the feudal lords. Against the soldiers of a benevolent man, deceptions are of no use; they are effective only against a ruler who is rash and arrogant, whose people are worn, out; they are effective only against a state in which the ruler and his subjects, superiors and inferiors, are tom apart and at odds. Therefore a tyrant like Chieh may practice deception upon another Chieh, and, depending upon how cleverly he proceeds, may happily achieve a certain success. But for a Cbieh to try to practice deception against a sage like Yao would be like trying to break a rock by throwing eggs at it, or trying to stir boiling water with your bare finger. He will be like a man consumed by fire or drowned in water.

"As for the relations between superior and inferior under the rule of a benevolent man, the various generals will be of one mind, and the three armies of the state will work together Subjects will serve their lord and inferiors will serve their superiors like sons serving a father or younger brothers serving an elder brother. They will be like hands held up to guard the face and eyes, arms clasped to protect the breast and belly. Try to attack such a ruler by deception and you will see the hands fly up in warning and then dart forward in attack.

"Moreover, if the benevolent man rules a state which is ten *li* square, the people for a hundred *li* around will act as listeners for him; if he rules a state of a hundred *li*, a thousand *li* will listen for him; and if be rules a state of a thousand *li*, the whole region within the four seas will listen for him. He will receive clear intelligence and warning, and the whole region will draw about him in unity. Thus the soldiers of a benevolent man, when gathered together, will form themselves into companies; when spread out, they will form in ranks. In striking power they are like the long blade of the famous sword Mu-yeh; what comes beneath it will be cut off. In keenness they are like the sharp point of Mu-yeh; what falls upon it will be pierced through. Drawn up in square encampment and surrounded by sentries, they will be like a solid rock; what butts against it will be smashed, crushed, broken, defeated, and forced to fall back."

"When rulers of evil and war-loving states carry out their sly expeditions, who can they get to accompany them? Obviously they must employ their own people. But if their own people favor the benevolent ruler, look up to him as to a father or mother, and rejoice in him as in the fragrance of iris or orchid, and on the contrary regard their own superiors as so many wielders of branding irons and tattooing knives, as their foes and enemies, then, human nature being what it is, even if the wielders of branding irons and tattooing knives, as their foes and enemies, then, human nature being what it is, even if the people should be as cruel and violent as the tyrant Chieh or Robber Chih, how could they be willing to fight for the sake of men they hate and do harm to one they love? This would be like trying to force men to do harm to their own fathers or mothers. They will surely come, therefore, and give warning to the benevolent ruler, and in that case how can the evil rulers hope to carry out their deceptions?

"Therefore, when the benevolent man rules the state, he grows day by day more illustrious. Those among the other feudal lords who lead the way in paying allegiance to him will find safety, those who lag behind will be in danger, those who oppose him on too many points will find their territory stripped away, and those who turn against him will perish. This is what the *Odes* means when it says:

The martial king raised his banners,
Firmly he grasped his battle-ax.
Blazing like a fierce fire,
Who then dared oppose us?"

"Very good," replied King Hsiao-ch'eng and the lord of Lin-wu. "And may we ask what ways and what modes of ac-tion the true king should follow in employing his soldiers?"

Hsun Tzu said, "Such detailed matters are of minor im-portance to Your Majesty, and may be left to the generals. What I would like to speak about, however, are the signs which indicate whether the king and the feudal lords are strong or weak, whether they are destined to survive or to perish, and the circumstances which insure safety or invite danger.

"If the ruler is a worthy man, the state will be ordered; if he is incompetent, the state will be disordered. If he honors rites and values righteousness, the state will be ordered; if he disdains rites and despises righteousness, the state will be dis-ordered. The ordered state will be strong, the disordered one weak. This is the basis of strength and weakness.

"If superiors have the qualities that command respect, then inferiors can be employed. If superiors do not command re-spect, then inferiors cannot be employed. If inferiors can be employed, the state will be strong; if not, the state will be weak. This is a constant rule of strength and weakness.

"To honor rites and seek to achieve merit is the highest manner of action. To work hard for one's stipend and value integrity is the next highest manner. To consider merit above all other things and despise integrity is the lowest manner. This is the constant principle of strength and weakness.

"He who treats his officers well will be strong; he who does not will be weak. He who loves his people will be strong; he who does not will be weak. He whose government decrees are trusted will be strong; he whose government decrees are not trusted will be weak. He whose people are unified will be strong; he whose people are not unified will be weak. He whose rewards are generous will be strong; he whose rewards are meager will be weak. He whose punishments are held in awe will be strong; he whose punishments are regarded with contempt will be weak. He whose supplies and armaments are complete and efficient will be strong; he whose supplies and armaments are crude and inefficient will be weak. He who uses his soldiers with caution will be strong; he who uses them rashly will be weak. He whose strategies proceed from a single source will be strong; he whose strategies proceed from several sources will be weak. This is the abiding rule of strength and weakness.

"The men of Ch'i place great emphasis upon skill in personal attack. He who by such skill comes back with the head of an enemy is rewarded with eight ounces of gold levied from the men who accomplished no such deed, but outside of this there are no regular battle rewards. If one is faced with an enemy who is weak and small in numbers, such methods may achieve a certain temporary success, but if the enemy is numerous and strong, one's own forces will quickly disintegrate. They will scatter like birds in flight, and it will be only a matter of days before the state will be overthrown. This method of employing soldiers will doom a state to destruction; no way leads to greater weakness. It is in fact hardly different from going to the market place and hiring day laborers to do one's fighting.

"The rulers of Wei select their foot soldiers on the basis of certain qualifications. They must be able to wear three sets of armor, carry a crossbow of twelve-stone weight, bear on their backs a quiver with fifty arrows, and in addition carry a spear. They must also wear helmets on their heads, a sword at their waist, carry three days' provisions, and still be able to march a hundred li in one day. When men have met these qualifications, their families are exempted from corvee labor and are given special tax benefits on their lands and houses. Thus, although individual soldiers may grow old and their strength wane, their privileges cannot be readily taken away from them, and in addition it is not easy to train a sufficient number of new recruits to replace them. For this reason, though the territory of the state is large, its taxes are meager. This method of employing soldiers puts a state in grave peril.

"As for the rulers of Ch'in, they have only a narrow, con-fined area on which to settle their people. They employ them harshly, terrorize them with authority, embitter them with hardship, coax them with rewards, and cow them with punish-ments. They see to it that if the humbler people hope to gain any benefits from their superiors, they can do so only by achieving distinction in battle. They oppress the people before employing them and make them win some distinction before granting them any benefit. Rewards increase to keep pace with achievements; thus a man who returns from battle with five enemy heads is made the master of five families in his neighborhood. In comparison with the other methods I have mentioned, this is the best one to insure a strong and populous state that will last for a long time, a wide expanse of territory that yields taxes. Therefore Ch'in's repeated victories during the last four generations are no accident, but the result of policy.

"So the skilled attackers of Ch'i cannot stand up against the armed infantry of Wei, and the armed infantry of Wei cannot stand up against the fierce officers of Ch'in. But neither could the fierce officers of Ch'in come face to face with the well--regulated troops of the dictators Duke Huan of Ch'i or Duke Wen of Chin, nor could the troops of Duke Huan or Duke Wen possibly hold out against the benevolence and righteous-ness of King T'ang or King Wu. Before such a force they would be like something burned and shriveled, something flung against a rock.

"The soldiers of states like Ch'i, Wei, or Ch'in are all merely seeking reward or striving for some profit. They are following the ways of hired laborers or tradesmen, and as yet have not understood what it means to honor their superiors, conform to regulations, and fulfill their moral obligations. If one of the other feudal lords were truly able to imbue his people with a sense of honor, then he could rise up and menace them all without difficulty. Therefore, to attract men to military service and recruit soldiers as they do, to rely upon force and deception and teach men to covet military achievements and profit—this is the way to deceive the people. But to rely upon ritual principles and moral education-this is the way to unite them. When deception meets deception, the victory may go either way, depending upon the cleverness of the combatants. But to try to use deception to meet unity is like trying to hack down Mount T'ai with an awl—no one in the world would be stupid enough to attempt it! Thus, when the true king leads forth his troops, there is no doubt of the outcome. When King T'ang set out to punish Chieh, and King Wu to punish Chou, they had only to give a wave of their hands and a nod, and even the most powerful and unruly nations hastened to their service. Punishing Chieh and Chou then became no more difficult than punishing a lone commoner. This is what the 'Great Oath' means when it speaks of 'Chou, the lone commoner.'

"Those whose soldiers achieve a major degree of unity may control the world; those whose soldiers achieve only a minor degree of unity may still be strong enough to menace" their enemies close by. But those who attract men to military service and recruit soldiers, rely upon deception, and teach men to covet military achievements and profit—their soldiers will sometimes win, sometimes lose, but do neither consistently. At times such men will contract their sphere of influence, at times they will expand it; at times they will survive, at times they will go under, like rivals struggling for supremacy. Military operations of this kind are like the raids of robber bands; the gentleman has nothing to do with such ways.

"Thus, for example, T'ien Tan of Ch'i, Chuang Ch'iao of I Ch'u, Wei Yang of Ch'in, and Miao Chi of Yen were all men who were popularly said to have been skilled in the use of soldiers. Yet, though these men achieved varying degrees of cleverness and might, they all followed essentially the same methods, and none of them ever got so far as to bring true harmony and unity to their armies. They all relied upon sudden seizures, deceptions, stratagems, and swift overthrows, and for this reason their armies were no different from robber bands. Duke Huan of Ch'i, Duke Wen of Chin, King Chuang of Ch'u, King Ho-lu of Wu, and King Kou-chien of Yueh were all able to attain harmony and unity in their armies, and it may therefore be said that they at least entered the realm of the true way. And yet they never grasped the essentials of the matter. So they were able to become dictators, but not to become true kings. These are the signs of strength and weakness."

"Excellent!" exclaimed King Hsiao-ch'eng and the lord of Lin-wu. "And now may we ask how to become a good general?"

Hsun Tzu replied, "In knowledge, nothing is more important than discarding what is doubtful; in action, nothing is more important than avoiding mistakes; in undertakings, noth-ing is more important than to be without regret. Only make sure that you will not regret the undertaking, and then you need not worry about whether it will be successful or not.

"In regulations and commands, strive for strictness and authority. In rewards and punishments, strive for consistency and aptness. In establishing encampments and depots, strive to make them well-guarded and secure. In troop movements, strive for an air of gravity and deliberateness, at the same time striving for alertness and rapidity. In observing the disposition and movements of the enemy, strive to obtain the most complete and penetrating reports, and see that they are checked for reliability. In meeting the enemy in battle, proceed on the basis of what you understand thoroughly, not on the basis of what you are in doubt about. These are called the six arts.

"Do not think only of maintaining your rank as a general and shudder at the thought of losing your command. Do not press too hard for victory and forget about defeat. Do not be too stern with your own men and despise the enemy. Do not fix your eyes on gain alone and take no thought for loss. Seek ripeness in all your plans and liberality in your use of supplies. These are called the five expedients.

"There are three cases in which a general refuses to obey the command of his ruler. Though threatened with death, he cannot be made to take up a position that is untenable. Though threatened with death, he cannot be made to attack where there is no hope of victory. Though threatened with death, he cannot be made to deceive the common people. These are known as the three extremities.

"If the general, having received his commands from the ruler, relays them to the three armies, and sees to it that the three armies are properly regulated, that the officers are assigned to their proper ranks, and that all matters are correctly disposed of, then the ruler will have no particular occasion to rejoice nor the enemy to feel resentment. This is called the highest type of service.

"Plan before any undertaking, and carry it out with circumspection; be as careful about the end as you are about the beginning, and end and beginning will be alike. This is the most auspicious policy. The success of all undertakings rests upon circumspection; their failure derives from negligence. Therefore, when circumspection prevails over carelessness, the result will be good fortune; when carelessness prevails over circumspection, the result will be annihilation. When planning prevails over personal desires, the result will be progress; when personal desires prevail over planning, the result will be disaster. Fight as though you were trying only to hold your ground; march as though you were already in battle; regard any success you achieve as merely lucky. Be cautious in strategy and never neglectful; be cautious in your undertakings and never neglectful; be cautious in dealings with your officers and never neglectful; be cautious in using your men and never neglectful; be cautious in regard to the enemy and never neglectful. These are called the five things that must not be neglected.

"He who carefully observes the six arts, the five expedients, and the three extremities, and who disposes of all matters with assiduity and circumspection, never allowing himself to be neglectful, may be called a true general of the world. He par-takes of a godlike intelligence!"

"Very good," said the lord of Lin-wu. "And now may I ask about the regulations of the king's army?"

Hsun Tzu replied, "The general dies with his drums; the carriage driver dies with the reins; the officials die at their posts; the leaders of the fighting men die in their ranks. When the army hears the sound of the drums, it advances; when it hears the sound of the bells, it retreats. Obedience to orders is counted first; achievements are counted second. To advance when there has been no order to advance is no different from retreating when there has been no order to retreat; the penalty is the same. The king's army does not kill the enemy's old men and boys; it does not destroy crops. It does not seize those who retire without a fight, but it does not forgive those who resist. It does not make prisoners of those who surrender and seek asylum. In carrying out punitive expeditions, it does not punish the common people; it punishes those who lead the common people astray. But if any of the common people fight with the enemy, they become enemies as well. Thus those who flee from the enemy forces and come in surrender shall be left to go free." Kai, the prince of Wei, was enfeoffed in Sung, but Ts'ao Ch'u-lung was executed in the presence of the army. The Yin people who submitted to the leaders of the Chou army, however, were allowed to live and were cared for the same as the people of Chou. Hence, those close by sang songs and rejoiced, and those far off hastened to the Chou leaders with the greatest speed. There was no country so re-mote and out of the way that it did not hurry forward to serve them and find rest and joy in their rule. All within the four seas became as one family, and wherever the report of their virtue penetrated, there was no one who did not submit. This is what is called being a true leader of the people. The Odes refers to this when it says:

> From west, from cast,
> From south, from north,
> There were none who thought of not submitting.

"A true king carries out punitive expeditions, but he does not make war. When a city is firmly guarded, he does not lay siege to it; when the soldiers resist strongly, he does not attack. When the rulers and their people of other states are happy with each other, he considers it a blessing. He does not massacre the defenders of a city; he does not move his army in secret; he does not keep his forces long in the field; be does not allow a campaign to last longer than one season. Therefore the people of badly ruled states delight in the report of his government; they feel uneasy under their own rulers and long for his coming."

"Excellent," said the lord of Lin-wu.

Ch'en Hsiao said to Hsun Tzu, "When you talk about the use of arms, you always speak of benevolence and righteousness as being the basis of military action. A benevolent man loves others, and a righteous man acts in accordance with what is right. Why, then, would they have any recourse to arms in the first place? Those who take up arms do so only in order to contend with others and seize some spoil!"

Hsun Tzu replied, "This is not something that you would understand. The benevolent man does indeed love others, and because he loves others, he hates to see men do them harm. The righteous man acts in accordance with what is right, and for that reason he hates to see men do wrong. He takes up arms in order to put an end to violence and to do away with harm, not in order to contend with others for spoil. Therefore, where the soldiers of the benevolent man encamp they command a godlike respect; and where they pass, they transform the people. They are like the seasonable rain in whose falling all men rejoice. Thus Yao attacked Huan Tou, Shun attacked the rulers of the Miao, Ya attacked Kung Kung, T'ang attacked the ruler of the Hsia, King Wen attacked Ch'ung, and King Wu attacked Chou. These four emperors and two kings all marched through the world with their soldiers of benevolence and righteousness. Those nearby were won by their goodness, and those far off were filled with longing by their virtue. They did not stain their swords with blood, and yet near and far alike submitted; their virtue flourished in the center and spread to the four quarters. This is what the Odes means when it says:

> The good man, the gentleman,
> His forms are without fault;
> His forms are without fault;
> He corrects the countries of the four quarters."

Lu Ssu said to Hsun Tzu, "For four generations now Ch'in has won victory. Its armies are the strongest in the world and its authority sways the other feudal lords. It did not attain this by means of benevolence and righteousness, but by taking advantage of its opportunities, that is all."

Hsun Tzu replied, "This is not something that you would understand. When you talk about opportunities, you are speaking of opportunities that are in fact inopportune. When I speak of benevolence and righteousness, I mean opportunities that are in fact great opportunities. This benevolence and righteousness which I speak of are the means whereby government is ordered properly, and when government is properly ordered, then the people will draw close to their superiors, delight in their rulers, and think it a light matter to die for them. Therefore I have said that matters pertaining to the army and the leadership of the generals are of minor importance. Chin has been victorious for four generations, yet it has lived in constant terror and apprehension lest the rest of the world should someday unite and trample it down. These are the soldiers of a degenerate age, not of a nation which has grasped the true principle of leadership. Thus T'ang did not have to wait until he had cornered Chieh on the field of Ming-t'iao before he could accomplish his overthrow; King Wu did not have to wait until his victory on the day *chia-tzu* before he could punish Chou for his evil deeds. They bad already assured victory for themselves by all their earlier deeds and actions. This is what it means to employ the soldiers of benevolence and righteousness. Now you do not try to get at the root of the matter, but look for a model in superficial appearances. This is the way to bring disorder to the world!"

Rites are the highest expression of hierarchical order, the basis for strengthening the state, the way by which to create authority, the crux of achievement and fame. By proceeding in accordance with ritual, kings gain possession of the world; by ignoring it, they bring destruction to their altars of the grain and soil. Stout armor and sharp weapons are not enough to assure victory; high walls and deep moats are not enough to assure defense; stem commands and manifold penalties are not enough to assure authority. What proceeds by the way of ritual will advance; what proceeds by any other way will end in failure.

The men of Ch'u make armor out of sharkskin and rhinoceros hides, and it is so tough it rings like metal or stone. They carry steel spears made in Yuan, sharp as the sting of a wasp, and move as nimbly and swiftly as a whirlwind. And yet Ch'u's troops were defeated at Ch'iu-sha and their general, T'ang Mei, was killed; and from the time when Chuang Ch'iao turned against the king of Ch'u, the state was torn apart. Surely this did not come about because Ch'u lacked stout armor and sharp weapons. Rather it was because its leaders did not follow the proper way. They had the Ju and Ying rivers to protect them, the Yangtze and the Han as their moats; they were bounded by the forests of Teng and shielded by Mount Fang-ch'eng. And yet the Ch'in forces swept down and seized the Ch'u capital city of Yen in Ying as easily as one might shake down a dry leaf. Surely it was not because Ch'u lacked natural defenses and barriers to protect it. Rather it was because its leaders failed to follow the proper way. The tyrant Chou cut out Pi Kan's heart, imprisoned Chi Tzu, and made the punishment of the burning pillar. He murdered and massacred without season and his ministers and people were filled with terror and gave up all hope of saving their lives. Yet, when the armies of King Wu came sweeping down, none of Chou's commands were obeyed and he found he could not rally his people about him. Surely it was not because his commands were not stern enough or his punishments not manifold. Rather it was because in leading the people he failed to follow the proper way.

In ancient times the only weapons were spears, lances, bows, and arrows, and yet enemy states did not even wait until these were used against them, but submitted at once. Men did not build walls and battlements or dig ditches and moats; they did not set up defenses and watch stations or construct war machines, and yet the state was peaceful and safe, free from fear of outside aggression and secure in its position. There was only one reason for this. The leaders illumined the Way and apportioned all ranks fairly; they employed the people at the proper season and sincerely loved them, so that the people moved in harmony with their superiors as shadows follow a form or echoes answer a sound. If there were any who did not follow commands, then and only then were punishments applied. Therefore, the rulers had only to punish one man and the whole world submitted. Men who bad been punished bore no ill will against their superiors, for they knew that the fault lay in themselves. Therefore, the rulers seldom had to use punishments, and yet their authority was recognized by all. There was only one reason for this: they followed the proper way. In ancient times, when Yao ruled the world, he executed one man, punished two others, and after that the whole world was well ordered. This is what the old text means when it says, "let your authority inspire awe, but do not wield it; set up penalties but do not apply them."

It is the way with all men that, if they do something only for the sake of winning rewards and benefits, then, the moment they see that the undertaking may end unprofitably or in danger, they will abandon it. Therefore rewards, punish-ments, force, and deception are in themselves not enough to make men put forth their full efforts or risk their lives for the state. If the rulers and superiors do not treat the common people in accordance with ritual principles, loyalty, and good faith, but rely solely upon rewards, punishments, force, and deception, oppressing them and trying merely to squeeze some kind of service and achievement out of them, then when an invader comes, if entrusted with the defense of a threatened city, they will surely betray their trust; if led into battle against the enemy, they will invariably turn and flee; if assigned to some difficult and demanding task, they will certainly run away. The bonds that should hold them will melt, and inferiors will turn upon and seize control of their superiors. Rewards and punishments, force and deception may be the way to deal with hired laborers or tradesmen, but they are no way to unify the population of a great state or bring glory to the nation. Therefore, the men of ancient times were ashamed to resort to such ways.

Lead the people by magnifying the sound of virtue, guide them by making clear ritual principles, love them with the utmost loyalty and good faith, give them a place in the government by honoring the worthy and employing the able, and elevate them in rank by bestowing titles and rewards. Demand labor of them only at the proper season, lighten their burdens, unify them in harmony, nourish them and care for them as you would little children. Then, when the commands of government have been fixed and the customs of the people unified, if there should be those who depart from the customary ways and refuse to obey their superiors, the common people will as one man turn upon them with hatred, and regard them with loathing, like an evil force that must be exorcised. Then and only then should you think of applying penalties. Such are the kind of men who deserve severe punishment. What greater disgrace could come to them? If they try to profit by evil ways, they find themselves confronted by severe punishment. Who but a madman or a fool, perceiving such an outcome, would fail to reform?

After this the common people will become enlightened and will learn to obey the laws of their superiors, to imitate the ways of their ruler, and will find rest and delight in them. Then, if men should appear who can train themselves to do good, improve and rectify their conduct, practice ritual 'principles, and honor the Way, the common people will as one man show them deference and respect, will favor and praise them. Then and only then may you think of doling out rewards. Such are the kind of men who deserve lofty titles and generous emoluments. What greater glory could come to them? If they fear to suffer some loss by their virtuous ways, they find themselves supported and sustained by titles and emoluments. What man is there alive who would not wish to receive the same?

With lofty titles and generous emoluments clearly held out before him, and explicit penalties and deep disgrace unmistakably hovering behind him, though a man might have no wish to reform his ways, how could he help himself? Therefore, the people will flock about their ruler like water flowing downward. Where he is present, he commands a godlike respect; when he acts, he transforms the people (and they become obedient) The violent and daring are transformed to sincerity; the prejudiced and selfish-minded are transformed to fairness; the quick-tempered and contentious are transformed to harmony. This is called the great transformation and the highest unity. The *Odes* refers to this when it says:

> The king's plans were truly sincere,
> And the country of Hsu came in submission.

There are three methods by which you may annex a neighboring state and bring its people under your rule: you may win them over by virtue, by force, or by wealth.

If the people of a neighboring state respect your reputation, admire your virtuous actions, and desire to become your subjects, they will throw open their gates, clear the roads, and welcome you to their cities. If you allow them to follow their old customs and remain in their old homes, the common people will all rest easy and will willingly obey your laws and commands. In this way you will acquire new territory and your power will increase; you will have added to your population and your armies will be stronger than ever. This is what it means to win over a neighbor by virtue.

If the people of a neighboring state do not respect your reputation or admire your virtuous actions, but are awed by your authority and intimidated by force, then, although they will feel no loyalty to you in their hearts, they will not dare to resist annexation. In such cases, however, you will have to enlarge your garrisons and increase your military supplies, and your government expenditures will increase likewise. In this way you will acquire new territory but your power will decrease; you will have added to your population but your armies will be weaker than before. This is what it means to win over a neighbor by force.

If the people of a neighboring state do not respect your reputation or admire your virtuous actions, but are poor and are looking for some way to get rich, are starving and in search of plenty, then they will come to you with empty bellies and gaping mouths, attracted by your food alone. In such a case, you will have to issue supplies of grain from your storehouses in order to feed them, hand out goods and wealth to enrich them, and appoint conscientious officials to look out for them, and only after three years have passed can you put faith in their loyalty. In this way you will acquire new territory but your power will decrease; you will have added to your population but the state will be poorer than before. This is what it means to win over a neighbor by wealth. Therefore I say, he who annexes a state by virtue is a true king; he who annexes it by force will be weakened; and he who annexes it by wealth will be impoverished. From ancient times to the present it has always been the same.

It is easy enough to annex territory; the difficult thing is to stabilize and maintain control over it. Ch'i was able to annex Sung, but could not hold on to it, and so Wei snatched it away. Yen succeeded in annexing Ch'i, but could not hold on to it, and so T'ien Tan seized control of it. Han's territory of Shang-tang, a region several hundred li square, rich and well inhabited, chose to become part of Chao, but Chao could not hold on to it, and hence Ch'in took it away. He who is able to annex territory but not to hold on to it will invariably be stripped of his acquisitions; he who can neither annex territory nor hold on to what he has will surely be destroyed. He who can hold on to territory will invariably be able to acquire more. When one can both acquire and hold on to territory, there is no limit to the amount he can annex. In ancient times T'ang began with the region of Po and King Wu began with Hao, both of them areas of only a hundred li square. The reason they were able to unite the world under their rule and win the allegiance of all the other feudal lords was simply this: they knew how to secure their hold upon their territory.

Secure your hold on the aristocracy by means of ritual; secure your hold on the people through government. With ritual well ordered, the aristocracy will submit to your rule; with the government fairly administered, the people will feel safe. With the aristocracy submissive and the people content, you will attain what is called a situation of great stability. If you remain within your borders, you will be unassailable; if you march to battle, you will be strong. What you command will be done, what you forbid will cease, and the undertakings of a true king will be complete in you.

4. THE FIVE ELEMENTS PHILOSOPHY

The dualistic ideas of yin-yang, *the passive and active forces in the universe, are fairly well known by Western readers and were reflected in the Daoist excerpts above. As Chinese thinkers continued to speculate on the dynamic properties of the universe and ways to systematize that understanding, they developed the accompanying philosophy of Five Elements. The metaphysical system of five basic elements was particularly related to popular Daoism and the magical and alchemical traditions associated with them. Here again, we see the attempt to divine an underlying structure to the universe, one based on understandable properties and processes. Perceiving a connection between the characteristics of various natural elements and phenomena, ancient Chinese thinkers developed a complex system that characterized their world. In its connection to nature, we can see the influence of Daoism. In its search for structure, we can see a plan that would also appeal to the Confucian mindset.*

This system certainly is related to concepts in traditional Chinese medicine and it has surely endured in the more metaphysical thinking of some martial artists, most prominently demonstrated by the fact that the famed Miyamoto Musashi, organized his Book of Five Rings *according to the Five Elements rubric. Even today, some masters of* kendo, *Japanese fencing, use a Five Elements perspective in analyzing* kata.

THE FIVE AGENTS

Similar in concept to the yin-yang theory is that of the five agents (wu-hsing). Like the yin and yang, the agents are not physical substances but metaphysical forces or modes which dominate or control certain periods of time, commonly the seasons, in a fixed succession. It is fairly obvious how the mode or element of wood should be assigned to the season of spring, associated with the color green and the direction east. In like manner fire is assigned to summer, its color red and direction south; metal to autumn, its color white and direction west; and water to winter, its color black and direction north. However, there are five agents and it is accepted that they proceed in the order in which they produce or "beget" each other, i.e., wood produces fire, fire produces earth, earth produces metal, metal produces water, etc. Since there are only four seasons, earth, with the color yellow, is commonly assigned a position in the center, aiding the other elements in their governing of the four seasons.

The correspondences derived by analogy according to this system are too numerous to be explained in detail. The principal ones, illustrating how all facets of the divine and natural worlds were classified by these five agents, are listed in diagram form.

A TABLE OF CORRESPONDENCES FOR THE FIVE-AGENTS SYSTEM

THE FIVE AGENTS

Correspondence	Wood	Fire	Earth	Metal	Water
Seasons	Spring	Summer		Autumn	Winter
Divine Rulers	T'ai Hao	Yen Ti	Yellow Emperor	Shao Hao	Chuan Hsu
Attendant Spirits	Kou Mang	Chu Yung	Hou T'u	Ju Shou	Hsuan Ming
Sacrifices	Inner door	hearth	inner court	outer court	well
Animals	sheep	fowl	ox	dog	pig
Grains	wheat	beans	panicled millet	hemp	millet
Organs	spleen	lungs	heart	liver	kidneys
Numbers	eight	seven	five	nine	six
Stems	*chia/i*	*ping/ting*	*mou/chi*	*keng/hsin*	*jen/kuei*
Colors	green	red	yellow	white	black
Notes	chueh	chih	kung	shang	yu
Tastes	sour	bitter	sweet	acrid	salty
Smells	goatish	burning	fragrant	rank	rotten
Directions	East	South	center	West	north
Creatures	scaly	feathered	naked	hairy	shell-covered
Beasts of the Directions	Green Dragon	Scarlet Bird	Yellow Dragon	White Tiger	Black Tortoise
Virtues	benevolence	wisdom	faith	righteousness	Decorum
Planets	Jupiter	Mars	Saturn	Venus	Mercury
Officers	Minister of Agriculture	Minister of War	Minister of Works	Minister of Interior	Minister of Justice

5. THE PLATFORM
SCRIPTURE

The Indian religion of Buddhism established itself in China in the second century A.D. A complex religion in its own right when it arrived, Buddhism was further elaborated and interpreted in China and later in Japan. The Mahayana traditions of East Asia (as opposed to the Theravada traditions of South Asia) found fertile ground in the Chinese and Japanese spirit. Of particular interest to martial artists is the development of the Buddhist sect that would come to be popularly known by its Japanese name, Zen.

It is widely believed that Zen Buddhism had a decisive influence on the philosophy of many contemporary martial systems, particularly those of Japan. This contention can be debated, and some of the discussion can be found in later excerpts in the reader. There is, however, an early and enduring association of Buddhism with various martial systems, particularly empty-hand systems of the type not particularly useful in the armies of the day. Bodhidharma, the historical figure associated with the spread of Buddhism into China, is said to have taught his monks various exercises to improve their fitness. While these exercises may or may not have been the type of animal forms associated with Chinese boxing systems, the important fact is that the mythological linkage of Buddhism and boxing is a strong one. And it has been strengthened by the stories of the fabled Shaolin monastery and its warrior monks, as reflected in numerous contemporary stories, films, and television productions.

We can see the significant impact of indigenous Chinese ideas on Buddhism in Zen. All Buddhist follow the teachings of Buddha, who maintained that all life is suffering that can only be relieved through the correct perception of reality, a perception that sees through subject/object dualism, and leads to a transcendent connection with the universe. The concept of satori, or enlightenment, literally refers to the blowing out of a candle, symbolic of the end of any concept of individual existence. As a school of Buddhism, Zen follows the teachings of Buddha but emphasizes an instinctive and experiential grasp of truth that is not reliant on the study of scripture. In the Zen tradition, teaching and reflection and meditation are merely mechanisms to lead one to the direct experience of insight. In this, we can see broad similarities between the Zen and Daoist traditions—note that the imagery of polishing a mirror appears here, as it does in the previous selections from Laozi.

The work that follows is an excerpt from an early and important Chinese text that gives the flavor of this influential Buddhist sect. It is written by the Sixth Patriarch, Hui-neng, and details how he, an illiterate acolyte responsible for pounding rice, comes to sudden enlightenment in the Zen tradition.

From *The Platform Scripture*

4

One day the Fifth Patriarch suddenly called his dis-ciples to come to him. When we had already assembled, he said, "Let me say this to you: Life and death are serious matters. You disciples are engaged all day in making offer-ings, going after fields of blessings only, and you make no effort to achieve freedom from the bitter sea of life and death. If you are deluded in your own nature, how can blessings save you? Go to your rooms, all of you, and think for yourselves. Those who possess wisdom use the wisdom (*prajna*) inherent in their own nature. Each of you must write a verse and present it to me. After I see the verses, I will give the robe and the Law to the one who understands the basic idea and will appoint him to be the Sixth Patriarch. Hurry, hurry!"

5

After the disciples had received these instructions, they each retired to their own rooms. They said to each other, "There is no need to calm our minds and devote our attention to composing verses to present to the priest. Head Monk Shen-hsiu is an instructor of rituals. When he acquires the Law, we can of course follow and stay with him. We do not have to write verses." They were satisfied. None dared present a verse.

At that time there were three corridors in front of the hall of the Great Master, Offerings were made there. It was planned to paint there on the walls as records the pictures of the transfiguration of the assembly depicted in the *Scripture about the Buddha, Entering into Lanka.* and also pictures of the five Patriarchs transmitting the robe and the Law so that these Stories might prevail in future generations. The artist Lu Chen had examined the wall. He was to begin work the next day.

6

Head Monk Shen-hsiu thought, "These people would not present verses to show their minds because I am an instructor. If I do not present a verse to show my mind, how can the Fifth Patriarch see whether my understanding is shallow or deep? 1 shall present the verse of my heart to the Fifth Patriarch to show him my ideas. It in good to seek the Law, but not good to seek the patriarchate. It would be similar to that of the ordinary people and I would be usurping the holy rank. If I do not present a verse to manifest my mind, I shall never acquire the Law." He thought for a long time but found it an extremely difficult matter. He then waited until midnight, and without allowing anyone to see him, went to the wall in the middle of the southern corridor and wrote a verse to manifest what was in his mind, thus wishing to seek the Law. "If the Fifth Patriarch sees the words of this verse—the words of this verse . . . If they are not acceptable, it is of course because the obstruc-tion of my past deeds is so heavy that I am not qualified to obtain the Law. The Patriarch's holy opinion is difficult to guess but I shall be satisfied in my mind."

At midnight Head Monk Shen-hsiu, holding a candle, wrote a verse on the wall of the south corridor, without anyone knowing about it, which said:

> The body is the tree of perfect wisdom (bodhi)
> The mind is the stand of a bright mirror.
> At all times diligently wipe it.
> Do not allow it to become dusty.

7

After Head Monk Shen-hsiu had finished writing the verse, he returned to his room to retire without anyone seeing him. The next morning the Fifth Patriarch called court artist Lu to come to the south corridor to paint the pictures of the *Scripture about the Buddha, Entering into Lanka.* Suddenly the Fifth Patriarch saw the verse. After reading it, he said to the court artist, "I will give you thirty thousand cash and will be much obliged to you for your coming from afar. But we will not paint the transfigurations. *The Diamond Scripture* says, 'All characters are unreal and imaginary.' It is better to keep this verse and let deluded people read it. If people practice according to it, they will not fall into the Three Evil Stages. People who practice according to the Law will enjoy great benefits."

Thereupon the Great Master called all the disciples to come and burn incense before the verse so that everyone would see it and a sense of reverence would arise in all of them. "All of you read this. Only those who understand this verse will be able to see their own nature. Those who practice according to it will not fall."

The disciples all read the verse and a sense of reverence was aroused in them. They said, "Wonderful!"

Thereupon the Fifth Patriarch called Head Monk Shen-hsiu into the hall and asked, "Was this verse written by you ? If you wrote it, you should receive my Law."

Head Monk Shen-hsiu said. "Please pardon me. In fact, I did write it. Yet I dare not seek the position of the patriarch. I hope Your Holiness will be compassionate and see if your disciple possesses a small amount of wisdom and understands the basic idea."

The Fifth Patriarch said, "The verse you wrote shows some but not complete understanding. You have arrived at the front door but you have not yet entered it. Ordinary people, by practicing in accordance with your verse, will not fail. But it is futile to seek the supreme perfect wisdom while holding to such a view. One must enter the door and see his own nature. Go away and come back after thinking a day or two. Write another verse and present it to me. If then you have entered the door and have seen your own nature, I will give you the robe and the Law." Head Monk Shen-hsiu went away and for several days could not produce another verse.

8

A boy was reciting this verse while passing by the rice-pounding area. As soon as I heard it, I knew that the author had not seen his own nature or understood the basic idea. I asked the boy, "What verse were you reciting a little while ago?" The boy answered, "Do you not know that the Great Master said that life and death are important matters? He wishes to transmit the robe and the Law to someone. He told the disciples to write and present a verse for him to see. He who understood the basic idea would be given the robe and the Law as testimony of making him the Sixth Patriarch. The head monk by the name of Shen-hsiu wrote in the south corridor a verse that frees one from the attachment to differentiated characters. The Fifth Patriarch told all the disciples to read it. Whoever understood this verse would immediately see his own nature, and those who practiced according to it would be emancipated."

I replied, "I have been pounding rice here for more than eight months and have not been to the front of the hall. Will you, sir, lead me to the south corridor so that I might see this verse and pay reverence to it? I also wish to recite it and to fulfill the conditions for birth in the Buddha-land in my next life."

As the boy led me to the south corridor, I immediately paid reverence to the verse. As I did not know how to read, I asked someone to read it to me. After I heard it, I immediately understood the basic idea. I also composed a verse and asked a person who could read to write it on the wall of the western corridor to manifest what was in my own mind. It is useless to study the Law if one does not understand his own mind. Once a person understands his own mind and sees his own nature, he will immediately understand the basic idea. My verse says:

> Fundamentally perfect wisdom has no tree.
> Nor has the bright mirror any stand.
> Buddha-nature is forever clear and pure.
> Where is there any dust?

Another verse says:

> The mind is the tree of perfect wisdom.
> The body is the stand of a bright mirror.
> The bright mirror is originally clear and pure.
> Where has it been denied by any dust?

Monks in the hall were all surprised at these verses. I, however, went back to the rice-pounding area. The Fifth Patriarch suddenly realized that I alone had the good knowledge and understanding of the basic idea but he was afraid lest the rest learn it. He therefore told them, "He does not understand perfectly after all."

9

The Fifth Patriarch waited till midnight, called me to come to the hall, and expounded *The Diamond Scripture*. As soon as I heard this, I understood. That night the Law was imparted to me without anyone knowing it, and thus the method of sudden enlightenment and the robe were transmitted to me. "You are now the Sixth Patriarch. This robe is the testimony of transmission from generation to generation. As to the Law, it is to be transmitted from mind to mind. Let people achieve enlightenment through their own effort."

The Fifth Patriarch said, "Hui-neng, from the very begin-ning, in the transmission of the Law one's life is as delicate as hanging by a thread. If you remain here, someone might harm you. You must leave quickly."

10

After I received the robe and the Law, I left at midnight. The Fifth Patriarch personally saw me off at the courier's station at Chiu-chiang. I then understood the instructions of the Patriarch. "Go and work hard. Carry the Law to the south. Do not preach for three years, for it is not easy for this Law to flourish. Later when you spread the Law and convert people, when you skillfully guide deluded people and open up their minds, you will not be different from me." Having said goodbye, I started south.

6. Divine Record of Immovable Wisdom (Fudochi Shinmyo Roku)

The Zen monk Takuan Soho was a precocious thinker, elevated to an early place of prominence during the turbulent years of the late sixteenth and early seventeenth centuries in Japan. He is best know to us for his remarkable friendship with the famous swordsman, Yagyu Munenori.

The Yagyu family was one blessed with a succession of able warriors. Yagyu Mitsuyoshi distinguished himself in battle in the service of his lord and eventually came to the attention of Tokugawa Ieyasu, who would emerge victorious in the struggle to achieve dominance over Japane's warring feudal lords, establishing a government that would endure from 1603 to 1868. The Yagyu family were retainers of the Tokugawa house and Mitsuyoshi's son, Munenori, was appointed fencing teacher to the shogun.

An able and accomplished swordsman, Munenori was also an individual interested in the deeper implications of martial study. His growing friendship with Takuan served to deepen his reflection and the developing philosophy he was forming. As an aid to his close friend, Takuan penned a treatise designed to show Munenori how the experience of training in swordsmanship could help reveal the deeper truths expounded by Buddhists. In its focus on the workings of the mind, the Fudochi Shinmyo Roku *reveals a sophistication of thought that has engaged the attention of many later thinkers—some martial artists and some not. Certainly the clarity of focus Takuan writes of, the ability to remain centered and flexible enough to deal with all events, is something that modern martial artists acknowledge as essential in sparring. The sense that zazen, the seated meditation characteristic of the sect, can help in inculcating this ability is part of the reason why Zen influence persists in the modern martial traditions.*

THE MIND THAT TARRIES

Suppose you see in a glance a sword coming at you and decide to block it with own. Then your mind stays with the sword and, neglecting your own moves, you allow the opponent to slash you. This is called the mind that tarries.

Suppose you do see the opponent's sword come, but do not allow your mind to stay with it. Suppose, instead, that in response to the coming sword, you do not think of striking back or form any idea or judgment, but the moment you see the sword raised you move in, your mind not tarrying, and grasp the sword. Then you should be able to wrest from the opponent the sword intended to slash you, and turn it into one which to slash him. . . .

In Buddhism, the mind that tarries is called maya.

FUDOCHI, OR IMMOVABLE WISDOM

Fudo (in the term *fudochi*) does not mean the immobility of a stone or a tree. The mind which moves over there, to the left, to the right, in the ten directions and in the eight directions, but does not tarry anywhere for a second, has *fudochi*. . . .

Likewise, the Fudo Myo-o symbolizes the human mind that does not move, the body that does not unsettle. Not unsettling means not staying with anything.

Glancing at something and not allowing the mind to stay with it is called fudo. If your mind stays with something, the various judgments that are in your head will begin to stir variously. The mind that stays is not moving even if it appears to be.

For example, suppose ten men come at you, each with a sword. If you deal with each one and do not allow your mind to stay with what you do, forgetting one move in order to deal with the next, you should be able to let yourself work adequately with all ten of them.

GOING BACK TO THE STARTING POINT

Now, when someone who has trained from the beginner's stage reaches the rank of "immovable wisdom," he is said to turn around and settle back to where he began. To explain this in relation to your swordsmanship, the beginner does not even know how to hold his sword, so there is no way for his mind to tarry. if someone strikes at him, he instinctively responds, giving no particular thought to it.

As he learns various things, however, and as you teach him how to hold up his sword, where to put his mind, and many other things, his mind comes to tarry in many places, and even when striking at someone he comes to feel not entirely free in many ways. But days, months, and years pile up, and as he continues to train, he becomes oblivious of his mind, whatever posture he may take or however he may hold his sword. In the end he comes to feel as he did at the outset, when he knew nothing, had learned nothing.

SCARECROW AS THE ULTIMATE CASE

The National Teacher Bukkoku of Kamakura has this poem:

> Though be doesn't have the mind to stand guard,
> not useless in the mountain paddy is that scarecrow,

THIS APPLIES TO EVERYTHING.

A scarecrow in a mountain paddy is a doll equipped with a bow and an arrow. Birds and beasts see it and run away. The doll has no mind whatsoever, but because deer become frightened and run away and its purpose is met, it is not all useless. What it does is comparable to the deed of someone who has reached the ultimate stage in any field of endeavor. in such a person, only the arms and legs and the body work, and as the mind does not tarry anywhere for a second, you cannot tell where it is. Without thought, without mind, he thus attains the rank of the scarecrow.

An ordinary mortal who is completely stupid cannot make himself conspicuous, because he has no wisdom in the first place. Similarly, an outstanding man of wisdom does not make himself conspicuous because he has reached the depths. It is the knowing fellow whose wisdom shows who is funny. You must find the behavior of monks these days funny. I am embarrassed by it.

NOUMENON AND PHENOMENON

We speak of noumenal training and phenomenal training.

Noumenal training, as I said earlier, aims for the state where you do not concern yourself with anything and you discard your mind. Its stages are as I have written above.

Without phenomenal training, however, all you will have will be theories in your head, and neither your arms nor your legs will work. Phenomenal training, as applied to swordsmanship, entails the "five points" concerning posture and the various other things to be learned.

Even if you knew the noumenon, it would be useless unless you could employ techniques freely, Similarly, even if you could handle your sword well, it would not be any good if you were in the dark about the state where the noumenon ultimately lies. Noumenon and phenomenon ought to be like the two wheels of a cart.

WITHOUT ENOUGH SPACE OF TIME

There is a phrase, "without enough space of time to allow a strand of hair. . ." For example, when you clap your hands, the sound comes out instantaneously. Between the clapping and the sound is there not enough space to allow a strand of hair. it is not as if you clap your hands, then the sound thinks about it and comes out after a space of time. The same moment you clap your hands, the sound comes out.

If your mind stays with the sword that someone swings at you, a space of time will result. During that space of time your own move will be forgotten. If even a strand of hair can't get in between the moment your opponent strikes at you and the moment you react, the opponent's sword might as well be yours.

Zen dialogue stresses this responsive mind. Buddhism abhors the mind that stops and stays with something, and calls it klesa. What is prized is the mind that flows torrentially and never stops, like a ball riding a swift current.

ZEN SECT

In the Zen sect, if asked, "What on earth is the Buddha?" you are to raise your fist. If asked, "What is the ultimate meaning of Buddhist Law?" you are to say, even before the question is finished, "A spray of plum flowers," or "an oak tree in the garden." The point is to not deliberate on the right or wrong of your response. What is prized is the mind that does not stay.

KNOWING THE MIND

To explain the mind with words, it exists in others as well as in yourself, and does good or evil things day and night, in accordance with its karma. The mind leaves the house or destroys a country, and depending on its owner, it may be good or evil. Because, however, few explore and bring to light what the mind is really like, everyone continues to be misled by the mind. . . . Those who happen to have brought its nature to light have a hard time putting what has been learned into practice.

The ability to speak eloquently of the mind may not mean enlightenment on the subject. Even if you hold forth on water, your mouth does not become wet. Even if you speak eloquently of fire, your mouth does not become hot. You cannot know the real water and real fire without touching them; you cannot know them just by explaining them from books. likewise, even if you speak eloquently of food, hunger will not be cured. The ability to speak is not enough for knowing the subject at hand.

In our society, both Buddhists and Confucians expound on the mind. But as long as they do not behave as they preach, they have yet to know the mind. Until each person explores the mind in himself and knows it fully, the matter will remain unclear.

PLACE FOR THE MIND

Where to put your mind?

If you put your mind in the move of the opponent's body, you will be distracted by that move. if you put it in his sword, you will be distracted by his sword. if you put it in your desire to strike the opponent, you will be distracted by that desire. If you put it in your own sword, you will be distracted by your sword. If you put it in your desire not to be struck, you will be distracted by that desire. If you put it in the opponent's posture, you will be distracted by his posture. In short, there is no place to put your mind, they say.

Someone said: "If you put your mind elsewhere, it will stay in whatever place it has gone to, and you will be defeated by your opponent. So stuff your mind into the area under your navel and don't let it go anywhere Simply keep it rolling in response to the opponent's moves."

This is understandable. Nonetheless, from the viewpoint of an advanced stage in Buddhism, to stuff the mind under the navel to prevent it from going elsewhere is low, not advanced, in stage. . . . (In any event,) if you stuff your mind under your navel in your attempt not to let it go elsewhere, you will be distracted by that attempt and end up not taking full initiatives, not feeling very free.

Someone asked: "if stuffing my mind under my navel hampers my moves, makes me feel unfree, and prevents me from taking full initiatives, where in my body shall I put it?"

I responded by saying: "If you put it in your right hand, you will be distracted by your right hand and won't be able to take full initiatives. If you put it in your eyes, you will be distracted by them and won't be able to take full initiatives. If you put it in your right foot, you will be distracted by your right foot and won't be able to take full initiatives. No matter where it may be, if you put your mind in one place, any of the other places won't be able to take full initiatives."

"Well, then, where shall I put it?"

"If you don't put it anywhere," I said, "your mind will fill your whole body, extend and spread all over. Then, it will serve your hand when the hand needs it, your foot when the foot needs it, your eyes when the eyes need it. Because it fully exists wherever it is needed, it will serve any place it is needed . . .

"If you stop thinking of some place to put it, your mind is bound to extend and spread all over and fill your whole body. Without putting your mind in any place, you must let it serve wherever it is needed at each moment, depending on your opponent's move. . . .

"Devising ways not to let your mind stay in one place depends entirely on training. Not letting your mind stay anywhere is the goal and of vital importance. If you don't put it anywhere, it will be everywhere.'"

THE BE-MIND AND THE NO-MIND

The be-mind (ushin) is the same as the "false mind" (mo-shin). It is the "mind that exists," and becomes one-sided about anything. We call such a mind the be-mind because it has things to think about and thereby generates ideas and judgments. The no-mind (mushin) is the same as the "true mind" (honshin). Neither congealing nor taking definite shape, it is a mind devoid of ideas and judgments, a mind that extends and spreads throughout your body, filling your whole being. . . . if the no-mind becomes a good part of you, you will not stay with one thing or neglect a single thing, it will be in your body like brimming water, coming out and serving whenever needed. . . . if you have something to think about in your mind, you are but are not hearing someone speaking to you. This is because your mind stays with that something you are thinking about. Your mind tilts to one side with that something, and as it does, you don't hear while hearing, you don't see while seeing. . . . If you try to rid your mind of that something, that attempt, in turn, becomes something in your mind. if you don't try, that something will go away on its own, leaving you with the no-mind.

AN EMPTY GOURD ON THE WATER

If you put an empty gourd on the water and touch it, it will slip to one side. No matter how you try, it won't stay in one spot. The mind of someone who has reached the ultimate state does not stay with anything, even for a second. It is like an empty gourd on the water that is pushed around.

THROW YOUR MIND AWAY

Don't let your mind stay with hands that are holding a sword about to strike. Forget your striking hands. Simply strike and slash your opponent. Don't put your mind in your opponent. Keep in mind that the opponent is void, you are void, and so are your striking sword and your hands holding it. And never be distracted by the voidness of it all.

The Zen master Wu-hsueh of Kamakura, when captured and about to be beheaded during the War of Great T'ang, said in verse: "Like a flash of lightning cut the spring breeze!" At this, we are told, the man about to behead him threw down his sword and ran away.

Wu-hsueh must have meant this: The moment the sword is swung up is like a flash of lightning, with no mind or idea in it. There is no mind in the striking sword, in the executioner, or in me, the man being executed. The executioner is void, the sword is void, and so am I the man about to be struck. The man striking is not a man, his striking sword is not a sword, and I, about to be struck, am no more than a flash of lightning. So cutting me is like cutting a wind blowing in the spring sky. Nothing stays, that's it. Soldier, cutting a wind, you won't feel a thing.

When you do everything like this, completely forgetting your mind, you have attained the rank of a superior hand. When you dance a dance, you take up a fan and take steps. When you do so, as long as you can't forget yourself, trying to improve the movements of your hands and feet and to dance a dance better, you can't say you are accomplished. While your mind stays with your hands and feet, your performance won't be interesting. Whatever you do while you haven't discarded your mind altogether will be bad.

SEEK THE RELEASED MIND

This is Mencius' word. What it means is that you Must search and seek the mind that has been released and bring it back to yourself. For example, if your dog, cat, or chicken is released and goes off some place, you will search and seek it and bring it home. Similarly, if your mind, which is your master, takes to an evil path and runs away, why don't you seek it and bring it home, says Mencius. This is quite understandable.

Nevertheless, a man by the name of Shao Kang Chieh said, "You must release your mind." This is just the reverse. What he means is that if you keep your mind in check, it will become exhausted and won't work like a cat, and that therefore lest your mind stay with you and become tainted, you must use it well, leave it alone, and chase it off, wherever it may be.

The mind becomes tainted and stays on, so don't let it get tainted, don't let it stay on, but find it and bring it back to yourself—this is what you say to someone at the beginner's stage. Try to become like a lotus that does not become tainted with mud.

There's nothing wrong with being in the mud. A well-polished ball of crystal does not become tainted even in the mud. Treat the mind like a ball of crystal, and let it go where it wants to.

If you constrain your mind, you will be unfree. You put your mind on a tight rein only while you are a beginner. If you continue to do so all your life, you will never reach the advanced stage, but end up remaining at a low stage.

While you are in training, the state of mind that Mencius prescribes, "Seek the released mind," will work well. At the ultimate stage, what you need is Shao Kang Chieh's dictum, "You must release your mind."

II. GUIDES

H AVING LEARNED SOMETHING about terrain of the martial path from the types of sources presented in Section I, followers of these ways are left to a daunting experience. Students follow a Way that demands persistence, discipline, and ruthless introspection. The various styles and systems of the martial arts vary, but they are similar in that they require the development of tremendous physical skills that take years to develop, and also insist on an integration of things of the body with things of the mind.

To say that such an undertaking is complex is an understatement. It is also challenging and frustrating, an experience that requires physical, psychological and spiritual effort that can be exhausting and painful in many ways.

Because of the complexity of the psychological dynamic inherent in this sort of effort at mind-body integration, teachers play an absolutely essential role. Teachers preserve past insights, guide trainees along a challenging path, watch carefully and correct relentlessly. They are there to guide trainees along the way, to encourage them, and to show each of us that we are capable of far more than we could ever have imagined. If we grow tired, or fearful, or discouraged, the teacher serves as a living embodiment of the tradition we follow, a reassurance that our actions are not in vain, and an affirmation of the reality we seek.

It is not that the martial path is impossible to navigate without such guides, only that an already daunting task is much more difficult without them.

There are other reasons why martial arts masters play a central role in these traditions. In the days when masters trained warriors for actual combat, it made little sense to write important lessons or techniques down, since this would in essence give them away to anyone who came into possession of the document, friend or foe. As a result, many of the old written sources we have are highly cryptic in nature. And they are that way in part to guard secrets—only someone who understood the "key" of the system would be able to penetrate the vague and stylistic prose.

Even given a written source, there is yet another reason for the need for a teacher. Insights about training are notoriously difficult to write down. We are discussing highly experiential phenomenon that are hard to express in words. To talk or write, for instance, about the experience of the flow of *ki* is not the same thing as experiencing it. Nor does it quite help the student learn how to cultivate that experience. The martial arts are mostly learned by doing.

Yet the human urge for preserving insight (even its pale reflection) for later generations is a strong one. And martial arts masters have not been immune. It is quite often the case that past masters have left us either more concrete pronouncements on organization or philosophy or elliptical, poetic utterances the significance of which are revealed only after reflection and effort. But they are valuable nonetheless. By looking at the record of what others have set down, we come to understand a little more deeply how these arts developed (it was, after all, the masters who have shaped these traditions), more fully grasp their rationale, and see, perhaps, a hint of common experience that stretches across the centuries.

1. TAIJI

The art of taiji *(t'ai chi) is a "soft" form of Chinese boxing* (quanfa – fist method) *that has become extremely popular in the West. Part of its spread has to do with the fact that individuals of any age can participate in its practice. A taiji form is flowing and gentle, emphasizing slow movements that place little or no strain on the body—a type of moving meditation. It is also the fact, however, that taiji is deeply complex and offers the more ambitious student correspondingly more difficult and complex training—paired forms, self-defense and combat applications, and weapons use. In addition, taiji is firmly grounded in the Daoist philosophical tradition. It stresses balance, gentility and a sensitivity to the energy of the world and the people around us. As you read the selection below(attributed to a thirteenth century teacher), note the many areas of commonality it shares with the concepts put forth by Laozi, the mention of Five Elements concepts, as well as the strong emphasis on the use of intrinsic energy (ch'i in this selection).*

TREATISE BY MASTER GANG SAN-FENG

Once you begin to move, the entire body must be light and limber.
Each part of your body should be connected to every other part.

In T'ai Chi practice, the entire body should coordinate into one complete unit. Once you begin to move, the entire body should move, and not just the hand, leg, elbow, and so on. As a beginner you should observe this principle at all times.

The universe moves and exercises its influence in a coordinated manner. For example, when the earth rotates the entire planet moves. Imagine what would happen if only part of the earth rotated while the rest of the planet remained stationary. As the system of balance and harmony was upset, drastic changes would occur throughout the universe.

T'ai Chi was created as a system of mental and physical discipline which human beings could understand and follow, and which is based on universal principles of 'balance and harmony. When you practice T'ai Chi, the first basic principle that you follow is: "Once you begin to move, the entire body must move as one."

Merely moving an arm or a leg is not practicing in a T'ai Chi manner. The body must be coordinated, relaxed, comfortable, peaceful, and mentally alert. In this way you will be able to maneuver the body in any direction, at will; when the mind wishes to move, the body will instantaneously follow its command.

A mistake often made by students who are new to the art of T'ai Chi is that of allowing the various parts of the body to move separately, in an uncoordinated manner. This is due to the fact that the parts of the body are not connected. When the hand moves, the rest of the body should respond in a totally coordinated manner. This will result in a well-controlled movement and help in the development of internal energy, which will eventually lead to the process of internal power projection.

The internal energy should be extended, vibrated like the beat of a drum. The spirit should be condensed in toward the center of your body.

Let us review here the important factors involved in the exercise of ch'i when practicing the T'ai Chi Form, as discussed in chapter 2. You should drive your internal energy outward from the center of the tan t'ien and extend it with sufficient pressure (not too much and not too little) so that the tension upon its surface is like that on the head of a drum. The ch'i will then vibrate like the beat of a drum when set in motion. The most important principle in the cultivation of ch'i is that you should extend your ch'i to the maximum margin of allowable pressure.

Cultivating your ch'i will also stimulate the power of your spirit, which should be drawn inward toward your, center point and condensed into the bone marrow. Stronger ch'i will help to elevate the power and the amount of the spirit. Do not let the spirit extend outward and get lost. Rather, let it be condensed inward and recycled.

When performing T'ai Chi, it should be perfect; allow no defect. The form should be smooth with no unevenness, and continuous, allowing no interruptions.

When you consider T'ai Chi as a discipline art and yourself as a martial artist, your attitude should be that of looking for perfection, which means that you continue to improve your study and practice until there is no defect.

The T'ai Chi meditative movements must be very smooth and even, just as if you were trying to draw a perfect circle without the aid of an instrument. You begin with a rough draft and try to draw as evenly and smoothly as possible in every direction. Although a perfect circle may only be possible in theory, as you continue working toward this goal you will be acting in a manner that is close to the required smoothness and evenness.

The internal energy, ch'i, roots at the feet, then transfers through the legs and is controlled from the waist, moving eventually through the back to the arms and fingertips.

Master Yang Chien-hou (1839-1917), son of Master Yang Lu chan, liked to remind his disciples of this principle many times during his daily T'ai Chi instruction.

After achieving some success in ch'i awareness practice, the T'ai Chi student should learn how to lower his ch'i feeling down to the ground and then project it upward from his feet through his legs. Therefore, in T'ai Chi practice, always keep your knees bent slightly to allow flexibility; never straighten your legs completely. This will allow the vibration of your internal energy to be transmitted from your feet through your knees to your waist.

Note that the T'ai Chi Classics use the term root, which emphasizes the importance of the feet. Both feet must always stay firmly attached to the ground, as strongly as the roots of a big tree. Also, the feeling of internal energy must penetrate deep into the ground, instead of merely being attached to the surface.

After projecting the ch'i upward, your waist serves as a transmitter; it controls, guides, and distributes the direction and amount of internal energy.

Keep your back and your entire torso in a vertical position, to allow the vibrations to travel freely upward through your back to your shoulders. Keep your shoulders completely relaxed to allow the transmission of ch'i down to your elbows and up to your fingertips. Always keep your elbows dropped and relaxed; your wrists are relaxed, but not limp.

When transferring the ch'i from your feet to your waist, your body must operate as if all the parts were one; this allows you to move forward and backward freely with control of balance and position. Failure to do this causes loss of control of the entire body system. The only cure for such a problem is an examination of the stance.

Ch'i carries tremendous amounts of vibration, requiring a high degree of coordination of the entire body. Your torso and limbs, your hands and legs, must be coordinated both physically and mentally with every other part of the body. All the parts should relate to each other as one inseparable unit, especially when you transfer your ch'i from the root upward. Success in this will allow you to maneuver your entire body—forward, backward, upward, downward—at will. You will be able to control any situation.

If the body is not coordinated, you will not be able to control your body system. According to the advice given in this T'ai Chi treatise (added at a later date by an unknown T'ai Chi master), "The only cure for such a problem is an examination of the stance."

Just as a weak foundation is unable to support a tall, strong building, a poor stance in T'ai Chi form will lead to poor coordination of the entire body, and this will prevent the student from being able to maneuver his body as one integrated unit.

Application of these principles promotes the flowing T'ai Chi movement in any direction: forward, backward, right side, and left side.

When you perform your T'ai Chi movements in a totally coordinated manner, your body is light and limber, and each part of your body connects to every other part. Your T'ai Chi form is very smooth and continuous, your ch'i vibrations are extended, and your spirit is condensed and centered.

The ch'i transfers from your feet upward through your legs to your waist, and eventually through your back to your arms and fingertips. This allows you to develop your mind to guide your body, so that you can move in any direction at will: forward, backward, to the right or left, up or down.

In all of this, you must emphasize the use of the mind in controlling your movements, rather than the mere use of the external muscles. You should also follow the T'ai Chi principle of opposites: when you move upward, the mind must be aware of down; when moving forward, the mind also thinks of moving back; when shifting to the left side, the mind should simultaneously notice the right side-so that if the mind is going up, it is also going down.

T'ai Chi emphasizes the development of the mind rather than the muscles, since the mind can be developed infinitely, beyond any limits of time and space.

In T'ai Chi practice you allow your mind to follow the T'ai Chi principle of opposites: the principle of Yin and Yang. Physically, your body can move in only one direction at a time—for example, a move to the right side. Yet in such a move there are other possibilities: moving to the left side, upward, downward, backward, forward. Thus, when you move in one direction, your mind should be simultaneously aware of the other possibilities.

When you have achieved the practice of yielding and totally relaxing yourself, your body will be able to respond freely to the direction of the mind. Theoretically, this type of training will allow the physical body to move as rapidly as the body's mental processes. Although in actuality limitations on physical movement may exist, the discipline will result in a body that is more limber and movements that are more controlled.

Such principles relate to Tai Chi movement in the same way that uprooting an object, and thereby destroying its foundation, will make the object fall sooner.

In the practice of T'ai Chi movement, Uprooting Power follows the principle presented, previously: the most efficient method of destroying an object's foundation is to uproot it. T'ai Chi masters have widely emphasized this principle in relation to Push Hands practice. By allowing the mind to focus downward, the opponent will resist in an upward direction and therefore allow you to uproot him easily and efficiently.

Besides clearly separating the positive and negative from one another, you should also clearly locate the substantial and insubstantial. When the entire body is integrated with all parts connected together, it becomes a vast connection of positive. and negative energy units. Each positive and negative unit of energy should be connected to every other unit and permit no interruption among them.

Since the Yin/Yang theory is the main principle of T'ai Chi philosophy, when you perform T'ai Chi movements the entire body must separate clearly into the positive and negative portions. For example, when your weight is placed more heavily on your right foot, the right side of your body will be substantial (positive, or Yang) and the left side insubstantial (negative, or

Yin). When you are moving forward, the front side of your body will be Yang and the rear or back portion of your body will be Yin. Conversely, when you are moving backward, your back will be Yang and your front will be Yin.

If your hand is moving forward, with the palm facing you, the back of your hand will be Yang and the palm will be Yin. In relation to your arm, the entire hand would be considered Yang and the arm, as it followed the forward direction of your hand, would be Yin. In relation to your other hand and arm, the entire moving hand and arm would be Yang while the other hand and arm would be Yin.

The same principle can be applied to the entire body. The body consists of a large number of positive and negative energy units. Each small unit of Yin and Yang must connect to every other unit in a coordinated manner, with no interruption among them, in order to maneuver the entire body in a balanced Yin/Yang manner. Connecting to each other also means coordinating with each other: neither the Yin nor the Yang can act independently, without regard for the other's motion.

In Long Forms your body should move like the rhythmic flow of water on a river or like the rolling waves of the ocean.

When you study T'ai Chi, each meditative movement is a complete unit within the T'ai Chi system. As you combine your forms into a larger and longer system, you should regard all of the forms as having become one long form, just as, if you were to pour many cups of water into a large container, you would then have one container of water, instead, of many separate, smaller units.

When you perform the forms you should also allow your internal energy to drive your entire body to flow, so that it moves continuously, like water flowing in a river or like the rolling waves of the ocean.

In the Long Form, Ward Off, Rollback, Press, Push, Roll-Pull, Split, Elbow, and Lean Forward are called the forms of the Eight Diagram (Pakua), the movement encompassing the eight directions. In stance, moving forward, backward, to the right side, to the left side, and staying in the center are called the Five-Style Steps. Ward Off, Rollback, Press, and Push are called the four cardinal directions. Roll-Pull, Split, Elbow, and Lean Forward forms are called the four diagonals. Forward, backward, to the left side, to the right side, and center are called metal, wood, water, fire, and earth, respectively. When combined, these forms are called the thirteen original styles of T'ai Chi.

The T'ai Chi Form originated as the thirteen postures of meditation. These are the eight postures, or directions—the Ward Off, Rollback, Press, and Push forms comprising the four cardinal directions, and the Roll-Pull, Split, Elbow, and Lean Forward forms, comprising the four diagonal directions—in combination with the five different ways to maneuver the eight meditative postures: forward, backward, to the left side, to the right side, and staying still in the center.

Through observation, the ancient Chinese defined the nature of human life according to five categories: metal, wood, water, fire, and earth. Metal represents hardness and penetration; as you move forward you act with the character of metal. Wood represents flexibility combined with strength; it is yielding and growing. When you move backward, your action has the character of wood. Fire and water act in opposite directions, but both are characterized by aggressiveness and pliability. They are yielding, piercing, uncertain, and powerful. When you move to the right or left side, you embody these attributes. Earth represents stability, immobility, motherhood, the center, the calmness of the origin. When you remain in the center, you adopt the nature of earth.

2. KANO JIGORO AND JUDO

At the turn of the twentieth century, Japan was fortunate in having a number of martial artists who worked tirelessly to promote their arts and demonstrate the relevance they could have in the contemporary world. This was a particular area of concern for the Japanese, who, in a rush to modernize and develop into an international power on par with those of the West, looked away from older traditions and embraced Western science and technology. With the crushing of a final samurai rebellion in 1876 (an event popularized in the recent film The Last Samurai) *by a conscript army trained along Western lines, the practicality of traditional martial arts was called into question, and their lustre as cultural activities waned as well.*

The educator Kano Jigoro, a martial arts enthusiast, took it upon himself to synthesize the various schools of jujutsu into a unified, rationalized system. He stressed the broad positive impact of martial arts training in his new system of judo, emphasizing its role in promoting physical and mental health for modern Japanese, and its attraction as a competitive sport. In the process, he revolutionized the modern martial arts. The scientific analysis of techniques and their modification to make practice safe for all, the use of rule-bound "sparring" in training and competition, his creation of a centralized organization to maintain standards, as well as the practice of training in a uniform called a gi *and denoting rank by the use of colored belts, are all innovations pioneered by Kano that have been adapted by many of the modern martial arts systems today.*

From *Modern Bujutsu and Budo* BY DONN F. DRAEGER

JUDO

There is no boundary in the way of flexibility, and the heart shall see no enemy.
—MIFUNE KYUZO

Modern judo is commonly described as a sport, a fighting art, a spiritual discipline, a system of physical education, and a recreational activity. It is to some extent all these things, and more. Exponents fully dedicated to judo consider it to be a "way of life. But a full appreciation of the true nature of judo is yet to be attained by the vast ma-jority of its six million exponents. This is because personal interests have narrowed the scope of judo; many of its important aspects have been played down in favor of a few specialized ones.

In order that judo may be seen in its true light, it is necessary to examine the original Kodokan Judo, because this is the link between Japanese feudal-age or classical judo and the sport-contest kind of judo that is so internationally popular today.

Kano Jigoro (1860-1938) was the founder of Kodokan Judo. In the personality of Kano the man, his rational genius as an educator and his personal philosophy as an idealist were of great importance in determining the nature of the original Kodokan Judo. Kano the educator sincerely believed that the prosperity of any nation depends on the fullness of that nation's energy, the latter determined by the excellence of the moral quality of its citizens' minds and the vigor of their bodies. As a boy Kano suf-fered from bad health. Because of his physical weakness he was often the victim of bullies, who beat him unmercifully. Because he was deeply concerned over the deplorable state of his health, Kano sought to correct it. He embarked on a program of physical exercise, participating in baseball, rowing, gymnastics, and hiking. Two years later Kano noted with great satisfaction that he had improved his health and now possessed a reasonably strong body. Nevertheless, the real turning point in Kano's life came with his decision to study *jujutsu* (the art of flexibility).

Kano enrolled in the Tenjin Shin'yo Ryu in 1877 under the tutelage of Fukuda Hachinosuke, who had been a disciple of Iso Mataemon, the founder of the ryu. The Tenjin Shin'yo Ryu was devoid of any martial aim in the Meiji era, but it still had the reputation of being an effective art of self-defense. Fukuda provided rigorous training for his few disciples, who soon proved to be less devoted to their study than was Kano. At every training session Kano found his interest in jujutsu increasing, al-though the severity of the physical exercise was taking its toll. The specialty of the Tenjin Shin'yo Ryu was *ate-waza*, or "striking techniques," and *katame-waza*, or "grappling techniques." Kano's tattered and torn *uwagi* (training jacket), preserved today by the Kano family as one of its treasures, gives evidence of the vigor with which he undertook his training. His injuries were many. Outside the dojo, Kano was frequently chided by companions for self-doctoring wounds received in jujutsu training. They complained that "Kano's ointment," a concoction that Kano applied liberally to his bruises and abrasions, smelled so bad that his presence was known to them even before he came into sight.

Fukuda's death brought Kano under the technical guidance of Iso Masatomo, a son of the founder of the Tenjin Shin'yo Ryu. But Iso's death forced Kano to continue his study of classical bujutsu elsewhere. He joined the Kito Ryu in 1881 and enlisted the services of an instructor named Iikubo Tsunetoshi. The Kito Ryu, too, at this time lacked martial fiber. Iikubo teachings, called *ran* (implying "freedom of action"), were considerably different from the jujutsu of other ryu. Iikubo demanded only moderately vigorous physical training, more attention being given to abstract symbolism in connection with physical technique. Emphasis in the Kito Ryu was laid on *nagewaza*, or "throwing techniques."

The cumulative effect of training in the styles of the Tenjin Shin'yo Ryu and the Kito Ryu not only further improved Kano's physique but gave him an insatiable ap-petite for yet more knowledge about jujutsu. He made an academic study of other classical bujutsu ryu, especially the methods of unarmed combat prescribed in the martial curricula of the Sekiguchi Ryu and the Seigo Ryu. At this time Japan was influenced by a current of thought that had turned most of its urban citizens against traditional institutions, customs, and beliefs. Kano lamented the fact that classical jujutsu had thus fallen into disuse. With the decline of jujutsu, the prestige of many legitimate experts was also lowered. Many skilled exponents, because of their social and even economic plight caused by the lack of disciples, turned to giving burlesque performances or to issuing challenges to all comers for the amusement of an admission-paying audience. Kano, however, regarded jujutsu as an object of national culture, a cultural asset worthy of the respect of the nation. He therefore resolved to restore jujutsu to its rightful place.

Kano began his self-appointed task by recasting jujutsu in a very special way, one that was both attractive and useful to the members of Meiji society. In 1882, Kano emerged with a synthesized system and established himself, under the humblest of circumstances, at the Eisho-ji, a temple in the Shitaya area of Tokyo. Kano called his new system Kodokan Judo, and began teaching nine disciples in a dojo of only twelve *tatami* (rice-straw mats used for flooring, each approximately three feet by six feet).

Kodokan Judo is a highly eclectic system. Kano liberally borrowed ideas from established classical Japanese sources. In selecting the name Kodokan, for example, Kano was well aware of the existence of a Kodokan at Mito, Ibaragi Prefecture. The Mito Kodokan was founded by daimyo Tokugawa Nariaki in the nineteenth century to further academic learning; there scholars like Aizawa Seishisai and Fujita Toko developed the chauvinistic kind of nationalism that inspired the overthrow of the Tokugawa bakufu and the nationalistic ideology of the leaders of Meiji and later eras. Kano's word "Kodokan" is homophonous with that of the Mito Kodokan, though the first ideogram of the two words differs. However, the general meaning of both Kano's Kodokan and that of Mito indicates a common spirit of cultural endeavor. Kano's Kodokan means: *ko* (lecture, study, practice), *do* (way or doctrine), and *kan* (hall or place), that is, "a place for studying the way."

The general concept and purpose of classical budo as a spiritual discipline used as a vehicle for attaining self-perfection appealed to Kano. He clearly intended his Kodokan Judo to be the vehicle to *michi o osameru*, or "attain the way." Kano deliberately chose the word "judo" in preference to "jujutsu" to describe his system in order to emphasize the importance of the philosophical aspect inherent in do as "a way of humanity." But Kano also had more mundane reasons for this choice. He wrote: "Many jujutsu ryu often indulged in such dangerous practices as throwing by rather unfair means, or by wrenching limbs. This led not a few people who had occasion to witness those wild exercises to deprecate jujutsu as being dangerous and harmful to the body. Moreover, there were some ill-disciplined jujutsu ryu, the disciples of which made themselves obnoxious to the public by willfully throwing down innocent people or by seeking quarrels. It thus turned out that the word jujutsu carried with it an unfavorable association in the minds of some in higher classes. Hence my desire was to show that my teaching, in marked contrast to jujutsu teachings [as] interpreted by the men of those classes, was quite free from danger and was not to be used as a means for reckless aggressiveness. . . . [My system] if taught under the name jujutsu might prove unacceptable to persons of the higher classes."

In Kano's words, aside from his obvious disdain for the reputation of Meiji-era jujutsu, we can also feel the degree of his preoccupation with social class-consciousness. The fact that Kano came from an affluent and influential merchant family, to-gether with his high level of education, made him extremely aware of social class differences in terms of class morals. It was this awareness that caused him to teach Kodokan Judo only to people of the highest moral qualities; Kano never intended his system to be taught indiscriminately to any and all people.

Kano's use of the word "judo" presented a problem. Some two centuries earlier, the Jikishin Ryu had become the first ryu known to have used the word "judo," but several other classical ryu soon followed suit. This fact made Kano insist on the use of the prefix "Kodokan" in order that his judo teachings might be distinguished from the judo of the classical styles.

THEORY OF KODOKAN JUDO

Kano accepted the practical aspects of *ju no ri*, or "the principle of *ju* (flexibility)," which had already been developed and was in use by the exponents of many classical bujutsu and budo. There were many interpretations of *ju*, however, some of which Kano regarded as gross misunderstandings of the working of this principle. These errors, if applied to Kodokan Judo, distort its theory, making it unrealistic and incapable of practical implementation. When the principle of *ju* is wrongly interpreted, there is an obvious conflict between theory and practice. In many ways these erroneous opinions still influence modern-day judo, and thus the principle of *ju* is worth further examination.

Classical bujutsu and budo exponents use the expression *Ju yoku go o sei suru* to describe the basis of the spirit and mechanics of their many different component systems. Kano's acceptance of this aphorism as applicable to Kodokan Judo shows him to have been one of its strongest expositors. From his detailed study of jujutsu, Kano found evidence of the fact that there was not a universal acceptance of the principle of *ju*, although only a minority failed to subscribe to it. He further discovered that among those jujutsu systems in which the principle was accepted, there were many interpretations that were unscientifically based.

"Ju yoku go o sei suru" may be loosely translated as "Softness controls hardness" or "Weakness controls strength"; it implies a certain naturalness of manner and action that is made the *sine qua non* of the execution of all techniques. For Kano, however, the meanings of "ju yoku go o sei suru" stem from Taoist teachings as expressed in the *Lao-tzu* (also known as the *Tao Te Ching*). This is an extremely important point, for it determines the intrinsic meaning of *ju* as applied to Kodokan Judo. The *Lao-tzu* declares that "reversing is the movement of the Tao," and makes of this phenomenon a law of nature that supports the idea that "the most yielding things in the world master the most unyielding." There is no direct mention of softness or hardness, nor of weakness or strength, which suggests that no precise limits are possible for either yielding or unyielding. Thus, in the multiple situations in which yield-ing and unyielding operate, the act of yielding can be made with strength, specifically, a flexible kind of strength. That which yields is not necessarily soft or weak in a quantitative sense, though its act of yielding may be so in a relative sense, and it only is temporarily softer and weaker than that which opposes it by being unyielding.

Kano was too much of a realist to be confused by abstract Chinese philosophy. From his study of the Kito Ryu he learned to appreciate the ancient and complex Chinese doctrine of *yin-yang* (*in-yo* in Japanese). The oneness of these two elements comprises the basis of the Kito Ryu theory of mechanics. *Ki*, meaning "to rise," is equated with yang (yo), a positive factor; *to*, meaning "to fall," is equated with yin (in), a negative factor. Yang implies light; yin implies shade. The action and interaction of these mutually participating and sustaining, inseparable aspects of nature regulate the use of strength in the execution of Kito Ryu techniques. Thus, varying interpretations of the expression "Ju yoku go o sei suru" did not disturb Kano's keen mind. He recognized the distinctions being made between softness and hardness, weakness and strength, as being formal distinctions, not absolute ones. Kano was also aware of the failure of some jujutsu ryu to make the necessary practical interpretation, thus being led down the path of solely aesthetic endeavor, resulting in ineffective techniques.

Kano's fervent desire as a youth to attain physical fitness allowed him to recognize and appreciate the merit of physical strength in athletic endeavor. In fact, Kano embodied his respect for physical strength in the element of *rentai-ho* (method of physical training), one of the aspects of his "three-culture principle", which makes Kodokan Judo a system of physical education. It was Kano's idea to argue not against the development and use of physical strength but rather the misuse of that strength. Kano endorsed his disciple Arima Sumitomo's comment: "Instances often oc-cur in which it is found advantageous for one to employ an unusually large amount of strength or to exert strength directly against strength in defeating an enemy. . . . It follows, therefore, that a strong man can avail himself of judo to a more decided advantage than a less strong man." It was natural that Kano placed great reliance upon the Tenjin Shin'yo Ryu interpretation of ju—the submissive quality of the body that subordinates it to the mind—that makes it a principle of flexibility of mind in meeting and adapting oneself rapidly to sudden emergencies. This concept had already been expressed as *karada o shite seishin ni jujun narashimeru jutsu*, or "the art of making the body obedient to the mind," by Terada Kan'emon, the fifth headmaster of the Kito Ryu and founder of the Jikishin Ryu. Thus, for Kano, the principle of ju was never without practical physical implications; for the body, directed by the flexible mind, is to react with similar mechanical flexibility as it adapts itself to a situation encountered suddenly.

The principle of ju as applied to the mechanical execution of judo techniques was for Kano the basis for the act of combining one's strength with that of the opponent so as to bring about the latter's defeat. Jujutsu systems earlier recognized the same principle in the same way, as can be seen by the expression *Kureba mukae, sareba okuru*, which means "When the opponent comes, welcome him; when he goes, send him on his way." The *go-go ju, ni-hachiju* (five and five is ten; two and eight is ten) theory of jujutsu evolved from that, and is summarized as follows: "If the enemy pushes with five units of strength, pull with five units of strength; the result is ten units. If the enemy pulls with eight units of strength, push with two units of strength; the result is also ten units."

Kano applied scientific reasoning to such jujutsu expressions and clarified their somewhat cryptic quality by postulating a unit-of-strength theory of his own: "What then does this 'gentleness' or 'giving way' really mean? . . . Let us say that the strength of a man standing in front of me is represented by ten units, whereas my strength, less than his, is represented by seven units. Now, if he pushed me with all his force I would surely be pushed back or thrown down, even if I used all my strength against him. But if instead of opposing him I were to give way to his strength by withdrawing my body just as much as he had pushed, taking care at the same time to keep my balance, then he would naturally lean forward and thus lose his balance. In this new position he may become so weak, not in his actual physical strength, but because of his awkward position, as to have his strength represented for the moment by only three units instead of his normal ten. But meanwhile, I, by keeping my balance, retain my full strength, as originally represented by seven units. Here, then, I am momentarily in a superior position, and I can defeat my opponent by using only half of my strength, that is, half of my seven units, or three and one-half, against his three. This leaves one-half of my strength available for any [other] purpose. If I had greater strength than my opponent I could of course push him back. But even if I wished to, and had the power to do so, it would still be better [more efficient] for me first to give way, because by so doing I should have greatly saved my energy and exhausted my opponent's."

Kano's application of the principle of ju, then, is that of using the body not to collide with forces applied by the opponent but rather through clever maneuvering to combine with them to upset the opponent. Kano, well versed in dynamics, also approved of Arima's statement: "The degree of power is determined by the weight of a given body and the speed of its motion, so that the greatness of weight and the agility of movement are important factors in judo. Viewed in this light judo is not an art to be wondered at; on the contrary, it merely employs strength in the most effective way." The principle of ju for many jujutsu ryu, as well as for Kano, incorporates two aspects, those of yielding and resisting. Kano objected to those who believed that yielding was the only facet of the principle. He notes: "The way of gaining victory over an opponent is not confined to gaining victory only by giving way. . . . Sometimes an opponent takes hold of one's wrist. How can someone possibly release himself without using his strength against this opponent's grip? The same thing can be asked when somebody is seized around his shoulders from behind by an assailant. . . . These are forms of direct attack." In suggesting that Kodokan Judo techniques operate on the basis of both yielding and resisting, Kano also explodes the fiction that Kodokan Judo is purely a defensive system: "If [that] were true it would imply that judo techniques are useless unless the opponent attacks first, and if this were so it [judo] would indeed be a restricted form of combat."

Kodokan Judo, like many jujutsu systems, operates on the basis of kobo-itchi, that is, the aspects of attack and defense are but one and the same thing, priority of aspect being determined in a given situation. Kano demonstrated the aggressive nature and superiority of Kodokan Judo over the Yoshin Ryu jujutsu, based on defense and led by Totsuka Hikosuke. In 1886 under the auspices of the Tokyo police, a tournament was arranged between adherents of the Yoshin Ryu and Kodokan Judo. Fifteen men were selected on either side to demonstrate their respective styles of combat. The Kodokan won a brilliant victory, losing only two matches and drawing one. Saigo Shiro played no small part in this triumph. Using his technique of yama arashi (moun-tain storm), Saigo devastated his opponents with masterly throws. It is not generally known, however, that Saigo's technique was one he had learned earlier from the Daito Ryu style of aiki-jujutsu.

AIMS OF KODOKAN JUDO

There has always been an assumption by many exponents of Kodokan Judo that the system that they practice is superior to any other in the field of hand-to-hand tactics. Indeed, Kano himself gives evidence of his belief that Kodokan Judo is in all ways superior to anything ever developed in the Japanese martial arts and ways. We see this best in Kano's choice of the formal name Nippon Den Kodokan Judo, an expression that implies "the best budo of Japan." This prestigious and boastful appellation appears on all certificates of dan rank. The validity of its implied meaning, of course, cannot be substantiated, but it is indicative of the confidence and faith that Kano placed in his beloved Kodokan Judo.

Having clearly defined the principle of ju, categorically denying that yielding or giving way is its only mode of operation, Kano states: "If thus the principle of giving way cannot cover all the methods used in contests . . . is there any principle which really covers the whole field? Yes, there is, and that is the principle of maximum efficient use of mind and body." In his academic study of jujutsu, Kano discovered the expression *shin-shin no chikara o moto no yuko ni shi o sum*. This stresses the importance of the economical use of energy, both mental and physical. Restated by Kano, it is the following: "Whatever be the object, the best way of attaining it shall be the best use of energy directed to that purpose or aim." This statement Kano announced in 1923 as *seiryoku zen'yo*, or the principle of "the best use of energy." This principle is the basis of the Kodokan ideal.

In this principle Kano sees energy as a living force, not simply as physiological vigor. Through judo training one learns how to abide by the principle. But higher values were in Kano's mind as he exhorted all exponents of Kodokan Judo to follow the principle. Training in Kodokan Judo for the purpose of acquiring a physically sound body (*rentai-ho*), or for the purpose of developing expert contest skill (*shobu-ho*), is termed *kyogi* judo by Kano, that is, judo in the "narrow sense," because it stresses only technique. Kyogi judo is to be replaced by *kogi* judo, or judo in the "wide sense," in which *shushin-ho*, or mental cultivation in terms of moral standards, leads to the perfection of the self. Thus, physical perfection of the self is not sufficient in itself, for no matter how healthy an exponent becomes through his practice of judo, no matter how skillful he is, "If he does not benefit society," says Kano, "his existence is in vain." Rentai-ho, shobu-ho, and shushin-ho form the three elements of what Kano referred to as his "three-culture principle," a principle that makes Kodokan Judo a form of physical education.

Kano wished judo training to be undertaken not only in the dojo but also outside it and so make of its physical aspects the focus of human endeavor for the progress and development of man. Whereas the exponents of kyogi judo may be technically mature, it is only with their realization of kogi judo that they become socially mature. Kano's outlook here is conditioned by the

Confucian precept of "extending one's scope of activities to include other people and activities." In this way it amplifies the avowed purpose of classical budo, which in some ryu is quite vague in terminology except when dealing with the seeking of individual perfection. Kano defines Kodokan Judo, in terms of the principle of seiryoku zen'yo, thus: "Judo is not a method of making the best use of mental and physical energy for purposes of attack and defense alone, rather it is a method by which this principle [seiryoku zen'yo] can be assimilated and applied in all spheres of life." Following this train of thought, Kano evolved his second great principle, which he called *ji-ta kyoei*, or the principle of "mutual prosperity" (mutual assistance, cooperation, and welfare).

The principle of mutual prosperity became the keystone of Kano's hopes for international social harmony. The basic elements of Kano's ji-ta kyoei are found in the tenets of the classical bujutsu and budo ryu. Exemplary among these tenets are the teachings of the Yagyu Shinkage Ryu (Edo line), which features swordsmanship of a kenjutsu type. Kenshi of the Edo Yagyu Shinkage Ryu regard their training in kenjutsu as being kogi kenjutsu, and more commonly refer to it as *seiho* or *heiho*. They seek self-perfection through training according to prescribed sword techniques, but such an endeavor is always only a means to a greater end. In the doctrine of the Edo Yagyu Shinkage Ryu, seiho is the declared aim of the exponent who seeks to perform "good deeds" for Japanese society. Kano's emphasis on doing good for society, however, has a considerably broader sphere of application, that is, the entire international community. Kano expected that exponents of Kodokan Judo everywhere, through their common interest in training and learning, would learn to use the principle of seiryoku zen'yo, and to understand that this is possible only when there is mutual cooperation. This realization, in turn, leads them, in Kano's words, "to a very high state where the differences between oneself and others have been transcended," and they are able to apply the principle to the daily activities of their lives, there to influence others so as to make their lives similarly wholesome and useful to mankind.

TECHNIQUES AND TRAINING METHODS

Any honest and thoroughgoing analysis of Kano's original Kodokan Judo techniques reveals the fact that all of them without exception were in some manner already being used by the older classical bujutsu or budo systems. Thus what was collectively designated by Kano as the Kodokan *go kyo no waza*, or "the five principles of technique," as well as those techniques standardized in the Kodokan katame-waza, the category of grappling techniques, stem from the mechanics and theory of sources with which Kano was familiar. Modern judoists using effective contest throws like *seoinage, haraigoshi*, and *osotogari* to down their opponents, or judoists who gain a contest victory through the immobilization of their opponent with techniques like *kesagatame*, *jujime*, and *ude hishigi jujigatame*, owe a real debt to sources older than Kodokan Judo; this is no less true in the practice of *ate-waza*, the assaulting techniques of Kodokan Judo in which the exponent uses various parts of his body as weapons against the anatomical weaknesses of the opponent. Rudimentary forms of Kano's original Kodokan techniques can be seen in the tactics of the Yagyu Shinkage line of "empty-hand" combat (itself derived from the influence of the Kage Ryu and the Tenshin Shoden Katori Shinto Ryu), the Kito Ryu (based on the Tenshin Ryu), the Jikishin Ryu (influenced by the Kito Ryu), the Tenjin Shin'yo Ryu (based on the Yoshin Ryu, the Shin no Shinto Ryu, the Fukuno Ryu, the Isogai Ryu, and the Miura Ryu), the Sekiguchi Ryu (greatly influenced by sumo tactics), and those ryu, such as the Seigo Ryu, that deal with *kumi-tachi*, combat by grappling.

As regards Kano's originality in devising new techniques for his Kodokan Judo, he was an adapter rather than an adopter of existing ones. It is in this sense that Kano demonstrated considerable originality of thought. Two criteria conditioned Kano's efforts in the design of Kodokan techniques: (1) to base all techniques on scientific principles, and (2) to remove all crude and dangerous practices from techniques. Both of these important considerations were prompted by the social needs of Meiji society.

Kano's refinement of old techniques along scientific lines was based on the fact that the empty-hand techniques with which he was familiar appeared to him to be unscientific. But on the basis of what is known today of those techniques, the validity of Kano's criticism is suspect; perhaps it would be fairer to criticize the technical ability of the men in Kano's time who used those techniques. Nevertheless, in view of the wide range of opinions with regard to the principle of ju, there were many techniques performed in Kano's time that used this principle in an unacceptable manner, and he did seek to make it possible to use mechanical efficiency in the techniques that he adapted for use in Kodokan Judo.

Kano's concern for the personal safety of those using Kodokan Judo techniques brought about a refinement of techniques that were once battlefield methods or methods of self-defense for use in civil scuffles in which the safety of the loser was unimportant. The resulting refinement of such techniques for use in Kano's judo made of them a kind of sport-play activity. And so Kano established certain rules governing the execution of techniques, and clearly described and defined certain prohibited actions.

Perhaps Kano's biggest contribution to empty-hand techniques was that of requiring opponents to grip each other by the garments when executing them. While this feature can be found in some of the older bujutsu and budo forms, gripping is almost absent in the truly classical arts of combat, the bujutsu, where it would have proved to be not only a dangerous practice but one that would rarely have been possible because combatants usually wore some kind of armor. The act of gripping fulfills both of Kano's aims in his adaptation of older techniques for Kodokan Judo. Not only does gripping lend more efficient leverage against the opponent, but it affords a high margin of safety for the one being thrown; in the latter case the thrower can control the pattern and rate of fall of his opponent, making a safe landing possible instead of leaving his victim to gravity.

In many ways Kano stands as a heretic vis-à-vis the classical bujutsu and budo traditions. For example, in devising Kodokan Judo training methods he defied the classical concept of yugen insofar as this term implies "mysterious skills." To some degree this is a direct refutation of yomeigaku philosophy, which formed the very backbone of all classical learning methods. Kano did not agree that it was necessary to acquire technical and spiritual maturity both through experience and through penetration of the hidden depths of the of the *okuden*, or secret teachings; for if this were admitted, Kano's own study, particularly that made in a purely academic way, would mark him as being deficient in many respects in his knowledge of classical bujutsu. Kano also placed less reliance on kan, or intuition, in learning, replacing it with rational thought and analysis based on a "method of instruction in conformity with modern science."

Kano decried the lack of systematic teaching methods that would make things like learning *ukemi* (taking falls) a less dangerous task. In most jujutsu systems the thrower would hurl down his victim and the latter would have to fall as best he could. Kano had seen with his own eyes the crippling results of this practice. He therefore devised a special manner in which ukemi was to be learned without running undue risk of injury. It is this feature of Kodokan Judo that satisfies one criterion of good physical education, that of safe and systematic teaching methods, and further identifies the orthodox Kodokan manner of teaching. Thus the tendency of some modern judoists to omit systematic ukemi exercises from training is not the "new development" that it is sometimes claimed to be by its advocates; it is rather a reversion to the old, crude, and unsystematic practices of jujutsu.

The central point on which Kodokan Judo rests as a system of physical education is Kano's demand for a state of equilibrium among the elements of his "three-culture principle," those of. rentai-ho, shushin-ho, and shobu-ho. In regard to the last, Kano says: "I did not attach exclusive importance to the contest side of training . . . but aimed at a combination of contest exercises and training of mind and body." Skill, for Kano, is an important aspect of training, to be sure, but as a goal of judo training it is inferior to that of skill used as a means to the greater social aims of Kodokan Judo. Kano also clearly announced his dislike for Spartan training methods that rely upon "survival of the fittest." "Correct judo training," says Kano, "must not cause overexertion."

In order for Kodokan Judo to satisfy other criteria of good physical education, Kano insisted that all training must give full regard to the harmonious development of the human body. Such a development is impossible in a contest-oriented kind of training in which the major emphasis is on *ran-*

dori, or "free exercise." Kano's own experience with the *ran* system of the Kito Ryu had given him the idea for ran-dori; in the Kito Ryu, trainees were urged to *ran o toru*, "take freedom in action." But Kano saw ran-dori as being incomplete in itself. He concluded: "What is deficient in ran-dori must be supplemented by kata [prearranged form]."

Kata, long the basis of classical bujutsu and budo, was extremely important for Kano, who not only made it the theoretical base for Kodokan Judo but insisted that judo cannot be a good system of physical education without sufficient use of kata in the training schedules of all exponents. Kata confers on judo the means by which it becomes balanced physical education, transforming kyogi judo—ran-dori, or contest-centered judo—into kogi judo, a cultural or educational discipline, which is the essence of Kodokan Judo. Kano's deliberate designation of *nage no kata and katame no kata*, the prearranged forms of throwing and grappling, respectively, as *ran-dori no kata*, or prearranged forms of ran-dori, shows his intention that these two kata are to be used as the theoretical basis for ran-dori training.

Kano declared ran-dori, kata, and shiai to be the primary elements of judo training but also made judicious use of lectures and *mondo*, question-and-answer periods, in directing the technical development of his disciples. The value of these latter two training methods in stimulating the intellectual development and moral training of judo exponents is very real. Kano considered that the personal character of all of his disciples was the real test of their value, and always required them to conduct their lives in a dignified manner. By his own outstanding example Kano inspired all who came to the Kodokan.

Kano's ideas on human virtues can be categorized as (1) those developing and influencing others and (2) those affecting one's own life. The former category includes the cultivation of a sense of honor, the avoidance of luxurious habits, a sense of justice, a sense of righteousness, kindness and discernment, an adherence to good etiquette, and honesty; the latter category includes the development of good mental health, control of the passions, achievement of physical fitness, the development of courage, preparedness, mental acuity, persistence and determination, readiness in emergencies, temperance in all things, and esteeming not victory over an opponent but the way in which victory is striven for.

JUDO TODAY

Kano remarked: "Nothing is of greater importance than education; the teaching of one virtuous man can reach many, and that which has been learned by one generation can be passed on to a hundred." Modern-day exponents of judo will do well to reflect on Kano's words in light of the original form and concepts of Kodokan Judo that have been described. Because Kano believed that Kodokan Judo could contribute to the peace of the world and improve the general welfare of mankind, he made very determined attempts to internationalize judo. He traveled abroad eight times to further this goal. While in London in 1933. Kano spoke of his plans for a world judo federation and die dissemination of the teachings of Kodokan Judo throughout the entire world: "The spirit of judo. which has as its ideal world peace, concurs with the international spirit: and in this respect, if an international judo federation comes into existence, it will mean the establishment of a real international organization." In 1952, though he did not live to see it, Kano's dream of an international judo body was realized. That organization, the International Judo Federation, is the senior world body for judo and is composed of national federations from over seventy nations. The aims and purposes of the federation, as stated in article four of its statutes, are as follows:

1. To promote cordial and friendly relations among the members, and to coordinate and supervise Judo activities in all countries of the world.
2. To protect the interests of Judo throughout the world.
3. To organize and conduct World Judo Championships and Judo competitions in the International Olympic Games Program, in conjunction with the Regional Unions.
4. To organize the Judo movement throughout the world on an international basis, and to promote the spread and development of the spirit and techniques of judo.
5. To establish technical standards.

Prior to the end of World War It, judo in Japan rose to an all-time high of technical perfection. Although exponents looked forward to competition, the real purpose of all training was seishin tanren, or spiritual forging. The prohibition against carrying on martial arts and ways declared by SCAP in 1945 included judo and resulted in its technical stagnation. When judo was finally reinstated in 1947, Kano Risei, adopted son of Kano Jigoro and third president of the Kodokan, made resolute efforts to rebuild the technical integrity of Japan's judo tinder the aegis of the Kodokan. He organized the Zen Nippon Judo Renmei (All-Japan Judo Federation) in 1949 and assumed leadership over the administrative and technical aspects of judo.

Although aware of the cultural values of Kodokan Judo, Kano Risei's policies nevertheless placed emphasis on judo as a competitive sport. This emphasis began with the organization of the first truly national Japanese judo championships in 1948. Judo in Japan today is primarily a sport, much to the dissatisfaction of many traditionalists who view judo as a Japanese cultural activity. Nevertheless, the way all judo training is conducted today continues to be one in which experts for world and Olympic competitions are formed.

3. FUNAKOSHI GICHIN AND KARATE-DO

Ask most people to name a martial art and they will likely respond, "karate." This "empty hand" martial art has spread across the world in various forms, whether in the more "orthodox" form of Japanese karatedo *or Okinawan* karatejutsu, *or as Korean* taekwondo. *Even the various "hard" boxing systems of China popularly know as "kung-fu" are confused in the popular imagination with karate.*

Funakoshi, like Kano, was an innovator who ensured that a traditional art he valued would survive into the modern age. The story of karate is an interesting one because it demonstrates not only that techniques and systems change through the years, but also how the philosophical rationale of a martial arts system can be modified to better fit the times. Karate is a dramatic case in point—a "peasant" form of empty-hand fighting from one of Japan's conquered territories that was made more attractive to the Japanese by tying its rationale to more "mainstream" cultural elements. And, in a curious twist of fate, when Japan's armed martial arts forms were forbidden for a time during Allied occupation, karate (as an unarmed system) escaped the ban, experienced a popularity on a par with older martial systems and ultimately achieved worldwide prominence.

From *Modern Bujutsu and Budo* BY DONN F. DRAEGER

> True karate-do is this: that in daily life, one's mind and body be trained and developed in a spirit of humility; and that in critical times, one be devoted utterly to the cause of justice.
> —FUNAKOSHI GICHIN

There are more than seventy different Japanese systems of karate-do; some thirty more systems prefer to designate their teachings karate-jutsu. There is, however, in all of these systems, to varying degrees, the influence of what was originally a plebeian Okinawan form of combat. Distinctive Japanese taste has influenced the original Okinawan teachings to produce a characteristically Japanese kind of karate-do that is primarily devoted to the study and practice of unarmed methods of hand-to-hand sparring and grappling. Japanese karate-do, properly taught, is a balanced system of spiritual discipline, physical education, self-defense, and competitive sport.

Cultural exchanges between Japan and the Ryukyu Islands have existed since pre-historic times. But the fact that these islands had nothing much to offer the outside world until the Chinese developed gunpowder in the ninth century A.D., and later, from the twelfth century onward, required sulphur in large quantities for their war against the Mongols, kept China and Okinawa from entering earlier into large-scale trading or tributary relationships.

In the seventeenth century the Japanese overlords of Okinawa made possible a limited knowledge in Japan of both Chinese and Okinawan combative arts. But it is only in the Meiji era that we have evidence of the Japanese government's interest in Okinawan fighting arts. An alert Japanese army doctor noticed the unusually well-proportioned and strong physiques of certain Okinawan conscripts in Okinawa; subsequent investigation revealed that such physiques were due to the practice of what the Okinawans called *te*, meaning "hand." Te is a category of hand-to-hand combat including both unarmed and armed combat. It developed under the strong influence of Chinese *wu shu* (martial arts), especially those of the *ch'uan fa*, or "fist way," types brought to Okinawa by Chinese monks, merchants, and traders. Okinawan *te* developed as a plebeian form of fighting.

The Japanese officials on Okinawa approved the inclusion of te in the physical education curriculum of Okinawan schools in 1902 because it served a military purpose, that of conditioning future conscripts. Te, as adapted for the purpose and general aims of physical education, eventually became known as *karate-jutsu*, the ideograms for which mean "Chinese hand art."

No historical proof has been found to show that Okinawan te or karate-jutsu was systematically taught in Japan before the Taisho era, though it is probable that individuals traveling between the Ryukyu Islands and Japan's southernmost main island, Kyu-shu, had some knowledge of these arts. The present emperor, while touring Okinawa in 1921 as the crown prince, witnessed a demonstration of karate-jutsu and was so favorably impressed that he included the event in his formal report to the Japanese government. Official Japanese curiosity about Okinawan combative arts led the Ministry of Education to invite an Okinawan expert to Japan. Funakoshi (Tominakoshi) Gichin (1869-1957) of Shuri, an elementary school teacher, was selected to travel to Japan because he was the most literate exponent of the Okinawan art of te; but there were many other native exponents more skillful than he. Funakoshi had appeared at the Butokuden in Kyoto in 1917 in a preliminary effort to familiarize Japanese government officials and the members of the Butokukai with te and karate-jutsu. Bur it was not until his second visit, in 1922, that he made the first public demonstrations of karate-jutsu in Japan.

To increase his chances of interesting the Japanese public in karate-jutsu, Funakoshi deliberately made his appearances only before intellectuals. He gave impressive demonstrations and lectures on the physical and spiritual merits of karate-jutsu to audiences composed primarily of artists and attorneys; Funakoshi reasoned that professional people who possessed keen minds generally tend to have unfit bodies. He stressed the fact that training in karate-jutsu strengthens even the weakest body, and that a person of small stature like himself could develop and maintain good health through such training. Funakoshi selected volunteers from his audiences to test his resistance to blows and to efforts to force him to lose his balance; no member of any audience succeeded in making Funakoshi wince or tumble. His calm and dignified appearance had a remarkable effect upon all who witnessed his demonstrations, and it was not long before his teachings gathered a considerable number of devotees. Funakoshi also demonstrated and lectured on karate-jutsu at Kano Jigoro's Kodokan and at universities, where his dynamic presentation of his art greatly inspired educators and students alike.

Funakoshi's method of introducing karate-jutsu in Japan brought only a small portion of the Okinawan art before the Japanese public, that portion which Funakoshi deemed to be most appropriate to his purpose and most likely to gain the approval of his intel-lectual audiences. His popularity as an instructor grew rapidly, and with it the public's curiosity to learn more about this effective method of hand-to-hand combat. By 1924, Keio Gijuku University in Tokyo had adopted karate-jutsu as physical education; Tokyo Imperial, Shoka (Hitotsubashi), Waseda, Gakushuin, Takushoku, Chuo, Meiji, Nihon, and Hosei universities soon followed Keio's example. The great popularity of karate-jutsu among Japanese university students soon gave this art a larger following in Japan than on Okinawa.

Funakoshi remained in Tokyo directing the establishment of a new style of karate-jutsu based on the mechanics of the Shuri te that he had learned from Azato Anko. Mabuni Kenwa, a former fellow student of Funakoshi during the time that both were studying Okinawan te under a teacher named Itosu Yasusune, arrived in Japan to organize the development of his own style of karate-jutsu in 1928. Itosu was an exponent of the Shuri te originated by Matsumura Munehide; the latter was also the teacher of Azato. In spite of these fundamental relationships, Funakoshi's style of karate-jutsu dif-fered vastly from Mabuni's style, especially after Mabuni trained under the guid ance of Higaonna Kanryo (1888-1951), a master of Naha te. Thereafter, Funakoshi and Mabuni went their separate ways as instructors of distinctly different styles.

Though Funakoshi favored the Shuri te style, he made a number of modifications to it. His son Yoshitaka acted as Funakoshi's instructor; his teachings were radically new and formed the basis of the original Japanese style of karate-jutsu. Mabuni developed what he first called the Hanko ("Half-heart") style. Later he preferred the name Shito; this name derives from the alternate readings of ideograms found in the names of his former teachers, *shi* for the *ito* of Itosu, and *to* for the *higa* of Higaonna. On Okinawa, in the absence of Funakoshi and Mabuni, Miyagi Gogyun (Chojun), a senior disciple of Higaonna, became a leading master of a style of karate-jutsu that he called Goju; this name derives from the influence of the Chinese ideograms go, meaning "hardness," and *ju*, meaning "softness." Miyagi selected this name for his teachings because his Goju techniques are based on maintaining a balance of resistive and flexible actions.

During his stay in Japan, Funakoshi developed a long line of disciples, each of whom has played a very influential role in the development of a modern Japanese kind of karate-do technique expressing the individual styles of these men. Most prominent among Funakoshi's senior disciples in Japan are Takagi Masatomo, Nakayama Masatoshi, Ito Ken'ichi, Otsuka Hidenori, and Konishi Yasuhiro. Moreover, Yamada Tatsuo is of primary importance in the development of the Japanese style of kempo, "fist way." Mabu-ni's disciples, too, have greatly affected the Japanese development of karate-do, but their teachings remain more under the influence of Okinawan technique than do those of Funakoshi's disciples. Kokuba Kosei is one such outstanding disciple. After study with Mabuni, Kokuba followed Motobu Choki, a Shuri te specialist who learned from Mabuni, Itosu, and Azato; Kokuba also studied for a time with Funakoshi. Both Mabuni's and Miyagi's teachings, as interpreted by Sawayama Masaru, have also influenced the development of Japanese kempo; but it is Miyagi's last Japanese disciple, Yamaguchi Gogen, who must be credited with founding a typically Japanese Goju style of karate-do.

The rapid proliferation of Japanese karate-do cannot, however, be credited to the teachings of any one man or the influence of a single sect. Many skilled exponents have influenced the formation of Japanese karate-do and have shared in promoting its growth. From the traditionalist's point of view, however, Funakoshi must be considered the "father" of Japanese karate-do, insofar as he is responsible for making various important innovations in Okinawan karate-jutsu that have brought this art closer to Japanese taste. In 1935 Funakoshi changed the concept kara, which was originally written with an ideogram meaning "China." By substituting another ideogram, also pronounced "kara," Funakoshi changed the meaning to "void" or "empty." Thus, Funakoshi's new karate-jutsu meant "empty-hand art." Two years later Funakoshi discarded the word "jutsu" in favor of "do." Thus karate-do was born in Japan, and the literal meaning is "empty-hand way." In Okinawa, Funakoshi's changes angered many exponents, who considered them to be gross insults to tradition. But by 1938 almost all Okinawan exponents were accustomed to calling their systems either karate-jutsu or karate-do.

To facilitate the dissemination of his teachings, Funakoshi established a central dojo in Tokyo in 1936 and, after much deliberation, gave it the name Shotokan. The ideograms that are read "Shoto" are Funakoshi's pen name as a calligrapher; *kan* means "hall." Funakoshi never referred to his style of karate-do as the Shotokan Ryu; in fact, he was categorically opposed to the use of the feudal term "ryu" for his newly developing karate-do. Thus the use of the expression "Shotokan Ryu" among modern exponents to bolster claims to authenticity through affiliation with Funakoshi's teachings has no valid basis. Funakoshi's son Yoshitaka, however, organized the Shoto-kai

(Shoto Association), and this organization became the basis for the founding of the Nippon Karate Kyokai (Japan Karate Association) in 1957.

The presence of Okinawan masters of karate-jutsu in Japan brought about a reasonably wide dissemination of their original teachings, but it also caused an even wider interpretation of these teachings by masters and disciples. Intense rivalries among masters were generated as each tried to outdo the others in skill; these rivalries were inflamed by loyal disciples who sought to establish the superiority of their master or sect over all others. The scope of techniques, as well as methods of training, were greatly expanded by this professional jealousy and friction.

With Japan's entry into war with China in 1937, and its participation in World War II, karate-jutsu and karate-do were officially recognized as valu-able adjuncts in the training of soldiers and sailors. The mass participation of some of Japan's finest young men resulted in a prodigious development of new unarmed karate-like techniques. After Japan's defeat, and during the period when most martial arts and ways were prohibited, karate-like systems continued to flourish; the Allied Powers believed these systems to be little mote than methods of physical education in the manner of "Chinese box-ing." The technical progress of karate-jutsu and karate-do in the 1950's and 1960's was characterized by the formalization of the techniques, tactics, and training methods of each sect. This in turn made obvious the very great dif-ferences among the various sects, and created in many experts the desire to formulate a Japanese national standard for karate-do. Toward this end the participation of great numbers of high school and university students in karate-do competitions brought popular appeal to the sport aspect of karate-do and made it a sport of national importance.

ESSENCE, AIMS, AND TECHNIQUES

The very strong influence of Chinese ch'uan-fa on Okinawan te and karate jutsu is carried over in lesser degree to the Japanese styles of karate-like technique. Te that developed at Shuri was under the direct influence of *wai-chia*, the so-called "external systems" of ch'uan-fa; that at Naha was affected by the *nei-chia*, the "internal systems"; while te at Tomari was a com-bination of the two forms. Japanese karate-do absorbed many features of the external styles but was relatively uninfluenced by the internal forms.

The concept expressed in the *Lao-tzu* as "The most yielding things in the world master the most unyielding" indicates the most important character-istics of the internal systems. The effect of the "soft" and pliable actions of the internal systems depends on *nei-kung*, or "internal power," which in turn is released through the interaction of the will (*i*), vital energy (*ki*), and mus-cular strength. Internal systems make much *wu-kung*, exercises that gear glands and mind to physical effort. External systems rely on the use of *wai-kung*, or "external power." They are characterized by "hard" and rigorous muscular exertion in which quickness of eye, hand (fist), and foot are all essential. No system of ch'uan-fa, te, karate-jutsu, or karate-do is an absolutely "soft" or "hard" system, but may be categorized as being one or the other depending on the priority given to one or the other aspect in the execution of techniques.

Okinawan combative arts are not intrinsically under the influence of Buddhism because at the time of the founding of these arts Buddhism was not popular in Okinawa. The linking of Okinawan fighting arts and of Japanese karate-jutsu and karate-do to Buddhist religion or philosophy, especially Zen, is a modern innovation and one that is considerably newer than the systems it allegedly spiritually invigorates. In particular, the quasi-Buddhist teachings that are sometimes associated with Japanese karate-do are without foundation in the original form established by Funakoshi. These teachings are largely due to the personal interests of those exponents who seek to satisfy their consciences in justification of hand-to-hand combat, or who otherwise seek to bring esoteric aspects into their art in support of claims to higher ideals than are contained in systems involving purely physical sparring and grappling. The fanciful imaginations of writers who are largely without experience in karate-like disciplines have enhanced the erroneous belief that karate-do and Buddhism are inseparable.

Funakoshi had very specific things in mind when he replaced the original ideogram "kara," meaning "China," with that meaning "empty." The fact that pure Japanese karate-do does not involve the use of weapons other than parts of the body gives literal substance to the translation of "karate" as "empty-hand." But the obvious conflict of that rendering with the fact that Okinawan karate systems always include the use of specific weapons was one reason why Funakoshi's change of ideogram angered the traditionalist exponents in Okinawa. Funakoshi clarified the apparent paradox and gained support from his fellow countrymen. He declared that the use of the ideogram "kara" (empty) was based on the concept of "hollowness," meaning "unselfishness." Thus the "emptiness" suggested by the newly chosen ideogram refers to the state of rendering oneself "empty," or egoless, for the purpose of an unhindered development of spiritual insight. This new meaning for "kara," Funakoshi insisted, gave a philosophical essence to what heretofore had been basically a physical art. But Funakoshi never intended that farfetched philosophical abstractions be made of his concept of kara. He leaves a clear definition in his writings: "As a mirror's polished surface reflects whatever stands before it and a quiet valley carries even small sounds, so must the student of karate-do render his mind empty of selfishness and wickedness in an effort to react appropriately toward anything he might encounter. This is the meaning of kara, or "empty," of karate-do." Beyond this expression of the meaning of "kara" there seems little need for the many and varied interpretations given to it by modern karatephiles.

As early as 1926 both Higaonna and Itosu on Okinawa had argued that te should be revised as a *shugyo*, a system of austere discipline, making of its then essentially combative and physical nature a spiritual one. Both of these great masters insisted that te was not an art to be used for harming human beings but one in which technique combines with spirit to solve daily problems and avoid physical conflicts. Neither Higaonna nor Itosu taught people whose individual characters were known to be bad. But it was the impetus given to karate technique by Funakoshi, who clearly taught it as an exercise for die mind and body to form personal character, that led to the establishment of Japanese karate-do in 1935.

The Okinawan prototypes of Japanese karate-jutsu and karate-do evolved from the efforts of people from the lower social classes whose morals, ethical standards, general interests, and level of education all differed vastly from those of the aristocratic Japanese warriors. This plebeian environment in which karate techniques developed in Okinawa, together with the fact that they also developed in a plebeian environment in twentieth-century Japan, make it obvious that there is no direct connection between Japanese karate-like systems and the classical Japanese martial arts. It is also apparent from detailed studies made of the pre-Edo period *bushi*'s fighting arts that these professional warriors had little interest in the empty-hand aspects of combat because the accepted manner of engaging the foe entailed armed combat; unarmed scuffling was regarded as peasant activity, beneath the dignity of the bushi's social position. Bushi, armed with lethal weapons like the long sword, were capable of rendering all unarmed techniques ineffective.

The great social changes that occurred during the Edo period included the decay of the classical warrior institutions, the appearance of a class of men known as samurai many of whom were not only effete but also only nominally warriors, and the rise of the commoners to a position of social importance. Methods of unarmed combat, though at times useful to the samurai when engaged in civil scuffles, did not constitute their major martial study. But the commoners' interest in empty-hand arts was both natural and widespread. They had long been denied the use of weapons, a fact that makes their preference for unarmed combat understandable. But it is quite apparent from the historical records that many commoners sought to gain social prestige through participation in disciplines in which weapons were used in such martial ryu as they were permitted to join or were able to found for themselves.

In this manner the commoners became familiar at first hand with the spirit and practices of the warriors. They borrowed liberally from the warriors' martial culture the aspects they greatly admired or believed to be essential to their own systems of discipline. In some ways the commoners were original, but by and large they were adapters, not adopters, of warrior systems. They were also guilty of misrepresenting warrior beliefs, customs, ethical standards, and martial practices through exaggeration or lack of understanding. But the commoners' interest in empty-hand disciplines, made with an inquiring attitude of mind, continued through the Meiji and Taisho eras. This set the scene for the rapid acceptance of Okinawan karate-jutsu among the general citizenry of Japan.

Japanese karate-jutsu and karate-do exhibit certain characteristics of the classical warrior spirit and ethos. Funakoshi used the expression *mizo no kokoro*, which means "a mind like water," to emphasize the importance of making the mind calm when facing an emergency or an adversary. This imagery indicates that the calm mind, like still water, accurately reflects all that comes before it. Thus the exponent who gains this mental state will be both psychologically and physically prepared to deal with whatever action an adversary takes. But Funakoshi's use of this expression is not entirely original, for it stems from a plethora of metaphysical concepts involving *fudoshin* (immovable mind) that were in common use by Japanese swordsmen in the sixteenth and seventeenth centuries. Another favorite expression of Funakoshi is also rooted in the classical warriors' traditions: *tsuki no kokoro*, or "a mind like the moon," which refers to the necessity of maintaining surveillance over one's surroundings at all times. By this symbolism is meant that, like the wide range of illumination produced by the unclouded moon as it sends its light earthward, so the mind must be aware of all conditions surrounding the body. This attitude is expressed in classical martial arts as *zanshin*, and is also included in the function of *kan-ken futatsu no koto*, perceiving with both the eyes and the intuitive mind.

Nakayama Masatoshi, as a disciple of Funakoshi in 1931, witnessed the master's rigid discipline in connection with *tsuki no kokoro*. Funakoshi was quick to criticize his disciples for any relaxation in their alertness. In training he would deliver sound kicks and blows to those trainees who failed to maintain a proper bearing. Even outside the dojo he was a taskmaster. "He would quickly tip up a bowl of rice into the face of any disciple who handled it in such a way as to weaken his defense," says Nakayama, and, without injuring the user, would also "show how an adversary could jam improperly handled chopsticks down one's throat even as the user ate with them." Funakoshi never ceased to maintain vigilance. "Even while walking outdoors," recalls Nakayama, "he would never turn a corner close to a wall but make a wide circuit to avoid being surprised."

Funakoshi's concern with the practical aspects of self-defense did not result in an over-emphasis on proficiency in physical technique. Important as technique obviously was for Funakoshi, training meant the individual's confrontation with obstacles in order to develop an improved power of persistence in endeavor and the consequent ability to overcome hardship. The performance of karate-do, in this sense, is a vital matter for Funakoshi, and is highly reminiscent of the Taoist religious doctrines in which nature is to be confronted; exercise is the means by which mind and body are improved and the span of life is increased.

When asked about it, Funakoshi invariably characterized karate-do as a system of defense, but always within the concept of *kobo-itchi*, where *hen-o*, or response to an emergency, includes *sen no sen*, the highest form of attack initiative, as well as *go no sen*, the lowest form, depending on the appropriateness of one or the other in a given situation. What mattered most to Funakoshi was that the trained exponent should refrain from contention, but that if pressed, he should respond naturally, instinctively, and spontaneously to the threat of the attack. But above all, Funakoshi declared karate-do to be a medium for character building and the final goal of training to be the perfection of the self, which is implicit in the classical interpretation of do. The maxims displayed in the dojo of the Japan Karate Association summarize Funakoshi's highest hopes for karate-do: (1) character, (2) sincerity, (3) effort, (4) etiquette, and (5) self-control.

In gentle contrast to Funakoshi's concept of karate-do, and in marked opposition to many of the karate-like systems that have developed since Funakoshi's death, is the ideology of Konishi Yasuhiro, who founded the Shindo Shiizen Ryu in 1934. Konishi trained under both Funakoshi and Motobu Choki. For Konishi, the Taoist philosophy of life is the basis of all training. He explains: "People often use the word 'conquest' in speech. When a mountain climber comes to the summit, he says immediately that he conquered such and such a mountain. And if one endures such hardships as heat or cold well, he says that he mastered the conditions. This is all merely an illusion. What seemed like having conquered is really . . . a state of accommodation without any opposition to nature. It is a state of God and man united in one body. This results in [inner] peace and is a natural state in which [the distinction between] enemy and friend does not exist."

Konishi, also the holder of a kendo *kyoshi* (teaching license), brought various ideas from the realm of swordsmanship into his teachings, which he prefers to call karate-jutsu. In particular, emphasis on zanshin, the ability of an exponent to gain dominance over an opponent through an alert state of mind and the maintenance of proper physical posture, characterizes Konishi's techniques. Thus the spiritual aspect dominates the physical. A decidedly strong bias of antiviolence cloaks Konishi's karate-jutsu in its stringent ethic, a fact that makes clear that jutsu forms are not without higher ideals despite what advocates of do forms sometimes erroneously believe.

Training in the manner demanded by Konishi is made for the purpose of developing a wholesome human being, one who is both mentally and physically sound. Through dedication to training carried out over a protracted period of time, *shin* (mind), *gi* (technique), and *tai* (body) are united in the proper proportions. When this is accomplished the trainee becomes aware of his moral obligation to be useful to society.

Kata, or prearranged formal exercise, is the basis for discipline in Konishi's karate-jutsu; it is therefore the starting point of all training. Through the sufficient use of kata a trainee gains control over his mind and body and thus comes to understand that karate-jutsu technique is to be applied only for the purpose of controlling undesirable personal traits in oneself and in others. Karate-jutsu must never be used to foster a malicious spirit. But kata alone, notes Konishi, is not sufficient to produce the fullest development of the individual. Accordingly, trainees are required to participate in controlled bouts with fellow trainees; to this end competition becomes one facet of training.

Otsuka Hidenori(b.1892), who founded the Wado Ryu in 1939, has developed what is perhaps the purest form of Japanese karate-do. The essence of Otsuka's teachings derives from his long experience with classical bujutsu. He began to study the jujutsu of the Shindo Yoshin Ryu when very young—in 1898, at the age of six—and attained the menkyo (license) level of proficiency in 1921 under the tutelage of Nakayama Tatsusaburo Yokiyoshi. Otsuka began his study of karate-jutsu under Funakoshi in 1922. A. deep concern for human welfare is evident in Otsuka's teachings. For him, *ten-chi-jin* ("heaven-earth-man, principle-way") is a harmonious union to be respected and sought through adherence to austere discipline (shugyo). A *waka* (a standard verse-form containing thirty-one syllables) describes Otsuka's aspirations for those who engage in any bujutsu or budo:

> Bu no michi wa   Have no regard for martial
> tada aragoto to   aspects [when training],
> na omoi so   but rather adhere to the
> Wa na michi kiwame   way of peace [harmony and
> Wa o motomu michi   tranquillity].

Karate-do for Otsuka is thus primarily a spiritual discipline. All exponents of the Wado Ryu demonstrate great ability in coping with armed and unarmed attack. This ability stems from the fact that Otsuka has welded the facet of yielding according to the principle of flexibility (*ju no ri*) to karate-like techniques. This results in many of the harsher resistive elements of sparring technique that characterize most styles of karate-jutsu and karate-do being removed from the Wado style. But the "softness" of "Wado Ryu technique is less subtle than that of the internal systems of genuine Chinese ch'uan-fa The absence of "softness" in technique represents, in Otsuka's opinion, an uneconomical use of the body, for a great expenditure of energy always accompanies the use of "'hardness." Otsuka is one of the Japanese pioneers in the development of the relaxed-arm thrust punch coupled to a rapid withdrawal of the punching fast to effect a focusing of energy As regards the popular practice of hardening certain parts of the body by deforming them in order to reduce their sensitivity to pain. Otsuka totally rejects such inane ideas.

Yamaguchi Gogen has developed his Japanese Goju style of karate-do as *seishin no mono*, that is, "a thing of the spirit." There is in the balance of "hard" (go) and "soft" (ju) actions displayed by Yamaguchi's performance of technique a confirmation of what is suggested by the name Goju, and also what is perhaps the best example of the influence of Chinese nei-kung (internal power) on a Japanese style of karate-do. Exponents of Yamaguchi's Goju karate-do, therefore, are expected to place emphasis on the development of internal power through the use of special exercises. These exercises are performed to bring posture, movement, and breathing into a harmony that teaches the body to act as a whole, unified in concentrated effort. Breathing is vigorous, but is performed slowly and in a rhythm that is precisely timed. Inhalation is made as if "smelling" the air, while exhalation is made forcefully and with the emission of sound that stems from air forced outward by the muscular contraction of the abdomen.

The pursuance of do, or the way, through the discipline of karate-do is for Yamaguchi a display of patience, fortitude, and perseverance. Karate-do in its broadest sense "is a way of peace," he claims. "Karate-do means not to be beaten, but also not to strike others." Human morals differ among different individuals and peoples, but karate-do, says Yamaguchi, can guide all people to right behavior. The do is thus a way to live correctly, and he who fails to do so, Yamaguchi believes, is a coward. Training in karate-do, when properly carried out, leads one to the discovery of a nonaggressive way of life.

4. Ueshiba Morihei and Aikido

Here, again, we have the story of a gifted traditionalist who worked to create a modern martial art that would fit the need of the times. Ueshiba's art of aikido is interesting for a number of reasons. It has an elegant philosophy that stresses non-violence and has proven tremendously attractive to students all over the world. Its use of circularity and ki projection seems to create a link with mainland Chinese traditions while also being influenced by traditional Japanese sword, spear, stick, and unarmed systems. And finally, in Ueshiba Morihei we have a Shinto mystic intent on fusing things of the body with things of the spirit. While the reader may not totally agree with the writer's characterization of Ueshiba as the greatest martial artist who ever lived (Stevens, it must be noted, is a student of aikido), he is certainly among the most interesting.

From *Abundant Peace* by John Stevens

Morihei was undoubtedly the greatest martial artist who ever lived. Even if we accept every exploit of all the legendary warriors, East and West, as being literally true, none of those accomplishments can be compared to Morihei's documented ability to disarm any attacker, throw a dozen men simultaneously, and down and pin opponents without touching them, recorded scores of times in photographs, on film, and by personal testimony.

How did Morihei become invincible?

One factor was his vast practical and theoretical knowledge of Eastern and Western martial arts. Like Aizu-Wakamatsu in Fukushima, Morihei's birthplace, Tanabe, was a "treasury of the martial arts," with one important difference; the influence of the Shinto cult of Kumano was so pervasive that the martial traditions originating in Wakayama always had a more spiritual cast than the win-at-any-cost methods of the Aizu fighters.

In his youth Morihei learned of the Aioi Ryu (probably an offshoot of the Sekiguchi Ryu) from the stories told about his grandfather, a famous exponent of the art. This and related systems stressed the importance of freely applying the "hard" and the "soft" according to each particular situation.

Morihei's first real training in the martial arts began with *sumo*, traditional Japanese wrestling. It was due to the head-on collisions common in *sumo* that Morihei started to toughen his skull by pounding it against a pole or stone hundreds of times each day. Since *sumo* requires powerful hips and legs, the young Morihei did a lot of jogging in the heavy sand and shallow water along the seashore to build those muscles. Another requirement of *sumo* is good balance; one must not let any part of the body (except of course for the feet) touch the ground. This precludes "sacrifice throws" in which one goes down first, hoping that one's momentum will carry the opponent over and down. One must overpower the opponent to win. While there is certainly an ele-ment of flexibility in *sumo*—even 4oo-pound mountains of flesh must be able to touch their foreheads to the ground with their legs stretched straight out—in general the em-phasis is on the hard elements of pushing, thrusting, and lifting.

In Tanabe, Morihei also learned to wield a harpoon with deadly accuracy, a skill that demands a sharp eye, strong arms, and perfect balance even on a rocking boat.

It is unclear exactly how much Morihei practiced during his brief sojourn in Tokyo as a teenager. He apparently visited several *dojos* and trained a bit at the places mentioned in Part One, but because of his preoccupation with getting his business started and his poor physical condition (beriberi), Morihei did not make much progress.

Following his induction into the Imperial Army, Morihei received instruction in the use of firearms and the basics of Western military science. He continued to excel at *sumo* and also became highly proficient in the do-or-die combat art of bayonet fighting. In those days military encounters still involved hand-to-hand fighting, and in actual combat a soldier could not afford to let an enemy score a single point against his body. Other than an explosive thrust, there are no techniques in bayonet fighting; consequently, everything depends on timing—or "anticipation," as it is called in the Japanese martial arts. One must either instantly perceive an opponent's window of vulnerability and move in decisively or else immediately evade and counter an attack by "opening" to one side or the other.

The importance of Morihei's early training in *sumo* and bayonet fighting and their respective emphasis on keeping one's center of gravity low and entering directly (*irimi*) should not be overlooked.

Morihei's first systematic training in the classical Japanese martial arts began around the same time as his induction into the service. He enrolled in the *dojo* of Masakatsu Nakai, master teacher of Goto Ryu Yagyu Jujutsu. This *ryu* (school) originated in the body techniques employed by the illustrious Yagyu family of warriors; it was modified by several different masters over the centuries and then formed into a composite system in the nineteenth century. In Yagyu martial art systems, mind plays just as important a role as technique. In fact, mental power—an unperturbed, immovable mind—will always prevail over brute strength. A famous anecdote, told to every Yagyu trainee, goes like this:

Iemitsu, the third Tokugawa shogun, received a tiger as a gift from the Korean court. Iemitsu challenged the famous Shinkage Ryu swordsman Yagyu Tajima Munenori to subdue the beast. Yagyu immediately accepted the challenge and strode confidently into the cage. Just as the beast was about to pounce, he thumped the snarling animal on the head with his iron fan. The tiger shrank back and cowered in a corner. The Zen monk Takuan, who happened to be present, chided Yagyu, "That is the wrong approach." Takuan then entered the cage unarmed. When the tiger reared to attack, Takuan spat on his hands and gently rubbed the tiger's face and ears. The ferocious animal calmed down at once, purring and rubbing itself against the monk. "That's how you do it!" Takuan exclaimed.

Nakai was highly regarded for both his skill at the martial arts and his noble character. There is a tale that once during an early open *jujutsu* competition in Osaka, one of Nakai's disciples defeated a top Kokodan *judo* man. Upset by the loss, Jigoro Kano, then still a hot-tempered young man, issued a challenge to Nakai's senior disciple. Nakai severely scolded Kano for such intemperate behavior: it is improper for a master instructor to engage a lower-ranked trainee merely because he happened to defeat a disciple. Both the teacher and the disciple must reflect on the reason for the defeat and then apply for a rematch when they feel that they are ready.

Since Nakai was additionally proficient in sword, spear, and *jo* techniques, it is likely that Morihei trained in those arts during his four and a half years of appren-ticeship. Morihei received a Goto Ryu Yagyu Jujutsu teaching license from Nakai in 1908 at age twenty-five. Even though Morihei studied a number of different systems, this is the only full teaching license he obtained.

After his son's discharge from the army, Yoroku built a *dojo* for Morihei; Morihei instructed there as well as sponsoring the visits of famous *jujutsu* and *judo* teachers.

After acquiring formidable physical and mental strength, Morihei found himself in Hokkaido, where he was initiated into the mysteries of *aiki* by Sokaku Takeda of the Daito Ryu.

While many traditional elements were absorbed into the system, it must be stated categorically that the Daito Ryu was the creation of one man and one man only, Sokaku Takeda. The core techniques that Sokaku inherited from Tanomo are said to have originated with Minamoto (Genji) Yoshimitsu around A.D. Yoshimitsu's son moved to Koga and established the Takeda clan; the art was secretly transmitted among family members from generation to generation. In 1754 the Takeda clan shifted its base of operations to Aizu-Wakamatsu, and there the system, known as *oshiki-uchi* or *odome*, was taught to high-ranking samurai men and women.

As noted previously, these techniques were passed along to Saigo Tanomo, who combined the highly effective blows, locks, pins, and throws of *oshiki-uchi* with the harmonization and breath control methods of *aiki-inyo*. This unified system was taught to Sokaku, who in turn added other elements based on his extensive firsthand experience in combat. For instance, Sokaku learned from his big battle with the construction gang that the regular *seigan* stance (with sword held horizontally) was ineffective when con-fronted by a swarm of attackers. The *jodan* stance (with sword held over one's head) was far superior, facilitating lightning-fast counters, and Sokaku incorporated such knowledge into his teaching.

The Japanese martial arts world is extremely conservative, and anyone presumptuous enough to create a new school was immediately hit with a barrage of criticism. To avoid trouble, Sokaku, who initially called his system the Yamato Ryu, decided to change it to Daito Ryu and had formal documents drawn up tracing the lineage back to Yoshimitsu. Daito was the name of Yoshimitsu's mansion and further referred to the Daito (Great East) Prosperity Sphere then being promoted by Japanese imperialists. Sokaku thereafter styled himself thirty-fifth Grandmaster of the Daito Ryu.

(Quite similarly to Morihei, Sokaku continually modified his techniques over the years, and there are distinct differences in the way his early and later disciples execute them. These discrepancies have resulted in several schisms within the Daito Ryu, the most serious breach being between Sokaku's son Tokimune and Sokaku's one-time designated successor Yukiyoshi Sagawa.)

At any rate, the thirty-two-year-old Morihei was easily defeated, for the first and only time in his life, by a skinny gnome twenty-five years his senior. Sokaku told Mori-hei, "If there is any reserve or hesitation, even a skilled practitioner can be easily defeated. Hear the soundless sound, see the form-less form. At a glance, control your opponent and attain victory without contention. This is the inner meaning of *aiki*."

In Hokkaido, Morihei was initially given instruction in the "108 Basic Techniques" of Sokaku's Daito Ryu. Many of these techniques—for example, *shiho-nage, chokusen irimi nage, ikkyo* through *gokyo, suwari waza*, and *hanmi-*

hantachi—are still prac-ticed, in greatly altered form, in present-day Aikido and may be considered the roots of certain Aikido movements. However, there are many other movements that have nothing to do with the Daito Ryu.

Sokaku opened Morihei's eyes to the potential power of *aiki* timing, breath control, and the unity of body, sword, and stick techniques. Nevertheless, Morihei learned very little from Sokaku following the first period in Hokkaido, and in fact complained to confidants that Sokaku showed him nothing new during later visits to Ayabe and Tokyo. On his part, Morihei pursued his own independent studies of different traditions. In short, the influence of Sokaku's Daito Ryu on the development of Aikido should not be overemphasized. As Morihei clearly stated, "The direct influence of Sokaku's Daito Ryu techniques on the formation of Aikido is not that great. It was but one element among many."

What are some of the other martial arts Morihei studied?

Around age forty-two Morihei seems to have secluded himself in the mountains of Kumano and practiced Kuki Shin Ryu, a secretly transmitted martial art devised by mountain ascetics (*yamabushi*). Many of Morihei's *jo* techniques evidently originated from this ryu because the chief weapon of the ascetics was their staff/walking stick, which they carried with them at all times.

Incidentally, the Kuki Shin Ryu is closely associated with several of the modern *nin-jutsu* schools. In the early days, Morihei occasionally demon-strated *ninja* techniques, as in the following anecdote:

His disciples asked Morihei if the feats attributed to *ninja* were really true. "You have been watching too many movies," Morihei said. "Grab your swords and sticks, and I'll give you a real demonstration of *ninjutsu* right out in die open." Ten or so disciples surrounded Morihei in the center of the *dojo* and attacked simultaneously; they felt a stream of air as Morihei disappeared and then heard him calling to them halfway up a staircase twenty feet away. When they requested another feat, Morihei yelled, "Are you trying to kill me just to entertain yourselves? Each time one performs such techniques, his life span is reduced by five to ten years."

Ninjutsu is the antithesis of Aikido. It is an art based on stealth, deception, and, dirty tricks; yet even with their reliance on the vaunted "techniques of invisibility" and an arsenal of exotic weapons, none of the famous *ninja* of the past could have stood a chance against the divine techniques of Morihei, for-mulated in accordance with the principles of love and harmony.

Among other disciplines that Morihei investigated were the Take-no-uchi and Kito Jujutsu Ryus, Hozoin Ryu spear fighting, and several schools of swordsmanship, notably the Yagyu Ryu and the Katori Shinto Ryu. At Ayabe, Morihei concentrated on Hozoin Ryu spear techniques, hanging sponge balls in the trees all around him and then spearing them as accu-rately and as quickly as possible for hours and hours. Morihei had a close relationship with the Yagyu Ryu swordsman Kosaburo Shomojo for many years; despite variations, Morihei's basic sword stance and pair techniques were those of the Yagyu Ryu.

Because of his extensive travels in China, Morihei had wide exposure to that na-tion's martial arts traditions; somewhat surprisingly, he seems not to have taken much interest in them, not even *t'ai-chi*, which appears to have the most in common with Aikido. Since there were no Chinese masters on the same level as Morihei, he likely dismissed, perhaps unjustly, mainland martial arts as unworthy of serious study.

Morihei had an incredible ability to assimilate martial arts techniques. One day a famous classical Japanese dance teacher visited the Kobukan to request instruction in the halberd (*naginata*). Morihei hesitated a bit because he had little experience with that particular weapon, which was mainly used by females. Charmed, however, by the lovely teacher, he consented. Morihei ordered a disciple to obtain a popular novel in which the hero is a master of *naginata*, place the book on the Shinto altar, and see that he not be disturbed for the remainder of the day.

When the dance instructor returned for her lesson, Morihei showed her a series of beautiful moves. Later, after the woman had performed them on stage, she was told by a surprised *naginata* master, "What wonderful techniques! Where did you learn them?"

His puzzled disciples asked Morihei how he was able to master the *naginata* so quickly.

"The hero of the novel visited me while I was in a trance and taught me his secrets" was the reply—Morihei's fanciful way of saying that the universally applicable principles of *aiki* enabled him to formulate techniques freely with any type of weapon. Similarly, when Morihei had his disciples read popular novels to him, upon hearing the famous battle scenes described, Morihei would leap up and act out the heroes' movements.

Although Morihei absorbed an enormous number of martial arts techniques from diverse sources, it is incorrect to think of Aikido as derivative of the older traditions. Aikido, Morihei insisted, is a totally new and revolutionary system, independently created with a special set of principles and ideals.

Morihei's genius for the martial arts was coupled with extraordinary physical strength and stamina. In Hokkaido, Morihei built up his already formidable power through heavy farm work with specially weighted tools, wrestling with huge logs, and long-distance running. Even in his fifties, Morihei seemed nearly as wide as he was tall. "Scrubbing his back during a bath," an early disciple recalls, "was like polishing stone. His stomach muscles were so thick that they formed a triangle." Morihei's grip was crushing, leaving bruise marks for days on the spots he had held or merely touched. Once Morihei inadvertently broke the wrist of a *karate* master by lightly blocking a punch with his fingers.

Tales of his unbelievable ability to move boulders and lift logs abound. Once, in Takeda, his disciple Yukawa, whose nickname was Samson, was furiously attempting to uproot a small tree. "Too much strain! Too much strain!" Morihei laughed as he grabbed the five-inch-diameter tree and yanked it cleanly from the earth.

Morihei retained his muscle tone well into his seventies and in Iwama did twice as much farm work twice as fast as the teenage trainees. In purely physical terms, Morihei was one of the strongest men ever to tread this earth.

In addition to his fantastic muscular strength, Morihei discovered how to plug into the unlimited current of breath (*kokyu*) and *ki* power that circulates through the universe. Put in the simplest possible terms, *kokyu*, the Japanese equivalent of the Sanskrit *prana*, is the vital breath of life, and *ki* is the waves of energy that emanate from *kokyu*. Every Japanese art underscores the importance of fostering breath and *ki* power. One's *kiai*, a forceful inner and outer projection of *kokyu* and *ki* power, indicates the level of one's coordination of body and mind. *Kiai* is usually thought of as merely the shout emitted at the instant a technique is executed. For most trainees, this is true, but for advanced practitioners a *kiai* is a perfectly concentrated burst of energy, only part of which is audible.

Morihei's *kiai* was, not surprisingly, irresistible. "Use your *kiai* as a weapon," he instructed his disciples. His could be heard more than half a mile away; even when he was not shouting out loud, he projected terrific waves. Once, during a service at a Buddhist temple, Morihei joined the congregation in the recitation of the *Heart Sutra*. Although Morihei was chanting at the same level as the others in the group, the priest felt as if the sounds rising from Morihei were solidly pounding him on the back.

On another occasion, Morihei was demonstrating before the president of a large newspaper company, when the president thought to himself, "This is all fake." At that instant, Morihei let loose with an explosive kiai, and all the flashbulbs in the cameras of the news photographers went flying out of their sockets.

Morihei was often photographed and filmed having a bunch of men pushing against him with all their might without being able to budge the suddenly immovable fixture. Morihei could even perform the feat with a stick held out horizontally from his body while five or six men attempted to force it sideways; Morihei kept them at bay and then flipped them down with a slight twist of his wrist. Several of Japan's top baseball players became Morihei's students after swinging their bats full force against Morihei's sword; instead of knocking the sword from Morihei's hands, the proud athletes were stunned to have their bats driven back in their own direction.

In these cases, Morihei was subtly attuned to the others' outflow of *ki* and could imperceptibly counter it with a stronger flow of his own. Morihei devised a series of *kokyu-ho* techniques to help his disciples develop breath and *ki* power. Some, like the "unbendable arm," can be learned by anyone in a few minutes; others, like throwing one's opponent without touching him or her, require a lifetime of training.

Extensive training, physical strength, and breath and *ki* power are still not enough; to be really invincible one needs an uncanny sixth sense.

For years and years, Morihei's disciples tried to catch him off guard— Morihei promised a teaching license to anyone who could do so—but even at night there was some part of the master that was ever awake: "Who is that trying to sneak up on me?" Morihei revealed that beams of energy continually radiated from his body and that as soon as a hostile force entered that field, he was instantly alerted.

Once a disciple who noticed that Morihei always evaded to the right when he attacked him with a straight blow dared to cross up his teacher by immediately striking in that direction. Morihei stood right where he was in front of the startled swordsman: "What on earth are you doing?"

Another time, a young disciple facing Morihei with a sword drought of launching a sneak attack; Morihei's eyes opened wide with a frightful glare, and that was the end of that. At a celebration, several disciples wondered among themselves if Morihei would be vulnerable after drinking sake; Morihei, on the other side of the room, whirled around and scowled at them.

A noted *karate* instructor became Morihei's pupil after visiting the *dojo* and being told nonchalantly by the Aikido master, "Strike me if you can!" So saying, Morihei turned his back on the expert, who swung away without coming close to the elusive elf.

As soon as Morihei entered a *dojo*, he immediately paid his respects to the Shinto altar. After doing so during a visit to a *dojo* of one of his disciples, he called the instructor over and berated him: "Why did you neglect to chant the morning service today? The *kamisama* is lonely!"

Once a sculptor was commissioned to do a bust of Morihei's muscular upper torso. When it was finished, Morihei checked the rear of the bust and said, "This muscle and this muscle are not quite right." Upon closer examination, the sculptor was shocked to find it so. Morihei knew exactly how his back looked even though he couldn't see it!

Typically, Morihei attributed his sixth sense to divine protection. A disciple accom-panying Morihei on a trip, noticing that Morihei had closed his eyes to nap, thought, "Now is my chance!" The elated disciple reached for his fan to strike Morihei on the head. Morihei's eyes shot open.

"My guardian deity tells me that you are thinking of hitting me over the head. You wouldn't do such a thing, would you?"

Whatever the source, all of the great martial artists developed a similar sixth sense, perhaps acquired from the decades of peering into the inner reaches of the human heart and having a mind set forever in the training hall.

2

Morihei ceaselessly refined his unique art; consequently, Aikido underwent numerous permutations during the Founder's forty-year teaching career.

The signboard at Morihei's first *dojo* in Ayabe read *Daito Ryu Aikijutsu*, but following his move to Tokyo and the subsequent founding of the Wakamatsu Dojo, his system was known as, among other things, Kobukan Aiki-Budo, Ueshiba Ryu Jujutsu, Tenshin Aiki-Budo, and finally, from 1942, Aikido.

The Aiki-Budo of the period 1932-1942 was rigorous, direct, and practical. In this decade, Morihei's tremendous physical power and technical prowess were the dominant elements; it was hard-style, aggressive *budo* characterized by razor-sharp execution of the techniques and muscular strength. A spiritual element was always present in Morihei's presentation of the art, but because his disciples repeatedly faced challengers and because the country was preparing for and then engaged in war, the techniques had to be 100 percent effective. Extensive use was made of devastating blows to anatomical weak points (*atemi*); throws were carried out with full extension to bring an opponent down and out, and pins were applied with joint-wrenching and bone-crunching force. Weapons study centered on the combat arts of spear, bayonet, and sword fighting.

An early disciple relates: "People hesitated to challenge Morihei because of his reputation, but we assistant instructors were continually put to the test by *judo* men, *kendo* men, *sumo* wrestlers, boxers, and just plain street fighters. We always attempted to avoid such confrontations, but usually there was no alternative. And once the contest commenced, there is no way we would allow ourselves to be defeated."

Two instruction manuals and one film were produced under Morihei's supervision during the Aiki-Budo years. (A series of techniques was photographed in the Noma Dojo in 1936 but never made public; Morihei also had a hand in the compilation of a textbook on arrest techniques for the Military Police Academy.)

Budo renshu appeared in 1933. The pictures were drawn by Miss Kunagoshi with several of the live-in disciples posing as models. Morihei evidently intended the book to be a kind of license presented to advanced students: "Read this book, train diligently, and that will enable you to be enlightened to the inner principles of the martial arts and become a true master."

The manual opens with a collection of Morihei's *doka* ("songs of the way"). These are didactic poems, written in the 5-7-5-7-7-syllable *waka* form, by masters to inspire and instruct their disciples. *Doka* rarely have much literary merit, and Morihei's were no exception; their primary purpose is to reveal the essence of an art in a few pithy phrases. Morihei's *doka* run from the commonsensical:

One who is
well prepared
for anything that arises
will never rashly draw
his sword in haste.

Progress comes to those who train and train;
reliance on secret techniques will get you nowhere.

to the practical:

If the enemy assumes
a lower stance,
remain in the middle stance
unwavering,
immovable.

When an enemy
rushes in
to strike,
step to the side
and cut him down instantly.

to the mysterious:

Penetrate reality
by mastering the
kiai YAH!

Do not be deceived by the enemy's ploys.
The active and passive spirits perfectly harmonized,
forming the cross of aiki;
advance ever onward,
pouring out manly vigor.

The short text is a similar jumble of the plain, the practical, and the eso-teric. In spite of all the material published under his name, Morihei had absolutely no literary ability—his multifaceted mind precluded him from collecting his thoughts into coherent sentences. It was his disciples and scholarly friends who edited his words into more or less comprehensible form. (I have taken similar liberties; all of the quotes that appear in this book were culled from the huge corpus of oral and written literature.)

The most interesting statements in the text, no doubt directed toward his many followers in the military, are these:

The true martial art is the one that defeats an enemy with-out sacrificing a single man; attain victory by placing yourself always in a safe and unassail-able position.

True *budo* is for the sake of peace and harmony; train daily to manifest this spirit throughout the world.

Since the illustrations in *Budo renshu* were roughly sketched, they are difficult to follow; in 1938 *Budo*, professionally photographed with Morihei himself posing for the pictures, was typeset and privately circulated. The manual opens with these words: "Budo is a divine path formulated by the gods, the basis of the true, the good, and the beautiful; it reflects the absolute and unlimited inner workings of the universe. The virtue acquired through assiduous training enables one to perceive the essential principles of Heaven and Earth." Morihei goes on to say, "Purify the body and mind, link yourself to the Divine, manifest the hidden, and strive for enlightenment." In addition to the standard body techniques—*tai-no-henko, irimi nage, shiho-nage, kote-gaeshi, ikkyo* through *gokyo,* and *kokyu-ho*—this manual includes sword, spear, and bayonet techniques. It also includes the warning "This manual is not to be shown to non-Japanese."

By far the most interesting relic of the Aiki-Budo era is a film shot in Osaka in 193 5 when Morihei was fifty-two years old. Morihei, then at his physical peak, is shown whirling around the *dojo,* throwing his disciples halfway across the room, pinning them with precise holds, and deftly dealing with armed attacks. At first, Morihei appears to be merely a supremely skilled technician and strong man; it is not until the end of the film, when he is grabbed full strength by ten men, that viewers realize that they are witnessing something inexplicable. Morihei emits a peculiar kiai, and they all fly off him and hit the mat.

While the core techniques remained essentially the same, Morihei's techniques, reflecting changes in his philosophy, became softer and more circular in postwar Aikido. He now maintained that if one has the power to walk, it is possible to practice Aikido. One man wanted to learn Aikido more than anything but was advised not to do so by his doctor. The man had been very ill as a youth, spending years in and out of hospitals, and was extremely weak physically. Morihei went out of his way to teach the man simple warm-up exercises and then later to engage him in sword partner practice. After the student built up some strength in his arms and legs, Morihei had him practice seated techniques. The man persevered, eventually becoming an instructor. Other young trainees were assigned to massage duty, working on Morihei's legs and shoulders to strengthen their wrists for Aikido training.

Morihei's gradual ascent into the highest realms of pure *ki* and *kokyu* power had a deleterious effect on some of his later followers. In his final public demonstration, the phantomlike Morihei downed his partners by simply waving his hand or pointing his finger at them. Morihei, of course, had reached such a fluid stage after sixty years of solid training. Unfortunately, many modern practitioners favor this "no touch" approach, throwing each other about with a flick of the wrist or a cockeyed, off-balance toss of the shoulder. If your partner is going to fall down anyway, why worry about proper distancing, lack of vulnerability, or concentrated power?

Morihei's mind was forever in the training hall, and each minute of the day was a time for him to practice, but he also engaged in special sessions. In the prewar period these would take place on Mount Kurama, near Kyoto. Morihei would take two or three disciples with him for a twenty-one-day training session. The small group lived on rice, pickles, miso soup, and wild herbs. Morihei would rise at 5:00 A.M. to pray. After morning prayers and misogi, they would swing heavy swords 500 times and then practice footwork. From ten o'clock to noon they trained in body techniques. Afternoon training ran from three to five; the disciples took turns acting as Morihei's partner as he ran through series after series of techniques. In the evening the disciples would review the day's training.

Every three days, Morihei would announce at midnight, "Time for night training." The disciples could discern nothing in the pitch-darkness, but Morihei cried out to them, "Watch out for the rock on your left! Duck to avoid the upcoming branches!" He armed them with wooden swords and commanded them to attack. At first, none of the disciples had the slightest notion where their teacher was; gradually, however, they sensed his presence to the right or left and speeded up their attacks. Then Morihei turned the tables: he chased after them, bringing his razor-sharp blade within a hair's-breadth of their headbands. (Incidentally, many famous Japanese warriors engaged in ascetic training on Mount Kurama over the centuries; the *tengu* said to be residing there was a master of military science.)

In the postwar years, similar sessions took place at Atago Mountain near Iwama and in Tokyo at the ruins of Toyama Military Academy, site of one of Morihei's old haunts. Morihei was devoted to training in the dead of night, in the light of the full moon, thrusting and thrusting against a tree, pounding and pounding a heavy wooden sword against a stack of thick branches. (Morihei would not allow the use of lanterns or flashlights at night: "Samurai have to learn how to see in the dark!" He also scolded his disciples for walking on his right side, blocking his controlling hand: "Keep on the left where you can be protected.")

Morihei's instruction was not systematic. He insisted, "Aikido has no techniques." That is, the movements are rooted in natural principles, not abstract or rigid formulas. He would explain such-and-such a movement as a function of such-and-such a deity or divine principle, demonstrate it, and have his trainees attempt it. Questions were discouraged—if there was a problem, Morihei would show die technique once more, saying, "See what I mean?" Occasionally he gave cryptic hints such as "Surge forward from the Great Earth" or "Billow like the Great Waves" and "Use One to Strike All!"; but in general the basic principle was "Learn and forget! Learn and forget! Make the tech-niques part of your being!"

Proficiency is acquired only through long and diligent training; overly detailed explanations and excessive rationalization of the movements simply serve to confuse and eventually trivialize what is divinely inspired. That is why Morihei said, "An instructor shows only a very small part of Aikido. Through ceaseless, diligent training, discover the ramifications of each technique, slowly, one by one, instead of piling up technique after technique."

In his later years, especially when he was sequestered in Iwama, Morihei tended to run through techniques in a series of related movements and emphasized the sword and *jo*. On the other hand, he would show up unannounced at the Tokyo *dojo*, demonstrate a whirlwind of techniques, and then dash out. A disciple once said to him, "When you are in the *dojo* I can perform the techniques perfectly, but when you leave I cannot recall a thing." Morihei replied, "That is because I link your *ki* with mine and invisibly guide you. If you are ever in doubt or in trouble, just think of me and I will assist you."

Morihei studied many kinds of weapons over the years but ultimately settled on the sword and the *jo* as his "instruments of purification."

In *Budo* Morihei stated: "The sword of *aiki*, in which Heaven, Earth, and human beings are harmonized, empowers one to cut through and destroy all evil, thereby restoring this beautiful world to its innate purity." A *doka* from this manual goes:

> The penetrating brilliance of a sword
> wielded by a man of the Way
> strikes at the enemy
> lurking deep within
> one's own body and mind.

In *Takemusu Aiki*, a collection of Morihei's postwar talks, he related this tale:

One night, as I was swinging my sword in my garden, I was suddenly confronted by an apparition armed with a sword. At first I could do nothing against him, but gradu-ally I began parrying his lightning-fast attacks. The apparition returned the following two evenings and then vanished. Thereafter, whenever I held a sword, I lost all sense of sword, opponent, time, and space; I was breathing in the universe—no, the universe was contained within me. One swing of the sword gathers up all the mysteries of the cosmos.

Morihei's swordsmanship was so free-form that it raised criticism in some quarters for being too unorthodox; in truth, however, Morihei's sword was the real *kendo*—he unfailingly assumed the appropriate stance and reacted naturally to any attack.

In his last years, Morihei employed the *jo* as an instrument of purification in the divine dance he performed before training to calm his spirit and cleanse the *dojo*. *Misogi-no-jo* is a heartfelt prayer for peace and harmony expressed through the medium of the staff and body movements.

Everyone agrees that Morihei was a different person in the training hall. He seemed to spring to life as he entered the *dojo*, and his disciples marveled at how much bigger he appeared in his training uniform. Morihei was frequently smiling and laughing, but when he performed *misogi-no-jo* or held a sword, he was no longer a human being but a vehicle for the Great Spirit of Aiki. His eyes flashed, energy radiated from his body, and all became deathly still. "When he held a sword," his disciples relate, "he turned into one of those wrathful deities that slay evil."

Morihei was indifferent to organizational problems and handled die presentations of licenses and later *dan* rankings rather haphazardly. As noted above, he was only briefly under the auspices of the Daito Ryu and never possessed die full teaching license of that *ryu*. He gave *mokuroku* ("catalogue of techniques") to a few of the early disciples and/or copies of *Budo renshu* and *Budo* to others as a kind of license. When Kobukan instructors began teaching at outside institutions, they needed credentials and were subsequently supplied with *dan* rankings similar to those of *judo*. (A number of old-timers were unaware that the Headquarters Dojo had issued them such rankings.) Following the establishment of the Aikikai in 1948, a regular *kyu-dan* ranking system was instituted. Evidently, Morihei considered the eighth *dan* rank equivalent to the *menkyo-kaiden* teaching license of the old martial arts systems and awarded this rank to his top prewar and postwar disciples. Several others received ninth and even tenth *dan* ranks from Morihei, who tended to hand out such favors to those whom he liked and who asked for them. Among Morihei's senior disciples, the question of who received what rank and why is, and will likely remain, muddled.

Throughout his career, Morihei was constantly refining and expanding his art—"This old man must still train and train," he said not long before his death—and thus taught differently at different stages of his life. There is a definite continuum between prewar and postwar Aikido, but the techniques themselves evolved considerably. Morihei gave his disciples permission to film his techniques but warned, "Today's techniques will be different tomorrow." Hence, there is no standard Aikido; each of the direct disciples focused on those aspects he most readily understood and with which he had the most affinity, and then went on to develop an individual style based on his own experiences. Morihei encouraged this: "Learn one technique, and create ten or twenty more. Aikido is limitless." Given the great differences, though, it is sometimes hard to believe that all of them sat at the feet of the same master. The best advice in judging the different interpretations of Aikido is this: "Do not look for the differences; look for what is the same."

5. MIYAMOTO MUSASHI

Musashi is a well-known figure among martial artists in the West due to the publishing success of his Book of Five Rings. *His personal history is discussed at length in Section III, but here we may note that fictionalized versions of his life have made him a mainstay of the Japanese press and movie industry. For many martial artists, the fascination with Musashi rests in the fact that he was an "old school" samurai who penned his insights on fighting even as the types of service demanded of a warrior class changed. While his reflections are, in many ways, prosaic, the fact that in his career he emerged victorious from many duels adds a sense of real authority to his writing.*

From *The Book of Five Rings* BY MIYAMOTO MUSASHI

THE GROUND BOOK

Strategy is the craft of the warrior. Commanders must enact the craft, and troopers should know this Way. There is no warrior in the world today who really understands the Way of strategy.

There are various Ways. There is the Way of salvation by the law of Buddha, the Way of Confucius governing the Way of learning, the Way of healing as a doctor, as a poet teaching the Way of Waka, tea, archery, and many arts and skills. Each man practices as he feels inclined.

It is said the warrior's is the twofold Way of pen and sword, and he should have a taste for both Ways. Even if a man has no natural ability he can be a warrior by sticking assiduously to both divisions of the Way. Generally speaking, the Way of the warrior is resolute acceptance of death. Although not only warriors but priests, women, peasants and lowlier folk have been known to die readily in the cause of duty or out of shame, this is a different thing. The warrior is different in that studying the Way of strategy is based on overcoming men. By, victory gained in crossing swords with individuals, or enjoining battle with large numbers, we can attain power and fame for ourselves or our lord. This is the virtue of strategy.

THE BOOK OF THE VOID

The Ni To Ichi Way of strategy is recorded in this the Book of the Void.

What is called the spirit of the void is where there is nothing. It is not included in man's knowledge. Of course the void is nothingness. By knowing things that exist, you can know that which does not exist. That is the void.

People in this world look at things mistakenly, and think that what they do not understand must be the void. This is not the true void. It is bewilderment.

In the Way of strategy, also, those who study as warriors think that whatever they cannot understand in their craft is the void. This is not the true void.

To attain the Way of strategy as a warrior you must study fully other martial arts and not deviate even a little from the Way of the warrior. With your spirit settled, accumulate practice day by day, and hour by hour. Polish the twofold spirit heart and mind, and sharpen the twofold gaze perception and sight. When your spirit is not in the least clouded, when the clouds of bewilderment clear away, there is the true void.

Until you realize the true Way, whether in Buddhism or in common sense, you may think that things are correct and in order. However, if we look at things objectively, from the viewpoint of laws of the world, we see various doctrines departing from the true Way. Know well this spirit, and with forth tightness as the foundation and the true spirit as die Way. Enact strategy broadly, correctly and openly.

Then you will come to think of things in a wide sense and, taking the void as die Way, you will see the Way as void.

In the void is virtue, and no evil. Wisdom has existence, principle has existence, the Way has existence, spirit is nothingness.

Twelfth day of the fifth month, second year of Shoho (1645)
Teruro Magonojo SHINMEN MUSASHI

6. Yamaoka Tesshu, Zen Swordsman

Another mystic, Tesshu was a practitioner of Zen Buddhism. In many ways he embodied the ideal of the martial artist. He was a fearsomely skilled fighter who never took a life. He was actively and productively engaged in the political events of his time, playing a role in the difficult Japanese transition from rule by a shogun to control by a modern government headed by the Emperor. He was a gifted calligrapher whose works are still studied by aspiring artists today. And he believed that the martial way, sincerely pursued, could lead individuals to enlightenment. In fact, his training methods in swordsmanship were designed to help students see beyond the sword in their hands, to a type of transcendence. In this, his ideas have helped shape the ideology and philosophy of the modern form of Japanese fencing known as kendo, which, while very different from Tesshu's swordsmanship, is nonetheless designed to be something "more" than mere training in the use of a weapon.

From *The Sword of No Sword* BY JOHN STEVENS

Known as "Ragged Tetsu," Tesshu had another nickname: "Demon Tetsu." Whatever Tesshu took up, no matter how minor, he gave it his all. Although Tesshu's father was not much of a martial artist, the Ono clan counted many illustrious swordsmen in its past, and Choemon was eager to have his energetic son follow in the footsteps of his ancestors. The boy was introduced to swordsmanship at age nine by the *Shinkage Ryu* master Kusumi Kantekisai, and thereafter never missed a day of practice. Upon the family's move to Taka-yama, Tesshu received instruction from Inoue Kiyotora, a highly regarded swordsman of the *Ono-ha Itto Ryu*.

In Edo, Tesshu enrolled in the Kobukan, the national military institute, and made the rounds of the famous training halls (*dojo*) in the area. Tesshu, a massive six-footer with tremendous strength, became the scourge of Edo training halls. He once shattered a two-inch-thick wallboard in the Kobukan kendo hall with one of his thrusts. Several dojos prohibited Tesshu from making strikes to his opponent's *kote* (wrist protector) for fear of a broken arm. Tesshu always carried his training gear with him; whenever he heard the sound of bamboo swords he would rush in and request to participate. At joint training sessions, most swordsmen would take a breather following each contest. Not Tesshu— he kept his helmet on and faced one swordsman after another. His friends joked, "Demon Tetsu likes swordsmanship better than eating or sleeping."

Regardless of the nature of their visit, callers to Tesshu's residence inevitably found themselves in his garden crossing swords with their host. When deliverymen made their morning rounds, Tesshu, naked save for his loincloth (*fundoshi*), would invite them to strike with all their might on any part of his body. The deliverymen naturally tired of bruising their knuckles on their strange customer's rockhard frame and asked Tesshu's brother to intercede on their behalf.

"But I'm simply conditioning my body," Tesshu explained. "We samurai must be ready for anything."

"That may be true," his brother said, "but you are scaring away all the deliverymen. How are you going to get provisions?"

"All right, all right!" Tesshu laughed. "Pass the word that there will be no more early morning training."

During those first years in Edo, Tesshu engaged in thousands upon thousands of contests with the best swordsmen of Japan. He never relaxed his warrior's bearing, not even in the toilet or when asleep. Accidentally awakened by a friend one night, Tesshu, who slept with his practice sword, was on his feet in an instant, counter-attacking.

One day, however, the confident twenty-eight-year-old demon met his match in Asari Gimei (Yoshiaki), master swordsman of the *Nakanishi-ha Itto*

Ryu. As soon as Tesshu learned that this renowned swordsman was in town, he applied for a contest. The arrangements were made and the two swordsmen came together. The contest lasted half a day. Tesshu attacked furiously, but Asari turned aside each blow, keeping Tesshu at bay the entire time. Finally, they came together in a clinch, their swords locked at the handles. Tesshu used his superior height and weight to knock Asari to the floor.

Asari got up and they faced each other in the middle of the hall. "What do you think about this match?" Asari asked Tesshu.

"It was a tough fight, but luckily I was able to win," Tesshu replied proudly.

"No, I am the winner," Asari asserted.

"You are mistaken. I won," Tesshu maintained.

"Just before you knocked me down, I scored a clean strike against your chest protector."

"That's impossible. I didn't feel a thing."

"Check your chest protector."

Tesshu did so and discovered three broken bamboo strips on the protector. Tesshu, refusing to believe he had lost, shouted indignantly, "These marks were made by insects and I never noticed them before!"

Later that day, Tesshu's brother-in-law Deishu, a witness to the contest, visited Tesshu's home and told him, "You know, Asari was telling you the truth."

"Yes," Tesshu confessed. "I realize that myself."

As was the custom in those days, Tesshu became the disciple of the one who defeated him. Asari was even more intimidating in regular practice. The first time the two faced each other with wooden swords, Tesshu was unable to put Asari on the defensive. In fact, Asari, half Tesshu's size and twelve years older, repeatedly forced Tesshu all the way back to the wall of the training hall. Asari's *kiai* (spiritual force) was irresistible. Finally, Asari drove Tesshu right out of the dojo into the street, knocked him down, and unceremoniously slammed the door in his face.

Whenever Tesshu closed his eyes, he would see Asari standing before him like a mountain, bearing down on the bewildered trainee. Troubled by this constant vision, Tesshu redoubled his efforts, both in the training hall and on the meditation cushion. Zen master Ganno advised him, "If an opponent frightens or confuses you, it means you lack true insight. Solve the koan of 'Originally not one thing exists' (*honrai muichibutsu*) and nothing will obstruct you."

Even though Tesshu managed to solve this koan after ten years of contemplation, he still could not shake the perplexing apparition. Tesshu consulted with Tekisui, abbot of Tenryuji, who presented the swordsman with this koan taken from Tozan's Five Ranks:

> When two flashing swords meet there is
> no place to escape; Move on coolly, like a lotus flower blooming
> in the midst of a roaring fire, And forcefully pierce the Heavens!

(This is rank number four, mutual integration. A true practitioner moves without hesitation through the confusion and chaos of the sensual world, avoiding all duality.)

Every minute for the next three years, Tesshu butted his head against this koan. During breaks in conversation, Tesshu would cross two pipes, trying to figure out the problem; while eating, he put his chopsticks together like two swords. Tesshu always kept a pair of wooden swords near his bed. If a possible solution presented itself at night, Tesshu would jump out of bed and ask his wife to grab a sword and confront him.

In his forty-fifth year the many years of hard training and ceaseless introspection culminated in Tesshu's great enlightenment. On the morning of March 30, 1880, as Tesshu sat in zazen, the meaning of Tekisui's koan revealed itself. He lost all sense of time and space; Asari's threatening sword vanished.

> For years I forged my spirit through the study of swordsmanship,
> Confronting every challenge steadfastly.
> The walls surrounding me suddenly crumbled;
> Like pure dew reflecting the world in crystal clarity, total
> awakening has now come.

That same morning Tesshu went to Asari's dojo to test his awakening. As soon as Asari crossed swords with Tesshu, he knew his disciple had realized the state of "no-enemy." Asari withdrew his sword and declared, "You have arrived." It is said that after he officially designated Tesshu his successor as thirteenth Headmaster of the Nakanishi-ha Itto Ryu, Asari never picked up a sword again.

Shortly thereafter, Tesshu established the *Muto Ryu*. *Mu-to*, "no-sword," was not a new concept. Tesshu considered himself a restorer, rather than an innovator—his favorite quotation from the Confucian Analects was: "Do not make up your own teachings but cherish the ways of the ancients"—and his system (*Ryu*) was firmly based in the traditions of the past. Following his designation as the tenth Headmaster of the Ono-ha Itto Ryu by Ono Goyu, Tesshu henceforth referred to his school as the *Itto Shoden Muto Ryu*, "The No-Sword System of the Correct Transmission of Ito Ittosai."

Although Tesshu had a small makeshift dojo on his property, once he founded the Muto Ryu a larger training hall was needed. Tesshu used his retirement fund from the government to construct a hall he named the Shumpukan. The name refers to a poem by Bukko Kokushi, a thirteenth century Chinese priest who came to Japan to teach warrior Zen to the Kamakura Shoguns. When Bukko was still on the mainland, his temple was raided by fierce Mongol troops. As the soldiers rushed forward with their swords drawn, Bukko looked up calmly from his meditation and recited this poem:

> In heaven and earth no spot to hide;
> Bliss belongs to one who knows that things are empty and that
> man too is nothing.
> Splendid indeed is the Mongol longsword
> Slashing the spring wind like a flash of lightning!

Not total barbarians, the Mongols were impressed enough by Bukko's composure to leave the priest unharmed.

"Spring wind" in Japanese is "*shumpu*." Tesshu's Shumpukan (kan means hall) was not merely a gym where one learned to hit others over the head with a stick; it was a holy "place of the Way" where the spirit was forged and awakening fostered.

> Using thought to analyze reality is illusion;
> If preoccupied with victory and defeat, all will be lost.
> The secret of swordsmanship?
> Lightning slashes the spring wind!

At the Shumpukan, Tesshu placed little emphasis on complicated explanations or rational analysis of technique. He rarely corrected his trainees' hand or foot work. Unlike other schools of swordsmanship where trainees were told, "If your opponent assumes such-and-such a stance, take such-and-such a stance in response," new Muto Ryu swordsmen were instructed to devote themselves exclusively to *uchi-komi* for at least three years. *Uchi-komi* is "attack training," repeated straight blows to the opponent's *men* (top of the head). The important element was never to retreat or hesitate; swordsmen must keep up the attack until they drop. It was not that Tesshu dis-regarded technique; forbearance can be developed no other way. When students complained of a lack of progress after a year's training, Tesshu thundered, "You've just begun!" Pointing to his abdomen, he continued, "You must experience swordsmanship here!"

Three years of uchi-komi training had many benefits: the body naturally became hardened; one developed strong arms, a powerful grip, sharp vision, and stable hips; one's movement gradually became free-flowing, characterized by forceful blows and sweeping attacks; unconcerned with winning and losing, totally absorbed in the moment at hand, one attained presence of mind. (Critics of this system referred to Muto Ryu training as "wood-chopping.")

For advanced swordsmen, Tesshu had more severe forms of training. Tesshu initiated a special method he termed *seigan*. "Seigan" is a Buddhist term meaning "vow," such as Shakyamuni's vow to attain enlightenment, or a Bodhisattva's vow to save all sentient beings. In this instance, it was a vow to challenge death in order to attain the ultimate principles of swordsmanship.

There were three kinds of seigan. The first seigan was generally preceded by a 1,000-consecutive-day practice period. On the final day of the period, the candidate was required to engage in a two-hundred-contest seigan with the other swordsmen in the dojo. With the exception of a brief pause for a lunch of rice gruel and pickled plums, the swordsman stood continuously (i.e., *tachi-kiri*, as seigan was also known), facing fresh opponents one after the other. The contests ran from early in the morning until two hundred were completed some time in the afternoon.

Successful candidates were eligible, after further training, for the second seigan: six hundred matches over a three-day period, following the same format as the first seigan.

The supreme test was the third seigan, a seven-day, one-thousand-four-hundred-contest marathon which taxed the outer limits of the swordsman's physical and spiritual endurance. Tesshu wrote:

Swordsmanship should lead to the heart of things where one can directly confront life and death. Recently, swordsmanship has become a mere pastime with no bearing on matters of importance. In order to counter this tendency, I have instituted a one-week, one-thousand-four-hundred-match training session. Initially, the swordsman will find the contests similar to regular training; however, as the number of consecutive matches piles up, it will assume the dimensions of a fight to the finish—one must rely on spiritual strength. This is real swordsmanship. If single-minded determination is absent, one will never advance regardless of the years spent in training. Thus I have established this special method of training to test the resolve of my swordsmen. Fortify your spirit and throw yourselves into this practice!

Two accounts remain of swordsmen who underwent seigan:

Kagawa Zenjiro was the first candidate: "On day one, the matches began at 6:00 a.m. Ten opponents took turns facing me and except for a short lunch break, I didn't sit down or remove my training gear until I completed the two hundred contests around 6:00 that evening. It was demanding, but I was in reasonably good condition. However, one of my fellow trainees visited my home later to relay this message from Tesshu Sensei: "You are slacking off. You must try harder,"

"The second day, I resolved to give it my all. Tesshu, too, had instructed my opponents to show no mercy. By mid-afternoon I was suffering greatly from fatigue. I somehow completed the required number of matches and limped home. My legs were so badly swollen I was unable to get up to go to the toilet. Near the end of the third day, I was staggering around the dojo, barely able to stand. Just then a former trainee entered the hall to be one of my opponents—A sneaky, ill-mannered lout, notorious for his unfair tactics, he liked nothing better than to injure his opponents seriously. My pain and weariness vanished; I focused entirely on my devious opponent. Even if he smashed my skull, he too would fall. Raising my sword high above my head I was about to leap across the dojo to meet him when Tesshu suddenly called out, 'Excellent! Excellent! Stop now!' Puzzled because I had not finished the quota of matches, Tesshu told me not to worry and to return home. I neither ate nor slept that night. My wife helped me to my feet the next morning. It was raining, but I couldn't raise my arms to hold an umbrella so she threw a blanket around me. I went to the training hall certain this would be my last day on earth—I was determined to die rather than not complete the seigan. When I arrived at the dojo, Tesshu was waiting for me. 'Ready to continue?' he asked. 'Yes,' I immediately replied. To my surprise, Tesshu ordered me to stop, and had the other trainees complete the remainder of the session." Because Kagawa had realized the "sword of no-sword" Tesshu had no need to test him further.

Yanagita Genjiro completed the two-hundred-match seigan on the final day of his thousand-day training period. He then practiced five hundred more days in a row and undertook the three-day, six-hundred-match seigan. Blows received from the short, thick Muto Ryu bamboo sword (*shinai*) were extremely painful. Yanagita recalled: "After the first day my head was full of lumps and my body covered with bruises, but I did not feel weak. On the second day I began to suffer. I thought I would have to give up halfway. I managed to continue and near the end of the day I experienced 'self-less-ness'—I naturally blended with my opponent and moved in unhindered freedom. Although my spirit was strong, my body was weak. My urine was dark red and I had no appetite. Nevertheless, I passed the final day's contests with a clear mind; I felt as if I was floating among the clouds."

Tesshu was not impressed with such hardship. He told his disciples: "When I was twenty-four I participated in a joint training session and engaged in one thousand four hundred matches over a seven-day period. I do not remember feeling tired or being in pain. There is victory and defeat in swordsmanship, but forging the spirit is far more important. What is the secret? The mind has no limits. Use such a mind when facing your opponents, incorporate it in your movements, and you will never tire regardless of how many days and how many contests you have. Study this and practice harder!"

Unfortunately, no firsthand accounts survive by the two swords-men who completed the seven-day seigan: Kominami Yasutomo and Sano (Tojo) Jisaburo, (Sano's "memorial" seven-day seigan took place after Tesshu's death.) According to Shumpukan records, eight swordsmen successfully completed a one-day, two-hundred-match seigan. Ogura Tetsuju and Yanagita Genjiro made the one-thouand-day practice that included a one-day seigan. Yanagita also completed a three-day seigan as did Kagawa Zenjiro. Two swordsmen, Kominami Yasutomo and Sano Jisaburo, underwent all three seigan: one-, three-, and seven-day. Another swordsman made a one-day *kata* seigan consisting of 2,750 movements. Successful completion of a seigan was accompanied by presentation of certificates, catalogs of techniques, and memorial training gear. However, the records are not clear on this point and it appears that the system was not uniformly applied.

Depth of spirit alone is not enough; it must be combined with technical prowess to create true swordsmanship. To foster proper technique, Tesshu had his trainees follow the classical kata of the Itto Ryu. When mastered, "kata," set forms that cover the entire range of techniques, enable a swordsman to adjust to any contingency. Unlike the contrived, artificially constructed kata of many other schools, Muto Ryu kata are all derived from actual combat conditions. There are fifty basic Muto Ryu kata—to perform the entire sequence requires nearly thirty minutes—plus a series of highly advanced kata. Again, emphasis is placed on the fundamentals: at least three years should be spent on perfecting the first five kata.

Regular practice in the Shumpukan ran from 6:00 to 9:00 in the morning. The live-in disciples rose at 4:00 to clean the grounds, sweep the training hall, and prepare the equipment. By 6:00, seventy to eighty swordsmen had gathered. Tesshu would circle the dojo, sometimes letting his disciples strike his helmet, sometimes countering in a flash and flipping them to the ground. There were no lengthy explanations—the only admonition was "Train harder! Train harder!"

Tesshu developed a kind of sixth sense, frequently surprising his disciples by telling them exactly what they were thinking. When asked about this "magic power," Tesshu told them: "It is nothing out of the ordinary. If your mind is empty, it reflects the 'distortions' and shadows' present in others' minds. In swordsmanship no-mind allows us to see the perfect place to strike; in daily life it enables us to see into another's heart."

To Tesshu, the prime requisite of a swordsman in unyielding determination. When a friend asked for the secret of swordsmanship, Tesshu instructed him to seek the guidance of the Asakusa Kannon. The friend paid a visit to the temple housing that image, but received no revelation. Dejected, he was about to return home when he noticed the calligraphy board hanging above the statue. It read: "Giver of Fearlessness."

Fearlessness, coupled with ceaseless training, is the secret of swordsmanship. Many Muto Ryu swordsmen lacked natural ability, yet, through diligent practice, they were able to defeat the most skilled technicians. The motto of the Shumpukan was: "Throw yourself into practice."

One year during the special thirty-day winter training period a member of the Shumpukan was to be married, and the live-in disciples asked Tesshu for permission to attend the ceremony. He had this to say: "Practice, particularly these special sessions, is more important than anything else. There are always good reasons for taking off, however, once a commitment is made, it must not be broken." Tesshu allowed no exceptions. Ogura Tetsuju received a special dispensation from his three-year Zen retreat to visit Tesshu on his death bed. Tesshu refused to see him, sending this message: "The three years are not up yet."

Tesshu insisted that no-sword swordsmanship was ultimately pure spirit.

Near the end of his life, Tesshu's movements were extraordinarily supple and he could defeat an opponent without even touching him. Students had sore spots on the places where Tesshu had merely pointed his sword at their bodies.

A week before his death, Tesshu called all his trainees together for a final practice session. Tesshu told them, "I'm dying. My physical strength is gone. I am barely able to stand. Not a trace of competitiveness remains. I'll now prove to you all that Muto Ryu swordsmanship is a thing of the spirit. If any of you display the slightest reserve today, the Muto Ryu will perish with my death."

Sano was the first to attack. Without regard for Tesshu's terminal illness, Sano charged forward. Just as he was about to bring his sword down with all his might, a tremendous force spun him around. Upon recovery, he cut loose with a two-handed thrust; in the twinkling of a eye, Sano was crushed to the floor. Seven or eight disciples came forward and all went flying in the same fashion. "This is the sword of no-sword."

The day before his death, Tesshu asked why the customary sounds were not rising from the dojo. The senior disciples, he was informed, had decided among themselves to call off the practice in order to be by Tesshu's side in his last hours. "What!" Tesshu thundered. "The best way to honor me and the Muto Ryu is to get in that hall right now and practice your hearts out!"

Although Tesshu awarded a number of certificates to various disciples, it appears that only Hasegawa Unhachiro received a *men-kyo-kaiden* teaching license, and this may have been presented to him posthumously. Since one of Tesshu's treasured swords and the Shumpukan files passed to Kagawa Zenjiro, he is commonly reckoned as the second Headmaster of the Muto Ryu. Kagawa's top disciple was Ishikawa Ryuzo who, in turn, instructed the three main Muto Ryu exponents of the twentieth century: Navy Chief of Staff Kusajika Ryunozuke, Chief Justice Ishida Kazuto, and Dr. Murakami Yasumasa, Murakami Sensei, the only surviving member of the three, currently heads the Muto Ryu and maintains the *Shumpukan Bunko* (Library) which preserves many of the original records. The techniques and training methods of the Muto Ryu were never widespread—today, for example, there are no more than fif-teen Muto Ryu swordsmen—and critics, then and now, say its meth-ods are too severe and its principles too deep for wide application. That may well be: Tesshu was never interested in popularizing the Way of the Sword as a sport or pastime. To Tesshu, one good swords-man was worth 10,000 mediocre trainees.

7. Yagyu Munenori

Takuan Soho's swordsman friend, son of Yagyu Mitsuyoshi, and fencing instructor to the Tokugawa shogun, Yagyu Munenori was a martial artist whose eminence demanded not only technical excellence, but deep reflection on the dynamics of developing martial skill and the justification for utilizing it. In this, he is clearly a samurai—the name means those who serve—articulating his ideas regarding the social place and function of the fighting man. But he is also more than that. Munenori is an individual concerned with ethical action, of ultimate purpose, and the role of martial training in leading the person to enlightenment. When reading these excerpts from the Yagyu family's scrolls on swordsmanship, it is clear that Munenori was a product of his times. His concern with governance, the social order, and the correct role of the warrior have been shaped by the Confucian ideology promulgated by the Tokugawa Shogunate. He has read his Laozi as well. And, of course, the flavor of Zen has permeated his musings, an echo of the insights of his close friend Takuan.

The Death-Dealing Blade BY YAGYU MUNENORI

Weapons Are Unfortunate Instruments

Here's what was said in the past: "Weapons are unfortunate instruments. Heaven's Way hates them. Using them when there is no other choice—that is Heaven's Way."

Suppose you ask how this is so. What the statement says is that the bow and arrows, the sword, and the halberd are weapons, and that they are ominous, unfortunate instruments. Whereas Heaven's Way is the way to keep things alive, these choose to kill, and in this they are indeed unfortunate instruments. In other words, Heaven's Way hates them because they go against it.

But the statement says killing man by using a weapon when there is no other choice is also Heaven's Way. Suppose you ask what the point of this is. Even though in the spring winds flowers bloom and the green increases, when the autumn frost comes, leaves fall and trees wither. This is the judgment of Heaven's Way. There is logic in striking down something when it has peaked. When someone rides his luck and does evil, you strike him down when his evils have peaked. In that sense, using weapons is said to be also Heaven's Way. At times, because of one man's evil, thousands of people suffer. So you kill that one man in order to let the thousands live. Here, truly, the blade that deals death could be the sword that gives life.

Strategies: Small and Large

There are ways of using weapons. If you don't know how to use them, you will be killed while meaning to kill. When you think of it, among the military strategies the one that entails two swords as you confront someone means only one loser and one winner. This is strategy on an extremely small scale. Winning or losing will involve little gain or loss.

When a single man wins and the state wins, and when a single man loses and the state loses, that is strategy on a large scale. Here, a single man means the general; the state, the various armies under his command. The various armies are the general's arms and legs. Making the various forces work well means making the general's arms and legs work well. For the various forces not to work is for the general's arms and legs not to work. When you and someone confront each other with swords, you win by making your arms and legs work at will. Likewise, a general wins a battle by using his forces and by plotting well.

Governance and Swordsmanship

A man in the position of general must be able to set up camp and maneuver his army for battle not only on the actual battlefield where victory or defeat is decided, but also within the confines of his mind. The latter is the art of war in the mind.

Not ignoring a disturbance when governance is good is the basis of the art of war; so is foreseeing a disturbance from the various developments in the state and stopping it before it breaks out. When the country is governed well, it is also part of military strategy to appoint this man to this governorship, that man to that mayorality, and to give attention to the remotest corners of the land to strengthen the defense of the state.

Schemes of a governor, mayor, magistrate, or village head for personal gain will mean hardship for the governed and spell the beginning of the collapse of the state.

The ability to understand this and to plot to prevent the personal schemes of a governor, mayor, magistrate, or village head from ruining the land is comparable to the ability to judge your opponent's stratagems by observing his moves in a sword fight. You must be attentive and observant. Something of greater utility can be learned from swordsmanship.

Serving Your Lord

Your lord may be flanked by sycophants, who when facing him feign an air of morality, but who when looking down at the ruled give an angry glance. Such men, unless you lie low before them, will speak ill of you for something good you have done. As a result, the innocent suffer and the sinful thrive. Understanding this is more important than the ability to judge your opponent's stratagems in a sword fight.

The state is you lord's; so are the people. Those who serve in his vicinity are his subjects, just as those who serve him in the distance. Closeness or distance scarcely matters. For the lord, his subjects are his arms and legs; the legs may be a little distant, but they are no different from the arms. Because they feel pain the same way, the arms and the legs are neither closer nor remoter. When such is the case, if those who are close exploit those who are distant, those who are distant will suffer despite their innocence and resent their lord, who should come under no such cloud.

Those close to the lord are few—five to ten at the most. Those distant are many. Those who are many will turn away from him if they resent him. Those few and close, who from the beginning think only of themselves and not of their lord, and serve him in a way that makes the people resent him, in an emergency will vie in turning away from him. When that happens, who will think of the lord? His aides are responsible for such a development; he is not to blame. It is hoped that this will be understood, and that those in the distance will not be placed outside the lord's benevolence. To grasp this truth under any circumstance is in itself part of military strategy.

Strategic Thinking in Everything

Whether a friendship remains unchanged or not from beginning to end also depends on grasping the truth, and so requires something not unlike strategic thinking. Even companionship during a gathering relies on timely judgment and therefore a strategic mind. If you fail to grasp truth, you may stay too long when you should not and end up being blamed for something groundlessly; or you may speak out without reading the workings of someone else's mind, thereby inviting a quarrel and in the end ruining yourself All this depends on whether you grasp the truth or not.

Arranging various things in your living room through selection of an appropriate spot for each piece also requires incisive judgment of the room. Here again, something not unlike strategic thinking is needed. No matter what the subject, there is one truth, and it would do no wrong to apply that to government.

It is a prejudice to think that swordsmanship is meant solely to slash an opponent. It is meant not to slash an opponent, but to kill evil. It is a way of allowing ten thousand men to live by killing a single evil man.

What is recorded in these three volumes may not go out of this house. But that is not to make this school of swordsmanship a secret. This record is made for transmis-sion to those who are worthy of it. Without transmission, these volumes might as well not exist. May my descendants keep this in mind.

The Great Learning is the Gate for the Beginner

To reach a house, you must first enter the gate. The gate is a pathway leading to the house. After passing through the gate, you enter the house and meet its master. Learning is the gate to reaching the Way. After passing through this gate, you reach the Way. Learning is the gate, not the house. Don't mistake the gate for the house. The house is located farther inside, after the gate is passed. Because learning is the gate, don't think that the books you read are the Way. Books are a gate for reaching the Way.

There are those who remain in the dark about the Way, no matter how much they study, no matter how many ideographs they learn. They may read the classics as easily as if they were paraphrases by ancient scholars, but because they are in the dark about the truth, they cannot make the Way their own. Even so, it is difficult to reach the Way without learning. At the same time, someone who has studied hard and talks smoothly may not necessarily be someone who has illuminated the Way. But again, there are those who naturally live according to the Way without study-ing anything.

Exhaust All Knowledge and Master Everything

The *Great Learning* says: "Exhaust all knowledge and master every-thing." Exhausting all knowledge, means knowing everything that is generally known in society and the principle of everything that exists, leaving nothing unknown. Mastering everything means that when you have come to know the principle of everything, there is nothing you don't know, nothing you can't do. When you have exhausted things to know, you have mastered all the things to do. If you have not, you can-not do anything.

While you don't know about something, you have doubts about it. Because you are doubtful, that something does not leave your mind. if the principle of that something becomes clear, nothing will remain in your mind. This is what is meant by exhausting all knowledge and mas-tering everything.

When nothing remains in your mind, everything becomes easy to do. You learn the Way of everything in order to brush aside whatever may be in your mind. At first, because you know nothing, you do not have doubts or any such thing in your mind. Only after you begin learning do things come into your head that prevent you from doing anything with ease. When the things you have learned leave your mind completely, forms and the like disappear; and as you perform each skill in your own field, it becomes easy regardless of the form. Without violating the form, you perform it unconsciously, correctly.

The same holds true in swordsmanship. Training after you have learned a hundred sword positions, after thoroughly learning whatever body position , eye position, or form there may be, is training in a state where you have exhausted all knowledge. When you have exhausted all the forms and all those forms cease to exist in your mind—that is the state where you have mastered everything. When you have exhausted all the various forms and piled up accomplishments through training and practice, movements come to exist in your arms, legs, and body, not in your mind; and whatever you do you do freely, in disregard of the forms, but not violating them. When you reach that point, you do not know where your mind is—even the Demon of Heaven or a heretic won't be able to pinpoint its whereabouts. The forms exist for reaching that state. When you have acquired them, they cease to exist.

That is the ultimate end of all disciplines. The final state of any discipline is where you forget what you have learned, discard your mind, and accomplish whatever you set out to do without being aware of it yourself You begin by learning and reach the point where learning does not exist.

The Mind and the Spirit

That part of the mental makeup positioned inside to develop detailed plans is called the mind, and that part that carries out those plans, the spirit. The mind may be compared to the master, and the spirit to his servant. The mind stays inside and uses the spirit. If the spirit becomes overworked, it may stumble. You must have the spirit tethered to the mind so that it may not be carried away.

In swordsmanship terms, the firming up of your body below the waist may be said to be the mind, and the actual exchange of blows after the fight has begun, the spirit. Keep the spirit under the tight control of your body below the waist. Don't allow it to take an impetuous attack stance. It is vital to maintain calm by having the mind pull back the spirit and by not allowing it to be dragged along by the spirit.

8. ISSAI CHOZAN

Karl Friday is a specialist in Japanese history. He is also a highly trained martial artist, an adept in the Katori Shin-ryu school of swordsmanship. As a result, he unites scholarship and martial skill in the best tradition of what the Japanese call bunbu ryodo *(the way of learning and the way of the sword in accord). His translation and analysis of this eighteenth century parable on the mental dynamics of martial skill are so complete that they need no further introduction.*

The Cat's Eerie Skill BY ISSAI CHOZAN

PREFACE

Turbulence and combat are a part of the lives of all creatures. From the smallest to the greatest, no species is utterly free of violence, least of all man, who has learned to kill not only for food or for self-defense, but in anger or hatred, for profit, and even for pleasure. Yet this creature, man, using the same hands with which he fashions tools of destruction, creates art that celebrates life; using the same mind with which he plots rapine, conceives philosophies that celebrate peace and harmony.

Among the myriad solutions mankind has proposed for taming its savagery none is as intricate or intriguing as the cultural and conceptual traditions surrounding the Japanese practice of the *bugei* (the military disciplines, or, more popularly, the martial arts). In late medieval and early modern Japan, martial training appropriated the status—as well as the forms, the vocabulary, the teaching methods, and even the ultimate goals—of religion and the fine arts. By the eighteenth century they had evolved into a complex cultural phenomenon in which various physical, technical, psychological, and philosophical factors were believed to intertwine and interact to produce a coherent path that guided both the physical and the moral activities of those who followed it.

The intricate entanglement of tactical, corporeal, mental, and spirit-ual concerns lies at the heart of classical Japanese martial art, and yet it is often only poorly understood. Scholars and aficionados alike have long been intrigued by the compelling paradox of samurai martial culture and its equation of perfection of the arts of violence with perfect non-violence. But to resolve this enigma, modern observers have tended to fall back on simplistic notions like an unattaching "Zen mind" that transcends and neutralizes the moral consequences of killing.

While this idea is not entirely wrong, it misses a critical point: to the early modem samurai, proficiency in combat and spiritual enlightenment were not contending, or even sequential, achievements; they were interactive and interdependent developments—inseparable aspects of the same phenomenon—to be experienced simultaneously. It was, by this time, a fundamental premise of bugei instruction in Japan that the ability to utterly transcend any attraction to violence was *essential* to the perfection of combative skills. Pundits, drawing out the implications of a world view (formed at the nexus of Buddhism, Taoism, Neo-Confucianism, and Shinto thought) that stressed monism and the interpenctration of all things and all actions, were insisting chat the study of fighting arts not only could but *must* eventually become a path to broader development of the self.

One of the best illustrations of the reasoning that underlay this con-clusion is Issai Chozan's eighteenth-century parable about the nature of ultimate proficiency in the fighting arts, *Neko no Myojutsu* ("The Cat's Eerie Skill"). Issai, whose real name was Tanba Jurozaemon Tadaaki, was a retired retain-er of the Sekiyado domain in Shimosa Province (in what is now Chiba Prefecture), and a prominent scholar of Shinto, Buddhism, Confucianism, Taoism, and military science. He published *Neko no Myojutsu* in 1727, when he was sixty-nine years old as part of a thirty-volume work entitled *Inaka Soji* ("The Country Chuang Tzu").

The text centers on a discussion among a group of cats, concerning their failure to defeat an unusually ferocious rat. Issai uses the cats' skills and shortcomings as illustrations of successive levels of achievement in martial ability.

NEKO NO MYOJUTSU—THE CAT'S EERIE SKILL

There was once a swordsman named Shoken, whose home was in-vaded by a huge rat that would appear and run about, even in broad daylight. Closing the rodent up in one room, he set his house cat to capturing it, but the rat charged, leaped at the cat's face, and bit her, causing the cat to squeal and run away. Nonplussed by this result, the swordsman borrowed several neighborhood cats who had made names for themselves as extraordinary rat-catchers, and turned them loose in the room. But the rat sat quietly in a corner until one of the cats approached, whereupon it leaped out and bit him. Seeing this terrible sight, the other cats froze with fear and could not advance.

The swordsman became enraged and, taking up a wooden sword, went after the rat himself to beat it to death. But the rat slipped beneath the wooden sword untouched, while the swordsman struck sliding doors and Chinese paper screens, tearing them to shreds. That spirited rat bound through the air with lightening-like speed, and even leapt at the swords-man's face, attempting to bite. At length, drenched with perspiration,

Shoken summoned a servant. "I have heard tell," he said, "of a peerless cat about six or seven leagues from here. Borrow it and have it brought here."

The servant dispatched a man. But when he returned with the cat, the animal did not look especially clever, nor did its body appear in any way remarkable. Be that as it may, when the cat was placed in the room, the rat did not move from its corner, while the cat walked nonchalantly across the room, caught it, and dragged it back to Shoken.

That evening, all the cats assembled in the swordsman's home, with this Elder cat in the seat of honor. The other cats came forward, kneeled, and said, "We are all felines of some reputation, long-trained and skilled in this art. Not only rats, but even weasels and otters, we slap down and carve up with our claws. But we have never heard of anything like this ferocious rat, Through what skill were you able to bring it down? We humbly beseech you to share with us your wondrous art."

The Elder cat laughed and replied, "You are all young kittens. Although you are experts in your work, you have not until now heard tell of the methods of the true Way. And so when you meet with the unexpected, you are taken unaware. Nevertheless, let us first hear of the extent of each of your training and practice."

A shrewd black cat came forth from the group. "I was born," it began, "to a house of rat-catchers and have set my heart on that path. I can leap over a seven-foot folding screen or squeeze through a tiny hole. I have been unsurpassed in speed and acrobatics since I was a kitten. I can feign sleep or inattention, and have never failed to catch rats even when they run along the roofing beams. And yet today I faced a rat of unimaginable prowess, and was defeated for the first time in my life."

The Elder cat replied, "What you have mastered is rehearsed form. Thus you cannot escape your calculating mind. The ancients only taught technique in order to show the Way. And so their techniques and forms were simple and few, and yet they contained within them all the ultimate principals of the art. In this later age, many pursue technique and form exclusively, somehow or other putting together various tricks and mastering cleverness, while never equaling the prowess of the ancients. They use their talent, and contest one another in form and technique, but even the zenith of cleverness amounts to nothing. The small man, who perfects technique and concentrates on skill, must always be thus. Skill is the use of the body and the will, but it is not based in the Way. When one focuses on cleverness one falls into deceit, and often one's own skills and tricks are turned against oneself. Reflect upon this and learn it well."

Thereupon a large, tiger-striped cat stepped forward. "To my thinking," it said, "martial art requires the ability to move with *ki*. I have, therefore, long practiced breathing exercises. I have built up my *ki* so that my *tanden* is firm and full—as if it reaches from Heaven to Earth. I strike down my enemies with this alone, securing victory even before I advance to fight. I seize rats with it, answering their every attempt at change of tactic, just as the echo answers the voice it follows. I have no conscious thought of employing technique, and yet technique bubbles forth spontaneously. I can strike down rats running along ceiling beams just by staring at them; and then I take them. But this mighty rat came forth without form and left nothing in passing. What is one to make of this?"

The Elder cat rejoined, "You have trained at harnessing the impetus of your vital energy, but you count only on your ego. This is not the Good in the true sense of the Good. You go forth ready to shatter the enemy, and he comes forward to shatter you; what happens when he cannot be shattered? You seek to dominate and crush him and the enemy seeks to dominate you; what happens when he cannot be dominated? Why must it be that your will will always be strong and your enemies' always weak? The power that you think fills Heaven and Earth is but a representation of the real ki. It resembles Mencius' 'flood-like ki,' but it is not the same. His is vigorous because it carries perspicacity; yours is vigorous because it is carried by your might. Thus its application is likewise different. It is like the main currents of the Yang-tze and Yellow Rivers or the might of a single night's flood. What happens when an enemy cannot be bowed by the force of your ki? It is said that a cornered rat will turn to bite a cat. He fights for his life, trapped, and with no other hope. He forgets his life, forgets his desires, and thinks only of the battle. He thinks nothing of his body. Thus his will *is* like iron. How can such an animal be made to submit by the force of one's ki?"

And then a gray, somewhat aged cat came quietly forward to speak. "As you say, though ki may be vigorous, it has portents. And that which has portents, however faint, can be detected. Thus I have long disciplined my heart such that I do not overawe or struggle; I harmonize and do not oppose. When the enemy is strong, I yield tranquilly to him. I engulf his technique like a curtain enveloping a stone thrown against it. I offer even the strongest rats nothing to fight. And yet this rat today neither bowed to force nor complied with yielding. It came and went like a ghost. I have never seen the like of this."

The Elder cat said, "What you are calling harmony is not a natural harmony; it is a contrived harmony. You seek to evade the enemy's attacking spirit, but when there is even the slightest presence of mind on your part, the enemy can perceive it. You self-consciously attempt to harmonize, and your spirit becomes muddied and lazy. When one acts out of forethought, one obstructs one's natural perception. And when one obstructs one's natural perception, sublime actions cannot come forth from anywhere. But when one follows one's intuition, without thinking and without doing, one has no presages. And when one has no presages, one can have no enemies under Heaven.

"But this is not to say that all of what you have trained at is of no value. If the Way permeates all its manifestations, all actions hold ultimate principle within them. The ki activates the functions of the body. When the ki is magnanimous, it can harmonize with all things without limit. When the ki is in harmony, one ceases to fight with force, yet is not readily broken even when striking metal or rock.

"Nevertheless, where there is even a speck of self-conscious thought, all becomes artifice, This is not the naturalism of the Way. Therefore those you face do not capitulate, but become antagonistic. What sort of art should one use? Only be selfless and respond naturally.

"The Way has no ultimate. You should not think, from what I have said, that I have reached the zenith. A long time ago there was a cat in a village near mine. It slept all day long and showed no vigor of spirit. It was like a cat carved of wood. No one ever saw it catch a rat. And yet wherever that cat went, there were no rats nearby. It was the same wherever it had been. I went to it to ask why this was, but it didn't answer. Four times I asked and four times it gave no answer. It was not that the cat was ignoring me, but that it did not know *how* to answer. It did not know how it did what it did. What is known is not said, and what is said is not known. This cat had forgotten self and others. It had returned to a state of nonentity. It was like King Wen of Chou, who attained divine warriorship, and killed not. I am still far from attaining the level of that cat."

Shoken had been listening to these words as if dreaming. He then came forth and bowed to the Elder cat, saying, "I have long studied the art of the sword, but have not yet reached the ultimate in that path. But, having heard your ideas this evening, it seems that you have attained complete mastery of this path of mine. I beg of you: show me the inner secrets."

The cat replied, "Nay, I am a mere animal; rats are my food. What do I know of human activities? But one thing I once furtively overheard is that swordsmanship is not just about striving for victory over others. It is, in a phrase, the art that looks upon the profound and clarifies life and death. One who would be a samurai must always train in this art and nurture this will. Hence one must first permeate the principles of life and death, never deviating and never wavering, using no cleverness or thought, keeping one's heart and ki in harmony, without distinguishing self from others, and being undisturbed like the depths of a spring. Thus one will adapt and respond spontaneously to change.

"When the faintest thought of entities enters one's heart, there is relativity. When there is relativity there is an enemy and a self, who can confront one another and fight. In this state [one cannot] respond freely and spontaneously to change. One's heart has already fallen into the realm of death and lost its brightness of spirit; how can one stand and fight clearly in this state? Even if one wins, it would be but an accidental victory. This is not the true objective of swordsmanship.

"This state of nonentity should not be equated with an arrogant vacuity. The spirit is originally without form; it stores no things. When it hoards anything at all, the ki will be drawn to that place. And when the ki is drawn to anyplace at all, adaptability cannot function unrestricted. It goes too much where it is directed, and it does not reach where it is not directed. Where there is too much, one's strength over-lows and cannot be stopped. Where it does not reach, it starves and cannot be used. It cannot respond instantly with changes. The formlessness of which I speak holds nothing and is drawn to nothing. In it there is no enemy, and there is no self. It only responds to what comes, and leaves behind no tracks. The *I-ching* says, 'Without calculation and without artifice, being still and unmoving: this is what enables one's senses to penetrate all under Heaven.'" One who studies swordsman-ship in light of this principle is close to the Way."

Shoken then asked, "What is meant by 'There is no enemy, and there is no self?'"

The cat answered, "There is an enemy because there is a self. Where there is no ego, there is no enemy. Enemy is simply a name for something in opposition, like yin to yang or fire to water. Wherever there is form there must be opposition. When there is no form in one's heart, there can be nothing to oppose it. When there is nothing to oppose one, there is no fight. Thus there is no self and there is no enemy. When one forgets both self and other, becoming like the undisturbed ocean depths, one is in harmony and at one with all. Although one strikes down the enemy's form, one is not conscious of it; nor is one unconscious of it. One is without deliberation and moves only with one's instincts. When one is completely unattached to all thoughts, the world is one's own world, and one makes no distinctions between correct and incorrect, or like and dislike. All these come from the line between pain and pleasure or gain and loss in one's own mind. Heaven and Earth are expansive, and yet there is nothing to be sought after outside one's own mind.

"The ancients said, 'When one's eyes focus only on dust, the Three Worlds seem shabby and narrow; when one's heart is carefree, one's whole life is rich and abundant." [This means that] when even a speck of ambition enters one's vision, one cannot keep one's eyes open. This happens when things enter into a place that was originally clear, and empty of things. This is an allegory for the mind and spirit. [Mencius] said that in the midst of millions of enemies, even though one's body can be crushed to dust, one's heart is one's own. Even a mighty foe cannot control one's mind and spirit. Confucius said, 'Even a common man cannot be robbed of his will.' If one is confused, this very mind aids one's enemies.

"This is all I have to say. Only reflect on it and seek yourselves. A teacher can only transmit the technique, and shed light on the principle. To realize the truth of it is in oneself. This is called 'acquisition through direct experience. It may also be called 'mind-to-mind transmission,' or 'transmission outside the teachings. This is not a matter of turning one's back on the teachings, for even the teacher cannot but convey them. Nor is it only Zen. From the lessons of the sages to the goals of the arts, all acquisition through direct experience is 'mind-to-mind transmission' and 'transmission outside the teachings.' The teachings themselves are only to point out what is already in oneself, albeit invisible. One does not receive such knowledge from a teacher. It is easy to teach, and easy to listen. But it is difficult to find what is in oneself and to make it one's own. This is called 'seeing reality. It is like rousing from an erroneous dream, and thus may also be called 'awakening.' There is no difference between these terms."

COMMENTARY

In this compelling allegory, Issai describes the highest form of fighting ability as something beyond the achievement of physical skills, tactical brilliance, and even psycho-spiritual power. He identifies absolute, flawless proficiency in combat as a state in which one rises above all possible opponents by deactivating all possible opposition. The ultimate warrior is one in such perfect harmony with the natural order that he transcends both any interest in fighting and any need to fight.

This state is, however, qualitatively different from the sort of benign pacifism through strength commonly envisioned by modern, especially Western, martial art aficionados. The latter, exemplified by David Carradine's character in the popular 1970's television series *Kung Fu*, centers on the dismissal of aggression and ego, and on the deliberate avoidance of conflict. The consummate warrior of this ideal renounces war.

But in the classic Japanese ideal, a perfect warrior is still a warrior, performing the functions of a warrior, just as the master cat described in the parable was still a functioning cat. The cat kept its neighborhood free of rats, even though it did no overt hunting or killing. In the same way, bugei philosophers like Issai did not advocate abandoning the world and repudiating violence, the way a monk does, but mastering violence and becoming able to defend the realm and serve justice without needing to actually fight.

In *Neko no Myojutsu*, Issai not only characterizes what perfect martial skill involves, he illustrates why this must be the case. The cats of the parable describe increasingly sophisticated approaches to martial art, yet each approach is inherently and irredeemably flawed.

The swordsman's house cat appears to have relied on its physical strength and speed alone. But, Issai warns, no matter how strong or how fast one is, there will always be someone stronger or faster—as Shoken's pet quickly learned. This is precisely the reason that warriors develop martial arts and train in the first place: conditioning and the application of well-conceived tactics can enable relatively small or slow fighters to defeat larger or faster ones. The second cat in the parable had reached near-perfection of skill at this level. But, reminds Issai, while physical skills and tactical cunning give one a significant edge against most opponents, the very best will not be taken in; some will even find ways to exploit these devices to their own advantage.

A more sophisticated alternative to relying on either brawn or brain is to focus instead on developing sufficient psycho-spiritual presence to be able to dominate and overawe opponents into submission by sheer force of will. This is the line of attack favored by the third cat in Issai's tale. Becoming able to crush opponents with the power of one's spirit makes it possible to transcend corporeal limitations—for the spirit, unlike the body, need not weaken with age or illness. It also robs adversaries of any way to discern or anticipate one's stratagems—for there are none to be discerned. There is, therefore, an appealing mystique to fighting in this manner. Nevertheless Issai dismisses this as a relatively unreliable, and low-level, approach to combat. A more sophisticated method yet, is to focus not on overwhelming the opponent, but on yielding to him—deflecting all opposing force, and flowing around it like water in a stream. This gives opponents nothing to strike at, and leads them to defeat themselves. But even this, says Issai, falls short of perfect skill in martial art, for at this level non-violence is still an artifice that can be detected and exploited by an opponent.

Through the voice of the Elder cat, Issai argues that to reach the ultimate in combative skill—to place himself beyond all possibility of defeat—a warrior has to eliminate all self-conscious thought or guile, and act spontaneously, in complete harmony with Nature. Only by doing this can he free himself from reliance on physical, mental, or spiritual tools, and the risk of meeting an opponent who is better with them.

This premise is easy enough to understand, but the ramifications of accepting it are profound. For the desire to fight, to win, to see justice done, or even to survive are all manifestations of self-conscious thought, and all must be transcended in the quest for perfect martial art. And thus a journey that begins with a craving for certain victory must, if followed to its logical end, take one beyond outcomes, beyond fighting, and beyond even the self.

9. WARRIOR POETRY

Poetry, which as a written form has the capacity to communicate a more emotional and less rational dimension to experience, has often been a way for martial artists to try to speak about their art. These selections from various Japanese schools of spear arts illustrate the various ways in which students of the Way have attempted to present their insights and experiences.

Songs of the Way of the Spear

Hozoin School (about AD 1600)

By what I did yesterday, I win today;
This is the virtue of practice.

Remember the old saying, The plan for a day is a cock's crow,
The plan for a life is something serious.

In the knightly arts, first see that you yourself are right,
And after that think of defeating an opponent.

The unskilled man does not know his own faults.
And yet dreams vainly of defeating another.

The Way is first of all about one's own defects;
After that, you can defeat others.

Without knowing the stains and faults in one's own self,
How empty to dream of victory over others!
In the knightly arts, if a man's will is right
There is no doubt of his ultimate victory.

Don't think to win just by force;
There is hard in the soft, soft in the hard.

'Softness is just weakness', some say;
But know there is a difference between softness and weakness.

When making an attack, do not be careless;
There is a waiting in action, an action in waiting.

In all the turns of the combat, never must one get controlled
by the enemy—
This is what is always to be remembered.

In a contest, you must be aware of the distances and the timing;
But do not lose sight of the awareness which is beyond them (zan-shin).

When you penetrate deep to the simple awareness (zan-shin)
You will experience the state of being and non-being.

It is like a stream, which when flowing is pure;
If it stands still, it becomes putrid.

Against a strong opponent, though you lose still you get something out of it;
Do not think always in one straight line.

In a contest, first control your own mind;
Only after that think about technique.

If you have control of your mind, be careful not to lose it;
Hold the mind firm, and then make the thrust.

The hands waiting, the feet active without flagging;
Let the heart be that of a waterbird swimming.

When the short body and the long spear are a unity,
The enemy finds no opening to strike.

SABURI SCHOOL (SEVENTEENTH CENTURY)
There is no village where the moon does not shine,
But it is clear in the hearts of the men of poetry.

Though one think, 'I have thrown away the world, my body is naught',
Still when the snow falls, the night is cold.

The samurai who is gentle in his benevolence and in his duty and in his bravery,
He is not burnt up in fire nor drowned in water.

Though a man is well equipped and strong and great,
If he does not know the Way of the knight, he is as a stick or stone.

The beach pine has no voice;
When the wind blows, it sings.

The water does not think of giving it lodging
Nor the moon of lodging there
How clear the reflection!

The heart which can hear the frost forming on a cold night,
When confronted with an enemy, will snatch the victory.

KAGOSHIMA SCHOOL
In blind darkness (mu-myo, the technical Buddhist term for ignorance),
The rising and setting of the moon
No man knows.

On the surface of Sarusawa Lake the mist is thick..
What is floating and what sinking
No man knows

A   UM
Study the natural state of the heart;
Study it well to the limit of the two characters A and UM.

The two characters A UM are killing and saving in the palm of the hand;
At the instant of being and non-being, life and death, you rise
To the peak of three thousand lives and deaths.
One glance, and you attain freedom.

If the transparent (white) dewdrop of the self
Is put on a red maple leaf,
It is a ruby.

TENTO SCHOOL
It is vulgar to despise the other traditions.
The Buddha in every temple is to be revered.

In the shade of the evening, do not walk talking loudly and carelessly.
Is there someone lying in wait?

Don't argue about who does well and who badly;
Seek where you yourself fall short.

10. YANG FAMILY TRANSMISSIONS

The Yang style of taiji is probably the most commonly practiced form of this art today. A characteristic of Chinese arts has been the close guarding of teachings and the restriction of knowledge to individuals within the inner circle of the style. The role of the sifu, *teacher, has remained indispensable in the transmission of these arts. As a result, when compared with Japanese arts, written sources on Chinese systems are not readily available to Western readers. But times change. In what follows, the twentieth century master teacher known as Chen Man-ch'ing, discusses the need for preserving insights of past generations and making them widely available. His commentary on the oral traditions of the Yang family serves as a valuable record for students of all martial ways. The poetic commentary from Yang family manuscripts that follows Chen's exposition shows a commonality in the poetic inspiration of both Japanese and Chinese martial artists.*

EXPOSITION OF THE ORAL TRANSMISSION—
CHENG MAN-CH'ING

As a rule, martial artists who have acquired superior technique keep it secret and do not reveal it to others. It is also customary to transmit it only to sons and not to daughters. However, the sons are not always worthy and this leads to frequent loss of true transmissions. If, perhaps, a teacher has a favorite student then he will impart his technique, but always hold something back against unforeseen contingencies. If we go on in this way, can one really expect to see the flowering of our national martial arts?

Although I, Man-ch'ing, studied with Master Yang Ch'eng-fu, I do not dare to claim that I received the full transmission. However, were I to hold things back, or keep secrets and not make them public, this would be to horde treasure at the expense of the nation. For the past ten or so years, whenever I desired to commit them to paper in order to spread their popularity, this feeling stirred in my mind and I put the task aside. This happened over and over, for I feared the transmission would reach the wrong people. However, after careful consideration, and in the spirit of openness and generosity, I firmly resolved to faithfully record the twelve important oral teachings in order. Master Yang did not lightly transmit these to anyone. Each time he spoke of them, he exhorted us saying, "If I do not mention this, then even if you study for three lifetimes, it will be difficult to learn." If I heard these words once, I heard them a thousand times. This is how much he deeply cared, but he could not realize his great expectations. This was a cause of great pain to him. Nevertheless, I hope to provide the wise and brave men of the world with the means to study and develop, and enable all people to eliminate illness and enjoy longevity. This would be of profound benefit to the race.

1. Relaxation Every day Master Yang repeated at least ten times: "Relax! Relax! Be calm. Release the whole body." Otherwise he would say, "You're not relaxed! You're not relaxed! Not being relaxed means that you are ready to receive a beating."

The one word, "relax, " is the most difficult to achieve. All the rest follows naturally. Let me explain the main idea of Master Yang's oral instructions in order to make' them readily comprehensible to students. Relaxation requires the release of all the sinews in the body without the slightest tension. This is what is known as making the waist so pliant that all of our movements appear boneless. To appear boneless means that there are only sinews. Sinews have the capacity to be released. When this is accomplished, is there any reason not to be relaxed?

2. Sinking. When we are able to completely relax, this is sinking. When the sinews release, then the body which they hold together is able to sink down.

Fundamentally, relaxation and sinking are the same thing. When one sinks, one will not float; floating is an error. If the body is able to sink, this is already very good, but we need to also sink the ch'i. Sinking the ch'i concentrates the spirit, which is enormously helpful.

3. Distinguishing Full and Empty. This is what the Tai-chi ch'uan classics mean by, "The body in its entirety has a full and empty aspect." The right hand is connected in one line of energy with the left foot, and likewise for the left hand and right foot. If the right hand and left foot are full then the right foot and left hand are empty, and vice versa. This is what is meant by clearly distinguishing full and empty. To summarize, the weight of the body should rest on just one foot. If the weight is divided between two feet, this is double-weightedness. When turning one must take care to keep the *wei-lu* point and the spine in alignment, in order to avoid losing central equilibrium. This is of critical importance.

4. The Light and Sensitive Energy at the Top of the Head. This means simply that the energy at the top of the head should be light and sensitive, or the idea of "holding the head as if suspended from above."

Holding the head as if suspended from above may be compared to tying one's braided hair to a rafter. The body is then suspended in mid-air not touching the ground. At this moment it. is possible to rotate the entire body. If the head is independently lifted or lowered, or moved to the left or right, this will not be possible. Light and sensitive energy at the top of the head is simply the idea of suspending the head from above. This is all there is to it. When practicing the form, one should cause the *yu-chen* point at the base of the skull to stand out, then the spirit (*shen*) and *ch'i* will effortlessly meet at the top of the head.

5. The Millstone Turns But the Mind Does Not Turn. The turning of the millstone is a metaphor for the turning of the waist. The mind not turning is the central equilibrium resulting from the sinking of *ch'i* to the *tan-t'ien*.

"The millstone turns but the mind does not turn" is an oral teaching within a family transmission. It is similar to two expressions in the T'ai-chi ch'uan classics which compare the waist to an axle or a banner. This is especially noteworthy. After learning this concept, my art made rapid progress.

6. Grasp Sparrow's Tail Is Like Using a Saw. That is, the Roll-back, Ward-off, Press and Push of push-hands move back and forth like the

action of a two-man saw. In using a two-man saw, each must use an equal amount of strength in order for the back and forth movement to be relaxed and without resistance. If there is the slightest change on either side, the saw will become stuck at that point. If my partner causes the saw to bind, then even using strength will not draw it back, and only pushing it will free it and reestablish the balance of force. This principle has two implications for Tai-chi ch'uan. The first is to give up oneself and follow others. By following our opponent's position we can achieve the marvelous effect of transforming energy or yielding energy. The second is that at the opponent's slightest movement, one is able to anticipate it and make the first move. That is, when the opponent seeks to throw us with a pushing force, I anticipate this by first using a pulling force. If the opponent uses a pulling force, I anticipate this by first using a pushing force.

The metaphor of the two-man saw is really an extremely profound principle. This is a true oral teaching of a family transmission and one which brought me to a kind of sudden enlightenment. Being adept at anticipating an opponent's slightest movement means that I am always in control and my opponent is always at a disadvantage. The rest goes without saying.

7. I Am Not a Meathook; Why Are You Hanging on Me? T'ai-chi ch'uan emphasizes relaxation and sensitivity and abhors stiffness and tension. If you hang your meat on meathooks, this is dead meat. How can we even discuss sensitive *ch'i*? My teacher detested and forbade this, and so scolded his students by saying that he was not a "meathook." This is an oral teaching in the Yang family transmission. The concept is very profound and should be conscientiously practiced.

8. When Pushed One Does Not Topple, Like the Punching Bag Doll. The whole body is light and sensitive; the root is in the feet. If one has not mastered relaxation and sinking, this is not easily accomplished.

The punching bag doll's center of gravity is at the bottom. This is what the Tai-chi ch'uan classics describe as, "When all the weight is sunk on one side there is freedom of movement; double-weightedness causes in-flexibility." If both feet use strength at the same time, there is no doubt that one will be toppled with the first push. If there is the least stiffness or inflexibility, one will likewise be toppled with the first push. In short, the energy of the whole body, one hundred per cent of it, should be sunk on the sole of one foot. The rest of the body should be calm and lighter than a swan's down.

9. The Ability To Issue Energy. Energy and force are not the same. Energy comes from the sinews and force from the bones. Therefore, energy is a property of the soft, the alive, the flexible. Force, then, is a

property of the hard, the dead and the inflexible. What do we mean by issuing energy? It is like shooting an arrow.

Shooting an arrow relies on the elasticity of the bow and string. The power of the bow and string derives from their softness, aliveness and elasticity. The difference between energy and force, the ability to issue or not issue, is readily apparent. However, this only explains the nature of issuing energy and does not fully detail its function. Allow me to add a few words on the method of issuing energy as often explained by Master Yang. He said that one must always seize the moment and gain the advantage. He also said that from the feet to the legs to the waist should be one unified flow of ch'i. He told us that his father, Yang Chien-hou, liked to recite these two rules. However, seizing the moment and gaining the advantage are difficult ideas to comprehend. I feel that the operation of the two-man saw contains the concept of seizing the moment and gaining the advantage. Before my opponent tries to advance or retreat, I already anticipate it. This is seizing the moment. When my opponent has already advanced or retreated, but falls under my control, this is gaining the advantage. From this example we can begin to understand that the ability to unify the feet, legs and waist into one flow of ch'i not only concentrates the power and gives us stamina, but prevents the body from being disunited and allows the will to be focused. The above discussion covers the marvelous effectiveness of issuing energy. Students should study this concept faithfully.

10. In Moving, Our Posture Should Be Balanced, Upright, Uniform, and Even. These four words-balanced, upright, uniform, and even-are very familiar, but very difficult to realize. Only when balanced and upright can one be comfortable and control all directions. Only when uniform and even can our movement be connected and no gaps appear. This is what the Tai-chi classics call, "stand erect and balanced," and "energy is moved like reeling silk." If one does not begin working from these four words, it is not a true art.

11. One Must Execute Techniques Correctly. The "Song of Push-Hands" says, "In Ward-off, Roll-back, Press and Push, one must execute the correct technique." If one's knowledge is not correct, everything will become false. Let me tell you now that if in warding off, one touches the opponent's body, or if in rolling back, one allows one's own body to be touched, these are both errors. When warding off, do not touch the opponent's body; when rolling back, do not allow your own body to be touched. This is the correct technique. During Push and Press, one must reserve energy in order not to lose central equilibrium. This is correct.

I had read the words, "One must execute the correct technique," over and over in the "Classic of Tai-chi ch'uan" without really understanding them. Only after hearing this over and over from Master Yang did I grasp the proper measure and method. Without oral instruction, it is difficult to understand. There are many such examples. This is an authentic secret teaching of a family transmission. Students should begin with this to experience it for themselves, then they can grasp the proper measure and not lose central equilibrium. This is supremely important.

12. Repelling a Thousand Pounds with Four Ounces. No one believes that four ounces can repel a thousand pounds. What is meant by "four ounces can repel a thousand pounds" is that only four ounces of energy need be used to pull a thousand pounds, and then the push is applied. Pulling and repelling are two different things. It is not really that one uses only four ounces to repel a thousand pounds.

By separately explaining the words, "pull" and "repel," we can appreciate their marvelous effectiveness. The method of pulling is like putting a rope through the nose of a thousand pound bull. With a four ounce rope we can pull a thousand pound bull to the left or right as we wish. The bull is unable to escape. But the pull must be applied precisely to the nose. Pulling the horn or the leg will not work. Thus if we pull according to the correct method and at the correct point, then a bull can be pulled with only a four ounce rope. Can a thousand pound statue of a horse be pulled with a rotten rope? No! This is because of differences in the behavior of the animate and the inanimate. Human beings possess intelligence. If one attempts to attack with a thousand pounds of strength, and approaches from a certain direction, say head-on for example, then with four ounces of energy I pull his hand, and following his line of force, deflect it away. This is what we mean by pulling. After being pulled, our opponent's strength is neutralized, and at that moment I issue energy to repel him. This opponent will invariably be thrown for a great distance. The energy used to pull the opponent need only be four ounces, but the energy used to push must be adjusted to circumstances. The energy used to pull an opponent must not be too heavy, for if it is, the opponent will realize our intentions and find means of escape. Sometimes one can borrow the pulling energy, change the direction, and employ it for an attack. In other cases, the opponent realizes he is being pulled, reserves his force, and does not advance. In reserving his force, he has already put himself in a position of retreat. I can then follow his retreat, release my pulling energy, and turn to attack. The opponent is invariably toppled by our hand. This is a counter-attack.

All of the above was transmitted to me, Cheng Man-ch'ing, orally by Yang Ch'eng-fu. I do not dare keep this secret, but wish to propagate it more broadly. I sincerely hope that kindred spirits will forge ahead together.

SONGS OF THE EIGHT WAYS
(from Yang Family Manuscripts—Collected by Li Ying-ang,
attributed to Tan Meng-hsien)

THE SONG OF WARD-OFF
How can we explain the energy of Ward-Off?
It is like water which supports a moving boat
First make the ch'i in the tan-t'ien substantial,
Then hold the head as if suspended from above.
The whole body has the power of a spring.
Opening and closing should be clearly defined.
Even if the opponent uses a thousand pounds of force,
We will float lightly and without difficulty.

THE SONG OF ROLL-BACK
How can we explain the energy of Roll-back?
We draw the opponent towards us by allowing him to advance,
While we follow his incoming force.
Continuing to draw him in until he overextends,
We remain light and comfortable, without losing our vertical posture.
When his force is spent he will naturally be empty,
While we maintain our center of gravity,
And can never be bested by the opponent.

THE SONG OF PRESS
How can we explain the energy of Press?
Sometimes we use two sides
To directly receive a single intention.
Meeting and combining in one movement,
We indirectly receive the force of the reaction.
This is like a ball bouncing off a wall,
Or a coin dropped on a drum,
Which bounces up with a metallic sound.

THE SONG OF PUSH
How can we explain the energy of Push?
When applied, it's like water in motion
But within its softness there is great strength.
When the flow is swift, the force cannot be withstood.
Meeting high places the waves break over them,
And encountering low places they dive deep. T
he waves rise and fall,
And finding a hole they will surely surge in.

THE SONG OF PULL-DOWN
How can we explain the energy of Pull-down?
Like weighing something on a balance scale,
We give free play to the opponent's force whether great or small.
After weighing it we know its lightness or heaviness.
Turning on only four ounces,
 We can weigh a thousand pounds.
If we ask what is the principle behind this,
We discover it is the function of the lever.

SONG OF SPLIT
How can we explain the energy of Split?
Revolving like a flywheel,
If something is thrown against it,
It will be cast off at a great distance.
Whirlpools appear in swift flowing streams,
And the curling waves are like spirals.
If a falling leaf lands on their surface,
In no time it will sink from sight.

THE SONG OF ELBOW-STROKE
How can we explain the energy of Elbow-stroke?
Our method must be reckoned by the Five Elements.
Yin and yang are divided above and below,
And full and empty should be clearly distinguished.
The opponent cannot keep up with our continuous movement,
And our explosive pounding is even fiercer.
When the six energies have been thoroughly mastered,
Then the applications will be infinite.

THE SONG OF THE SHOULDER STROKE
How can we explain the energy of the Shoulder-stroke?
The method is divided between shoulder and back.
The posture "Diagonal Flying" uses the shoulder,
But between the shoulders there is also the back.
When suddenly an opportunity presents itself,
Then it crashes like a pounding pestle.
Yet we must be careful to maintain our center of gravity,
For losing it we will surely fail.

SONGS OF THE FIVE STEPS

SONG OF ADVANCE
When it is time to advance, advance without hesitation.
If you meet no obstacle, continue to advance.

Failing to advance when the time is right is a lost opportunity.
Seizing the opportunity to advance, you will surely be the victor.

SONG OF RETREAT

If our steps follow the changes of our body, then our technique will
   be perfect.
We must avoid fullness and emphasize emptiness so that our opponent
   lands on nothing.
To fail to retreat when retreat is called for is neither wise nor courageous.
A retreat is really an advance if we can turn it to a counter-attack.

SONG OF GAZE-LEFT

To the left, to the right, *yin* and *yang* change according to the situation.
We evade to the left and strike from the right with strong sure steps.
The hands and feet work together and likewise knees, elbows and waist.
Our opponent cannot fathom our movements and has no defense
   against us.

SONG OF LOOK-RIGHT

Feigning to the left, we attack to the right with perfect steps.
Striking left and attacking right, we follow the opportunities.
We avoid the frontal and advance from the side, seizing changing
   conditions.
Left and right, full and empty, our technique must be faultless.

SONG OF CENTRAL EQUILIBRIUM

We are centered, stable and still as a mountain.
Our *ch'i* sinks to the *tan-t'ien* and we are as if suspended from above.
Our spirit is concentrated within and our outward manner perfectly
   composed.
Receiving and issuing energy are both the work of an instant.

III. TRAVELERS: ANALYSIS AND INSPIRATION

INTRODUCTION

WHETHER AS FIGHTING ARTS, physical training, cultural pursuits, or mechanisms for personal development, the martial engage people intimately and profoundly on a number of levels. They deal with significant issues that are of universal concern—issues of control, fear, struggle, and identity. They are, in short, arts that contain within them the stuff of high drama and real significance.

This is perhaps why the martial arts have engaged the world's attention to the extent that they have. It is not simply that they are elegant physical systems, or effective means of unarmed self-defense. They can be that, certainly. But they are something more.

The answer to what that something more is, however, varies from person to person. And this variety stems, in part, from the complexity of these arts—fighting systems, cultural vehicles, spritual disciplines (sometimes all at once). So there are a variety of perspectives that can be taken when coming to grips with the martial arts—ways to understand the Ways, so to speak. The selections here provide some differing interpretations. There are scholarly reflections on the place of these arts in Asian and world culture, explorations of martial arts philosophies, and discussions of why this particular aspect of the East holds a fascination for the West. There are personal accounts of training and what this pursuit has meant for the individual, and, due to the inherent drama of the arts, there are also some selections that discuss or present fiction related to the martial arts.

1. The Martial and Other Japanese Arts

G. Cameron Hurst is a well-respected expert in Japanese history who has trained in various martial arts forms. In this selection, he places martial arts study within the broader context of trainng in traditional Japanese arts, demonstrating how socio-cultural elements have shaped structure and process within the bugei *(martial arts) and identifying characteristics they share with all* geido *(artistic ways).*

From *Armed Martial Arts of Japan* by G. Cameron Hurst

Japan's premodern martial arts exhibited certain characteristics in common with other forms of cultural expression, as we have seen. They shared organizational and ritual aspects designed to foster community and continuity; they shared similar means of transmitting teachings from generation to generation; and they shared basically similar philosophical concepts and methods of instruction. Here I would like to expand on these characteristics of the martial and other arts.

Organizational and Ritual Aspects of Ryuha

Ryuha were corporate groups controlling a particular asset. In the case of the martial and other arts, the asset was mastery of specialized cultural forms. Ideally, ryuha were based upon the long-standing principle that social relationships are bound by fictive kinship rules. Relationships between the ryuha head and his students tended to follow authority-intensive patron-client relationships. Heads of ryuha often assumed parentlike authority in the lives of their student-disciples, serving not only as teacher and role model but also as mentor, advisor, or even marriage go-between.

Some martial arts ryuha developed fully the iemoto pattern described in Chapter 4, in which successive generations of family members controlled the ryu. Examples include the Yoshida family of the various Heki-ryu archery schools and the Yagyu family of the Yagyu shinkage-ryu of swordsmanship, whose heads enjoyed tremendous prestige as official fencing instructors to the Tokugawa house. But comparatively few martial arts schools developed along these lines. Indeed, rather than use the term *iemoto,* the martial arts ryuha instructors themselves more commonly used the term *shihan.* Though meaning "teacher," it bears the sense of "exemplar" or "model" and is thus often rendered in English as "master." Instead of following the iemoto pattern, the schools more commonly split into subgroups, each operating independently and with little or no interference from the head's former master. Now, for example, there are, at the most conservative estimate, well over seven hundred schools of swordsmanship alone. The phenomenon of an enormous iemoto organization, as with the Urasenke tea ceremony school, whose iemoto today controls the activities of well over a million and a half students through a far-flung network of intermediate licensed instructors, was uncommon in the martial arts world.

The reason for the difference lies in the nature of the instructional system and the transmission of the corpus of school teachings. In martial arts schools transmission tended to be total. An individual who had mastered all the secrets of the school was fully certified to instruct his own students. Most often, such an individual opened a dojo and created his own school, whose style was slightly different from, though derivative of, his teacher's. The original founder rarely retained control over his students after they mastered the techniques. The case of the swordsman Kamiizumi Ise no kami, founder of the Kage-ryu, is a good example.

Kamiizumi attracted numerous outstanding students, many of whom received from him full certification of mastery and went on to teach their own students—over whom Kamiizumi exercised no control. Kamiizumi not only taught his students the entire corpus of his techniques but also granted them the authority to certify others. This process continued over the generations. Although there is a record of the transmission of the tradition beginning with Kamiizumi, each generation of fencers operated independently of one another, even to the point of starting their own ryuha with differing names.

Martial arts schools typically exhibited this pattern of discontinuity in headship apparently because of the closed nature of feudal society. The military government jealously discouraged too much association between warriors of various domains. It would have been virtually impossible for a swordsman from a Kyushu domain to learn swordsmanship at a Yagyu family dojo in Edo and then return to his domain and remain under the authority of the Yagyu iemoto. An extensive fencing ryuha that organized many warriors from different domains along strict iemoto lines was unthinkable for most of the Tokugawa period, although toward the end of the period it was much more common for bushi from different domains to train together in a common dojo. Training together led to precisely what the bakufu feared: interdomain plotting against the shogunate. Iemoto organizations were much more common in domain fencing schools, where the clientele was limited to samurai of one domain.

Similarly, the bakufu never approved a policy of testing its fencers—or other martial artists—in nationwide competition. If the superiority of one ryu had been demonstrated, perhaps the tendency for schools to divide would have been reversed, creating one huge iemoto organization for swordsmanship. The Yagyu iemoto served the shogunal house as fencing instructor but was never tested in any way, so he could hardly have been considered the best swordsman in Japan despite his exalted position. Even though swordsmanship developed into the highly competitive sport of fencing, competition in fencing never approached the popularity of the toshiya competition, whose victor was decreed the best archer in Japan. No other martial art developed like sumo, which apparently had a number of ryuha at the beginning of the seventeenth century but which later consolidated. Wrestlers from every domain were invited to contest for the title of best in the land in the biannual Edo sumo matches. This national competition ultimately eliminated the multiplicity of sumo ryuha, bringing the whole endeavor under the iemoto organization of the Yoshida Oikaze family.

Martial arts schools failed to develop the *natori*, or subordinate instructor, system still characteristic of flower arrangement, the tea ceremony, and other large iemoto groups. High-ranking students of the iemoto, as they attain a certain mastery, are allowed to teach beginners just as though they were the iemoto. Often these natori are given a name that includes one character from the iemoto's name and are incorporated into the extended iemoto family. They serve as the connecting link between the lowest students and the master. As the system grows, there can be three, four, five, or even six layers of natori between the iemoto and his lowest students. But a natori system was rarely established in the martial arts, primarily owing to the feudal fragmentation of samurai society. As corporate groups, however, martial arts schools shared with other ryuha the same concerns with organization and continuity. By Tokugawa times there was normally a formal training hall that served as the focus of the group's activity. In all forms of practice, not simply the martial arts, these dojo took on a semisacred character. The term *dojo* originally meant a place where religious instruction was conducted; only later was its use extended to other forms of training. A dojo usually housed a *kamidana,* an altar dedicated to a Shinto deity, or a *butsudan* (Buddhist altar). A portrait of the acknowledged founder or some other symbol dedicated to his honor was usually on display. Ceremonies to award certification of mastery of the ryu secrets, commonly involving the exchange of cups of sake, were solemnly performed before the portrait. These rituals served to enhance the group's corporate consciousness.

Because establishing authority was crucial to the reputation of a ryuha, each school invoked some form of authority from the past. One cultural organization might assert that a former emperor had issued an edict to its founder, granting him a monopoly over a certain activity. Tea ceremony schools tended to claim connection with Sen no Rikyu when he became venerated as the saint of tea. Alternatively, ryuha claimed divine transmission of their secret teachings to the founder by some deity. This was especially common among martial arts schools, many of which consequently became intimately linked with a particular deity and with a particular shrine or temple, the deity functioning essentially as a patron saint. Authority might also be enhanced by alleging transmission of the techniques from a famous historical person, like Minamoto Yoshitsune, or from a shadowy mountain monk or miracle-dispensing goblin. The transmission of authority from a revered person or deity was recounted solemnly in ryuha texts, which were transmitted to each succeeding ryuha head.

The head himself required personal authority to permanently differentiate his status from that of his pupils, especially in such physical activities as the martial arts, where the pupil might surpass the master in actual ability. In some ryuha, there might be a ceremonial costume that could be worn only by the iemoto. In the Kanze school of Noh, the drama *Yuminagashi* was originally taught to but one person each generation, the iemoto; and when he performed that drama, he wore a special costume. Likewise, when performing *Dojoji*, the iemoto wore a slightly different costume from his disciples'. Symbols of iemoto authority might also be secret or exclusive items— a special mask, fan, tea bowl, musical instrument, or sword. Thus the Kikutei family traditionally inherited the famous *biwa* (lute) called Iwao. The most crucial symbol of iemoto authority, especially in martial arts schools, was the possession of scrolls or other texts explaining the ryuha secrets.

Martial arts schools in Tokugawa times, then, consisted of a head instructor who was either a member of a family of professional teachers of the art or a legitimate successor within an authoritative line of masters, and his students. Meeting in a semisacred dojo, which was protected by the god of the training hall and contained a solemn portrait of the founder, the members of the ryuha were drawn together to learn the mastery of their art. The entire society was stratified, from the beginning student to the most advanced senior pupil, who was the master's primary assistant. As with other ryuha, martial arts students typically paid a set fee to receive instruction. It was paid on a monthly basis and varied over time and among schools.

But the students were far more than dues payers. Many boarded at the school; by the the end of the Tokugawa period there were sometimes even dormitory facilities to house students who came from other domains to study with the teacher. The students became extremely familiar with the instructor and his family, often establishing near familial ties or mentor-advisee relationships. Beyond the regular payment of instructional fees, students offered special ceremonial gifts (e.g., salted fish or sake) at specific times of the year as a means of displaying respect for their teacher.

The student-teacher relationship was considered important from the moment the student entered the master's charge. Usually accompanied by his parents and in formal dress, the would-be fencing or other martial arts student (the age of entry ranged from nine or ten to the mid-teens) visited the school for a formal meeting with the master, presented an appropriate registration present *(sokushu)*—usually a fan or a writing brush—and signed a pledge to study hard under the master's tutelage and keep the teachings secret.

The master, for his part, besides acting as teacher, spiritual mentor, and parent, provided a myriad of specific services for his students, from helping to arrange marriage partners to, most importantly, finding them employment as instructors. Students stayed with the master through a number of graded ranks, similar to the system of belts widely employed in the martial arts today. The ritual nature of the system and the camaraderie, often shrouded in secrecy, made it difficult for students to join and leave at will, as is often done today, when teaching is more often a business than a profession.

TRANSMISSION OF TEACHINGS

Practitioners of various cultural forms, including the martial arts, tended to remain with one teacher and stick with the endeavor. The art was not considered a pastime or a veneer to round off one's character, as it is more likely to be considered today, whether in Japan or abroad. It was considered a serious business; the art was respected, the iemoto was venerated, and the effects that practice had upon one's character were thought to be of considerable benefit—especially in the martial arts, which never completely lost the justification that warriors needed to maintain combat readiness.

Given the highly stratified nature of Tokugawa society, martial arts schools functioned as arenas of social mobility. At the end of the period, most expert fencers were drawn from the ranks of lower samurai, who were blocked from bureaucratic advancement within their domains by the severe restrictions of warrior society, or from among unattached, wandering samurai (ronin) without prospects or even from among commoners, a number of whom rose to head their own dojo and even to serve as instructors to daimyo. Many martial artists achieved a degree of status based upon actual achievement—the demonstration of physical superiority over others—denied them in other social arenas.

As in other cultural forms, fencers, archers, and other martial artists often took special ceremonial names. Martial arts genealogies bristle with names such as Sekishusai, Ryounsai, Ikosai, Ren'yasai—so-called *saimei* that were apparently adopted after taking Buddhist vows. Such names afforded recognition within the special world of the ryuha. But even without special names, demonstrated expertise conferred prestige and buttressed self-esteem. One Tokugawa vassal of low rank who never achieved any success as a retainer, Katsu Kokichi, took extraordinary pride in his achievements in the world of fencing, where he had few peers. It was one arena in which he could prove himself. Ryuha thus served important social functions. But while meeting the physical and emotional needs of followers, they were primarily concerned with the transmission of what were regarded as valuable cultural forms. The responsibilities of both instructor and pupil were informed by a tradition of loyalty to the founder, and group consciousness restrained tendencies toward individualistic indulgence. A person did not easily join or leave a martial arts school. In fact, given the inherent danger of the skill that instructors were going to impart to a would-be pupil, entry into the practice of swordsmanship in particular necessitated careful scrutiny of the background of the applicant and normally required the recommendation of a respected third party. In common with other cultural ryuha, moreover, martial arts schools extracted pledges from their students, often upon several occasions, as the process of transmission progressed.

The secrets of any ryuha could be transmitted from master to disciple in a number of ways. In medieval times, when fighting skills were still practical, teaching and transmission was primitive, immediate, often ad hoc. Not only were there no texts, but it was generally thought, by way of analogy with many forms of Buddhist expression, from Tendai to Zen, that transmission occurred largely by example, not through verbalization. In Japanese the term is *ishin denshin*, "nonverbal understanding," understanding that goes from mind (*shin*) to mind. This idea dates back to the beginning of Buddhist tradition and the esoteric transmission from the historical Buddha to his disciple Kashyapa in the Sermon on Vulture Peak. In religious texts this idea is often referred to with the terms *furyu monji* ("no reliance on the written word") and *kyoge betsuden* ("transmission outside the sutras"). The head of any martial arts or other school instructed his disciples in a manner analogous, then, to that of many religious teachers.

The earliest form of transmission of martial skills was called *kuden* (verbal transmission); the same term was used for the transmission of much esoteric knowledge in early Japan. But by late medieval times, instructions were often written in brief form, in texts called *kudensho* (writings of verbal transmission).

Indeed, the texts were often extremely brief, with lists of the names of techniques followed by the phrase *kuden*. The pre-Tokugawa martial arts texts extant in a few schools are rudimentary, with a focus on recounting legends of the founder of the school and with little instruction in or explication of techniques. There is often only a listing of several techniques, usually identified by hyperbolic names, like "flying dragon," or by the names of animals, like "monkey" and "rat"—terms that would not be readily understood by anyone without instruction from the teacher.

By the Tokugawa period, it was customary in all ryuha, including those of the martial arts, to write down the teachings of the school and transmit them to successful students formally, usually in scrolls but in some cases in bound volumes. The authority of the ryuha head lay in the absolute supremacy of his technique, at least in theory. He was the creative genius behind the techniques who in effect created his own private canon that became sacred only with transmission by successive masters to their disciples. The techniques were written down as *hiden, gokuden, gokui*—"secret transmissions"—or *tora no maki* ("tiger scrolls") and were valued by the students as the embodiment of the wisdom of the master. As a rule, transmission involved a mysterious or sublime form, but this was more difficult in performing arts, where an authence was involved.

Although the ability of a disciple might outshine that of his iemoto, the iemoto enjoyed hereditary symbolic authority to control the ryu. The virtually total authority of the master helps to explain the tendency for martial arts ryuha to proliferate. That is, if a disciple became more skillful than the instructor or differed over matters of instruction, he found it necessary to seek another teacher or start his own school. The tendency is still common in the contemporary martial arts world, where schools continue to proliferate essentially by segmentation.

Initiation into the secret techniques of the ryuha usually meant the award of a certificate of mastery, a license that carried with it the express right of the initiate to reproduce that form, whether flower arranging or swordsmanship. The licentiate system, as we have seen, accelerated the proliferation of martial arts schools, since the initiated were essentially taught everything and allowed to function on their own, rather than employed as secondary instructors, as with many other cultural arts. In schools with the iemoto system, even after the certification of mastery, the new licensee may have been able to reproduce the forms—perform certain Noh dances, play certain pieces on the biwa, or the like—but the iemoto maintained final authority and control over the kata themselves, the importance of which will become clearer in a moment. But because there was little room for a fencing school head, for example, to control the kata in each of numerous feudal domains, transmission tended to be complete. Those receiving certification became individual martial artists, capable of becoming school heads in their own right.

Transmission of teachings involved several levels, or grades. In the martial arts it was common to have eight levels, but there were many schools with five, and some were even reduced to three. Consequently, the typical iemoto organization was a hierarchical structure with the iemoto or shihan at the peak. He transmitted the teachings to the disciples in graded segments, awarding certification for mastery of a certain level (*mokuroku, chu mokuroku*) at an appropriate ceremony. The highest level was normally referred to as *kaiden* (complete transmission) or sometimes as *menkyo kaiden* (certified complete transmission); in most martial arts schools, receipt of certification qualified the recipient to become an independent teacher.

Although this method of training and certification was generally accepted as reasonable, it was not without its critics. In 1837, Matsudaira Awaji no kami Takamoto wrote a blistering attack on martial arts instructors. He claimed that the primary reason that instructors created elaborate documents of transmission, established various levels of mastery, and then made mastery difficult for students to achieve was simply to increase their fees. He charged that teachers not only refused promotion to those who had trained hard but also awarded certification to favored students without regard to actual ability. As a consequence, skilled students might lose confidence in their instructor and leave the school.

There were several forms of transmission in traditional cultural organizations. *Ichidai soden* (one-generation transmission) meant that the master's certification lasted only for the lifetime of the recipient; upon his death, the scrolls containing the ryu secrets passed back to the house of the iemoto. This form of transmission was quite common in many Tokugawa-period schools, including some schools of the martial arts. *Ichinichi soden* (one-day transmission) was a rare form used for certain special performances (like the *Azuma asobi* at the Kamo Shrine in Kyoto). The iemoto permitted others to be trained to perform a special piece on that day only, after which the right passed back to the iemoto.

Deiri soden (transmission through access) was granted to some individuals who were responsible for handling ryuha articles but not necessarily involved in learning the techniques themselves. They became members of the group because they "came and went" *(deiri)* in and out of the presence of the iemoto. In the Tokugawa period there were also instances of *kaeri soden* (returning transmission), usually because of a sudden death in the iemoto house. A proper successor had not been named, so the transmission was made temporarily to a high-ranking student. Later the house secrets were to be "returned" to the main iemoto house. *Ichoku soden* (edict transmission) referred to those forms of cultural authority that required the edict of an emperor, retired emperor, or shogun upon transfer.

Isshi soden (one-child transmission) is, as the name implies, a form in which but one child of the iemoto inherited the family's professional secrets. In Tokugawa times, this was most often the eldest son. There remain even today organizations in which the transmission has never deviated from the eldest son to eldest son pattern.

All these forms of transmission occurred in martial arts schools. There are numerous examples of isshi soden in schools where one family functioned as iemoto. In pre-Tokugawa times somewhat similar forms existed to limit the spread of the teachings, such as *ikkoku ichinin soden* (transmission to one person per province). Ichidai soden (one-generation transmission) was not unknown either. Whatever the form of transmission, however, transmission was by no means automatic or perfunctory. Bitter family quarrels over the transmission of the secrets were frequent. Though perhaps not of the magnitude of the family headship disputes that drove medieval warrior houses into open warfare, they were significant nonetheless. Difficulties with kaeri soden (returning transmission) were also common, such as the situation among the Yoshida family branches that controlled Heki-ryu archery.

Concern for the secrecy of the teachings transmitted was paramount in all arts organizations, but perhaps of greatest worry to those of the martial arts because the techniques in which students were being instructed were potentially lethal. Instruction to the wrong kind of person was a problem, so great care was exercised by most school heads to accept only pupils of outstanding character. In pre-Tokugawa times, when teaching was barely developed and not yet a profession upon which livelihood depended, instructors were more strict. But even in Tokugawa Japan, students were not automatically accepted without some check on their character. A bad student could clearly, by his behavior, embarrass the head of a tea ceremony or flower arranging school. But a student who misused the sword or spear to injure or kill someone was a far greater threat to both society and the reputation of the instructor.

Yet it was common for all arts instructors to extract pledges and oaths from students, swearing that they would not disclose the secrets of the school nor teach them to others without the explicit authorization of the master.

Heads of martial arts schools, especially swordsmanship, demanded pledges from students at virtually each level of certification. Martial arts pledges were similar in form to those of other schools. Called *kishomon*, they were normally sealed with the blood of the one making the pledge and written on special paper. Making such a pledge was an act of an entirely different magnitude from signing an application to join a karate club and agreeing to pay a monthly fee, as is often required today.

The paper on which the pledges were commonly written was *Kumano goo* paper, which came from Kumano Shrine, three venerable Shinto institutions in what is today Wakayama Prefecture. *Goo*, "Ox King" (or "Ox Jewel"), is a term of uncertain origin. It apparently derived from a secret rite in esoteric Buddhism and may have been an honorific for the historical Buddha. Written with other characters, the word also means "cow bezoar," a miraculous medicine supposedly produced from the liver and gall bladder of the cow and believed by the Chinese to have great efficacy.

Kumano goo paper talismans became popular in the early medieval period as faith in the deities of the Kumano shrines spared and as the shrines became the object of frequent pilgrimages. Yamabushi (mountain monks) and miko (female shrine shamans) sold the talismans. The talisman was a special sheet of paper on which were inscribed the five Chinese characters *Kumano gohoin* ("honored treasure seal of Kumano"). The inscription was written in a strange calligraphy—the characters were composed with small black crows, the crow being considered the messenger of the Kumano deities—and the paper was pressed with the vermilion seal of the shrines. Pasted to a doorframe, it drove away evil spirits; planted in a field, it scared away birds and the wind; and fixed to a pole in an irrigated field, it brought a bountiful harvest. As demand increased, Kumano goo paper became the major type of paper used by Japan's warrior class in writing a wide variety of pledges. By the Tokugawa period, it had become the standard paper on which oaths were inscribed to protect the secrets of a ryuha.

Written by the aspiring disciple, the oath normally contained an introduction and a number of formulaic phrases stating that the student would not show anyone nor tell anyone, parent or child, the secrets into which he was being initiated; nor would he show the scroll containing the secrets to anyone. All of this would normally appear on a separate sheet. On the next sheet, he pledged to keep his word, invoking the names of a variety of native and foreign gods. Some invocations were rather brief, but it was more common to be exhaustive, leaving no major deity unmentioned. Here is the pledge of an archery student.

1. I deem it a great honor to have imparted to me the secrets of the XX-ryu.

2. I shall concentrate on my training day and night without remission. If, unfortunately, I have no time to practice, I shall give up the bow.

3. I understand that as I progress in my training you will gradually unfold to me the secrets of your art, and that you will regulate my progress not according to the length of my discipleship but according to the skill and accomplishment I display. Realizing this, I shall never harbor any resentments against my teacher.

4. The verbal instructions and the written tradition which you give me I will never reveal even to my parents or brothers, much less to anyone else. If it should happen that after receiving the written tradition my house should die out, it shall be immediately burned or returned. It goes without saying that I shall not take pupils of my own until you give me a licence to do so.

5. I shall never indulge in criticism of other schools of archery. Should I ever offend against anyone of these rules, may I receive the divine punishment of Hachiman-bosatsu, Bunten, Taishaku, the Four Tenno, all the Great and Lesser Gods of Japan, the Two Gongen of Izu and Hakone, Temman Tenjin and the Ancestors of my Clan.

In sign whereof I lay my oath and set my seal.

A similar document from the Inatomi-ryu of gunnery adds to the above list the deities of Kamigamo, Shimogamo, Hirano, Imari, and Matsuo Shrines, the Mountain God of Hiyoshi Shrine, Goze Tenno of Gion Shrine, and the Gongen of Mounts Fuji, Hakusan, and Atago, among others, and the oath taker prays that they will visit leprosy upon him in this life and that Shaka and Amida will cause him to fall into Hell in the next life if he fails to keep his pledge. It was also common to include the Indian god Marishi (Marishi-ten, Marishisonten), a martial deity often depicted riding on the back of a boar while brandishing sword, bow and arrow, and spear in four hands.

Pledges were required no matter what the rank or social status of the student. Even the shogun was required to make such pledges to his swordsmanship instructor. Oaths from Shoguns Ieyasu to Ietsuna, written and duly offered to successive Yagyu-ryu heads, are preserved among the esoterica passed from one head to his successor.

PHILOSOPHY AND METHOD OF INSTRUCTION

The martial arts fall into the category of *geido,* "artistic ways," in Japan. There are literally hundreds of geido, but they can be classified into three basic types. Historically the first to appear were the aristocratic cultural forms created by the nobility in Heian times. They include playing a variety of Chinese and native stringed and wind instruments (biwa, *wakon, sho),* performing dances *(gagaku* and *sarugaku),* engaging in falconry, playing *kemari* (kickball), and composing poetry *(waka* and *renga).* Other aristocratic art forms developed later, in Muromachi times, among them Noh, flower arranging, the tea ceremony, garden design, and cooking. These are, in Nishiyama Matsunosuke's term, "polite accomplishments," enjoyed largely by the leisured upper class as recreation and entertainment. By Tokugawa times, however, a number of these enterprises had spread widely among the populace at large. The martial arts—archery, swordsmanship, use of the lance, equitation, gunnery, even ninjutsu—constitute a second type of artistic way. The third type includes forms of popular culture *(taishu geino),* ranging from mime, puppetry and juggling, to musical performances and dances, to comedy acts, recitations, and illustrated storytelling. The scope of artistic activities included in geido is thus extremely broad.

The martial arts share with other geido the characteristic of being a means to personally experience an art form. All of the geido involve, according to Nishiyama, actions that "create or re-create cultural values through the exercise of the whole body or a part thereof—dancing, performing, drawing, sniffing, tasting, speaking, playing, and so forth." While the actions do result in some form of cultural product, they are normally formless rather than objectified. That is, the resultant product is less important than the process of creating it. The value for the individual lies in the doing—the playing, performing, singing, shooting. In creation through the actions of the body, technique (waza) is primary. The practitioner must strive to develop the ability to perform requisite techniques to perfection. This concern for mastery of technique lies at the heart of every geido, from swordsmanship to the tea ceremony.

To master the techniques of an art, it was crucial to select a good teacher. Accordingly, instructors exhibited serious concern for their reputation. A swordsmanship instructor could gain a name, at least through the early Tokugawa period, by means of popular recognition of his successful duels or of battles in which he had distinguished himself Or as head of a well-known professional school, he could rely upon the weight of tradition. In later Tokugawa times, a teacher could win a reputation for defeating skilled fenders in extraschool matches *(taryu jiai).*

The instructor enjoyed almost absolute power over the student. His authority was supreme, his word unquestioned. But contemporary educational philosophy held that the instructor was of limited use; he was only an imperfect guide to personal mastery of the techniques involved. The master conveyed the techniques to the student, who through sheer repetition would ultimately, at least in theory, reach a perfect understanding on his own. Despite the production of numerous texts describing the various techniques (waza) and prescribed forms (kata), the tradition that true understanding could not be conveyed verbally or through instructional manuals, but had to be learned nonverbally, through experience (ishin denshin), never died.

Martial arts texts are replete with terms emphasizing that the realization of the meaning of the techniques is a nonintellectual process, that total bodily understanding can only be experienced. The texts include such terms as "to obtain with the body" *(taitoku)* and "to experience through the body" *(taikan)* and "to understand with the body" *(tainin)*. This idea is often expressed more colloquially by the phrase "to learn with the body" *(shintai de oboeru* or *karada de oboeru).*

The concept of body here requires some clarification to understand geido, especially the martial arts. Both Chinese characters in the compound *shintai* can read in Japanese as *karada,* "body." But the concept goes far beyond pure physicality, the existence of flesh and bones. The body is always meant to be regarded as that entity which houses the mind, or spirit. The Japanese sense is that while animals have a body of flesh, only human beings have a shintai. Training or education involving physical activity *(shintai katsudo)* makes no distinction between bodily training and mental undertanding, but instead assumes a unified mind-body approach. Not only martial arts texts but works on geido in general abound with phrases like *shinshin ittai* ("mind and body are one") and *shinshin ichinyo* ("mind and body are the same").

In martial arts ryuha as they developed in Tokugawa times, students were expected to endure extensive and exhaustive training, and after a certain period, one would naturally, of his own accord, come to master the techniques. Besides laying down the basic routines, the function of the instructor was to certify mastery of the required techniques. Ironically, the student was set on a course to learn techniques with minimal instruction, but mastery of the techniques had to be formally certified by the teacher. Similarly, in Zen Buddhism the practitioner does not really have a satori until the master acknowledges it.

In the Tokugawa period, when the necessity of engaging an enemy was little more than a theoretical problem for most warriors, the martial arts developed within the context of an intellectual inquisitiveness spurred largely by Neo-Confucian scholarship. In addition to discussing techniques, martial arts works, like works covering other forms of artistic expression, dealt with theory, mental constructs, and abstract principles like spirit and mind, borrowing heavily from the vocabulary of Buddhism, Confucianism, Daoism and Shinto. In swordsmanship, this tendency was especially marked; training and texts came to concentrate upon problems of the mind *(shin).* As Shimada Toranosuke, a well-known Jikishin kage-ryu fencer of the end of the Tokugawa period noted: "The sword is the mind. If the mind is not correct, then the sword will not be correct. If one wishes to study the sword, he should first study the mind."

By "mind," what martial artists were referring to was the mental attitude, the frame of mind, the psychological state necessary to face an opponent.

The ultimate mental disposition that one might hope to reach was called *mushin* (no mind), *munen* (no thought), or *honshin* (original mind). These were terms borrowed from Buddhism, especially from the Zen sect, and perhaps no work expresses this idea more clearly than *Fudochi shimmyoroku* by the Zen prelate Takuan. The title is usually translated in English as *The Marvelous Record of Immovable Wisdom*. In the work, written in the seventeenth century for his friend Yagyu Munenori of the Yagyu-ryu, Takuan discussed swordsmanship from a Zen point of view. The ideas are profound and have had an impact on the theory of martial arts ever since, even though Takuan was not himself a swordsman.

Ironically, Takuan seems not to have been all that influential in his day. Since then, his *Fudochi* text has been used by many, including the noted Zen scholar D. T. Suzuki and many Western writers on the martial arts, to emphasize the crucial role of Zen in swordsmanship. But Yagyu Munenori did not use Takuan's work for swordsmanship instruction until late in life. Even then he was apparently severely criticized for overemphasizing the mental aspects of swordsmanship.

In *Fudochi*, Takuan argues that you must never allow your mind to "stop" (focus upon just one thing) or you will be defeated by your enemy. He calls the nonstopping mind immovable wisdom: "Immovable means un-moving. Wisdom means the wisdom of intelligence. Although wisdom is called immovable, this does not signify any insentient thing, like wood or stone. It moves as the mind is wont to move: forward or back, to the left, to the right, in the ten directions and the eight points; and the mind that does not stop at all is called immovable wisdom." A mind that stops is a delusion, a *boshin* in Buddhist terminology. In swordsmanship, a mind that stops prevents the fighter from performing the correct action. Takuan likens the condition to the dilemma faced by the Thousand-Armed Kannon: "If the mind stops at the one holding a bow, the other nine hundred and ninety-nine will be useless." More specifically, for swordsmen,

> If one puts his mind in the actions of his opponent's body, his mind will be taken by the action of his opponent's body. If one puts his mind in his opponent's sword, his mind will be taken by that sword. If one puts his mind in thoughts of his opponent's intention to strike him, his mind will be taken by thoughts of his opponent's intention to strike him. If he puts his mind in his own sword, it will be taken by his own sword. If he puts his mind in his own intention of not being struck, his mind will be taken by his intention of not being struck. If he puts his mind in the other man's stance, his mind will be taken by the other man's stance. What this means is that there is no place to put the mind.

Takuan felt that the mind must be pure and flowing and not fix on one thought. He suggests that a fencer should not formulate a specific strategy: if he attacks me with a slashing attack from above, then I will counter by shifting my weight to the left and attacking his ribcage. The swordsman's mind must be unfettered. By stopping the mind nowhere, it is everywhere, and thus a natural and spontaneous reaction to the opponent is possible. This is what Takuan calls *mushin* or *honshin*. In other works, the same idea of a mind that flows through the body without fixating on anything is called *hoshin* (released mind) or *munen muso* (no concern, no thought) or *heijoshin* (normal mind). For swordsmen and other martial arts practitioners, the attainment of such a mental state was not an intellectual activity. Nor was it a religious activity. Few martial arts texts espouse Zen meditation, and few practitioners were followers of Zen. I have argued throughout this book that just because martial arts texts contain Zen Buddhist and other religious references, one should not assume that practitioners were religiously motivated. Similarly, while acknowledging the influence of Zen on martial and other arts, Minamoto Ryuen concludes that the mind-body unity articulated in Zen and the arts is different. Martial arts texts advocate not the simple mind-body unity of the Zen Buddhists—who after all are not concerned with physical activity but with motionless meditation—but a mind-body unity in which the two are in reverse correspondence with one another. That is, if the body is at rest, the mind should be active; if the body is active, the mind should be motionless. If the mind is in a defensive mode, the body is in attack posture, and vice versa.

In a 1837 critique of ryuha, Matsudaira Takamoto of Toyama domain, in a section entitled "Martial Arts Texts Cannot Be Trusted," argued that these texts are no more than collections of Shinto, Buddhist, and Confucian aphorisms collected from ancient manuscripts. He was of the opinion that since they were by and large compiled by rural scholars and priests with little knowledge of martial arts, the borrowed phrases of ancient wisdom contained numerous errors. He was especially critical of the many texts compiled by Buddhists. Because Buddhist terminology had nothing to do with martial arts, he argued, such texts were filled with "falsehoods and absurdities."

In fact, during the Tokugawa period, when Buddhism was officially frowned upon and a distinctly Confucian mentality had replaced the medieval Buddhist consciousness, few warriors chose exclusive Zen practice. The way the student could attain the proper mental state was through the type of practice espoused by the martial and other arts. As we have seen, this practice was often called *shugyo*, the word having been derived from religious training. But a more commonly used term in all geido of medieval and early modern times was *keiko*. Though it can be broadly understood as meaning "to learn," the term is an ancient Chinese expression first used in Japan in the *Kojiki* in the four-character compound *keiko shokon*, literally, "to reflect upon past ways to shed light on the present." Thus the distinct meaning *of keiko* was to take the past as precedent, but in medieval Japan it came to be applied almost exclusively to learning apart from pure intellectual study, specifically in the study of geido. As used in texts dealing with poetry composition, flower arranging, and fencing, keiko took on the sense of learning that requires polishing through repetition of established forms, a positive, engaged learning as opposed to a passive acceptance of received written material.

The term also had a certain attitudinal, or spiritual, sense. Keiko was more than an intellectual understanding of a body of material; it was intimately linked to mental attitude (kokorogamae) and involved a concern for the way one ought to live. In both a Confucian and a Buddhist sense, keiko meant "to learn the proper way of living (do) through mastery of one's art form." The English term "training" may be the most appropriate translation of keiko, which even today is commonly used to describe the process that a person goes through when studying the tea ceremony, flower arranging, poetry composition, dance, judo, or any of the traditional arts. Entering into the study of an art is a somewhat different experience from entering primary school or a cram school (juku), although these arenas of learning share certain attitudes. In keiko the emphasis is heavily upon the aspects of learning that improve character and mental development. Mastery of the way of tea, for example, as a means of personal fulfillment and development.

Keiko focused upon the mastery of forms (kata), which taught the disciple technique (waza). Since all geido had a focus on forms, many scholars have defined the Japanese cultural tradition as the "culture of kata." Among the martial arts, archery developed a kata tradition quite early, but with most martial arts it was in the late medieval period that people began to teach individual battlefield skills as specific techniques. Then a number of military geniuses created kata, based on their long years of military experience, as fixed ways of practicing necessary combat skills.

It was in the teaching of these highly individualistic techniques that specific ryuha emerged. Kata became the rules, the basic methods, by which techniques were transmitted from master to student within the ryu. Kata were believed to quickly and completely impart techniques to the students. The method of instruction was for the student to repeat the kata, over and over, under the guidance of the master. Learning involved a rote imitation of the teacher's kata, with no resistance, no attempt to embellish, and commonly with no explanation of the individual moves. Constant polishing of the moves, inner reflection on the process down to the tiniest detail of stance or hand position, it was believed, would ultimately result in an understanding—again through the body, which includes the mind—not only of the teacher's technique but also of the requisite spirit.

Geido in Japan today preserve thousands of kata that were developed by the founders of ryuha, altered and improved over the centuries, and handed down through generations of masters and students as the most appropriate means to mastery. The students are subjected to the no-questions-asked repetition of fixed forms until the teacher deems progress sufficient to move on to the next stage. This method of instruction seems peculiarly antiquated and out of step with the freedom and individualism of modern educational ideas.

But ironically, total submission to authority is regarded as the best way to achieve individual creativity.

Kata mastery progresses through three stages. We find in many texts on geido reference to *shu, ha,* and *ri,* the developmental steps to mastery. *Shu* means "to preserve" and refers to the initial phase of study in martial and other arts. The novice simply "preserves" the tradition by constant repetition of kata, polishing both outward form and internal mental awareness until the technique become automatically replicable. But simple repetition could conceivably lead to (and in Tokugawa martial arts certainly did lead to) the ossification of the art, so the student must "break down" or "destroy" (ha) the kata that he has mastered, in order to move to the final stage of development, where he was "liberated" (ri) from the kata, and true creative individuality could express itself. The theory behind the mastery of secrets via kata memorization involved, then, a progression from total subservience to tradition to a level of individual creativity.

The number of people able to achieve mastery through a progression from shu through ha to ri was limited historically and is limited today. It was exceedingly difficult to reach mastery in many of the traditional, geido. For example, 1,384 people entered the Yabuuchi-ryu of the tea ceremony during the Tokugawa period, and only eleven reached the pinnacle kaiden rank.

The Japanese traditionally regarded keiko as being rigorous and, to a degree, still do today. Although many of the traditional arts were recreational and creative activities for leisure time (and are practiced as such today—the tea ceremony for brides, kendo for kids), there was and is an expectation that the student will give total devotion to the way of that art. Martial arts texts are full of terms like *shisshin* (devotion) and *doshin* (devotion to the way; literally "way-mind"). The idea is for the student to be exclusively and totally devoted to the mastery of the kata of the particular endeavor. In an almost religious sense, students should cut themselves off from the secular world and enter the world of their chosen art. They should find the time to concentrate on their art so that, sleeping or waking, every moment is devoted to mastery.

The great Muromachi Noh master Zeami said it for all geido in his discussion of the attitude required in mastering Noh: "One who would attain this Way must not engage in the non-Way." What he meant by "non-Way" was any other activity, any other form of learning or art form. A single-minded devotion to a particular way was widely advocated, then. Injunctions to concentrate wholeheartedly are especially common in martial arts texts. In Nakabayashi Shinji's words: "It is advocated in keiko that one ought to concentrate powerfully (but without stubbornness and contentiousness), obediently, and purely on the way. And one ought to focus single-mindedly on this way not just during the time one practices the techniques; keiko lies in achieving a unitary focus in all the aspects of one's daily life, so that in each and every activity, the way is one. A great number of martial arts texts express the idea that the way lies in the behavior and conduct of everyday life."

If someone is devoted to achieving total understanding of a single way, then paradoxically that understanding cuts across all ways. This is in accord with Miyamoto Musashi's claim that after years of devoting himself single-mindedly to martial arts, he came to be conversant with a variety of geido, all without the aid of a teacher.

2. ZEN AND SWORDSMANSHIP

D.T. Suzuki was instrumental in helping bring a sophisticated awareness of Zen to the West. His important work Zen and Japanese Culture *analyzes the ways in which Zen ideas and sensibilities have shaped and been shaped in turn by broader patterns in Japanese culture. In the selection below, it is obvious that the experience of martial artists such as Tesshu and Yagyu Munenori (referred to below by his formal titular name of Yagyu Tajima no kami) influenced Suzuki's analysis of the relationship between Zen and the martial arts. The power of Suzuki's analysis has played a significant role in reinforcing the Western stereotypical conviction that the Japanese martial arts have in large part been shaped by Zen when, in fact, their development has been the product of a complex seies of ideas.*

Zen and Swordsmanship BY D.T. SUZUKI

The sword is the soul of the samurai": therefore, when the samurai is the subject, the sword inevitably comes with him. The samurai who wishes to be faithful to his vocation will have first of all to ask himself the question: How shall I transcend birth and death so that I can be ready at any moment to give up my life if necessary for my Lord? This means exposing himself before the enemy's swordstroke or directing his own sword toward himself. The sword thus becomes most intimately connected with the life of the samurai, and it has become the symbol of loyalty and self-sacrifice. The reverence universally paid to it in various ways proves this.

The sword has thus a double office to perform: to destroy anything that opposes the will of its owner and to sacrifice all the impulses that arise from the instinct of self-preservation. The one relates itself to the spirit of patriotism or sometimes militarism, while the other has a religious connotation of loyalty and self-sacrifice. In the case of the former, very frequently the sword may mean destruction pure and simple, and then it is the symbol of force, sometimes devilish force. It must, therefore, be controlled and consecrated by the second function. Its conscientious owner is always mindful of this truth. For then destruction is turned against the evil spirit. The sword comes to be identified with the annihilation of things that lie in the way of peace, justice, progress, and humanity. It stands for all that is desirable for the spiritual welfare of the world at large. It is now the embodiment of life and not of death.

Zen speaks of the sword of life and the sword of death, and tl is the work of a great Zen master to know when and how to wield either of them. Manjusri carries a sword in his right hand and a sutra in his left. This may remind us of the prophet Mohammed, but the sacred sword of Manjusri is not to kill any sentient beings, but our own greed, anger, and folly. It is directed toward ourselves, for when this is done the outside world, which is the reflection of what is within us, becomes also free from greed, anger, and folly. Acala (Fudo Myoo) also carries a sword, and he will destroy all the enemies who oppose the practice of the Buddhist virtues. Manjusri is positive, Acala is negative. Acala's anger burns like a fire and will not be put down until it burns up the last camp of the enemy: he will then assume his original features as the Vairocana Buddha, whose servant and manifestation he is. The Vairocana holds no sword, he is the sword itself, sitting alone with all the worlds within himself. In the following *mondo*, "the one sword" signifies this sword:

Kusunoki Masashige (1294–1336) came to a Zen monastery at Hyogo when he was about to meet the overwhelming array of Ashikaga Takauji (1305-1358) at the Minatogawa, and asked the master, "When a man is at the parting of the ways between life and death, how should he behave?" Answered the master, "Cut off your dualism, and let the one sword stand serenely by itself against the sky!" This absolute "one sword" is neither the sword of life nor the sword of death, it is the sword from which this world of dualities issues and in which they all have their being, it is the Vairocana Buddha himself. You take hold of him, and you know how to behave where ways part.

The sword here represents the force of intuitive or instinctual directness, which unlike the intellect does not divide itself, blocking its own passageway. It marches onward without looking backward or sideways. It is like Chuang-tzu's dissecting knife that cuts along the joints as if they were waiting to be separated.

Chuang-tzu would say then: The joints separate by themselves, and then the knife, even after many years of use, is as sharp as when it first came from the hands of the grinder. The One Sword of Reality never wears out after cutting up ever so many victims of selfishness.

The sword is also connected with Shinto. But I do not think that it has attained in this connection so highly developed a spiritual significance as in Buddhism. It still betrays its naturalistic origin. It is not a symbol but an object endowed with some mysterious power. In the feudal days of Japan, the samurai class cherished this kind of idea toward the sword, although it is difficult to define exactly what was going on in their minds. At least they paid the utmost respect to it: at the samurai's death it was placed beside his bed, and when a child was born it found its place in the room. The idea was probably to prevent, any evil spirits from entering the room that might interfere with the safety and happiness of the departed or the coming spirit. Here lingers an animistic way of thinking. The idea of a sacred sword, too, may be interpreted in this way.

It is noteworthy that, when making swords, the swordsmith invokes the aid of the guardian god. To invite him to the workshop, the smith surrounds it with consecrated ropes, thus excluding evil spirits, while he goes through the ceremony of ablution and dons the ceremonial dress in which he works. While striking the iron bar and giving it baths of fire and water, the smith and his helper are in the most intensified state of mind. Confident the god's help will be given to their work, they exert themselves to the limit of their powers, mental, physical, and spiritual. The sword thus produced is a true work of art. The Japanese sword must reflect something deeply appealing to the soul of the people. They look at it, indeed, not as a weapon of destruction but as an object of inspiration. Hence the legend of Okazaki Masamune the swordsmith and his products.

Masamune flourished in the latter part of the Kamakura era, and his works are uniformly prized by all the sword connoisseurs for their excellent qualities. As far as the edge of the blade is concerned, Masamune may not exceed Muramasa, one of his ablest disciples, but Masamune is said to have something morally inspiring that comes from his personality. The legend goes thus: When someone was trying to test the sharpness of a Muramasa, he placed it in a current of water and watched how it acted against the dead leaves flowing downstream. He saw that every leaf that met the blade was cut in twain. He then placed a Masamune, and he was surprised to find that the leaves avoided the blade. The Masamune was not bent on killing, it was more than a cutting implement, whereas the Muramasa could not go beyond cutting, there was nothing divinely inspiring in it. The Muramasa is terrible, the Masamune is humane. One is despotic and imperialistic, the other is superhuman, if we may use this form of expression. Masamune almost never engraved his name on the hilt, although this was customary with sword smiths.

The No play *Kokaji* gives us some idea about the moral and religious significance of the sword among the Japanese. The play was probably composed in the Ashikaga era. The Emperor Ichijo (reigned 986-1011) once ordered a sword to be made by Kokaji Munechika, who was one of the great swordsmiths of the day. Munechika felt greatly honored, but he could not fill the order unless he had an able assistant equal in skill to himself. He prayed to the god of Inari, who was his guardian god, to send him someone fully competent for the work. In the meantime he prepared his sacred platform in due accordance with the traditional rites. When all the process of purification was completed, he offered this prayer: "The work I am going to undertake is not just for my selfish glorification; it is to obey the august order of the Emperor who reigns over the entire world. I pray to all the gods numbering as many as the sands of Ganga to come here and give their help to this humble Munechika, who is now going to do his utmost to produce a sword worthy of the virtue of the august patron." Looking upward to the sky and prostrating himself on the ground, he offers the gods the nusa symbolic of his most earnest desire to accomplish the work successfully. Would that the gods might have pity on his sincerity! A voice is now heard from somewhere: "Pray, pray Munechika, in all humbleness and in all earnestness. The time is come to strike the iron. Trust the gods and the work will be done." A mysterious figure appeared before him and help him in hammering the heated iron, which came out of the forge in due time with every desirable mark of perfection and auspiciousness. The Emperor was pleased with the sword, which was worthy to be treasured as sacred and merit-producing.

As something of divinity enters into the making of the sword, its owner and user ought also to respond to the inspiration. He ought to be a spiritual man, not an agent of brutality. His mind ought to be at one with the soul which animates the cold steel . The great swordsmen have never been tired of instilling this feeling into the minds of their pupils. When the Japanese say that the sword is the soul of the samurai, we must remember all that goes with it, as I have tried to set forth above: loyalty-self-sacrifice, reverence, benevolence, and the cultivation of other higher feelings. Here is the true samurai.

It was natural, therefore, for the samurai, who carried two swords—the longer one for attack and defense and the shorter one for self-destruction when necessary—to train himself with the utmost zeal in the art of swordsmanship. He could never beseparated from the weapon that was the supreme symbol of his dignity and honor. Training in its use was, besides its practical purpose, conducive to his moral and spiritual enhancement. It was here that the swordsman joined hands with Zen. Although it can also be gleaned from the way Yagyu divides his treatise into three parts, adopting the terms currently used in the Zen texts, notably in the "Blue Rock Collection": (1) "The sword that kills," (2) "The sword that gives life," and (3) "The sword of no-sword." The first part treats mainly of the technique of swordplay; the second touches upon the "mystical" Zen aspect leading to the final stage; and this, making up the third part, gives the author's understanding of the Zen experience as applied to the art or the way of the sword.

YAGYU TAJIMA NO KAMI ON THE "MYSTICAL SWORD"

All weapons meant to kill are inauspicious, and must never be used except on occasions of extreme urgency. If any at all is to be used, however, let it be known that it is only for the purpose of punishing evils and not for depriving one of life.

To understand this, learning is the first requisite. But mere learning will never do. It is an entrance gate through which one is to proceed to the residence proper to interview the master himself. The master is Tao (truth). Tao is above mere learning, but without learning one cannot expect to reach the ultimate Tao. Tao is reached when one's mind is entirely emptied of delusive thoughts and intriguing feelings. And when Tao is thus finally realized, you have the knowledge of all things, but this knowledge is not to obstruct your living in Tao. For learning and knowledge are after all meant to be "forgotten," and it is only when this is realized that you feel perfectly comfortable in your transaction of business of any kind. As long as you have the sense of something still missing or, on the other hand, clinging on to you, you will be haunted by the feeling either of insufficiency or of "being bound" by something, and there will be no freedom for you.

When a man in the beginning of his life is ignorant of everything, he has no scruples, finds no obstacles, no inhibitions. But after a while he starts to learn, and becomes timid, cautious, and begins to feel something choking in his mind, which prevents him from going ahead as he used to before he had any learning. Learning is needed, but the point is not to become its slave. You must be its master so that you can use it when you want it. You have to apply this psychology to swordplay. The swordsman must not harbor anything external and superfluous in his mind, his mind must be perfectly purged of all egocentric emotions. When this is carried out and the mind itself is "lost" so that even devils cannot trace its whereabouts, be can for the first time make full use of the technique he has acquired. No, he goes even further than this, because he now forgets all that he has learned, because he is the learning itself and there is no separation of learner and learning. Indeed, this is the ultimate goal of discipline in all arts where learning gained is learning lost.

However well a man may be trained in the art, the swordsman can never be the master of his technical knowledge unless all his psychic hindrances are removed and he can keep the mind in the state of emptiness, even purged of whatever technique he has obtained. The entire body together with the four limbs will then be capable of displaying for the first time and to its full extent all the art acquired by the training of several years. They will move as if automatically, with no conscious efforts on the part of the swordsman himself. His activities will be a perfect model of swordplay. All the training is there, but the mind is utterly unconscious of it. The mind, it may be said, does not know where it is. When this is realized, with all the training thrown to the wind, with a mind perfectly unaware of its own workings, with the self vanishing nowhere anybody knows, the art of swordsmanship attains its perfection, and one who has it is called a *meijin* ("genius").

Yagyu Tajima no kami then proceeds to tell us how certain "diseases" are to be avoided in order to be a perfect master of swordsmanship. In what has been cited above, we can readily see how closely the training in the art approaches that in Zen. Learning of the technique corresponds to an intellectual apprehension in Zen of its philosophy, and in both Zen and swordplay a proficiency in this does not cover the whole ground of the discipline. Both require us to come to the attainment of ultimate reality, which is the Emptiness or the Absolute. The latter transcends all modes of relativity. In swordplay, all the technique is to be forgotten and the Unconscious is to be left alone to handle the situation, when the technique will assert its wonders automatically or spontaneously. So in Zen conceptualization, whatever form it may take is to be thrown out of the mind when the Emptiness reveals itself, illumining a world of multiplicities. For this reason we assert that the principle of Zen discipline pervades all the arts as they are studied in Japan. The personal experience of an inner meaning in any art which a man may take up is all in all; the technique is not to be neglected, of course, but after all it is secondary. The "diseases" the philosopher of swordplay enumerates are discernible in any branch of art, and their knowledge will also help us greatly in the understanding of the Japanese culture generally.

An idea, however worthy and desirable in itself, becomes a disease when the mind is obsessed with it. The diseases or obsessions the swordsman has to get rid of are: (1) the desire for victory, (2) the desire to resort to technical cunning, (3) the desire to display all that he has learned, (4) the desire to overawe the enemy, (5) the desire to play a passive role, and lastly, (6) the desire to get rid of whatever disease he is likely to be infected with. When any one of these obsesses him, he becomes its slave, as it makes him lose all the freedom he is entitled to as a swordsman.

How are we to be free from all these diseases or obsessions? If any kind of desire that is present in the mind—even the desire to be free from a desire—interferes with the spontaneous activities of an inner harmony, what shall we have to do? The desire must be cherished somewhere and somehow, for otherwise nothing will be attained; even desirelessness must be desired sometime. How can this dilemma be solved? A second wedge is needed to get the first one out, but how do we get rid of the second one unless a third is inserted? This process will have to go on infinitely if we are desirous of driving the last one out. So with "the disease" Yagyu wants the swordsman to be free from, there will be no time for him to be diseaseless when the desire to be free from the disease is also a disease. It is again like pursuing one's shadow; however hard one may run after it, he can never succeed as long as his own existence persists.

In Zen we have the same problem. It is desired to be free from attachment, but we can never do away with attachment if this is desired in any manner. In terms of logic, a desire can be expressed in a form of statement, either positive or negative. For instance, we can say, "I desire this" or "I do not desire this." "To desire" is an attachment, "to desire not to desire" is also an attachment. To be unattached then means to be free at once from both statements, positive and negative. In other words, this is to be simultaneously both "yes" and "no," which is intellectually absurd. The Zen master holds up a stick and demands, "I do not call it a stick, and what would you call it?"

Or he would declare, "I hold a spade and yet I am empty-handed, for it is the way I accomplish turning the soil." Disciples of Zen are required to achieve this impossibility.

Toward the solution of this eternal dilemma, Yagyu quotes an old Japanese poem:

> It is mind that deludes Mind,
> For there is no other mind.
> O Mind, do not let yourself
> Be misled by mind.

The swordsman-philosopher undertakes to explain what these lines mean in connection with the solution of the enigma. He first distinguishes two kinds of mind, true or absolute and false or relative. The one is the subject of psychological studies, while the other is Reality, which constitutes the basis of all realities. In the poem quoted, mind is the false one and Mind is the true one. The true one is to be protected from the false one in order to preserve its purity and freedom unspoiled. But somehow a desire arises from the false relative mind and contaminates the true absolute Mind. Therefore, the former is to be carefully watched over. But who does this watching? It cannot be any other than the false one which is both the spoiler and the cleaner. For Mind, the true one, always remains pure and undefiled. This is indeed the strange experience we all have. Perhaps it is better to say that this is something inevitable to intellectualization, something unavoidable in language, and that, constructed as it is, the intellect cannot do any otherwise, for it is the very nature of the intellect that it involves itself in the contradiction and helplessly bemoans its destiny. As long as we have to use language in one way or another, we cannot help feeling a certain split taking place within ourselves, which is contradiction.

"Why" is a word useful only in a world of relativity where a chain of causes and effects has some meaning for human intellection. When we desire to transcend it the question ceases to have sense. A solitary mass of cloud somehow —nobody knows how—appears in the blue sky and, immediately spreading, covers its entirety, and we are unable to see beyond the veil. But somehow, again, we come to cherish a desire to penetrate it, we cannot help longing for the blue sky. We are thus again somehow urged to think that the clouds and the blue sky must be interrelated, though there is apparently no causal connection between the two. We are somehow to recognize the presence of the clouds along with the blue sky: we see somehow the presence of the blue sky in and with the darkness of the clouds. The clouds themselves then cease to be clouds— yes, they are there, and yet they cease to trouble us as such, as something veiling the blue. We then rest content with all things as they are, and feel free, emancipated from the bondage unnecessarily put upon us by our own igno-rance. The "why" loses its meaning, the contradiction is no more here, and we are happy in the enjoyment of freedom and inner harmony under the blue sky, which is to all our knowledge the storehouse of infinite possibilities, that is, the source of creativity. The blue sky, it goes without saying, is here metaphysically used for the Mind.

The old question, however, still remains: How do we get to the blue sky? Is there any "definable" way to approach it? We have used the term "some-how" throughout the preceding statements, but we all know that this is far from giving satisfaction to our intellect. But what we have to remember here is that the intellect cannot supersede itself. It is the intellect that raises the question, but it is not the intellect that answers it. It is life itself that solves all the questions, that is to say, it is *prajna*-intuition which sees directly into life. All the communication, therefore, that comes from this source can never be "definitely" described. So it is with Yagyu Tajima no kami in his treatise. As far as the novices, who are always intellectually possessed, are concerned, what he says is altogether unintelligible. He simply says that one has to go on disciplining oneself when one wishes to see the diseases disappear, and that when enough discipline is "accumulated" they will be removed by them-selves without one's being conscious of it. Zen in this case generally uses the term *kufu (kung-fu* in Chinese) which is synonymous with "discipline" or "training" *(shugyo; hsiu-hsing)*. *Kufu*, as defined before, means "employing oneself assiduously to discover the way to the objective." One may say, this is literally groping in the dark, there is nothing definite indicated, we are entirely lost in the maze. I am afraid, however, that this is as far as any mas-ter of Zen or swordsmanship can go with his disciples. He leads them until no more leading is possible, and the rest is left to their own devices. If it is a matter of intellection, the way to the goal may be "definitely" prescribed. But in things concerning one's personal experience, all that the master can do is to make the disciples realize that they are now at last in the dark or in the labyrinth and that they must resort to something very much deeper than mere intellection—something which they cannot obtain from another. The way to the objective, if there is such a thing in this training, is no other than the object which they thought was somewhere else than "the way" itself. The "seeking" or desiring is of course a preliminary step, but this step does not lead anywhere outside but within the seeker or desirer himself. The seeking and the seeker, the desire and the desirer, are identical. Thus naturally, there cannot be any intellectual guiding post. When the way and the wayfarer are one, what can the outsider do for him? An intellectual or logical pointer can never be more than a pointer or an onlooker. Personal experience and Prajna-intuition are the same thing.

Yagyu Tajima no kami sometimes calls the Mind the "Sword of Mystery," *Shimmyo-ken*. Being a swordsman, he inevitably emphasizes the activity aspect of the sword instead of its substantiality. That is to say, he wants to see the sword moving functionally. When the sword is held in his hands, it is at an undifferentiated center of a circle that has no circumference. It is ready either to assert itself or to negate itself. The negating is nonbeing and the asserting is being. The sword can be either, according to the situation it meets. Ordinary people are always one-sided. When they see a negation (nonbeing), they fail to see an assertion (being); when they see an assertion, they fail to see a negation. But the expert swordsman sees both negation and assertion at the same time. He perceives that a negation is not just the negation but implies an affirmation. So with the affirmation. This is the Mystery.

Yagyu the philosopher now turns to Lao-tzu and gives his interpretation: "Where what is eternal is in the state of non-being we may see the mystery [of being]; where what is eternal is in the state of being we may see the limits [of nonbeing]." By this, says Yagyu, Lao-tzu wants to make us see into the interfusion of being and nonbeing. Being does not remain as such, nor does nonbeing. They are always ready to change from one state to the other. This is the "fluidity" of things, and the swordsman must always be on the alert to meet this interchangeability of the opposites. But as soon as his mind "stops" with either of them, it loses its own fluidity. The swordsman, therefore, is warned to keep his mind always in the state of emptiness so that his freedom in action will never be obstructed. Fluidity and emptiness are convertible terms.

When there is no obstruction of whatever kind, the swordsman's movements are like flashes of lightning or like the mirror reflecting images. There is not a hairbreadth interval between one movement and another. When in his mind there is any shadow of doubt, any sense of fear or insecurity, this indecisiveness at once reveals itself in his sword's movements, which means a defeat on his part. When the Sword of Mystery is off its original "seat," no *myo (miao)* can ever be expected to manifest itself.

This sword stands as symbol of the invisible spirit keeping the mind, body, and limbs in full activity. But we can never locate it in any part of the body. It is like the spirit of a tree. If it had no spirit, there would be no splitting buds, no blooming flowers. Or it is like the spirit or energy *(ki, ch'i)* of heaven and earth. If there were no spirit, there would be no thunder, no lightning, no showers, no sweeping winds. But as to its whereabouts we can never tell. The spirit is no doubt the controlling agent of our existence, though altogether beyond the realm of corporeality. The Sword of Mystery must be made to occupy this invisible "seat" of spirit and control every movement in whatever external situation it may happen to find itself. It is thus to be extremely mobile, no "stopping" in any place at any moment. As soon as the moon is revealed from behind the clouds, it loses no time in casting its shadow wherever there is a body of water, no matter how large or how scanty it may be. An immense distance between heaven and earth is no hindrance to the moonlight to traverse. The swordsman's spirit must be like this. He may find it very difficult to act like this in every intricate situation he may encounter in life. Except for the Zen master who has gone through every stage of training and finds himself free from every psychic hindrance or attachment, it is no easy task to mix oneself in all social situations and human complexities and not get caught in them in one way or another. However this may be. it is up to the swordsman to preserve this state of spiritual freedom and nonattachment as soon as he stands up holding the sword in his hands. He may not be able to extend this experience in swordsmanship to any other branches of art, but within the limits of his special field he must be master of himself. Those who can apply experience attained in one field to another with perfect readiness are called men of "all-around fluidity." Such are rare; most of us are specialized. In all events, what is most important is to grasp the original mind of truth and integrity that knows no falsehood, and the rest will follow by itself.

From these lengthy paraphrastic statements of Yagyu's philosophy of the sword, we can see how much of Zen metaphysics has entered into the body of swordsmanship. People of the West, particularly, may wonder how Zen came to be so intimately related to the art of killing. Inasmuch as Zen is a form of Buddhism and Buddhism is professedly a religion of compassion, how can Zen endorse the profession of the swordsman? This is the criticism we frequently hear from the Western readers of my books. But I hope they have now come to understand what lies underneath swordsmanship and how this is related to the training of Zen. For, as most students of Oriental culture may understand by this time, whatever field of art the Japanese may study they always emphasize the importance of the "subjective" side of it, giving to its technique a secondary, almost a negligible, consideration. While art is art and has its own significance, the Japanese make use of it by turning it into an opportunity for their spiritual enhancement. And this consists in advancing toward the realization of Tao, or Heavenly Reason of the universe, or Heavenly Nature in man, or the emptiness or suchness of things. Thus the sword is no longer the weapon to kill indiscriminately, but it is one of the avenues through which life opens up its secrets to us. Hence Yagyu Tajima no kami and other masters of the profession are in fact great teachers of life.

3. Modern Bujutsu and Budo: Major Characteristics

Donn Draeger was one of the early, authoritative voices introducing the Japanese martial arts to the West. By virtue of his deep involvement with both modern and traditional forms of the bugei, Draeger was in a unique position to begin a conversation that explored the richness of martial culture, helping Westerners alter their perspectives from domination by stereotyped ideas like the magical "judo chop" to a better understanding of systems that have been shaped by complex historical and ideological currents. In the selection below, Draeger outlines the distinctions he sees between bujutsu *and* budo *(a system of categorization that is still hotly debated), and attempts to describe the important and varied ideologies that have influenced the Japanese martial arts.*

From *Modern Bujutsu and Budo* BY DONN F. DRAEGER

> *O imitators, you slavish herd.*
> —*Horace*

The modern cognate disciplines can be described in various ways. To the traditionalists and to those who regard classical bujutsu from the viewpoint of actual combat, the modern disciplines are nothing but an ass in a tiger's skin. An adherent of the spiritually oriented classical budo may view the modern disciplines as a brash and colossal sham, a mere empty shell. Conversely, the adept at modern disciplines is prone to regard the classical bujutsu as crude and anachronistic methods of bloodletting, and the classical budo as methods of seeking oblivion in the idealization of folly. He offers, as a more worthwhile goal for man's endeavors, the modern disciplines, which to him are the beacons of material progress illuminating the realization of useful and wholesome social aims.

The history of the modern disciplines begins after the overthrow of the Tokugawa bakufu in 1868. At that time, as we have seen, Japan was plunged into a period of modernization. The nation suddenly became aware of its crumbling defenses against the outside world, of its disrupted economy, and of the confusion in its social and political systems. Traditional institutions were being challenged, and the leaders of the Meiji government acted with revolutionary vigor to restore national and cultural unity. In the conflict that arose between the conservatives and the progressives, the course of leadership swung in favor of the latter, who maintained that almost all classical bujutsu were nothing but archaic technologies incapable of sustaining national defense. Bujutsu was quickly replaced as the national form of training for members of the armed forces by superior Western military and naval methods and technology. These gave to Japan a combat capacity better suited to its foreign policy of imperialistic expansion.

Though the condemnation of the classical bujutsu as fighting arts by the government was a matter of official national policy, these disciplines did not simply decay. It was primarily their romantic element, coloring the opinions of a minority of conservatives who envisioned the retention of classical warrior virtues as admirable personal values in modern society, that kept the classical bujutsu from disappearing completely. Classical budo, being spiritual disciplines divorced from all considerations of actual combat, and standing against the rising tide of personal liberation in the Meiji and Taisho eras, also did not enjoy a wide following. These disciplines primarily, and oddly enough, served the interests not only of a nonradical group of conservatives but also of radical activists and progressives; in the latter two cases classical budo was not so suprasocial as to be indifferent to politics.

Ultranationalists and militarists, both in and out of government, distorted the intrinsic purpose of classical bujutsu and budo, thus proving the truism that new uses can be found for any product of man's ingenuity; indeed, a hammer can be used to paint a house if it satisfies the expectations of whoever uses it in this absurd fashion. The forced change in the primary purpose of the classical disciplines entailed discarding certain of the integral elements of their respective compositions and a subtle shift in emphasis on the priorities of the remaining elements.

The intrinsic nature of classical bujutsu is manifested by the threefold relationship; (1) combat, (2) discipline, (3) morals. The forced change modified this relationship to the following: (1) discipline, (2) morals. Similarly, the intrinsic nature of classical budo comprises (1) morals, (2) discipline, (3) aesthetic form. This was changed to (1) discipline, (2) morals. It will readily be seen by these changes, made approximately a century ago, that the people advocating them made no distinction between bujutsu and budo; in their eyes, the two were equated. This is the overriding reason for the general misunderstanding of classical disciplines that prevails today, which helps explain why the majority of modern Japanese are unable to distinguish between these two very different kinds of classical disciplines, and furthermore, why they are unable to make any distinction at all between classical and modern disciplines.

But there is more behind the effect of these gross changes than is apparent at first glance. These changes were made to accommodate a new role for such ryu of classical martial arts and ways as could be adapted to the needs of the government. This new role was their use as a means of discipline for citizens. They created a new mentality and spirit in those who were forced by the educational system to participate in such activities, which they would not have done of their own volition; for as surely as the degree of brightness is not the only difference between a kerosene lamp and an electric light, the minds of the people using such disciplines will also differ. Because an external mode of life dictated what the inner life was to be, the activist disciplines altered the internal lives of the Japanese people. The Japanese government fully expected that this change in its citizens' mental outlook would take place.

A basic element of the inner self of any human being, called "spirit," is that inner being which controls the external self; no life is independent of spirit. The Japanese government sought to develop and control the spirit of its citizens by ordering them to participate in bujutsu or budo. *Seishin*, or "spiritual energy," which is generated through training in classical disciplines, was expected to heighten such attributes as courage and patriotic spirit, especially in the case of the soldier or sailor. In reality, the emphasis on enforced discipline tended to exaggerate the importance of spirit in physical endeavor. Every fighting man came to believe that seishin would enable him to perform on the battlefield with a mind that would make possible unfaltering and unerring decisions in any emergency. This concept of seishin helped to fabricate the myth that the Japanese fighting man was invincible in battle.

Along with the change in the primary purpose of the classical disciplines, the personal sentiments and morals of the modern Japanese citizen also differed from those of the classical warrior. "Change" means the creation of a new mode of life, as well as of new ideals in life and new morals for life. But it is also true that both the mode of life in the days of the classical warriors, and the attitudes of mind and spirit fostered by those times, did in some way affect the creation of a new Japanese mind and spirit. All changes are influenced by a spirit of reminiscence, and thus, so pervasive was the influence of classical martial culture on the Japanese people that it enabled them to attempt to preserve the stoic values of the warrior virtues in an entirely new form that was much more acceptable to their modern generation. And so appeared the first of what are today called the *shin budo*, or "new budo." "Shin budo" is a generic expression that encompasses the modern cognate disciplines, that is, those disciplines created after the collapse of the Japanese feudal system in 1868. Both bujutsu and budo forms are included in shin budo and must be differentiated.

For reasons already discussed, the modern disciplines are linked more in technique than in spirit to the classical martial arts and ways. This is partly because the modern disciplines center on the individual's rather than the group's concern for self-protection, and are also focused on the individual's desire to improve his physical and mental health. The developers of the modern disciplines were spurred in the task of creating new bujutsu and budo forms by the fact that many of the classical ryu were closed to them; the classical budo ryu, however, were less restrictive in membership than the bujutsu ryu. Classical ryu appeared to many people in Meiji Japan to be filled with unscientific attitudes and practices. Many of the ryu lacked realism. They functioned in a sphere of activities that were concerned with particularly narrow and vague values in which training was conducted in such a manner as to enable trainees to imagine that they had conquered figments of the mind that there was no question of actually surmounting.

The founders of the modern disciplines borrowed liberally from both the theory and the practice of such classical disciplines as they had studied or practiced. In order to enhance their own personal prestige and that of their new creations, many of these founders made exaggerated claims regarding connections with classical disciplines, cleverly choosing ryu genealogies that could not be proved to be false. But the great expenditure of thought and energy involved in synthesizing different elements of the classical disciplines into new forms also gave rise to numerous innovations that brought to many of the modern disciplines a substantial degree of originality. On the whole, the first modern disciplines founded exhibit a freedom of individual expression and a virility unknown in the classical disciplines.

CATEGORIES AND CHARACTERISTICS

The modern disciplines are usually characterized as methods of self-defense, or as tactics for sparring and grappling with an opponent. In the strictest sense none of the modern disciplines is a true martial art; it is even debatable whether these systems are genuine martial ways. Because of the wide range of their stated purposes and their emphasis on self-defense, there is really very little martial—warlike or combative—quality in these disciplines.

There are two major types of modern disciplines: bujutsu and budo. Both types are alive and vigorous in modern Japanese society, though their purposes are different. Budo forms enjoy a greater popularity because they serve a wider range of purposes, which are determined simply by personal interests and tastes. In order that something of the general nature of the component systems of the two major categories may be understood, it is useful to examine each category in terms of purpose, spirit, and technique.

BUJUTSU

Purpose
The major purpose of many modern bujutsu is to provide officially approved methods of hand-to-hand combat for people authorized by the government to deal with offenders against the social order; all study and application of such modern bujutsu is thus confined to the members of law-enforcement agencies and the armed forces of Japan. Other modern bujutsu are purely for use by average citizens as methods of self-defense and spiritual training.

Spirit

A spirit of combat morality, which is defensive in nature and which is intrinsic to the classical bujutsu, applies to their modern counterparts. A substantial number of systems of modern bujutsu are made even more highly moral, because of the need for humane application in civil life, by changing the ethical concept of the classical bujutsu of sanction for killing an enemy to the concept of endeavoring to restrain an assailant. Violence is to be met and controlled by restraining those responsible for it, not by taking their lives.

The classical emphasis on *seishi o choetsu,* or transcending thoughts about life and death, is carried over into modern bujutsu, though its significance there is somewhat less meaningful. This is because classical bujutsu are intended to be applied as principal systems of combat on the battlefield, where they operate on the basis of fatal *shinken shobu,* or combat to the death between professionally trained and highly skilled equals. The modern bujutsu, however, not only are secondary methods of combat that are mainly (but not exclusively) intended for use in civil life rather than on the battlefield, but always pit a highly trained professional technician against an almost always less-trained assailant. Thus, combat for the exponents of modern bujutsu becomes *shobu,* a matter of winning or losing in a serious hand-to-hand encounter. For these reasons the modern bujutsu are only quasi-martial arts.

Techniques

The care taken over the selection of techniques that brought the modern bujutsu into existence and that allows them to approximate their classical ancestors in spirit also allows the modern forms to be practical means of hand-to-hand combat for civil applications. Training, therefore, depends entirely on the use of *kaho,* or the method of practice that relies on the use of *kata,* prearranged form. So effective are the techniques of modern bujutsu that it is impossible to practice them in any form of free exercise; consequently, they are not sports.

The teaching of modern bujutsu is conducted by skilled licensed professional instructors. The method used by these instructors is a mixture of intuitive *(kan)* or psychological and rational or logical learning practices, the latter no doubt stemming from the influence of Western methodology. But by and large a *yomeigaku*[1] flavor permeates all teaching and learning.

Modern bujutsu deal with all aspects of unarmed and armed combat: armed defender against armed attacker, armed defender against unarmed aggressor, unarmed defender against unarmed attacker, and unarmed defender against armed assailant; defense against multiple assailants is also considered. All techniques are uncomplicated, and all are direct responses to

1. The phrase comes from the Wang Yang-ming (Oyomei) school of Confucianism—the school of intuition or mind which places an emphasis on knowledge as the basis for action.

attacks. The club and stick are the most prized weapons used in the execution of techniques because these instruments permit a wider range of controlled punishment of the assailant than do bladed weapons or firearms.

BUDO

Purpose

Modern budo consists of various systems used as spiritual training and religious cultism, forms of physical exercise or education, methods of self-defense for individuals in daily life, athletic and recreational activity, and sport. All of these systems purport to improve and integrate man's mental and physical energies in such a way as to bring him into harmony with the mores of a peace-seeking international society.

Spirit

The high degree of social tolerance that characterizes modern budo forms is an outstanding feature of these disciplines. They are open to all people, regardless of occupation or social station. In furtherance of their varied purposes, modern budo ignore the essence of the classical "sport of death" and substitute for it the "sport of life." The universalistic interpretation that is placed on *senjo,* or the place of battlefield combat, by the classical disciplines becomes for modern budo a kind of arena, the *embujo* for exhibitions and athletic performances or the *shiaijo* for sport contests. In the latter arena the idea of shinken shobu or shobu is replaced by that of *shiai,* a trial between two people in which an opponent replaces the enemy. The uncompromisingly severe martial spirit of the classical disciplines is alien to the modern budo systems. Moreover, the execution of modern budo techniques is never more than an approximation of real hand-to-hand combat, because the taking of life is only symbolic and the action is more in the spirit of a game or sport competition. Exponents of modern budo are required to adhere to highly restrictive rules that limit not only the techniques that may be used but also the precise manner in which they may be executed. Seishi o choetsu is thus at best only symbolically present, and in some modern budo this spirit is completely disregarded.

Do, or *michi,* which in the classical martial arts and ways is a "way" to be followed or that should be followed, is given a different emphasis in modern budo. Do becomes the way that *must* be followed by all exponents, a compulsion that gives to modern budo the nature of a forced activity.

Techniques

Kaho, the reliance upon the use of prearranged forms in training, is depreciated in all but a few modern budo in favor of a controlled kind of free exercise. Group instruction, led by *sensei* (instructors) of all levels of competence (and incompetence) replaces the classical method of a direct and highly personal relationship between *shihan* (master teacher) and *monjin* (disciple).

Intuitive learning (kan) is less important than is a rational approach to training. The trainee is made to participate in "lessons" taken over a prescribed period of time. These lessons are neatly scheduled as "package courses" of instruction and are expected to be the means through which the trainee eventually will become expert.

The majority of modern budo systems are applied as unarmed methods of grappling or sparring. The grappling systems are the descendants of the polytypic series of tactics that had its beginnings in the martially ineffective styles of classical jujutsu of the late Edo period; the sparring systems developed under the influence of Okinawan peasant arts of hand-to-hand combat. In the emphasis given to unarmed combat, modern budo exhibits a shallow eclecticism, and this is especially true of the newest forms. The founders of these new systems demonstrate that they have substantially forgotten, or perhaps have never understood, the fire in which the techniques of the classical systems were forged. Their lack of familiarity with weapons and with the exigencies of actual hand-to-hand armed combat has resulted, when combat becomes the prime purpose of study or application, in the creation of impractical exercises.

MODERN DISCIPLINES AND CLASSICAL CONCEPTS

It is useful to discuss further the connections between the classical and modern disciplines. When the nature of these connections is known, it is possible to understand that much of what passes for original thinking in the design of modern disciplines is, in reality, merely the repetition or amplification of ideas that have served the spirit and function of the classical disciplines for centuries.

Various institutions, customs, and beliefs of traditional Japanese culture—including both those that are indigenous to Japan and those borrowed from alien sources—are to be found in the modern disciplines. Shinto, Taoist, Confucian, and Buddhist concepts that are acceptable to the modern Japanese are revealed when the elements of modern disciplines are critically examined.

Those modern disciplines in which the sword is used as the principal weapon are regarded as the highest forms. It is highly unlikely that this preference will ever be destroyed. This is because the sword continues to be the premier weapon of Japan. But few modern swordsmen are consciously aware, as they wield their blades, of the fact that the precedence of the sword stems from ancient Shinto beliefs. Shinto's highest deity, Amaterasu Omikami (literally, "Heaven Shining Great August Deity"), the ancestral deity of the imperial family, considered the sword as enabling its possessor to "distinguish right from wrong, for the sword stands for justice, and helps the weak against the strong for humanity's sake." Thus, the sword is a divine object of worship, not merely an instrument for killing. For the early Japanese people, the sword always had the qualities of being "firm, sharp, and quickly decisive, wherein lies the true origin of all wisdom, in the words of ihe *Jinno Shotoki* ("The Records of the Legitimate Succession of the Divine Sovereigns," by Kitabatake Chikafusa; 1293–1354).

Taoist and Confucian concepts combine to form a complex philosophical amalgam that is not intended to be divided, in this view, the cultivation of the self dirough rigid disciplines is equated to "illustrious virtue," and it is considered axiomatic that one cannot perfect one's self without perfecting the selves of others. Furthermore, aside from the very obvious integration of Taoist and Confucian concepts in the overall doctrine of *do*, "cultivation of self" and "illustrious virtue" have yet another significance for exponents of modern budo.

The *Great Learning* (the *Ta Hsueh*, a chapter of the Confucian classic the *Book of Rites* and later designated one of the Four Books of Chu Hsi) makes reference to the "eight minor wires," that is, the eight steps to be taken in spiritual cultivation of the self. The second of these "minor wires," or "the investigation of things," can be interpreted in several different ways, but the result always involves a multiple, not a single, aspect of personal endeavor. The very fact that most modern exponents miss the significance of this multiplicity of endeavor in relation to their study and training in modem disciplines is reason enough why the matter should be explained here.

An exponent who proposes to strive for self-perfection through the medium of a single-system type of discipline fails to abide by the aspect of plurality in "the investigation of things." The criticism of T. S. Eliot comes to mind: "People are always ready to consider themselves people of culture on the strength of one proficiency." And it is patent that the *do* cannot be grasped by a single corner, let alone be achieved in this fashion. To attempt to do so is to alter the classical concept of the *do*. Thus the tendency of modern systems to develop as all-and-only specialties, that is, only an empty-hand or only a one-weapon system, is rejected by traditionalists as not being characteristic of true budo forms. The traditionalists offer, as proof of their case, the fact that all genuine masters *(meijin)* of classical disciplines, without exception, studied a wide range of different disciplines, never specialising in one alone, at least not before having achieved meijin status. As further evidence, the traditionalists point to the modern scene, where the absolute lack of true masters of the modern *do* forms among pure specialists, no matter what their technical perfection, corroborates this thesis.

Many of the dualisms of Chu Hsi Confucianism are found in the modern disciplines, where they have been transferred from the classical disciplines. The modern kendoist who crosses his training weapon with that of his opponent regards that act as *yuken* (in kendo terminology, "shinai contacting shinai"); when these same two training weapons are held apart, this action is termed *muken* (in kendo terminology, "no contact between shinai"). All kendo techniques operate from one or the other of these two aspects of Confucian thought. Yet it is doubtful whether the average modern kendoist realizes that the former condition stems from the Chu Hsi concept of *yukei,* or "having form," and the latter from its complement, *mukei,* or "having no form."

In fact, the ranking system used in many modem disciplines to popularize their teachings, the so-called *dan-kyu* system, is itself based on this very Chu Hsi dualism: exponents having *dan* (graded rank) are designated *yudansha* (those having graded rank), while those having no dan are termed *nm-dansha* (those having no graded rank). In the execution of kata, or prearranged form, the judoist or the adept of karate-do who exhibits the right proportions of stillness and movement utilizes the Chu Hsi concepts of *sei,* or passivity, and *do,* or activity, in his mental and physical attitude. The modem bowman, as he performs the necessary operations for shooting a single arrow in *kyudo* style, may scarcely be aware that he has performed yet another act of Chu Hsi dualism; that of *tai,* or essence, and *yo,* or function. Nor does the exponent of some styles of aiki-do generally realize that in spite of the great emphasis placed on *ki* (vital force), the Confucian reverse, *ri,* or reason, must be equally operative if harmony of spirit and action is to prevail.

Whether they are stated or unstated, believed or disbelieved, known or unknown, the dualisms of Chu Hsi can be identified as being operative in all types of modern disciplines, just as they are in the classical forms. Only through the operation of these polarities can the exponent demonstrate a quality of performance that gives a typically Japanese character to the physical action and the necessary emotional mood to accompany its presentation. A performance shorn of any aspect of the many Chu Hsi polarities is a "dead" performance, the result being evident in a lack of "body feeling" on the part of one or all performers. This defect indicates the lack of an "inner life" in those who are exhibiting their skill, the "inner life" that is an essential quality of the true expert, the meijin.

All modern disciplines, as well as the classical martial arts and ways, are activistic in nature. They appeal to the essentially nonreligious nature of the Japanese people but are not without distinct concepts of morality and religious feeling. The modern budo, in particular, seek a metaphysical foundation for their concept of morality. The ethical stimulus that modern budo aims to give its exponents proceeds naturally from Taoist and Confucian concepts more than from Zen precepts, which many modern exponents believe to be the essential source of their ethics; the classical concepts of bushido are only remotely reproduced in modern budo teachings. The Confucian way elevates the mind to a state in which the individual becomes one with the universe, in contrast to the Taoist way, whose basic concept is a negation of the self; this self-abnegation must be made through an identification with nature, which in turn produces an elevation of the mind above mundane distinctions like "this" and "other." Both the Confucian and the Taoist concepts find support in modern budo. At the same time, the modern budo forms follow the theme of social expediency postulated by Ogyu Sorai, which tends to weaken the relevance of many of the highly stringent ethical concepts of Confucianism.

So far as modern exponents are concerned, the natural dispositions of modern man including those in which his inclinations may produce immoral conduct, which were well understood by Motoori Norinaga and Ogyu Sorai, take precedence over abstract, idealistic moral patterns of behavior. For example, the ethical teachings of Confucianism and Taoism that underlay much of the ascetic conduct of the classical warriors have become, in modern budo, little more than romantic ideals. The naturalism of Hirata Atsutane, with its appeal to the Japanese spirit, is a good summary of the goals of Japanese exponents of modern budo today: "To comply with those natural dispositions is called the Way. . . . Since the True Way is as facile a matter as this, one should indeed stop acting like a sage and completely abandon the so-called mind, or the way of enlightenment, and all that is affected and Buddhaish. Let us, instead, not distort or forget this *Yamato-gokoro* [spirit of Japan], but train and regulate it so that we may polish it up into a straight, just, pure, and good spirit of Japan."

A similar naturalistic tendency, which conditions the acceptance of Confucian ethics in modern disciplines, also plays a strong role in the way in which modern exponents accept the influence of Buddhism. At the time that the first modern disciplines were being founded, all sects of Buddhism broke away from strict observance of rigid discipline; and the lessening of the old spirit of austere discipline, together with the growth of liberalism, had an effect on the nature of the modern disciplines. Then too Buddhism has always had much more significance as the "business of state" in Japan than it has had as a religion for individual Japanese. Therefore, Buddhism influences modern budo only insofar as it is useful for the realization of absolute truth within secular life. The recognition given by modern exponents to the sacredness of physical effort is a dominant feature in any sense of religion they may possess. Thus, if an exponent puts his whole heart and soul into his training, he is practicing "good Buddhism" in the sense that the Zen priest Takuan (1573-1646) meant when he said: "The law of the Buddha, well observed, is identical with the law of mundane existence. . . . The Way [Do] is practical only."

In the remaining chapters of this book, representative modern disciplines are discussed. While it is important not to lose sight of the connections between the modern and the classical disciplines, it is more important to recognize that, by and large, in the exercise of the modern disciplines in this age of scientific rationalism little attention is paid to the cryptic and intuitive world of the classical martial arts and ways.

Though the earliest of the modern disciplines can be evaluated with some degree of reliability as to their essence and their roles in and effects on society, nevertheless it should be borne in mind that these disciplines are constantly undergoing change. In addition, new modern disciplines are emerging. We hear of systems called *taido* and *aikiken-do,* and still other disciplines.

At the time of writing these are too young yet for any hard and fast conclusions to be drawn about their intrinsic nature, and their roles in society have yet to be determined. Therefore the remaining chapters of this book will deal in detail only with well-established modern disciplines, which are not necessarily the oldest of the modern disciplines.

Rather than repeat much of what has already appeared in reliable books on the history and development of the modern disciplines, and on the explanation of their techniques, each of the modern disciplines selected for discussion here will be treated along a new line. Emphasis is placed on the intrinsic nature of these disciplines as stated by their founders and by some of their most qualified and respected exponents. This presentation has a twofold purpose: first, the practicing exponent of modern disciplines will be furnished with a basis for comparing the original form with what is being practiced on the modern scene. In many cases a glaring difference between essence and modern interpretation will be revealed. The recognition of this difference may then be used by serious and dedicated exponents to help rectify the malpractices observed on the modern scene.

Secondly, for the uninitiated, for whom the modern disciplines are perhaps no more than an object of curiosity or simply an academic issue, this presentation will give a true picture of what the disciplines really stand for, an understanding that might not be achieved if one had to rely on chance observation of the perverted practices that riddle the modern scene and are made to pass for the genuine article.

4. KATA AND PATTERN PRACTICE

In the modern martial arts world, considerable discussion has centered on the reason for and the utility of traditional training methods as opposed to more "modern" approaches. Tradtionalists stress the use of pattern practice, while the excitement of free fighting seems to have more attraction for modern sensibilities. In this selection, Friday discusses the tradition and rationale for pattern practice in the martial arts, arguing for its central role as one of many elements that can help in achieving some of the more lofty goals of martial training. What is more interesting, he notes that the dispute about the usefulness of kata, often understood as a modern problem, is, in fact an argument that is centuries old.

From *Legacies of the Sword* BY KARL F. FRIDAY

If the essence of a ryuha can be found in the transmission of its ryugi—the body of knowledge that defines it—the essence of that transmission can be found in *kata*, the oldest and still the central methodology for teaching and learning in the traditional bugei. Few facets of Japanese martial art have been as consistently and ubiquitously misunderstood, even by those who practice them, as kata. Variously described as a kind of ritualized combat, exercises in aesthetic movement, a means to sharpen fundamentals such as balance and coordination, a type of moving meditation, or a form of training akin to shadowboxing, kata embraces elements of all these characterizations, but its essence is captured by none of them. Kata, in fact, defies succinct explanation.

The standard English translation of "kata" is "form" or "forms"; but while this is linguistically accurate, the nature and function of kata are better conveyed by the phrase "pattern practice." Fundamentally, kata represents a training method wherein students rehearse combinations of techniques and countertechniques, or sequences of such combinations, arranged by their teachers. In most cases, students work in pairs.[1] One partner is designated as the attacker or opponent, and is called the *uchitachi* (when he uses a sword), *uchite* (when he uses any other weapon), or *ukete* (when he is unarmed). The other employs the techniques the kata is designed to teach, and is called the *shitachi* (in sword training) or the *shite* (when training unarmed or with other weapons).

This sort of pattern practice provides continuity within the ryuha from generation to generation, even in the absence of written instruments for transmission. The kata practiced by a given ryuha can and do change from generation to generation—or even within the lifetime of an individual teacher—but they are normally considered to have been handed down intact by the founder or some other important figure in the school's heritage. "In order," observed Edo period commentator Fujiwara Yoshinobu, "to transmit the essence of the school *(ryugi no honshitsu)* to later generations, one must teach faithfully, in a manner not in the slightest different from the principles *(Jiri)* of the previous teachers." Changes, when they occur, are viewed as being superficial, adjustments to the outward form of the kata; the key elements—the marrow—of the kata do not change. By definition, more fundamental changes (when they are made intentionally and acknowledged as such) connote the branching off of a new ryuha.

One of the key points to be understood about pattern practice in the traditional bugei is that it serves as the core of training and transmission. In modern cognate martial arts, such as kendo or judo, kata is often only one of several more or less coequal training methods, but in the traditional ryuha, pattern practice was and is the pivotal method. Many

---

1. Westerners usually equate kata training with the solo exercises of Chinese, Okinawan, and Korean martial arts. But pattern practice in the Japanese bugei is fundamentally different from this sort of exercise. One important—and obvious—distinction is that kata in both traditional and modern Japanese fighting arts nearly always involve the participation of two or more people.

schools teach only through pattern practice. Others employ adjunct learning devices, such as sparring, but only to augment kata training—never to supplant it.

The importance of pattern practice comes from the belief that it is the most efficient vehicle for passing knowledge from teacher to student. On one level, a ryuha's kata form a living catalog of its curriculum and a syllabus for instruction. Both the essence and the sum of a ryuha's teachings—the postures, techniques, strategies, and philosophy that comprise a school's kabala—are contained in its kata. And the sequence in which students are taught, the kata is usually fixed by tradition and/or by the headmaster or the school. In this way pattern practice is a means to systematize and regularize training. But the real function of kata goes far beyond this.

Learning the bugei or other traditional Japanese arts is largely a suprarational process. The most important lessons cannot be conveyed by overt explanation, they must be experienced directly; the essence of a ryuha's kabala can never be wholly extrapolated, it must be intuited from examples in which it is put into practice. David Slawson, discussing the art of gardening, describes traditional learning as taking place through an "osmosis-like process, through the senses, with little theorizing into the underlying principles." His observations echo those of a late Tokugawa period commentator on the bugei:

> Theory *[narai]* is not to be taught lightly; it is to be passed on a little at a time to those who have achieved merit in practice, in order to help them understand the principles [of the art]. Theory, even if not taught, will develop spontaneously with the accumulation of correct training.

To fully appreciate the function of pattern practice as a teaching and learning device, it is important to understand just what is supposed to be taught and learned, and the relationship of this knowledge to kata. The essential knowledge—the kabala—of a ryuha can be broken down into three components: *hyoho*—or *heiho*—("strategy"), *te-no-uchi* ("skill" or "application of skill"), and *waza* ("techniques" or "tactics"). "Hyoho" refers to something along the lines of "the essential principles of martial art," wherein "essential" is taken in its original meaning of "that which constitutes the essence." As such, "hyoho" designates the general principles around which a ryuha's approach to combat is constructed: the rationale for choosing between defensive or offensive tactics, the angles of approach to an opponent, the striking angles and distances appropriate to various weapons, the proper mental posture to be employed in combat, the goals to be sought in combat, and similar considerations. "Te-no-uchi" constitutes the fundamental skills required for the application of hyoho, such as timing, posture, the generation and concentration of power, and the like. "Waza" are the situationally specific applications of a ryuha's hyoho and te-no-uchi, the particularized tactics in and through which a student is trained. Waza, te-no-uchi, and hyoho are functionally inseparable; hyoho is manifested in and by waza through te-no-uchi.

Kata, then, are compendiums of waza, and as such are manifestations of all three components. More importantly, they are the means by which a student learns and masters first te-no-uchi and then hyoho. As Fujiwara Yoshinobu observed:

> Technique and principle are indivisible, like a body and its shadow; but one should emphasize the polishing of technique. The reason for this is that principle will manifest itself spontaneously in response to progress in technical training. One should emphatically stifle any impulses to verbally debate principle.

In emphasizing ritualized pattern practice and minimizing analytical explanation, bugei masters blend ideas and techniques from the two educational models most familiar to medieval and early modern Japanese warriors, Confucianism and Zen.

Associating the bugei and samurai culture in general with Zen has become a time-honored habit among both Japanese and Western authors. And to be sure, kata training shares elements in common with the Zen traditions of *ishin-denshin,* or "mind-to-mind-transmission" and what Victor Hori terms "teaching without teaching." The former stresses the importance of a student's own immediate experience over explicit verbal or written explanation, engaging the deeper layers of a student's mind and by-passing the intellect; the latter describes a learning tool applied in Rinzai monasteries whereby students are assigned jobs and tasks that they are expected to learn and perform expertly with little or no formal explanation. Both force the student to fully invoke his powers of observation, analysis, and imagination in order to comprehend where he is being steered. Both lead to a level of understanding beyond cognition of the specific task or lesson presented.

But learning through pattern practice probably derives most directly from Confucian pedagogy and its infatuation with ritual and ritualized action. This infatuation is predicated on the conviction that man fashions the conceptual frameworks he uses to order—and thereby comprehend—the chaos of raw experience through action and practice. One might describe, explain, or even defend one's perspectives by means of analysis and rational argument, but one cannot *acquire* them in this way. Ritual is stylized action, sequentially structured experience that leads those who follow it to wisdom and understanding. Those who seek knowledge and truth, then, must be carefully guided through the right kind of experience if they are to achieve the right kind of understanding. For the early Confucians, whose principal interest was the proper ordering of the state and society, this meant habitualizing themselves to the codes of what they saw as the perfect political organization—the early Chou dynasty. For bugei students, it means ritualized duplication of the actions of past masters.

In point of fact, Confucian models—particularly the Chu Hsi neo-Confucian concept of investigating the abstract through the concrete and the general through the particular, but also the Wang Yang Ming (Oyomei) version of neo-Confucianism's emphasis on the necessity of unifying knowledge and action—dominated all aspects of traditional samurai education, not just the bugei. The central academic subjects of such an education were calligraphy and the reading of the Confucian classic texts in Chinese. Calligraphy was taught almost entirely by setting students to copy models provided by their teacher. Students would repeatedly practice brushing out characters that imitated as closely as possible those that appeared in their copybooks as the teacher moved from student to student to observe and offer corrections. Reading, too, was to be learned through what Ronald Dore describes as "parrot-like repetition." After the teacher slowly read off a short passage—usually no more than four or five characters and at most half a page—from the text, students were directed to recite the passage over and over again for themselves, until they had mastered its form. Once this was achieved, the teacher would offer some general idea of the meaning of the passage, and the students would return to their practice. Such instruction formed virtually the whole of a young student's first five to seven years of training. The method showed little concern for comprehension of contents and offered little or no systematic analysis or explanation of even the principles of Chinese grammar and syntax or of the meanings of individual characters. Rather, it was expected that once acquainted with enough examples, the student would acquire the principles underlying them in gestalt-like fashion. The idea was that learning to recite texts in this manner was a necessary preparatory step to true reading. Having mastered the former, the student at length moved on to the latter, revisiting the same Confucian classics he had been struggling through for years but now with the goal of comprehending their meaning rather than just their form. Toward this end teachers offered lectures and written commentaries on the texts, but the principal pedagogical tool was still individual practice and repetition, interspaced with regular sessions in which the teacher would quiz students on difficult passages and incite them to work their way through them.

In the light of this, the value medieval and early modern Japanese bugei instructors placed on kata should hardly be surprising. But the notion that "ritual formalism"—in which students imitate form without necessarily understanding content or rationale—can lead to deeper understanding and spontaneity of insight than rational instruction—in which the teacher attempts to articulate the general principles of a task and transmit these to students—is not entirely foreign to Western education either, as Victor Hori observes:

As a graduate student in philosophy, I taught prepositional logic to first- and second-year university students and noticed that the class divided into two groups, those who could solve the logic problems and those who could not. Those who could solve them started by memorizing the basic transformation formulae of prepositional logic. . . .. Having committed these formulae to memory, these students were thereby able to solve the logic problems because they could "just see" common factors in the equations and then cancel them out, or could "just see" logical equivalences. However, the other students, those who had not committed the transformation formulae to memory, were more or less mystified by the problems though many made serious attempts to "reason" their way through. . . . Those who had done the rote memory work had developed logical insight.

Pattern practice in Japanese bugei also bears some resemblance to medieval Western methods of teaching painting and drawing, in which art students first spent years copying the works of old masters, learning to imitate them perfectly, before venturing on to original works of their own. Through this copying, they learned and absorbed the secrets and principles inherent in the masters' techniques, without consciously analyzing or extrapolating them. In like manner, kata are the "works" of a ryuha's current and past masters, the living embodiment of the school's teachings. Through their practice, a student makes these teachings a part of him and later passes them on to students of his own.

It is important, however, not to lose sight of the fact that kata are a means to mastery of a ryuha's kabala, or expressions of that kabala; they are not the kabala itself. Mastery of pattern practice is not the same as mastery of the art: A student's training *begins* with pattern practice, but it is not supposed to end there. Kata are not, for example, intended to be used as a kind of database mechanically applied to specific combat situations ("when the opponent attacks with technique 7-A, respond with countertechnique 7-A.l, unless he is left-handed, in which case . . ."). Rather, pattern practice is employed as a tool for teaching and learning the principles underlying the techniques that make up the kata. Once these principles have been absorbed, the tool is to be set aside.

Viewed, then, from the perspective of a student's lifetime, pattern practice is a temporary expedient in his training and development. The eventual goal is for the student to move beyond codified, technical applications to express the essential principles of the art in his own unique fashion, to transcend both the kata and the waza from which they are composed, just as art students moved beyond imitation and copying to produce works of their own.

As he moves toward mastery of the ryuha's teachings, the bugei student's relationship with his school's kata evolves through three stages, expressed by some authorities as Preserve, Break, and Separate *("mamoru, yabureru, hanareru,"* or "*shu-ha-ri*"). In the first stage he attempts to move within its confines. He is made to imitate the movements and postures of his teachers exactly, and is allowed no departure from the ordained pattern. When he has been molded to the point at which it is difficult for him to move or react in any fashion outside the framework of the kata, he is pushed on to the next stage, wherein he consciously seeks to break down this framework and step outside it. He experiments with variations on the patterns he has been taught, probing their limits and boundaries, and in the process sharpening and perfecting his grasp of the principles that underlie the forms. Only when he has accomplished this can he move on to the final stage, the stage of true mastery. Here he regains his individuality. Whereas previously he merged himself *into* the kata, he now emerges fused *with* the kabala of the ryuha. He moves freely, unrestricted by the framework of the kata, but his movements and instincts are wholly in harmony with those of the kata.

HISTORICAL PROBLEMS AND CRITICISMS OF KATA AND PATTERN PRACTICE

Pattern practice is a time-honored and, when properly conducted, an efficacious means of training and transmission of knowledge, but it is not without its pitfalls. It is easy to imagine that a methodology centered on imitation and rote memorization could readily degenerate into stagnation and empty formalism. The historical record indicates that this was already becoming a problem for bugei ryuha in Japan by the late seventeenth century.

Certificates of achievement and similar documents left by fifteenth- and sixteenth-century martial art masters suggest that kata had become the principal means of transmission by this time. It was not, however, the only way in which warriors learned how to fight. Most samurai built on insights gleaned from pattern practice with experience in actual combat. This was, after all, the "Age of the Country at War," when participation in battles was both the goal and the motivation for martial training. A number of the most illustrious swordsmen of the age, moreover, including Tsukahara Bokuden, Kamiizumi Ise-no-kami, Miyamoto Musashi, Yagyu Muneyoshi, Yagyu Hyogosuke, Ito Kagehisa, Morooka Ichiu, Okuyama Kyugasai, Hayashizaki Shigenobu, and Takeuchi Hisamori, are known to have traveled about the country seeking instruction and/or engaging in duels and sparring matches. This practice, known as *kaikoku shugyo*, *kaikoku junyu*, or *musha shugyo*, is believed by many authorities to have been common among serious bugei students. Ordinarily, such students would begin their instruction with a teacher near their home, train with him until they had absorbed all they could, and then set out on the road, offering and accepting challenges from practitioners of other styles. Warriors defeated in such matches (if they survived unmaimed) often became the students of those who bested them.

Training conditions altered considerably in the decades after the battle of

Sekigahara. First, the new Tokugawa shogunate placed severe restrictions on the freedom of samurai to travel outside their own domains. Second, the teaching of martial art began to emerge as a profession. Adepts no longer divided their energies between training students and participation in war, as there were no longer wars in which to participate. Instead, they began to open training halls and devote themselves full time to instructing students, who paid fees for their training. And third, contests between practitioners from different schools (*taryu-jiai*) became frowned upon by both the government and many of the ryuha themselves.

One result of these developments was a rapid proliferation of new ryuha, spurred at least in part by the disappearing need for "masters" to prove their skills in public combat. A second was a tendency for ryuha, their kabala no longer subject to continual polishing and refinement through exposure to that of other schools, to become introverted in their training and outlook.

Under such conditions, kata came to assume an enlarged role in the teaching and learning process. For new generations of first students and then teachers who had never known combat, pattern practice became their only exposure to martial skills. As instructors slipped further and further away from battlefield and dueling experience, and as evaluation of student progress came to be based on performance in pattern practice alone, it became increasingly difficult to determine whether or not students—or even their teachers—actually understood the kata they were performing. In some schools, skill in pattern practice became an end in and of itself. Kata grew showier and more stylized, while trainees danced their way through them with little attempt to internalize anything but the outward form.

By the end of the seventeenth century, Ogyu Sorai and other self-styled experts on proper samurai behavior were already mourning the decline of the bugei and martial training. The warrior arts of ages past, they lamented, had degenerated into "flowery swordplay" (*kaho kenpo*) and gamesmanship. In the words of Fujita Toko, an early nineteenth century commentator,

> Tests of arms with live blades ceased to be conducted. When this happened, the various houses founded their own schools and practiced only within their own ryuha. Thus . . . [training] came to be like children's play wherein one studied only kata; the arts of sword and spear could not but decline.

It should be emphasized, however, that the potential problems inherent in pattern practice are just that: *potential* problems, not *inevitable* ones. Not all ryuha lapsed into kaho kenpo during the middle Tokugawa period. Some were able to keep their kata alive, practical, and in touch with their roots, their kabala in the hands of men who had genuinely mastered it. In this context Sorai seems to have drawn a distinction between the Toda-ryu and the Shinto-ryu on the one hand, and the Yagyu Shinkage-ryu and the Itto-ryu on the other. Nevertheless, a good many ryuha gradually reified methods and conventions they did not fully understand, and fossilized kata, passing on only the outward forms without fully comprehending the principles behind them. This danger may have been particularly acute for schools such as the Kashima-Shinryu under the Kunii family or the Yagyu Shinkage-ryu—in which the headship was restricted to a single family—as it was difficult to guarantee that each generation would produce a son equal to his ancestors in talent and diligence. Some schools appear to have avoided this potential pitfall more successfully than others, but in any event, by the end of the seventeenth century the shortcomings of pattern practice were provoking both commentary and responses.

In the early 1700s, several sword schools in Edo began experimenting with protective gear to allow their students to spar with one another at full speed and power without injury. This touched off a debate that continues to this day.

Proponents of sparring and the competitions that developed concomitantly argued that pattern practice alone cannot develop the seriousness of purpose, the courage, decisiveness, aggressiveness, and forbearance vital to true mastery of combat. Such skills, they said, can be fostered only by contesting with an equally serious opponent, not by dancing through kata. Pattern practice, moreover, forces students to pull their blows and slow them down, so they never develop their speed and striking power. Competition, it was argued, is also needed to teach students how to read and respond to an opponent who is actually trying to strike them.

Kata purists, on the other hand, retorted that competitive sparring does *not* produce the same state of mind as real combat and is not, therefore, any more realistic a method of training than pattern practice. Sparring also inevitably requires rules and modifications of equipment that move trainees even further away from the conditions of duels and/or the battlefield. Moreover, sparring distracts students from the mastery of the kata and encourages them to develop their own moves and techniques before they have fully absorbed those of the ryuha.

The controversy persists today, with little foreseeable prospect of resolution. It is important for our purposes here to note that it represents a divergence in philosophy that transcends the label of "traditionalists versus reformers" sometimes applied to it. In the first place, the conflict is nearly 300 years old, and the "traditionalist" position only antedates the "reformist" one by a few decades. In the second, advocates of sparring maintain that their methodology is actually closer to that employed in Sengoku and early Tokugawa times than is kata-only training. And in the third place, modern cognate martial arts schools—the true reformists—are divided over this issue: Judo relies exclusively on sparring to evaluate students, while aikido tests only by means of kata, and kendo uses a combination of kata and sparring in its examinations.

In any event, one must be careful not to make too much of the quarrels surrounding pattern practice, for the disagreements are disputes of degree, not essence. All of the traditional ryuha that survive today utilize kata as their central form of training. None has abandoned it or subordinated it to other teaching techniques.

5. The Classification of the Fighting Arts

The amount of serious writing on the martial arts has exploded in the last two or three decades. While no shortage of "how-to" manuals are still available, there are also many other works that explore the intellectual aspects of the martial arts. The Journal of Asian Martial Arts *has distinguished itself by publishing the best in both types of writing. This selection, written by Kimberley Taylor and myself, continues the discussion initiated by Draeger concerning the ways in which we can categorize and understand the martial arts.*

INTRODUCTION

In the realm of the martial as well as in other types of artistic endeavor, almost everyone has an idea of what constitutes that particular "art." It soon becomes apparent, however, that such certainty does not imply precision. This is a particularly vexing problem when we examine the term "martial arts"; there is no standard for the classification of the various fighting arts. It is true that there are a number of idiosyncratic systems for categorizing the martial arts and that they are employed with great gusto by laymen, practitioners, and even scholars. The problem is not that practitioners and observers within varying traditions cannot make distinctions based upon a variety of criteria; it is that, once the boundaries between traditions are crossed, there is very little agreement on the classification process.

The central challenge for scholars reflecting on the situation, however, is to see whether it is possible to develop a consistent, objective, and intelligible system for more precisely defining what we are talking about. Above all, we should strive to generate a system that is useful in explaining these arts in terms of general patterns and processes observed in human activity.

This paper presents a comparative summary of several definitions and classification schemes. An attempt is then made to use the insights gained to generate a system that synthesizes elements from a number of approaches into a conceptual framework that will contribute to the scholarly examination of the fighting arts. It is thus revealed as an activity whose inspiration is rooted in both the goals of Western academic discourse as well as the intellectual heritage of the Far East, since a primary interest of scholars, Confucian and otherwise, has long been the "rectification of names."

DEFINITIONS OF MARTIAL ARTS

The common, everyday meaning assigned to the phrase "martial arts" is said to include almost any fighting art, but especially those associated with Eastern cultures. As currently used, it is a term useful for the general public, but not for serious scholars of these systems (unless they are referring to the stereotyped ideas of the general public). This imprecision was identified by Donn Draeger, who defined martial arts on a narrower basis, and relying on the dictionary definition, characterized these phenomena as those war-based, combat systems intended for use on the battlefield.

Payne, in his *Martial Arts: The Spiritual Dimension*, on the other hand, stated that there is a definite separation between "martial arts" and simply fighting. The techniques may be similar, but the ultimate aim of the martial arts is to radically transform the student for the better, rather than to produce a better fighter. This definition might seem to be in direct opposition to that of Draeger, but certainly the picture containing both men's views is a bit more complex. Draeger clearly articulates an ethical dimension to some traditional Japanese combat arts. In a larger sense, since all these systems are created within a social nexus, they are implicitly invested with some sort of ethical component.

Reid and Croucher, in *The Way of the Warrior*, echo Draeger and point out that "martial" derives from Mars, the Roman god of war and, as such, deals with warfare. They then go on, however, to create a distinction between Eastern and Western "martial" approaches. The authors note that the word "marcial" was used by Geoffrey Chaucer in 1357 and so has a long history in English, but they also stress that "whereas Europeans have historically concentrated on perfecting the weapons of mass destruction, in Asia this process was preceded, and possibly at times checked, by a much more refined approach to human conflict, an approach that we usually call 'the martial arts.'" These martial arts all include, as a fundamental characteristic, the study of breathing.

It is obvious here that the writers are attempting to make an argument for an East/West dichotomy in fighting arts that gives Asian culture the moral and aesthetic high ground: Asians as profound, insightful, and refined (their study of the martial focuses on the pacific art of breathing) as opposed to Western warriors, obsessed with the development of "weapons of mass destruction." It is an interesting argument, revealing perhaps more of the predisposition of the researchers than of a grasp of history. As fashionable as it might be to portray the Western military tradition as a vast, technological juggernaut, it is not an accurate assessment of history. Personal weapons were *the* most important element in combat in European history for millennia. As late as the Napoleonic wars, the critical tool in battlefield supremacy was the bayonet, and while the face of battle has changed, it is a change only a bit more than a century old whose import was not driven home until public romanticism was shattered in the Great War.

THE OVERLOOK MARTIAL ARTS READER ■174

The argument for some sort of cultural aesthetic sense in Asia alone that led the members of its various societies to emphasize personal weapons requiring great skill is charming, romantic, and wrong. It is, however, an idea that is extremely difficult to eradicate—you have but to read Noel Perrin's *Giving Up the Gun* to be seduced by it. All fighting is dirty, destructive, and practical. Complex social, historical and economic reasons account for the disparate development of fighting systems between East and West, not the intrinsic moral superiority of Asian culture. Reid and Croucher and others of their persuasion load their characterizations with far too many value-laden terms to be of any use.

II Tools for Classification

II–1. Physical Attributes

When discussing fighting systems that are currently being practiced, perhaps the most fundamental classification scheme would be based on the physical attributes of the arts themselves. Within this general category, a number of distinctions can be made.

A) Armed/Unarmed

The presence or absence of weapons is quite often used as a primary way to classify fighting systems. Weapons may also be classified according to type or use. Swords may be cut or thrust weapons, spears are usually classified as thrusting, while various other pole-arms may be used to cut or thrust. Stick weapons and their systems are almost as varied as are sword systems and may also be classified as striking, thrusting or trapping (grappling) oriented. These types of weapon remain in the hand. Projectile weapons may be bladed (throwing knives, Japanese *shaken* and *shuriken),* pointed (javelins, arrows), blunt sticks (Australian boomerangs), rocks or balls (sling-stones, medieval siege machines, cannonballs, bullets), or explosive (modern artillery shells, bombs and missiles).

B) Distance

The distance between the combatants will vary depending on the fighting system. Distance is always a function of weapons and techniques utilized. The closest interval will be in the unarmed grappling arts with some differences seen here as between Japanese sumo (body to body), judo (one arm's length), and *aikido* (two arm lengths). The empty-handed striking arts are generally practiced at a greater distance, with variations among these arts as well. Systems which concentrate mainly on arm strikes (boxing, Chinese *wing chun)* use a distance of about one arm's length while those which include or concentrate on kicking *(karate, taekwondo, boxe francais)* will use a greater initial or combative distance.

Weapons arts will again increase the distance interval. Sword, spear and pole-arm arts tend to use the tips of the weapons to set the combative range, the ideal range being "one step." It is generally considered an ideal distance to be able to strike the opponent on one step or lunge. When weapons are mismatched, for instance when using a sword against a spear, each person will attempt to use his own ideal distance, the swordsman attempting to get inside the range of the spear and the spearman trying to keep him out.

Projectile weapons again increase the combative range and this will depend on the particular range of the weapon.

C) STRIKE/GRAPPLE

This distinction might, on first examination, appear to be another primary means of classification. A fighting system might be described as employing mainly strikes, as does boxing, Japanese karate, or Korean taekwondo. It may, on the other hand, be perceived of as a grappling art such as wrestling, Japanese judo, or Chinese *chin na*. Complications arise almost immediately, however. Such clear-cut theoretical distinctions sometimes blur in actuality: one has but to examine Funakoshi's *Karate-Do Kyohan* to see that a system widely regarded as the quintessential striking art also utilizes grappling techniques. While it is certainly true that modern systems seem to specialize in one area or another, many traditional arts included a variety of techniques in their curricula. Arts like Japanese jujutsu, *shorinji kempo*, and sumo, Korean *hapkido* and *hwarangdo*, and even Western professional wrestling demonstrate this tendency although they are all mainly unarmed arts.

In addition, arts using weapons can also be classified into striking arts, which would include all the stick arts (Japanese *jodo*, Okinawan bojutsu, Filipino escrima, Western cane and staff fighting, riot baton), the various sword, halberd and spear arts and even the projectile arts such as archery and riflery. Weapons can also be used for grappling as in the Japanese chain (*manriki-gusari*) and rope (*hojo-jutsu*) arts. Short sticks are also used during grappling within such systems as hwarangdo and jujutsu and in such distinct systems as the karate-derived *kubotan*, developed in the U.S.A. The police arresting systems which use sticks and hand restraints would qualify as weapons-assisted grappling arts. To further muddy the water, some weapons may combine both striking and grappling as does the Japanese *kusari-gama* (chain and sickle).

The complications arising from this strike/grapple distinction should suggest that utilizing a strike/grapple dichotomy as a primary classificatory tool is fraught with imprecision. So, too, are a variety of secondary distinctions which, while significant, may be seen as conditioned by other factors. These are discussed below.

D) LINEAR/CIRCULAR

Technique also conditions the physical characteristics of arts. One such technique-driven distinction is that of linear as opposed to circular motion. In grappling arts, aikido is often cited as a circular art and is opposed to judo, sumo or wrestling, which are presented as linear arts. This distinction becomes difficult to defend when the mechanics of the arts are examined closely. Even sumo with its crashing bodies uses a very subtle circular shifting of the hips to facilitate throws and this can be easily seen when watching juniors fighting experienced opponents. Mifune Kyuzo, judo *hanshi,* was noted in his later years for expounding on the circular essence of judo.

Striking arts are also often classified either as circular or linear. Karate and boxing are usually called linear while the Chinese arts of taijiquan and *pagua* are defined as circular. The same definition problem is found here, with many arts containing circular and linear elements in such a combination that it is often difficult to decide which predominates. The difficulties here are similar to distinctions made with the striking/grappling distinction. Despite a lack of precision, however, the linear/circular distinction continues to be used. It may well be in this case that, to the Western observer, the more esoteric arts are circular, since this stands in nice contrast to the stereotypical notion that Western culture is crude (and, hence, linear) in contrast to the exotic East.

E) Hard/Soft, External/Internal

These distinctions ignore the continuity between physical and psychological. A linear art is almost always described as hard and external, while a circular art is usually described as soft and internal. This distinction between internal and external arts is usually found in discussions of Chinese systems. We should note, however, that the martial arts are by nature syncretic and this dichotomy is also reflected in popular ideas that contrast *jutsu* with *do* systems, which have lent their name to a major classificatory system (see below). The distinguishing characteristics here relate to ideological as well as physiological elements and, in part, relate to goals (discussed below).

II-2 Functional Classifications

Closely related to physical characteristics is the question of physical efficacy. It is, of course, an important one in arts ostensibly devoted to "martial" pursuits.

A) Potential Damage

The relative effectiveness of fighting systems has been used to provide a classification system. Often this is simply a claim that one art or type of art is better than the rest, but a more serious approach is also possible. A classification system could be based on the ability of the specific techniques in a fighting art to cause damage. In this scheme, a purely defensive art (if one exists) would be least damaging, compared perhaps to wrestling, boxing, kickboxing, and then weapons arts. When considering the weapons arts, a classification on the technological sophistication of the weapon might be made with a scale including sticks, knives, swords, spears, guns, and then explosive munitions.

Classification based on these criteria at least has the benefit of being subject to objective measurement and distinction. If a primary function of martial activity is to bring force to bear on an object, then systems could be easily classified by virtue of the speed, accuracy, and efficacy of techniques and technologies. This classificatory dimension has influenced some discussion on the fighting arts and their "efficiency".

B) POTENTIAL USEFULNESS

A slightly more subtle classification than the potential for damage could be made if one considered the potential usefulness of each art. This potential usefulness may be completely unrelated to the stated goal of the specific art. In this case, some arts might be classed as suitable for self-defense in an urban setting (karate, aikido, boxing) while others might be useful for hunting (archery, target shooting), warfare (target shooting), entertainment (wrestling, karate, weapons arts), or even assassination and arson *(ninjutsu)*. Again, the stated goals of an art may not match the potential usefulness of that art.

II-3 Goal Definition

A) INTERNAL GOAL DEFINITION

The uses an art is put to are also affected by the people who practice it. The stated goals of an art could provide a classification system. Some fighting styles are intended for sporting use (kendo, judo, boxing, wrestling) although most will also state goals dealing with self-improvement, even if only to make the practitioners "more self-confident." Some fighting styles state that they are primarily for self-improvement (taijiquan, aikido), for fighting prowess (self-defense courses, Western jujutsu), and for many other things. These goals are internal, or self-defined, by the literature associated with the art or by the instructors.

Student Goal Orientation. Students may have various reasons to participate in a fighting art. The reasons given for learning karate might include self-defense, health improvement, flexibility training, spiritual development, sport participation, fighting skills, fantasy fulfillment, and even perhaps the desire to have a movie career.

Instructor Goal Definition. Instructors can also provide a range of reasons for teaching the fighting arts. These might include a responsibility to pass on what has been learned, a missionary zeal to share the benefits, a desire to make a living, a need to teach in order to continue one's own training, a need to impress others (students), or a desire to pass on other cultural information while using the training to keep the student's attention.

A distinction based on internal or self-defined goals is extremely difficult to construct by virtue of its sheer subjectivity. A classification system is, by definition, imposed by a detached observer to help clarify patterns in human behavior. To succumb to distinctions based on individually stated goals is to confuse "real" behavior with "ideal" constructs. Social scientists have long held that both categories are important. They are also adamant (and we may join them), however, in their contention that these two areas are distinct domains.

B) External Goal Definition

Certain goals may be imposed on arts and these could also be used in classification systems. To a large extent this idea is similar to that of potential usefulness described above, except that here the actual use of an art is examined. Fighting arts may be used by the police to provide their officers with self-defense, arrest or riot-control skills. The military might use fighting arts to promote aggressiveness, calmness under fire, balance or coordination, and to provide hand-to-hand combat skills to their special forces. Fighting arts such as taijiquan or aikido might be used by community health organizations as methods to reduce stress and improve health. Other organizations such as women's groups may promote fighting systems as methods of self-defense and raising self-esteem. Various cultural groups may use fighting systems (usually derived from their own culture) as a means of maintaining an ethnic identity in a new land.

It is important to note here that not all systems have such rational or highly rationalized goals. In addition, we must also acknowledge that goal statements rely on formal recognition of the particular function(s) these arts serve. The complex nature of human culture is such, however, that particular institutions can have formally recognized (or manifest) functions as well as unacknowledged (latent) functions. Here again, we are often relying on distinctions generated by individuals and groups whose very involvement robs their perceptions of the objectivity needed for attempts at formal classification.

II-4 Static and Evolutionary Systems

A) Finite or Open-Ended Training

Another distinguishing feature of fighting arts related to their goals is the difference between closed and open training periods. Closed training periods are seen in self-defense courses and in the basic training courses of the military; a certain set period of time is used to teach a specific set of skills. An open training period allows for lifelong learning which means that the art is presumed to be open-ended. There is always something more to learn and one does not stop being a student until one dies.

B) Codified Versus Evolving Techniques

A similar concept is that of closed or open skills. Closed skills are ones that are like the Japanese art of *iaido* or other arts with *kata* training, in which a skill is learned and is repeated in the same way each time in an attempt to perfect the ideal motion. Open skills are ones which are performed within a changing environment, such as those used for boxing or wrestling, systems in which the opponent makes the ideal motion virtually impossible.

Both A and B will be heavily conditioned by systemic goals (category 3).

II-5 Cultural Classification

After a broad look at areas such as the appearance and applicability of the art, the next questions asked of an existing system might concern its origin. These questions provide another set of tools which can be used to classify fighting systems.

A) COUNTRY OF ORIGIN

It is usually quite simple to classify an art on the basis of the country of its origin, and in the case of Japan and China, this is often done. There are, however, national prejudices which arise and often make even this classification difficult. Korean taekwondo is often claimed to be native to that country and to be quite ancient, yet a good case can be made that it was originally Japanese karate, which was introduced during that country's most recent occupation of the Korean peninsula. Advertisements are also seen for "Korean gumdo" which claim that it is the 3000-year-old sword art of the Korean royal family. In fact gumdo is simply kendo, an international sport of Japanese origin, at which Korea does quite well.

In Japan there are several forms of jujutsu which are claimed to have a Chinese origin, as shorinji kempo in fact has. Karate is also often assumed to be a Japanese art although many people recognize that it is from Okinawa (which was ruled by Japan while karate was being developed) and arrived in Japan in the 1920's. Many of the Okinawan karate schools point to China as the source of their art.

China itself is not free from these problems, since there is a traditional assumption that the hard, Shaolin temple fighting arts originated with the arrival of a Buddhist monk from India. There is little evidence to support this claim (indeed, there is some speculation that the Shaolin temple might have been less important to Chinese fighting systems than was previously assumed), but the sheer persistence of the Bodhidharma myth suggests problems in this area.

The whole question of provenance is a difficult one. When classifying arts from other countries, for example from Indonesia and the Philippines, the problems of successive waves of invasion and immigration will create questions as to the origins of many of their fighting systems. Social and cultural boundaries are (and were) porous. Transmission, influence, borrowing, and synthesis are universal patterns in human culture. We may wish to find the Ur-source of the martial arts, but it is almost certain that our wishes will be frustrated. In addition, since many of the arts in question were passed on in secret or through the type of master-pupil instruction that avoided committing insights to print, there is very little historical documentation to go on.

National claims for various martial arts are reflections of social currents in the here and now, not the historical developments of the past.

B) SOCIAL GROUP AFFILIATION/ASSOCIATION

Another way used to classify the fighting arts has been to look at the social group from which the art arose. The archetypal example of this is karate, which is usually said to have arisen from the oppressed classes of disarmed peasantry in Okinawa as a self-defense art to combat the Japanese samurai. The samurai class itself is also a source of many armed fighting systems in Japan, with the merchant, artisan and farmer classes identified as the source of many unarmed jujutsu arts. Class distinctions in China also provide distinct sources for the various fighting systems, some associated with the warrior class, and others with the monks.

Such a scheme may be applicable in some societies, but it must be recognized that not all human groups exhibit the social stratification that produces such clearly demarcated classes. In the final analysis, a distinction based on class affiliation may really rest on an appraisal of the political purpose and physical efficacy of various techniques: historically dominant classes tend to appropriate the best means of coercion at hand in an effort to secure their power; the have-nots typically are denied access to effective weapons systems.

II-6 Historical Classification

This area is closely related to the cultural approach discussed above. It has its appeal simply by virtue of the illusion of precision that dating things gives. Historical classification may be given order by the march of time, but it is also made more complicated. Fighting arts, as social artifacts, adapt and change through time. Some fighting systems may no longer be actively practiced, and their physical characteristics may be unknown. Others may have survived into the present, but their functions may have changed. Still others have altered technique and' purpose in response to social changes. As a result, a number of historically-oriented principles come into play.

A) TIME OF ORIGIN

The simplest time-based classification system would be to classify each fighting system according to the year it was created. This is quite likely impossible and is rarely attempted, but fighting systems are often assigned an era of origin. The Western fighting arts might be classified under such headings as prehistoric (prior to recorded history), classical (the Greek and Roman ages), medieval (the feudal ages), pre-modern (perhaps 1600 to 1800) and the modern eras. In each era a specific type of combat and appropriate fighting system would predominate. This same system of historical classification could be applied to Japan, China and any other country, with appropriate adjustment of the dates.

B) GENEALOGICAL ORIENTATION

A variant of the historical scheme is genealogy. It may be perceived as one classification system that has the potential to give specific information about the techniques and philosophy of any particular art investigated. Perhaps by specifying where a fighting system came from (the root arts) and which arts were developed from the system (the branch arts), one can get an idea of the content of the system itself.

It is, as any historian of the fighting arts can testify, rather more difficult to trace the family tree than might be expected. Not all students of an art have bothered to learn the history of their art and so may not be much help to the researcher. Even those who should understand the history may be tempted to embellish it to increase the prestige of the art. This process can be seen in the history of aikido which has recently been investigated by several people. The traditional "genealogy" traces the roots of aikido to the Minamoto family in the late Heian era. In fact, aikido was developed in the last generation. The immediate root art, the *Daito Ryu Aikijutsu*, may purport to be of ancient lineage but is, in fact, hard to trace beyond Takeda Sokaku. He based the Daito Ryu on several other arts, and Ueshiba Morihei seems to have followed the same syncretic pattern in his development of aikido. There are other examples of Japanese arts that claim very ancient roots but none of them much predate the Tokugawa era. Certainly their techniques are difficult to trace back before about 1600. The Chinese fighting arts are also difficult to trace. There is much argument about their sources, and the claims to a Korean lineage for gumdo just underline the difficulties of creating accurate genealogies.

In the West, with our admiration of a "new, improved" product, the opposite problem often exists. Instead of claiming an amazingly long lineage, handed down by secret oral transmission, many teachers claim to have invented brand new, wonderfully effective systems. There are quite a number of fighting arts that have been developed using combinations of techniques (take the best, and leave the rest) from karate, judo and aikido, or from Western and Eastern fighting arts, or from what have you. Again, it is difficult to obtain a genealogy of a martial art that claims to be brand new and unique.

Where accurate records exist, the genealogical system can be quite useful both to classify the arts and to provide further information on their techniques. A genealogical system of classification is, however, not universally applicable, due to the socio-cultural variations between the societies within which fighting systems have evolved.

C) TIME-DISLOCATED ARTS

History is, of course, a record of change. As such, an historical perspective serves not only to identify origins (where possible), but also to trace patterns of development. Along with a chronological classification of fighting arts by time and place of origin, we must develop a conceptual scheme for arts which are "dislocated" in time. These include the arts which Maliszewski called fossilized, those which have been practiced relatively unchanged beyond their own time. The Japanese battlefield arts that Draeger called the true martial arts (see below) would be included in this category, arts such as the *Tenshin Shoden Katori Shinto Ryu*, the *Yagyu Shinkage Ryu* and the *Niten Ichi Ryu*.

Dislocated systems must also include those arts which might be called "re-animated," those which have been revived by groups out of historical interest. These would include the medieval fighting arts practiced by the Society for Creative Anachronism, and others such as the Greek Olympic sport of *pankriatum*, the British art of the small-sword, and even some of doubtful historical existence (at least as currently practiced) such as the Japanese art of ninjutsu, and the ancient Egyptian fighting arts depicted on the pyramid walls. These last might be more accurately called "re-invented" rather than revived.

These historical systems quite rightly attempt to place the development of various martial systems within specific social contexts. In some cases, they anchor these arts in the developments of the past. In other cases, however, they merely desire to dowse some arts with the shifting sands of mythology. In either event, such historical embellishments explain the past but do little to clarify the present.

II-7 Philosophical Classification
A) INTERNAL CONCEPTS
Fighting arts will all contain an internal philosophy, which will usually be matched by the classifier to the stated or implied goals for that particular system. Some of these goals might include pragmatism (getting the job done any way necessary), sportsmanship (fighting fair), personal honor or responsibility (fighting your own fights, defending yourself), pacifism (avoiding trouble), nationalism and sacrifice (defending the country), and civic responsibility (keeping the peace).

B) EXTERNAL CONCEPTS
Certain philosophical or religious systems are applied to fighting systems and can be utilized in their classification. These belief systems are rarely involved in the creation of a particular art, except insofar as the creators are influenced by their own society. However, the philosophy of the surrounding culture will influence the fighting arts of that culture. Religions are often tied to martial arts as in the examples of Daoism (taiji, pakua, xingyi) and Buddhism (shaolin) in China, Christianity in Europe (medieval knights), and Islam in the Philippines (the Moro fighters), India (the Mogul) and the Middle East. Ethical systems may also be linked to fighting systems as was Neo-Confucianism in Japan (the Tokugawa era *kenjutsu*)

III PROPOSED CLASSIFICATION SCHEMES

There are, then, a variety of considerations that inform the possible ways we can define and organize the "martial arts," ranging from the specific to the general, some quite narrow in their schema and others merely narrow in their outlook. As this subject begins to garner more serious attention from writers, we may witness more attempts to come to closure on this issue. A number of the significant forays in this area are outlined below.

III-1 The Draeger/HIS System

The International Hoplological Society (IHS) of Hawaii was founded by the late Donn F. Draeger and is dedicated to research on weapons and fighting systems. Draeger, a widely known and respected practitioner and writer, outlined a two-part system of classification. In it, the martial arts were defined as combat systems designed for the battlefield. Other systems of fighting were classed as civilian arts, which are primarily empty-handed self-defense systems designed for urban environments. Draeger stated that both types of system will be found in cultures that have a hereditary warrior class and a disarmed civilian class. The two systems tend to produce different ethics, personalities and even aesthetics. Their differences are summarized below.

MARTIAL ARTS
1. Promote group solidarity.
2. Designed for battlefield use.
3. Designed and practiced as weapon arts.
4. Designed for natural terrain and climate.
5. Designed for wearing armour.
6. Use a wide range of weapons and skills.
7. Use genuine weapons rather (ban domestic tools.
8. Developed by professional fighting class.

CIVILIAN ARTS
1. For self-protection and home defense.
2. Largely urban based.
3. Mainly "empty-handed," limited weapons use.
4. Designed for ideal surfaces, roads, streets and floors.
5. Designed for civilian clothing.
6. Skills (and weapons) use is specialized and limited.
7. Weapons tend 1tobe domestic tools.
8. Part-time training at best.

The IHS System is precise and based on a solid grounding in scholarship but has a narrowly-focused subject matter. It springs from Draeger's central interest: *bujutsu*. The IHS system, tremendously useful in a discussion of the Japanese martial tradition, is not equally applicable to a wider category of fighting systems. Even a cursory glance reveals a number of problems: the characteristic of military arts being "designed for wearing armor," for instance, effectively wipes out a number of martial activities from inclusion as well as societies that developed them; "developed by a professional fighting class" would seem to eliminate the martial activities of conscript armies in the twentieth century as well as those of less complex societies throughout history. The IHS system is designed with the specific socio-cultural environment of pre-Meiji Japan in mind. As such, it is of limited cross-cultural utility.

III-2 Armstrong's Continuum

This classification was expanded by Hunter Armstrong to include both mortal and agonistic (competitive, sporting) combat systems. Mortal combat arts can be found in both martial and civilian arts, as can agonistic arts. A mortal martial art, under this system, would include many of the old Japanese sword and spear schools; it would also include modern military training in riflery. Agonistic martial arts might include kendo, a sport based on these old sword schools, or Western sabre fencing, which is based on the old cavalry sword skills. A mortal civilian art might be Ok in a wan karate or Japanese jujutsu if these are practiced for their injurious effects. The sporting aspects of these arts are seen in karate tournaments and in the sport of judo.

Modern fighting systems of martial origin and development, which are still martial in application, are not necessarily mortal combat systems. Armstrong used the example of the U.S. Marine Corps "pugil sticks," which are padded and used with helmets and gloves. The sticks are used to help develop the controlled aggressive attitude necessary in a soldier but are sporting in their application.

Armstrong elaborated on his system in a later paper. The classification system proposed was not intended to produce mutually exclusive categories, but it was expected that the individual arts would show limited crossover between classes. The categories presented were:

Battlefield mortal combat
    A. Single combat
    B. Group combat
Self Defense
    A. Single defense
    B. Group defense
Dueling arts
Agonistic arts
Psychological arts

This last category includes systems derived from older forms which are used to cultivate religious-philosophical-spiritual (R-P-S) concepts and goals.

Armstrong also provided a "combat totality chart" to help elaborate the system.

MELEE	TRANSITION	STATIC
battlefield	agonistic	non-combative forms
self-defense	duels	R-P-S training

The melee forms are used for strictly practical purposes either on the battlefield or on the street. These arts would include the use of gunnery, spear, halberd, and any other art associated with winning a war. The self-defense arts would include karate, some forms of jujutsu, and Western "all-in" fighting systems. In these systems there is little stress on either making a better person or on having a "fair fight" during the training process.

The transition arts are those which include a degree of competition with others, either in a sporting situation or in the highly structured combat of the duel. These arts are also intended to make their students better human beings through teaching such virtues as sportsmanship, persistence, and "fighting spirit." They include kendo, judo, "sport" karate, taekwondo, Olympic fencing, Olympic wrestling and boxing. Systems of dueling which are currently practiced are more difficult to name, but some using the sword persist in the German universities while some systems of knife fighting most suited to dueling may be found in the Philippines and Indonesia. Many of the traditional Japanese sword systems, especially those developed during the Tokugawa era, were designed for use without armor and in one-on-one situations. These might also be placed in the category of dueling arts although they are usually assumed to be battlefield or self-defense arts.

Static arts might include taijiquan, pakua, xingyi, aikido, iaido and other so-called "soft" arts. These are based mainly on kata or set form training and their main intent is to create better human beings. The particular techniques of these arts are derived from fighting skills, but the practical usefulness of any specific movement is said to be of secondary importance; its primary importance is spiritual.

Many of the specific fighting arts could shift along this scale, depending on how they are taught and on why students enroll. Iaido, for example, is also practiced competitively, and during the early Edo period, it was practiced as a self-defense system. Many of the "battlefield" arts featuring ancient weapons such as the sword and the spear have survived down through the centuries not for their practical benefits in winning a modern war but because they are now practiced as spiritual training. The same is true of many former self-defense systems using such exotic weapons as the sickle and chain (Japanese kusarigama).

Armstrong's expansion, simply by virtue of its inclusion of more categories of activity, is much more useful in an attempt at classifying ostensibly martial behavior around the globe. What he seems to be suggesting (and this point will be expanded on below) is a gradual increase in rules that condition martial activities as they proceed along a continuum from the battlefield to the R-P-S pole.

III-3 A Cross-Cultural Typology

Responding to what he felt were some of the limitations of extremely culture-specific or less scholarly systems of classification, one of the authors of this paper approached the fighting arts from an anthropological point of view. He argued that the social function of the fighter in any culture should be examined carefully and cautioned that, due to a lack of suitable terminology, investigators may lump different social institutions together under one heading of "fighting." The careful scholar, however, should consider the social organization and the technology of a culture together with the evolution of its combat systems.

Donohue argued that a true martial system, one that is a formally coded body of knowledge concerned with potentially lethal human conflict, will show a tight fit between the complexity of the system and the social sophistication of the culture. If there is a mismatch between fighting method and social complexity, then the "martial" activity will likely be performing a different role from that expected of a martial (warfare) system. One could thus expect highly formal martial systems in complex societies and relatively simple, "embedded" systems in less complex societies.

Three basic levels of social complexity are outlined. The simplest is an egalitarian society where most of the men of a certain age are expected to participate in raids, feuds, and other forms of conflict with other small groups. The middle level of complexity is represented by societies that are ranked, stratified or in the process of becoming a state. These societies have a class structure that permits the fighter to be defined as a member of a distinct group or that rewards fighting prowess with a distinct status in the group. The most complex level of social organization is that of the nation-state, in which large groups of well organized fighters are identified as professionals.

"Efficiency" in terms of a martial system is defined by how well it matches the social complexity of the group. The egalitarian society would be expected to show a fighting system that is "embedded" in the culture. That is, the weapons used to fight are also the tools used to live, and the tactics of the fight are the tactics of daily life. For example, a group that practices hunting with spears would also fight using those same spears, and their tactics would likely be those of the ambush. The battle would be short, confused, and characterized by relatively poor leadership and discipline. These groups would invest very little time in the training of the fighters, and fighting would simply be another role amongst many for each individual. As a result, the martial system would be defined as efficient, closely fitting the resources of the group.

The martial systems of the transition societies would be expected to show a more complex tactical awareness, with larger groups of fighters acting in coordination. These fighters would have a certain status in the community and would be supported by the group at large so that their training time could be increased accordingly. Depending on the technological sophistication of the group, the weapons of these fighters might be little better than those in a simpler society. Examples of these martial systems would range from the tribal warriors of the Maori or the Celts, through the Impi of the Zulu, to the feudal knights and samurai, who represented a distinct social class. Due to a low technological capacity, these martial systems must rely on extensive training and large group tactics to be effective. This can place a great strain on the group which must support large numbers of young men while they are out of the workforce training for war. Again, the economics of this system will ensure an efficient fit between the martial system and the social complexity.

In the most complex social systems, the martial systems will reflect the limits of the technological capacity. The weapons, tactics and training will all be quite costly to the society, but the ability to support them will also be present. As the technology of the weaponry improves in the state, the skills required of the fighter will change focus from the ability to fight individually to the ability to cooperate with others. The psychological training of these fighters becomes critical and the basic, physical training can take place in a very short time.

Donohue called the fighting system of the egalitarian society "combat forms," that of the transitional society "combat systems," and that of the state society "martial systems." There is a fourth type of fighting system that Donohue examined, the martially-inspired arts, or what are commonly referred to as the "martial arts." These are systems which are extremely inefficient, cross-cultural, and usually found in the most complex societies. They are self-limited to crude weaponry, use individual tactics, and require very long training periods. They are martially-inspired but are not martial in the sense that they are not useful for warfare. The people who participate in these arts do so not as a role, as a way of gaining status, nor as an occupation. Rather, they participate in these avocations because they provide them with a sense of identity either with the past or with their fellow participants. These arts may also serve as ritualized systems to perpetuate a specific worldview or to provide a means of ethnic identification for participants.

Under this definition, the martially-inspired arts cannot be considered equivalent to the Draeger/IHS definition of a martial art, yet it would seem that, in some instances, the same fighting systems (eg. kenjutsu, *yarijutsu*) are being defined. This dilemma is clarified if we introduce the concept of evolution through time. It is entirely possible that a martial art as identified through the Draeger/IHS system (i.e. one intended for battlefield use) was originally a combat system from a transitional society and most certainly does not represent a battlefield system of a modern state.

Such a cross-cultural classification system will serve quite neatly to provide a way of determining just what is meant by a "martially-inspired art." A martial art would be one which is inefficient in terms of its current social setting; characterized by the use of low-tech weapons, high training times, and stylized fighting techniques; and practiced as an avocation. This classification system essentially attempts to be free of opinion and prejudice (Reid and Croucher), to be applicable to all societies and times (a failing of IHS), and to sharpen the distinction between fighting systems that were about true combat (killing) and those that were about something else (a confusion endemic to public perceptions regarding the "martial arts").

If we accept such a system, then the Draeger/IHS system can be understood as referring to an historically-specific category of "battlefield arts" that excludes modern martial systems and which contains the sub-category of "martially-inspired arts." By expanding the scope of our inquiry even further, one could also accept Armstrong's classification system as it stands and then place the cross-cultural classifications of the three efficient fighting systems into Armstrong's "battlefield arts" category. The analytic categories utilized in discussion could then be tailored to the narrowness or breadth of the investigation at hand.

III-4 Other Social/Historical/Stylistic Systems

Reid and Croucher proposed a fundamental classification of fighting into two groups: fighting for entertainment, sport or ritual, all within the tribal or social group, and warfare, which was fighting between tribes or social groups. This cultural approach is slightly different from that suggested above. While the authors did not elaborate on this theory, it is obviously vulnerable on a number of points.

In the first place, a distinction between inter- and intra-group conflict is not always useful; according to their criteria, the American Civil War would not fall into the category of warfare, since it was fighting within a socio-political group. The problem, of course, lies in how the authors wish to define the concept of society. Since they do not provide such a definition, their initial effort at categorization is fatally flawed.

Reid and Croucher then refine their definition of martial arts by contrasting them to warfare, fighting sports and entertainment. Warfare skills are said to be cruder than martial-art fighting skills, to rely on heavier weapons, on mass attacks and on strength as opposed to skill. Here, again, we see the impact of a perspective hindered by ideological preconceptions, historical myopia, or socio-cultural naivete. Martial arts were not, according to these authors, developed to defend soldiers on the battlefield. Draeger would, at least in part, disagree with this contention, and history would bear him out. Similarly, they maintain that martial arts do not include sport fighting because the martial arts have only one objective, to neutralize an attack by any means available, as quickly as possible. We are thus quickly led to a problematic position (not the least of which is that we would be forced to eliminate kendo and judo from the category) that martial arts are simultaneously devoted to efficiency in dealing with attacks but are conditioned by an ideology that forbids the use of efficient weapons;

Reid and Croucher also maintain that the martial arts are not an entertainment, as were the gladiatorial fighting arts of the Romans. This leaves the martial arts in the realm of ritual fighting by default. While their argument concerning a ritual dimension to the "martial arts" is getting close to a significant point, subsequent ideas vitiate this insight. There is a ritual dimension to most, if not all, fighting; certainly any organized combat has ritual elements. How best to make the distinction? They obviously ignore the mortality element, perhaps a mistake in a case like gladiatorial contests, which were spectacle, sport, and fight to the death. There also seems to be an inconsistency between portraying martial arts systems as ritual in nature and yet simultaneously practical, since ritual always involves codification, which narrows the range of responses.

The authors further restrict the term "martial arts" by stating that they originated in the East and were not present in Europe or around the Mediterranean. Later in their book, however, Reid and Croucher give a classification scheme for martial systems based on national origin and include all the continents. At this time they state that Europe did indeed have martial arts but these were transformed over the years to fighting sports.

This attempt (admittedly not a central part of their work and one designed to merely define the locus of their inquiry) is thus so replete with contradictions as to be of little utility. Although the authors have identified some significant attributes in the arts they examine, the constellation of characteristics is not systematically related to a wider perspective.

Another classification system, using national origin, was used by Scott and Pappas in *The Fighting Arts: Choosing the Way* . These authors survey the martial arts of India, China, Japan, Korea, Thailand, Burma, Indonesia and Malaysia, the Philippines and the West. They divided the national arts into subgroups of "kick and punch," "grappling" and "weapons." This is problematic in terms of the sheer breadth of categories: merely examining weapons systems alone reveals so many different types (are Korean snipers martial artists?) that we are once more dealing with generalizations, not analytic categories.

"Genealogical" systems of classification often prove tempting to thinkers. Peter Payne hypothesized that the martial arts originated in India, migrated to China, and from there spread to other Asian countries in all directions. Reid and Croucher felt that the martial arts originated in Babylon some time before 3000-2000 BC and moved east to India and China where they developed more completely. If this point-source theory is accepted, then a genealogical chart could be created to classify all the Asian martial arts according to their proximity to the original source art.

As mentioned above, diffusionist theories dealing with cultural characteristics are with us always. The idea of a martial-arts prime mover, a point of single origin and a later diffusion is not very well accepted and for good reason. It is, of course, more than likely that different societies throughout time have decisively influenced one another. This is not an issue. The attempt to create a genealogical pedigree for martial arts is, however, a dead end. We will never get to the point where we can establish a verifiable genealogy of systems that has any kind of depth.

The Bodhidharma-karate link is a case in point. Did Bodhidharma bring a new form of fighting across the Himalayas to China? Did the monks of Shaolin pass it on? Did it reach Okinawa? Is karate's provenance ancient? It is impossible to say. The story is a myth and, as such, is important. Its importance does not lie in historical fidelity, however, but in the fact that it emphasizes an enduring notion that there is an association between karate and ethical and philosophical systems.

Payne also classifies the martial arts according to several pairs of characteristics: grappling/hitting, empty-hand/weapons, hard/soft and internal/external. The first two dichotomies are self-explanatory and rely on classifying the physical techniques which dominate the art to characterize it. An internal art is defined as one which uses "*qi*" or "*ki*" energy while an external art uses muscular strength. Internal arts also tend to be "soft" arts, having circular, indirect, relaxed and smooth techniques that travel on the exterior or outside lines of attack. External arts tend to be "hard" with linear, direct, focused, fast techniques that are aimed at the inside or center-line of the opponent.

Herman Kauz in *The Martial Spirit* also uses the soft/hard, empty-hand/weapons pairs. In this case, the soft/hard pair is synonymous with the internal/external pair. Although the internal/external division is most often applied to the Chinese arts, Kauz also uses them to separate such Japanese arts as karate (hard, external) and aikido (soft, internal). Kauz also adds a sport/non-sport pair to his classification list, and points out that students may study the martial arts for self-defense, physical exercise, or as a method of meditation. This "intention of the student" gives another potential classification method. Its weakness has already been commented upon.

Kauz indicates that the national origin of a martial art will, to a large degree, determine the characteristics of the system, which is part of the cultural heritage of each country. Here he is at least partially reflecting views similar to those of Scott and Pappas.

III-5 The Bipartite Systems
JUTSU/DO, ART/WAY, MODERN/TRADITIONAL

One of the most common classification schemes encountered in the literature is the bipartite system which most commonly uses the Japanese terms *jutsu* and *do,* usually translated as "art" and "way." It is a perspective at least partially fueled by Draeger's work but is a great deal less painstaking in its theoretical and scholarly underpinnings. This system is partly based on distinctions centering on the goal of the training, but care must be taken to distinguish between training in the same system for two different reasons or training in two arts which also have two different purposes.

In common usage, the jutsu and do systems are quite often opposed to each other in terms of goals but are built on the same root art. Jutsu arts are usually assumed to be practical, martial or self-defense oriented, and concerned exclusively with technique. Do arts are often described as flowery, complex, sporting, and aimed at spiritual goals. Commonly cited examples of these pairs are jujutsu and judo, kenjutsu and kendo, karate-jutsu and karate-do, batto-jutsu and iaido. All of these arts are related but are popularly understood as being practiced for different purposes.

Under these definitions, one might think it possible to take any art and identify a jutsu and a do form of training. A recent illustration of this phenomenon is the example of the art of aikido. A recently evolved do form, it has exhibited the development of a multitude of applications and stylistic fragmentation common to many martial arts. Its relative newness, however, makes the process much clearer. In the hands of Ueshiba Morihei, aikido came to embody a classically *do* orientation quite at odds with the spirit of Takeda's Daito-Ryu (and even the style of Morihei's early *aiki-budo).* It was further transformed and adapted into a sport form (Tomiki aikido), that placed an extreme emphasis on ki (under the guidance of Tohei Koichi) and retained the hard edge of the earlier aikijutsu days (Gozo Shioda's Yoshinkan style).

Toshishiro Obata, a student of Gozo Shioda, has written a book called *Samurai Aikijutsu.* It presents several techniques from the art of aikido, but the author recommends that they be done in an aikijutsu manner. He states, "The only criticism that we make, and it is a positive one, is that modern aikido has become remote from its roots, and in some cases completely severed from them, and as a result has lost much of its effectiveness". He recommended, in effect, taking the do form of aikido and by studying the sword and the knife, converting it once again to the jutsu form which is practical and useful. The irony involved in training to develop effective techniques for dealing with sword attacks in the closing decade of the twentieth century seems to escape the author. He is, however, not alone.

This process (and its attendant irony) has a long history in the West and has been performed several times with other arts such as karate and judo or even with combinations of these three arts to create jutsu systems for self-defense. Quite often these new eclectic forms were simply called jujutsu. In any event, some believe their jutsu label identifies them as hard-hitting, effective, and more "realistic" forms of martial arts.

There can be, therefore, a subjective quality to the jutsu/do distinction. It is possible to classify arts according to criteria other than whether they include or exclude meditation, kata, lectures on ethics and other teachings. Ellis Amdur provides a more subtle distinction of *jutsu* and do, within the context of aikido practice, but relying on the practitioner's intent for the difference. For someone practicing aikido in an "aikijutsu" manner, "aiki is a means of achieving harmony with another person so you can make them do what you want." In this case, empathy and spiritual intimacy are evoked for the sake of manipulating the other. With this aim in the practice, Amdur warns there is a real danger of becoming indifferent to others, of losing compassion. Amdur defines compassion as a real contact, a full acceptance of the self and the other. Aikido practiced in the "aikido" manner is a movement in the self and between the self and the other to establish an ethical relationship rather than to cause the other to do something. "Aikijutsu" then is doing something "to" another for some reason or purpose. It uses calculation and skilled means. "Aikido" is not the result of a decision to act, but rather the action is "through" the actor. Something occurs and the right action emerges without deliberation. This is a spontaneous, unreflected action in the service of a higher aim.

This conception is much more subtle than the usual distinction made between jutsu and do. For the purpose of categorization however, it is extremely problematic. The difficulty lies in the sheer vagary involved in determining psychological intent. Amdur's points remind us that there is a broad spectrum of human behavior within socially-created systems, but this knowledge does not arm us with conceptual tools that can define such systems.

The Japanese, a people of great subtlety, nonetheless do not seem hindered by such relativism. Differences are somewhat more specifically identified in Japan. Draeger, for instance, would view jutsu and do distinctions as the result of historical, evolutionary trends within the Japanese martial arts. Thus, while in the West the do forms often give rise to the jutsu forms simply by using the same techniques in a "more practical" way, in Japan the trend has historically been for the do arts to arise from the jutsu arts and for the two arts to become quite distinct. Kendo, the modern form of swordsmanship, is quite different both in its techniques and in its equipment from the older kenjutsu from which it derived. Lowry's *Autumn Lightning*, although somewhat fictionalized, does a nice job of exploring the spirit behind the evolution of the Yagyu Shinkage Ryu in these terms. A very recent example of this evolutionary process would be the difference between *juken-jutsu,* the World War II army bayonet training, and the newly developed sport of *jukendo.* We will return to this discussion, but for now we will examine the idea that fighting arts can be classified as jutsu (practical, direct, battlefield arts) and do (spiritual, self-improvement arts) without demanding that the two types of art be present in each system.

Stephen Turnbull reflects this notion when he discusses Japanese fighting systems under the terms *bugei (or* bujutsu) and budo. He states that the bugei are designed for actual combat or are practice designed for combat. These are arts which use the wooden sword or *bokkuto* and are performed using set-piece motions called kata (kenjutsu). The budo are defined as modern forms far removed from combat (kendo). They are "friendly combats" not life-and-death duels.

Turnbull states that the bugei are actually living fossils, having no practical use in warfare today, while the budo are more relevant to modem practice. The do emerged in the early 1700's, taking note of the need to develop human qualities as well as technical skills. There are several instances of jutsu arts which were renamed do arts if they came to be practiced for their own sake rather than for combat practice, but Turnbull notes that the modern usage of the term budo is different from this meaning.

The modern budo may be competitive or sporting with a reduced emphasis on kata and increased concern for safety. In the example of the Japanese sword, the kenjutsu arts which used the wooden sword and kata training were replaced by kendo which uses a bamboo sword and padding for safety. The budo also tend to use a different grading and licensing system than the bujutsu systems.

It must be noted again that there is little indication that the Japanese themselves used or use the terms "jutsu" and "do" in the way that they are commonly used in the West, any more than we have a set opinion on how to use the terms "art" and "way." Caution should be exercised before classifying a system simply on the basis of its name. This point was addressed by Draeger. Japanese bujutsu arts, according to Draeger, need three elements to be so defined. They must use the sword, they must use armor and they must contain elements of Esoteric Buddhism. The do arts are often associated with methods or "paths" to enlightenment or self-righteousness, but Draeger pointed out that there are other "paths" which are possible. Without an ethical basis for the martial virtues one is studying, what one ends up with is rowdyism and gangsterism. Thus, both the jutsu and the do systems contain an ethical basis in their training, so the widespread popular attribution of an ideology only to do forms is erroneous.

When one considers that many Japanese kenjutsu schools still flourish, despite their uselessness on the battlefield, for self-defense or for sport, it should be obvious that what has preserved them is their ability to inform or transform the students spiritually. Many of the Japanese bujutsu and budo are primarily concerned with making a better person of the student rather than turning out a better fighter. On the other hand, there are also fighting systems in Japan that are designed simply to create better fighters. It is important to remember this point when using the terms jutsu and do to classify the arts.

The jutsu/do classification, one type of bipartite system, is, by definition, extremely broad. It does make a useful point, however. Michael Maliszewski notes that modern nonacademic writing tends to lump all Asian systems of fighting under the term "martial art," defined as styles of combat originating in the Orient and which offer a "way of life" based on Eastern philosophy. He takes note of the Draeger/Armstrong/IHS classification system but argues that such precise terminology is difficult to apply when the individual art is examined due to the crossover from one category to another. The same difficulty is mentioned by Armstrong. Maliszewski suggests that the simplistic, more inclusive definition of martial arts may be more useful than would normally be suspected. In his paper, Maliszewski states, "the term 'fighting art' will be applied to those comprehensive systems of combat or self-defense which may involve unarmed tactics as well as the use of weapons and which, either historically or on the contemporary scene, derive their roots or teachings from combat systems designated as such within their respective cultural or geographical settings".

"'Martial ways' refer to those systems which, though having some association with the combative sphere, seek as their primary goal a radical psychological authentication or transformation of the individual".

Finally, he states that "'martial disciplines' will be used to refer to fighting arts and martial ways collectively." Students in either the fighting arts or the martial ways may experience features which would seem to apply to the other system but all would experience physical training which, hypothetically, could be used in a combative situation. This is in contrast to physical systems of meditation such as Yoga or Zen sitting.

Maliszewski's classification scheme thus falls readily into the bipartite classification system, defining a "fighting art" as technique driven (jutsu) and a "martial way" as self-improvement driven (do).

Many of the academic studies on the effects of martial arts training use this same bipartite classification and define "traditional" training as that which concentrates on or includes art/meditative aspects, stressing self-control, conflict avoidance, respect for others, kata training, and the study of philosophy. "Modern" training is seen as stressing the sport/competitive aspects, limiting the teaching to the physical aspects only. This separation between jutsu and do would apply strictly to the intention of the student or instructor with no difference in the particular techniques practiced.

In general, these studies suggest that the traditional (do or "way") training has profound psychological effects on the students while the modern (jutsu or "art") training has little effect or may raise aggressiveness somewhat. This might indeed point out an effective (and affective) difference between the two systems: the one aims at the mental/spiritual transformation of the individual and the other aims at producing a better fighter. It must be noted with caution, however, that older studies on seemingly "modern" training systems (Western boxing and wrestling) also show that the boxers and wrestlers were less aggressive after training and were less aggressive than people in other sports. Since these two sports cannot be called "traditional," having no spiritual/meditative aspects, and do not seem to have the same effect as "modern" training, it might be suggested that the bipartite model may not discriminate between all systems of fighting.

Donohue's cross-cultural typology can also accommodate the bipartite system if the three efficient fighting systems are defined as jutsu or technique (practicality) driven and the inefficient, martially-inspired arts (do) are defined as self-improvement driven.

IV. CONCLUSIONS

It is important for the further study of the fighting arts that good categorical systems be developed so that no confusion among the various types of fighting arts will interfere with the investigation. Some well-defined classification systems have been presented here and ways to integrate them have been suggested. Other common classification systems, which have been developed rather intuitively, have been described and their separate elements analyzed. Future classification schemes should be created with an awareness of what the author is trying to investigate so that the scheme is useful to the study. Any such scheme must be able to distinguish amongst all the various types of fighting art or specifically state which are being excluded.

Maliszewski's approach seems to be a good starting point for any real substantive analysis. Fighting arts are recognized as having either a current or historical relationship to actual utilization in combat. Maliszewski recognizes the complexity of various secondary characteristics (linear, circular, armed, unarmed, historical origins, etc.) but never loses sight of the common-sense evaluation of function. The category "martial ways" in his system would neatly accommodate the variety of philosophies, goals, and orientations inherent in the various arts under examination.

The formulation is, of course, a general one. It is also essentially a replication of the bujutsu/budo distinction with an overarching category (martial disciplines) to house the entire system. While accurate, therefore, its focus is (most appropriately) on East Asia. Jutsu and do classifications, along with linear/circular, hard/soft, external/internal suffer much the same drawbacks as the IHS system: they are attempts to apply criteria of specific systems to all systems.

In an attempt to expand the cultural horizons of researchers, one of the authors of this piece has suggested analyzing fighting arts with respect to their function in a society and in relation to the level of sophistication of that society. Arts might be further classified according to this concept of efficiency by examining how closely the fighting system matches the sophistication of the society. The development of this system of classification was motivated by the concept that, for a categorization system to be useful, it must demonstrate utility beyond a particular historical, social, and cultural setting. The IHS system, for example, is certainly valid for pre-Meiji Japan. It does not, however, work for fifteenth century Italy, and therefore, it is a narrower type of classification that does not permit us to establish basic ground rules for the systemic examination of "martial arts" worldwide.

Any system used must also be relatively clear. If Reid and Croucher think that the martial arts involve "neutralization," what do they mean? Are there varying levels of neutralization? Is killing one of them? Is the skill of a Roman legionary, who trained long and hard with the sword, spear and shield, an aspect of individual skill, the product of the study of their version of a "martial art," or part of the group-oriented, externally-directed, mortal activity they feel characterizes Western approaches to fighting?

The basic point in this theoretical exercise is to attempt to outline a discussion that will serve to create a classification system free of opinion or prejudice (Reid and Croucher), that is applicable to all societies and times (a failing of IHS), and that sharpens the distinction between systems that were concerned with true combat (killing) and were concerned with something else
(a confusion endemic to public perceptions regarding the "martial arts").

In some respects, the most useful classification system seems to be Armstrong's presentation of a continuum in human behavior surrounding fighting that exhibits behavior stretching from mortal to psychological functions. It demonstrates a nice awareness of the lack of clear-cut boundaries, which frustrate us in the effort to categorize. The only drawback in his scheme is perhaps that it might be difficult to place specific arts at a precise point on the continuum. For example, gladiatorial contests are most certainly mortal contests that simultaneously exhibit aspects of a battlefield encounter, duel, and self-defense situation, and could also conceivably have agonistic, psychological, and philosophical import ("we who are about to die salute you").

What is significant in Armstrong's work is a demonstration of increasing levels of formality, control, and rule-bound behavior in the continuum of human violent activity. We need to be extremely precise at this juncture. "Primitive" combat is often ritualistic in nature, yet generally less complex societies exhibit very little internal specialization and differentiation in terms of social activities and functions: men are also warriors, tools are also weapons. John Keegan's recent review *A History of Warfare* posits the idea that primitive fighting is ritualistic while modern war is not. What Keegan means, however, is that the primitive combat arena is conditioned by social conventions of a very broad type whereas modern battle is specialized and subject to different rules.

Fighting is a complex phenomenon on social, physical and psychological levels. Primitive fighting is "embedded" in other aspects of life. In more complex societies, it becomes more separated from other dimensions of human activity, hence, more formal. Yet it never entirely loses its confused nature. The battlefield melee, for example, has always been precisely what the term implies: a fevered jumble of anything-goes slaughter. As things get more refined in human society, they also get more organized—indeed, Keegan notes in another work that the purpose of military training throughout history is to impose a conceptual order on the inherently chaotic. This passion for order is a concern for organized armies at all places and times. Duels are even more rule-bound, since the reasons for fighting them, the mechanisms for delivering challenges, etc., as well as the tactics permissible, are all clearly and formally established. Self-defense situations, which might seem anomalous, since anything goes when you're trying to save your skin, are nonetheless conditioned by rules—in this case, rules of ethics, which condition outlook and behavior and place the individual in a defensive position. Agonistic arts are even more rule-bound (no hitting below the belt) and certainly the psychological arts are the most refined of all (iaido is a great example here: learn the ten *Zen Nippon Kendo Remmei Seitei-gata,* perform them exactly as demonstrated, and now do them for the rest of your life).

It must be admitted that the desire to bring "order-out-of-chaos" holds great appeal for the authors. It seems to fit well with the general pattern of human culture. It would permit us to fit all classification schemes along a continuum ranging from no rules to many rules. It would permit us to reconcile Donohue's typology with Armstrong's, since they are similar in intent, though different in articulation. Armstrong suggests that there is a gradual increase in rules that condition martial activities as they proceed along a continuum from the battlefield to the R-P-S pole. The cross-cultural typology posits that the more complex a society, the more rules are present, and the more formal and uniform behavior becomes. Combat forms are loosely controlled; combat systems more so; and martial systems, even more so. Martially-inspired arts take the whole human craving for structure to heights that transcend combat needs. By doing so, we even get beyond the efficiency debate (Is judo dangerous? It depends on who's doing it and that's not the point anyway), although it is possible to argue that a surfeit of rules in anything leads to inefficiency. Of course, the same caveat may apply to classification systems which may become inefficient when an excessive number of rules are involved.

If this particular exercise has any utility, it is in its attempt to get at some sense of the elemental nature of what we are talking about when we discuss the "martial arts." How do we reconcile differing opinions, orientations, and styles. What pulls all such activities together? What serves to distinguish them?

As illustrated above, it is possible to make discriminations based upon a series of infinitely narrow and/or subjective criteria. Once we do so, we immediately begin to leave some groups out of our discussion. This is something to avoid if we wish to appreciate the variety and complexity of the martial arts phenomenon.

At the same time, however, we cannot be so generalized in our discussion that we find ourselves retreating behind the facile comment of the cognoscenti that "it's hard to describe, but we know it when we see it."

By suggesting that a fruitful investigative system uses characteristics that are applicable cross-culturally and that, in addition, seem to be consonant with generalized human patterns regarding codification and structure, we would hope to have made some small contribution to the ongoing scholarly exploration of the martial arts.

6. The Liberal Arts and the Martial Arts

Donald N. Levine is an academic and scholar of some repute. His work attempts to draw a parallel between more academic pursuits and martial arts training. In the process he demonstrates the complexity of martial training, as well as making a case for ways in which such activities can assist us in better understanding other fields of endeavor.

From *The Liberal Arts and the Martial Arts*
by Donald N. Levine

A compleat rhetoric for liberal education must address the following six questions:
1. What is "liberal" about liberal education?
2. What kinds of cultural forms are most suitable for the constitution of a liberal program?
3. What kinds of individual capacities should liberal training foster?
4. What are the characteristics of training programs designed to cultivate those capacities?
5. What is the relationship between liberal and utilitarian learning?
6. What is the ethical justification of liberal learning?

In what follows I propose to clarity these questions by asking what we might gain by comparing the liberal arts with the martial arts—those forms of physical training and expression epitomized in the cultures of East Asia by *kung fu, t'ai chi ch'uan,* judo, karate-*do,* kendo, and *aikido.* My point is not to argue that some form of athletic training ought to be an integral part of the liberal curriculum, though on that question I find myself in accord with the views expressed by William Rainey Harper, who said, "The athletic work of the students is a vital part of student life. . . . The athletic field, like the gymnasium, is one of the University laboratories and by no means the least important one." My argument, rather, is that courses of training in the martial arts often constitute exemplary educational programs, and that we might learn something of value for the liberal arts by examining them closely. Just to propose this will perhaps seem to some an act of buffoonery. To suggest that the martial arts are worthy of consideration on the same plane at that usually reserved for the liberal arts—surely that is nothing more than a bad pun. So I must begin by justifying my brazenness in coupling the arts, liberal and martial.

Before proceeding to justify my topic, however, I must confess that one thing about it is indeed gauche. Its two contrasting terms, "liberal" and "martial," are not logically comparable. For "martial" refers to a kind of content—physical training for self-defense—while "liberal" refers to a quality of approach in training. A logical contrast to the martial arts would be either some other kind of physical training, or else some kind of nonphysical training—which, of course, is what we have in mind, what might be called mental or intellectual arts. The logical contrast to liberal would be . . . illiberal. If we provisionally define liberal arts as signifying pursuits undertaken for the sake of personal growth and self-development, then it is clearly the case that both the martial arts and the intellectual arts have both liberal and illiberal forms. So the comparison I want to make here is between the liberal (intellectual) arts and the (liberal) martial arts.

So rephrased, my topic will be justified by arguing that the very culture that originated and legitimated the basic conception of liberal arts we follow in the West supported, at the same time, a conception of martial training as an integral part of the ideal educational program; and that, moreover, the tradition that provided the matrix for the martial arts in the East saw them as a part of what can be called an Oriental program of liberal education as well. Once I have defended those propositions, I shall turn to the comparison that is the heart of this exercise.

I

To talk about liberal training is to talk about a form of education that emerged historically only in two very special cultures, those of classical Greece and China. In ancient Greece, this kind of educational aspiration was linked to the ideal of *paedeia*, the notion of using culture as a means to create a higher type of human being. According to Werner Jaeger, who wrote a celebrated book on the subject, the Greeks believed that education in this sense "embodied the purpose of all human effort. It was, they held, the ultimate justification for the existence of both the individual and the community." That ennobling education took two major forms that were equally praised by the writers of ancient Greece, albeit with different emphases at different times—the cultivation of combative skills, on the one hand, and the contemplative intellect, on the other.

To see the affinity between the martial arts and the arts of contemplation in ancient Greece, let us look at two notions central to Greek thought: the concept of *arete* and the understanding of the divine.

Arete, often translated by the word "virtue," was the Greek term that conveyed the notion of qualitative excellence. Arete signified a special power, an ability to do something; its possession was the hallmark of the man of nobility. The same term arete was used to designate both the special powers of the body, such as strength and vigor, and the powers of the mind, such as sharpness and insight. In the Homeric epics, martial prowess was the kind of arete that was preeminently extolled, but with Xenophanes and other writers of the sixth century B.C., the attainment of *sophia*, or intellectual culture, was hailed as the path to arete. Although Xenophanes wrote in a rather polemical vein against the older ideals of martial arete, most classical Greek writers embraced them both. Thus, the poet Simonides could write, "How hard it is to become a man of true arete, four-square and faultless in hand and foot and mind." For Plato and Aristotle, the list of preeminent virtues begins with courage, and ends with philosophic wisdom (with prudence and justice in the middle).

Although the Greeks are best known to us as the progenitors of secular science and philosophy, they are known to classical scholars as a God-intoxicated people as well. And, so far as I can tell, there are preeminently two human activities that are repeatedly described as divine in Greek thought —the achievements of victors in athletic contests, and the activities of philosophic speculation. Since earliest known history Greek gymnastic activity was connected with the festivals of the gods. The four great pan-Hellenic games, of which the Olympics was the most famous, were cloaked in religious symbolism; thus, both the Olympian and the Nemean games were held in honor of Zeus. As Norman Gardiner has written of the former, the games were "much more than a mere athletic meeting. It was the national religious festival of the whole Greek race." The poetry of Pindar celebrated this linkage with . . . Pindaric rapture. In his triumphal hymns for victors of the athletic contests, Pindar expressed the religious significance of the spectacle of men struggling to bring their humanity to perfection in victorious combat.

One finds the pursuit of metaphysical speculation described with tones no less transcendent. Greek natural philosophers of the sixth century created a conception of a cosmos under the rule of law that offered a focus for their religious ideals; and Pindar's contemporary, Heraclitus, developed a doctrine that located man in that cosmos, one that held that "through its kinship with the 'everlasting fire' of the cosmos the philosophical soul is capable of knowing divine wisdom and harbouring it in itself." A century later, Plato and Aristotle in different ways depicted the activity of philosophic contemplation of pure Being as the most godlike of human activities.

In the classic Greek synthesis, then, the arts of combat and the arts of intellect were conjointly eulogized. They were the vehicles of that supreme educational effort, the cultivation of the virtues, and of the journey to transcendence. In both, the Greeks found a supreme expression of their aesthetic quest, the beauty of the bodily form perfected, and the beauty of the universe refracted in the contemplation of pure cosmic forms.

By the end of the fifth century, however, the unity of body and spirit that Simonides and others idealized became fractured. Due to heightened importance of prizes and spectators, the athletic games became much more competitive. Athletics became professionalized; physical training no longer sought all-round development but aimed to produce strength at the expense of vitality, health, and beauty. Moreover, once the Greeks began to feel that the spirit was separate from or even hostile to the body, Jaeger tells us, "the old athletic ideal was degraded beyond hope of salvation, and at once lost its important position in Greek life."

During the Hellenistic period, the liberal program underwent changes that were fateful for the subsequent evolution of education in the West. Although athletic sports continued as a popular public spectacle, their formative role as part of liberal training declined markedly, and disappeared altogether by the time of the Christian period. There was a similarly progressive decline and eventual disappearance of artistic, especially musical, education, which had also been a major component of education in the classical period. What emerged as the sole respectable form of liberal education was literary studies.

During the Roman period the literary curriculum was further elaborated, particularly the study of grammar and rhetoric. Although early Christian fathers were suspicious of these pagan subjects, by the fourth century A.D. Christian leaders like Augustine embraced major elements of the classical curriculum. Consequently, when the barbarian invasions had swept aside the traditional Roman schools, the Christian church, needing a literary culture for the education of its clergy, kept alive many of the educational traditions that Rome had adapted from the Hellenistic world.

By the sixth century A.D. the clergy had rationalized the literary curriculum into the *trivium*—the art of logic, grammar, and rhetoric—and a few centuries later institutionalized the *quadrivium*—the ancient Pythagorean program of mathematics consisting of arithmetic, geometry, astronomy, and music.

In the ninth century, Charlemagne restored some semblance of higher studies, drawing on traditions that had been maintained in Italian and Irish monasteries. The Carolingian Renaissance, reinforced by the rise of scholasticism, the beginnings of law and medicine as professions, and the recovery of classical knowledge nourished the liberal arts curriculum until it was securely established in the medieval university. During the Renaissance this curriculum was enriched by an emphasis on the humanistic significance of the classic texts. The Reformation brought a renewed effort to subordinate the trivium and quadrivium to religious materials and purposes.

The liberal arts tradition (in its English manifestation) came to America with the Puritan divines in Massachusetts. Liberal education came to be instituted in the American college in a framework that combined Protestant piety and mental discipline. The mental discipline approach, justified in English and Scottish moral philosophy, held that mental faculties were best developed through their exercise. In the course of recitations in the areas of Latin, Greek, and mathematics, the student disciplined mental and moral faculties such as will, emotion, and intellect. As William E Alien wrote: "The student who has acquired the habit of never letting go a puzzling problem—say a rare Greek verb—until he has analyzed its every element, and understands every point in its etymology, has the habit of mind which will enable him to follow out a legal subtlety with the same accuracy."

The rapid modernization of American society after the Civil War gave rise to new perspectives on the role of higher education. Laurence Veysey has identified three rationales of academic reform, which came to compete with that of "mental discipline" in the late nineteenth century. He calls these the programs of utility, research, and liberal culture. The advocates of utility argued that the American university should prepare students to serve the needs of American society for skilled leadership in modern industry, business, and government. Inspired by the model of the German university, the advocates of research insisted that the sole mission of the American university should be the furthering of the frontiers of knowledge. The advocates of liberal culture, however, condemned utility for its crass philistinism, and research for its encouragement of what they considered sterile specialization. In their emphasis on a refined sense of value, through the study of language and literature, the advocates of liberal culture in late nineteenth century America harkened back to the humanists of the Renaissance. The discovery of an essential and irreducible humanity, which they called "character," was made possible by breadth of learning. This, together with the aim of self-realization, was the appropriate rationale for higher education according to such advocates of liberal culture as Barrett Wendell, Charles Eliot Norton, Andrew West, and Woodrow Wilson. Such was the intellectual background behind those well-known experiments in the liberal curriculum following World War I associated with the general education program at Columbia, with Alexander Meiklejohn at Amherst and Wisconsin, and with the Hutchins College at the University of Chicago.

II

Contemporary with the archaic and classical periods of ancient Greece, in China during the Chou dynasty we find an educational program that bears significant resemblance to that of the Greeks. The goal of education was to produce a broadly cultivated person, and this included training both in literary and martial subjects. The curriculum codified during the Chou period consisted of six subjects, often referred to as the liberal arts of classical Chinese education: rituals, music, archery, charioteering, writing, and mathematics. According to the historian Ping Wen Kuo, "A liberal education included five kinds of ritual, five kinds of music, five ways of archery, five ways of directing a chariot, six kinds of writing, and nine operations of mathematics. . . . The training was moral, physical, and intellectual in character. . . . The ideal of education of the time of the Chou seems to have been the harmonious and symmetrical development of the body and mind, and may be said to represent a combination of Spartan and Athenian ideals of education, which called for a training at once intellectual and moral, as well as physical and military."

During the latter sixth century B.C., Confucius articulated the conception of the ideal person to be produced by this Chinese version of paedeia. He defined that ideal as one who possesses wisdom and courage, who is also magnanimous and accomplished in courtesy, ceremonial, and music. He heavily stressed the virtue of sincerity and held that education was a means to gain an enlightened mind, enlightened in the sense of coming to grasp the remarkable harmonies of nature.

In later centuries this ideal of liberal learning was eroded as the study of Confucian texts became viewed in a more utilitarian vein, simply as preparation for the requirements of bureaucratic office. The martial subjects were dropped from the standard curriculum. However, new forms of martial training were incorporated in disciplines followed in Chinese monasteries. To understand that development, we must digress for a moment to ancient India.

When the Hindus rationalized a program of muscular and breathing training in the discipline of yoga, they created a system directed toward the perfection of the body with the intent of making it a fit instrument for spiritual perfection—a perfection consisting of beauty, grace, strength, and adamantine hardness. At an early stage in the development of Buddhism, systematic physical training became a central component of religious discipline. It is said that Gautama was so impressed with Indian fist-fighting as an effective method of unifying mind and body that fist art was incorporated into the framework of Buddhism. This can be seen in the images of certain gods of the Buddhist pantheon—the two Guardian deities, the Devas, and the twelve Divine Generals—who appear in ancient fist-fighting stances.

The movement of Buddhism to China was not only a fateful episode to the history of Buddhism but in the evolution of the martial arts as well. The agent of that migration was the Buddhist monk Boddhidharma, considered the twenty-eighth patriarch in a direct line from Gautama Buddha. In the sixth century A.D., Boddhidharma journeyed from India to China, where he introduced the form of Buddhism known as Dhyana (in Sanskrit), Ch'an (in Chinese), and Zen (in Japanese). While in China, Boddhidharma lived at the Shaolin Monastery in Honan Province. He found the monks there solely concerned with achieving spiritual enlightenment and negligent of their physical health. In fact, they were sickly and fell asleep during *zazen* (seated meditation). As a member of the *kshatriya* (warrior class) as well as a monk, Boddhidharma was very well versed in the fighting arts and understood the interdependence of mental, physical, and spiritual health. He introduced a series of eighteen exercises (the "eighteen hands of the Lo-han") to the monks for the improvement of their health and for their protection against dangerous forces. These exercises became the basis of Shaolin Temple boxing, which, along with other varieties of Chinese boxing, later influenced the development of the fighting arts in Japan, Korea, and Okinawa.

A second line of development in the liberal martial arts of Asia derives from another Chinese religious tradition, that of Taoism. T'ai chi ch'uan (grand ultimate boxing) was evolved to combine certain forms of Shaolin boxing with an emphasis on breathing and inner control based on Taoist breathing practices and medical lore. According to the most prevalent account of the origins of t'ai chi, a Taoist monk of the late Sung Dynasty (twelfth or thirteenth century A.D.), Chang San-feng, created the thirteen basic postures of t'ai chi as bodily expressions of the eight trigrams of the ancient text I *Ching,* and the five basic elements of ancient Chinese cosmology. Somewhat later, a school teacher named Wang Chang-yueh is believed to have linked those postures in a continuous sequence of movement that formed the disciplinary core of the t'ai chi training program.

Yet another set of innovations in the martial arts took place in Japan following the rise of the samurai class after the tenth century and the introduction of Zen Buddhism there in the twelfth century. From this time the culture of bushido, the "way of the warrior," developed gradually from ideas drawn from Buddhism, Confucianism, and Shintoism. Samurai training included unarmed combat, the use of weapons, literary subjects, and training in Zen Buddhism, which provided the courage to face possible death every day. Following the unification and pacification of Japan during the Tokugawa Shogunate, many samurai adapted that Buddhist strain to transform the martial arts from illiberal to liberal uses, vehicles for training that emphasized the spiritual development of participants.

After the suppression of the samurai under the Meiji regime in the latter part of the nineteenth century, new martial arts were specifically created as forms of liberal training. This was the same period, incidentally, when Yang Lu-Chan for the first time taught t'ai chi publicly, in Beijing; until then it had been a secret heritage carefully guarded by certain elite Chinese families. In Japan a number of masters sought to revive the old bushido-Zen ethic by creating new forms that were nonlethal in intent and designed to provide personal growth and spiritual uplift. In 1882, Jigoro Kano, an educator proficient in *jiujutsu*, founded the first Judo Institute in Tokyo. The change from jiujutsu to judo exemplifies, in terminology and practice, the self-conscious transformation of the martial arts from lethal weapons to means of self-development. The suffix *"jitsu"* means technique; jiujutsu was, thus, a technique for inflicting serious damage on an opponent. The suffix *"do"* means "way." It derives from the Chinese Tao, and in Japanese has connotations related to the outlook of Taoism. More fully, "do" means the way to enlightenment, self-realization, and understanding. As conceived by Jigoro Kano, judo—literally, the gentle way—adapted the best techniques from jiujutsu, eliminated the harmful ones, and modified others so they could be practiced safely. As practiced by Kano and his followers, the aim of judo is to perfect oneself by systematic training of the mind and body so that each person works in harmony with others.

Comparable developments took place a little later with other arts. Around 1905, when karate was introduced from Okinawa into mainland Japan, the symbol kara (signifying "Tang," or "Chinese,") was reinterpreted by invoking another meaning of the word kara: "empty." This was to allude not only to the idea of fighting with empty hands—without weapons—but also to the notion of "emptiness" in Zen, that is to say, emptiness of mind, mind like a mirror or water that reflects without distortion, and thus to connote the ideals of selflessness, austerity, and humbleness. Later, this philosophic component was stressed by adding the suffix "do," and some of the preeminent schools now refer to themselves as teaching karate-do; that is, the way of life centering on the empty hand.

In the early 1920's, when experiments to revive liberal learning began to flourish in the United States, a gifted master experienced in all the traditional Japanese martial arts, Morihei Ueshiba, evolved a new system which he called aikido. In this art, he created a program for the cultivation of *ki*, the cosmic energy that flows through one's body and is thought to produce health and spiritual uplift, and the capacity for *ai*, harmonious blending, a blending of the forces within oneself, with other people, and with the natural universe.

A major institutional locus of the martial arts in the Far East today is the educational system. They have come out of the secrecy of monasteries and esoteric cults into the curricula of school systems and the clubs of universities. Although divided into hundreds of specialized forms, which vary considerably in style, techniques, attitudes, and objectives, what can arguably be called their most rationalized forms—those that involve a coherent approach to dealing with aggressive attacks, a systematic approach to training, and a nontrivial grounding in philosophic beliefs—all pursue the goals of developing a harmonious blending of mental and physical powers, a sensitivity to the responses of others, the virtues of calmness and courage under stress, and some form of an experience of transcendence.

This survey of the paedetic curriculum in two great traditions suggests, then, that the coupling of the intellectual and the martial arts is no mere trick of the tongue. Indeed, my sketch suggests that developments within the two traditions where each was perfected exhibit some instructive evolutionary parallels, 1) By the sixth century B.C., both in Greece and China, an ideal and a program of liberal training had evolved, which included both intellectual and martial components. 2) In both cases, this ideal became corrupted in later centuries, as combative arts became commercialized in the Hellenistic period, and as Confucian training became bureaucratized. 3) During the sixth century A.D., a liberal component of the older curriculum became codified and institutionalized in those havens of ideal pursuits, the monasteries. 4) In the medieval period, these paedetic curricula became enriched and extended, with the firm establishment of the trivium and quadrivium in medieval universities, and of the arts of kung fu and t'ai chi ch'uan in Chinese monasteries. 5) In the late nineteenth century, mainly in the United States and Japan, the ideals of those curricula were revived and propagated in the form of new secular programs of liberal training.

III

Let us proceed now to draw on these suggestive parallels between the intellectual arts and the martial arts to address the set of questions I posed at the outset. To begin with, what is liberal about liberal education?

The terms in which Westerners are inclined to think about the distinction between education that is liberal and education that is not—or illiberal, or banausic—were classically formulated by Aristotle. Aristotle's emphasis was not so much on different kinds of subjects as on the spirit in which a subject out of utility, as reading, is useful because it enables one to find numbers in a telephone directory. Or one may pursue a subject because, as we would say, of peer pressure: It is the fashionable "thing to do." But by definition, to act from necessity is not the mark of being free; to seek for utility everywhere is not suited for men who are great-souled and free; and to follow some pursuit because of the opinion of other people, says Aristotle, would appear to be acting in a menial and servile manner. In contrast to these kinds of motives, Aristotle describes motives for the sort of learning that befits a free person: learning that is undertaken for its own sake, learning that is appropriate for promoting happiness and a good life. And, although Aristotle certainly does not deny the need to study the useful arts, he insists that they should not constitute the whole point of learning: People should study drawing, he urges, not merely to avoid being cheated in buying and selling furniture, but for the liberal reason that this study makes one observant of bodily beauty.

Now one does not need to turn to the martial arts to catch the import of Aristotle's distinction, although it may be useful to see how readily it can be exemplified in that domain. Illiberal training in the martial arts, then, would be undertaken out of necessity—learning to fight to prevent your community from being enslaved or slaughtered by an invader; or, for utility—to know how to defend yourself in case you happen to get mugged on the street. And there are other kinds of reasons for studying the martial arts that would render the pursuit illiberal—as when one trains because it is the glamorous thing to do, or to impress one's friends. By contrast, when the martial arts are taught and practiced in a liberal manner, it is for the sake of perfecting oneself as a human being and for acquiring a kind of culture that is intrinsically valuable.

At this juncture, I'd like to share an observation from my own experience with the martial arts that suggests an instructive elaboration on the Aristotelian notion of liberality in education. When I ask persons who have progressed rather deeply into the study of the martial arts why they are doing it, I get an answer that is typically different from what brings people to training in the first place. The reasons why people begin martial arts training are frequently illiberal: for self-defense, or to cure an ailment, or as an outlet for aggression, or because of social inducements. Once they have been training for a while, their motivations usually undergo some subtle change. By the time one has been actively training for a year or two, the reasons tend to converge on a single rationale: I'm training to perfect my mastery of the art. What emerges is the sense of a lifelong quest for perfection, wherein each moment is intrinsically satisfying, but the experience is framed as a part of an unlimited pursuit of growth and improved expression. One is reminded of what John Dewey wrote concerning the fine arts: that "the works of the fine arts are not merely ends in themselves which give satisfaction, but their creation and contemplation whet the appetite for new effort and achievement and thus bring a continuously expanding satisfaction." What this suggests is a criterion for liberal learning that amends the familiar classical definitions: that education is free and liberating insofar as it involves the quest for mastery of some domain of autonomous forms, forms that are in themselves the free creation of human spirit. And because that world of form is in principle limitless, this entails a connection with transcendence that is part of the attraction toward liberal learning.

So I would add, as another component of the generic definition of liberal education, martial and intellectual, that it is an enterprise devoted to the acquisition of cultural forms for their own sake. Having said this, my next question is then: what types of cultural forms are most suitable for a liberal program?

Once we have distinguished liberal education from the various illiberal forms of training—training for occupations, for solving particular social problems, for transmitting a certain tradition, and the like—there remains the more complicated problem of defining the best content for a liberal curriculum. Different philosophies of liberal education tend to take one of three positions. One position holds that the liberal curriculum should consist of a set of fundamental questions and plausible answers, e.g., those contained in a list of Great Books, or those simply having to do with the nature of the world, and man's place in it. A second position holds that the liberal curriculum should consist of the most important structures of organized knowledge, e.g., basic acquaintance with the principal disciplines of the humanities, social sciences, and natural sciences. A third position holds that the liberal curriculum should represent primarily those basic modes of inquiry and expression exemplified in the disciplines, e.g. how a scientist conducts experiments, or how a poet constructs a sonnet.

A strong case could be made for viewing each of these as the central principle for a liberal curriculum, and perhaps an even stronger case for a perspective that attempted to represent them all in some balanced way. But what all of them have in common is a stress on what Georg Simmel called objective culture: the external representations of reality and the externalized expressions of meaning that have been created in human history. The true cultivation of individuals, by contrast, takes place in what Simmel called subjective culture: the personal growth that comes about through the internal appropriation of cultural forms.

The advantage of looking at the martial arts in this context is that such training is almost exclusively concerned with the development of subjective culture—in this case, the competences of bodily movement that enable one to defend oneself in certain stylized ways. There is simply no way to think about the martial arts curriculum without dealing with the ways in which personal capacities of various sorts—perceiving, moving, responding—are nurtured and shaped and perfected. Thus, the martial arts curriculum provides a model for a kind of liberal training in which the principle of the learner's capacities is unmistakably and unavoidably at the center of attention. Although this principle was prominent in early nineteenth-century American notions of liberal intellectual learning, which focused on the goal of mental discipline, it has fallen by the way in contemporary discussions. The principle deserves, I believe, to be revived and viewed afresh as an important basis for organizing the modern liberal curriculum.

Once we have set the cultivation of subjective capacities as a primary goal of liberal education, however, we must deal with what is perhaps the most complicated of all the questions in the theory and practice of liberal education: What competences should be cultivated? And the obvious answer to that question is another question: What competences are there? Open ten books about competences, and you will find seventeen lists. How does one compose an inventory of competences that can be ordered and ranked so as to provide a set of priorities for liberal education?

Because I do not think this is a matter that can be resolved definitively for all time, or even that there is a single best way to resolve it at any given moment, I would not look to the martial arts for a model of how to solve it. The problem of identifying a basic list of competences is nearly as intractable in the martial as in the intellectual arts. But the martial arts can be helpful on the question, because they illustrate so transparently what the issues are and how one might grapple with them.

The complications here stem from the fact that disciplines emerge historically as concrete traditions, while technical competences can be generalized and used across a variety of disciplines. For example, aikido is a tradition that uses diffused energy, circular body movements, and wrist and elbow throws, while karate relies on concentrated energy, direct body movements, and punches, blocks, and kicks. Yet in both of them a basic movement is the straightforward punch. Moreover, both have a variety of defenses against said punch. So one could imagine a type of competence called punching and responding to punching, the first learnable within either of the two arts but usable beyond, the other requiring some new curricular effort to bring together a wide variety of defenses against punches into a single training program. Just in the last few years, in fact, some martial arts programs have come out with eclectic training approaches not unlike this.

There is, moreover, a set of generalized competences involved in various ways in all the martial arts that may be formulated as follows: Know oneself; know the other; and observe the right timing in one's response to the other. The idea of self-knowledge in the martial arts is tied to a concern for being centered. One must be in touch with the true center of one's being. One must be unified, the hands with the arms, the limbs with the torso, the body with the feelings and the mind. One must be poised in a state between relaxation and readiness to move—at all times. In the words of the seventeenth-century martial artist, Miyamoto Musashi, "Do not become tense and do not let yourself go. Keep your mind on the center and do not waver. Calm your mind, and do not cease the firmness for even a second. Always maintain a fluid and flexible, free and open mind."

And yet preoccupation with oneself and one's readiness to act, by itself, would be foolhardy. One must be alert to the dispositions and responses of others no less. One must be aware of the other's balance points, the "four corners" of his position in which he is vulnerable. One must sense the precise direction and intensity of an attack from the other. In aikido, the term ai, or harmony, refers in an important sense to the idea of blending effectively with the energy of one's attacker.

Finally, the relational field between self and other must be viewed in dynamic terms, such that the timing of one's response to the other is all important. It does no good to be centered in oneself, and aware of the flow of the other's energy, if one responds too soon, or too late, to the other's attack. So a great deal of emphasis in training focuses on these three areas: how to maintain one's own center; how to perceive and blend in with the energy of the other; and how to time one's responses with pinpoint precision.

What this suggests for the intellectual arts is that we might well start looking for basic forms of intellectual competence that are not tied to concrete traditions. In my judgment, this constitutes one of the most exciting challenges facing the academic profession today. Those who are honest about the matter acknowledge that a concrete tradition—sociology, say, or biochemistry—is rarely coterminous with a particular set of competences. I know, for example, that the distinctive skills needed to analyze social phenomena in the economistic terms of rational exchange, or the culturological terms of symbolic codes, are practiced across all of the social science disciplines, including cultural anthropology and economics. The challenge today is to take stock of the enormous changes in all the intellectual disciplines over the last few decades and, for purposes of liberal training, attempt to translate them into competence fields that can be truly defensible components of a future liberal curriculum.

Closely connected to the question of what subjective capacities are to be cultivated in the liberal curriculum is that of the kind of training program best suited to develop those capacities. On this question, I believe, training programs in the martial arts offer much that might be relevant to the design of training programs in the intellectual arts. Of many possible suggestions, let me mention two:

The first is the stress on practice—regular, systematic, unremitting prac- tice. The components of each art must be identified and laid out in such a way as to admit increasing mastery through incessant practice. As Miyamoto Musashi has written: "Practicing a thousand days is said to be a discipline, and practicing ten thousand days is said to be refining." One must practice continuously, and make a lot of mistakes, so that one can be corrected, and be ever on the lookout for ways to refine one's art.

Second, there is a sequence of phases in developing the practice of one's art. Gradations of rank, marked by a succession of tests that examine clear- ly defined levels of competence, form a crucial part of the training. Beyond that, there is a kind of progression, common to all arts, that I would call the road to the transcendence of mere technique. One begins by self-conscious- ly practicing a certain technique. One proceeds slowly, deliberately, reflec- tively, but one keeps on practicing until the technique becomes internalized and one is no longer self-conscious when executing it. After a set of tech- niques has been thoroughly internalized, one begins to grasp the principles behind them. And finally, when one has understood and internalized the basic principles, one no longer responds mechanically to a given attack, but begins to use the art creatively and in a manner whereby one's individual style and insights can find expression.

Notions like these seem to me enormously suggestive for training programs in the intellectual arts. As one of their possible implications, I would stress the importance of some specialization as an essential component of a truly liber- al education. There is simply no way to acquire any art to the point where it becomes truly effective as a means of advanced personal growth without the intensity of involvement that requires years of work and progressive mastery. Whether the capacity in question is knowing how to interpret an ancient text, or how to perform chemical experiments in the lab, or to formulate and ana- lyze a problem of public policy, an enormous amount of practice is required in order to be able to progress in some field from techniques to principles to expression (and, indeed, if you will, to develop a sense of personal ground- edness and sensitivity to the objects and knowledge of how and when to time interventions). That is the rationale, I believe, for including concentration programs as an integral component of a full curriculum in liberal education.

I V

I want now to discuss the question of the relationship between liberal and utilitarian learning. The rhetoric of liberal educators vacillates between two apparently contradictory positions. On the one hand, we say that liberal training is a good in itself, superior in worth to those illiberal pursuits that are merely practical. On the other hand, we often say that liberal education is really the most practical of all. Is this just double-talk, somewhat like saying: I never borrowed your book, and besides, I returned it to you last week?

Perhaps, but let us look at the martial arts once more to see if some clarification of this matter can be found. In the martial arts, the question of practical utility is always right at hand. In training dojos one often hears an instructor make some offhand reference to what might happen in real situations—"on the street," as they say. Yet nothing could be more clearcut than the difference between an applied training program in self-defense and a liberal curriculum in the martial arts. If you want to acquire some immediate skills for the street, I would say: don't take up one of the martial arts, but take a crash eight-week course in self-defense; just as I would say, if all you want is a job as a lab technician or an interviewer in a survey research organization, take a crash vocational course in those areas. Yet there is, I believe, a higher practical value in the liberal form of self-defense training. By proceeding to the point where one has mastered the basic principles of the art of self-defense, one has acquired resources for responding to a much wider range of threatening situations and a readiness to respond that flows from basic qualities of self-control, calmness, and courage that one has internalized as a result of years of dedicated training. It certainly would be advantageous to combine some techniques of practical self-defense with a liberal martial training—remember that Aristotle, after all, advocated that training in useful arts can be combined with liberal training—but then the former are enhanced by being grounded in a broader conception of the principles of direct combat. The argument may proceed similarly in regard to the liberal intellectual arts: by learning not merely the specific facts and techniques of a particular subject matter but its most basic principles and methods and by understanding these as exemplified in a range of fields, one has gained capacities that enable one to respond intelligently and independently, critically, and creatively, to the conditions of a complex and rapidly changing environment, the kind of environment in which all of us are now fated to spend our lives. This is like the ideal that Pericles attributed to the free citizens of Athens, "To be able to meet every variety of circumstance with the greatest versatility—and with grace."

The last question I want to raise in this comparative exercise may be put as follows: Isn't there something basically immoral in this program for liberal training? Doesn't it focus too much on the individual at the expense of the community? What's worse, couldn't it simply set people up—by training them in the arts—to carry out amoral or even vicious purposes? No matter how much the arts are glamorized, do they not only amount to sets of technical skills that can be put to evil purposes? And if my argument that liberal training produces a higher form of utilitarian competence is sound, then does it not follow that the person with an advanced liberal education has the capacity to be more evil than others?

Certainly this is a question that can never be far from the mind of those training in the martial arts. Indeed, the old masters in Asia were often very selective about whom they allowed to train with them, for they feared the consequences of putting their lore into the hands of those who might use these very potent powers for destructive purposes. In Japanese culture there is in fact a social type associated with that negative possibility—the *ninja*. The ninja is precisely one who has mastered martial techniques but puts them to selfish or destructive purposes. And I must say, before we liberal educators take too much pride in offering a wholly blameless product, that we must come to terms with the possibility of creating intellectual ninjas—people who are very adept indeed in the manipulation of linguistic and mathematical symbols, and other intellectual capacities, and use them in the service of the basest opportunistic motives and even for destructive purposes.

To say this is to raise the most fundamental issue of all about the liberal arts: the need for an ideological framework in which they find some ethical grounding. Precisely because the immoral potentialities of martial arts are so transparent, this question is harder to dodge. It is answered forthrightly by ethical formulations associated with the educational programs of all those martial arts I would call liberal today. In a manual of t'ai chi ch'uan, for example, one reads:

> The technique of self-defense implies a coherent vision of life that includes self-protection. The world is viewed as an ever-changing interplay of forces. Each creature seeks to realize its own nature; to find its place in the universe. Not to conquer, but to endure. The assumption is that there are hostile forces. One can be attacked by animals, by angry or arrogant people, or just by the forces of Nature, within and without. In the human world, attack is verbal and emotional as often as it is physical. The most subtle and manipulative struggles are the ones of which we are the least conscious. But the prescription for survival is always the same—integrity. [In the martial arts] this is more than a moral adage, it is a physical actuality.

The practice of aikido is suffused by the kind of ethical vision embodied in these words by its founder, Morihei Ueshiba:

> Understand Aikido first as budo and then as a way of service to construct the world family.

True budo is the loving protection of all beings with a spirit of reconciliation.
Reconciliation means to allow the completion of everyone's mission.
True budo is a work of love. It is a work of giving life to all beings, and not
killing or struggling with each other.... Aikido is the realization of love.

As college educators face the need to develop a fresh rhetoric for liberal
education, a rhetoric responsive to the enormous changes undergone in
recent decades by the academic world and the global environment, we may
do well to seek the insights and suggestions that can come from stepping
outside our customary universe of discourse on the subject. This is a process
we are familiar with from the numerous instances of cross-fertilization
among the intellectual arts and disciplines. The foregoing essay at comparison has explored one such channel of cross-fertilization, with the following
results:

1. We have raised the question of the difference between liberal and illiberal learning.
2. The experience of the martial arts suggests that one principle of the liberal program might be formulated as the cultivation of free cultural
   forms for their own sake.
3. We have asked about the kinds of cultural forms appropriate to a liberal
   program. The martial arts exemplify for us a neglected type of culture,
   that which concerns the perfection of the capacities of human subjects.
4. We have asked about the types of subjective cultivation that constitute a
   plausible inventory. The martial arts clarify for us the problem of distinguishing between concrete traditions and general technical capacities.
5. We have asked about the character of training programs appro p r i a t e
   to develop such capacities. The martial arts exemplify for us the significance of practice; of a phased program of development, from techniques
   to principles to expression; and of the need for specialized work to develop any capacity through that curriculum.
6. We have asked about the relation of liberality to utility. The martial arts
   exemplify the way in which liberally acquired powers are of especial utilitarian value in a complex and changing environment.
7. We have asked about the moral justification of liberal training. The martial arts provide models in which those questions are resolved through
   being linked to an ethical worldview.

7. The Martial Arts and the American Imagination

The martial arts have come under increasing investigation by scholars interested in exploring how culture and history have shaped them and investigating the varying and complex motivations people have for practicing them in the modern world. This selection discusses the internal psychological aspects of training and the emotional hold martial arts can exert on the psyche.

From *Warrior Dreams* by John Donohue

During a period when I was deeply immersed in my early research on the Japanese martial arts, which is to say, during a time when I was intensely involved in actual physical training, the terrors, demands and effects of these arts on their practitioners were never far from my mind. This was partly because, in the best tradition of participant-observation, I was experiencing some of these things myself. At night it was not uncommon that, in the fuzzy, half-conscious transition into sleep, I would involuntarily twist and twitch, still in the throes of training. Teachers and lessons, combat and form lived on even in my dreams.

I remember one dream very vividly. Unlike many of my other martial dreams, this one was deceptively placid. I was outside my home in the heavily shadowed streets of a suburban night, dressed in the dark uniform of a student of the traditional art of Japanese fencing, kendo. Curiously enough, I was also without the weapons used in such training. I was standing in the shadows quietly, merely observing the deserted streets. I gradually tilted forward until my body floated parallel to the ground, and began to propel myself down the street with my fingertips. I sped through the night, gliding invisibly past the occasional pedestrian or automobile. I felt disembodied, yet fully present, and also implicitly understood that I was invisible to the people I saw, and that this invisibility was somehow mysteriously linked to the garb I was clothed in. I flew through the night, a part of the darkness, gathering speed and momentum, until the dream faded.

There is an intensely personal dimension to the martial arts, but this should not obscure their group nature. Any cultural tradition, while undoubtedly a construct that reverberates through the silent world of the mind, is also by definition a shared experience that must be taught and learned within the social realm. We have seen how the impact of time and circumstance, the cumulative effect of social process, has acted to change ideas concerning the martial arts and the ways in which they are practiced. We noted that the martial arts seem attractive to contemporary Americans, and that this has to do partly with the fact that they fit so well with the stories Americans have told concerning fighters.

The American myth of the warrior has important things to tell us about the social dimension of martial arts practice as well. Although on one level the warrior myth (and the martial arts) glorifies the individual, it is simultaneously one that is justified only by its essentially social orientation. This is because the warrior hero ultimately labors in the service of others. In addition, this myth, like any tale, gains resonance only in the process of being told and retold to others—that is, within a social context. As contemporary American martial artists labor in their training halls, they attempt to give expression to visions of the martial arts that are conditioned by their own time, social place, and levels of understanding. This expression is one that, while intensely important from a personal perspective, is valuable in part because it also serves to anchor the individual within a particular community. It is not possible to adequately explore the question of the relevance of these arts today without acknowledging their role in the forging of a sense of social place and community.

Even martial artists themselves will acknowledge this fact. Their pride in their association with a martial arts school is obvious. It is articulated through dress and behavior and demonstrated by their constancy in training and their consideration for one another. As one instructor told me: "most people think they are coming here to learn self-defense; what they are really coming here for is to belong to something, to have friends."

It was previously related how the social and intellectual climate of the postmodern world has helped fuel interest in the type of nontraditional spiritual systems found in the martial arts. Uncertainty regarding what to believe, of the individual's place in the order of things, is a condition that seems to extend beyond the realm of the supernatural into that of the social as well. Theorists have long noted the sense of alienation, rootlessness, and lack of connection experienced in the complex societies of the contemporary world. While questions regarding identity, place, and purpose are universal ones all humans wrestle with, the particular conditions of life today seem to complicate the process of formulating creditable and satisfying answers. In a society characterized by rapid change in areas as different as technology and social roles, among highly mobile populations attempting to survive within a formal market economy, how are human relations created that generate a sense of stability, reassurance, and transcendent importance?

These are questions being asked (either implicitly or explicitly) by many people and institutions. In the fiercely individual, pluralistic society of late twentieth-century America, the pursuit of social linkage takes a number of forms. Certainly the discovery, revival, or outright creation of alternative traditions that attempt to incorporate the individual into a meaningful system of beliefs and behaviors is symptomatic of this quest for a sense of place. It is my contention that the martial arts are one such attempt.

If we examine some of the characteristics of the practice of the martial arts, this point may become clearer. It is interesting that the Asian symbolism and ritual trappings of *karate* have been retained and perpetuated in training halls embedded in the vastly different social environment of contemporary America. This suggests that the ritual nature of karate is not mere exotic window-dressing, but an important component of what makes karate so attractive to modern Americans.

Most people assume martial arts study is a process relating to the development of personal skill that will enhance the individual's stature. It is particularly interesting to note that such personal aggrandizement requires the martial artist, so deeply immersed in the myth of the rugged individual, to surrender autonomy and, in fact, become the member of a highly organized group. The mythology of the martial arts holds that these arts are at least partially esoteric in the way that they fuse physical and mystic technique. These stories' overtones lend credence to the belief that, while it may be possible to acquire some skill in the martial arts through training created by objective analysis and intellectual effort, true mastery is dependent on transmission of insight from a "master." Access to such individuals is typically gained through affiliation with a training hall and its associated organization. Once again, in pursuit of individual identity, the trainee is propelled into relations with the group.

The emphasis in martial arts training halls is therefore not one oriented around the whims of the individual, but rather emphasizes the need of the individual to conform to the customs, ideas, and practices of the group. In aspects as varied as dress, language, movement, and belief, students are relentlessly required to adhere to group principles. Membership in such groups is not a casual thing, and consequently individuals develop a complex and profound sense of group identity.

This group affiliation is of vital importance. It is through the group that the esoteric skills will be learned. The lore and customs of the group shape the process of transmission. Interaction within the community is, in essence, the mechanism through which insights and training take place. Finally, the group serves to validate the accomplishment of the individual. Like the warrior hero, the martial artist's achievements only take on meaning in regard to others.

As in any tightly knit corporate community, various symbols are utilized to signal membership and status. Since the art of karate has been utilized as a case study throughout our discussion so far, I will focus on it again, noting only in passing that the symbolic sets and ritual constructs for this art are very similar to those observed in other modern martial arts, particularly those in the Japanese and Korean traditions.

The karate training hall is a hierarchical society. Within this group, trainees participate and believe in a system for evaluating the worth of the individual by abstract standards which are unique to the group itself. Upon entering the *dojo*, the novice is plunged into a world where a type of achieved status, determined by the level of skill in the particular system being studied, organizes the social universe. All individuals can be easily placed within the social hierarchy by virtue of overt skill and even more subtle cues such as symbolic dress. All members wear a standard uniform—the *gi*—as well as belts whose colors indicate student rank.

Various *kyu* levels are associated with different colors, while *dan* grades are normally represented by black. The kyu/dan system of most modern martial arts systems was pioneered by Kano Jigoro for Kodokan judo. Originally, there were three belt colors: white and brown for kyu ranks, black for dan grades, but colors seem to have proliferated since then. As if to underscore the hunger for structure and hierarchy on the part of American martial artists, in many schools belts are awarded in practically all colors of the rainbow, different colors for each increment of advancement. Some schools even supplement belt color with "stripes" analogous to the hash marks common in the uniforms of the armed services.

Different ranks address each other with varying levels of formality—the bowing involved in the martial arts is by now so well known as to be almost not worth mentioning. Even the training hall itself is often symbolically demarcated into realms of higher and lower status.

Advancement in the closed society of the martial arts school is obtained through following the teachings of a special individual whose insight and experiences are unconditionally respected and valued, and who has himself undergone the process of initiation into the secrets of the system. This person occupies the pinnacle of this ranked society, and is the instructor. The form of address varies from school to school, but this individual is most typically addressed as *sensei*. Once again reflecting the seemingly contradictory American taste for hierarchy, it is now common for chief instructors to be referred to as "master" or variations on traditional Japanese titles such as *shihan*. An orthodox martial artist of the old school may remark that mastery is perhaps a goal but never the source of a title, but the student of society finds it highly significant. Contemporary society is predicated on equality and individualism, yet the bureaucratic, fragmented nature of modern life makes people aware that the self-made man is increasingly rare. The fact that thirty- year-old blue-eyed masters of esoteric martial systems seem to spring up like mushrooms is a significant occurrence in the contemporary American martial arts. It underscores the fact that martial artists are seeking an added dimension to things that will assist them in gaining a sense of control in their lives and that this dimension is manifest in the physical skill of extraordinary individuals within the martial arts community. All students, regardless of rank, come to feel strong emotional ties to their sensei, which are the product of the respect they have for this individual's physical skills and (ideally) spiritual development as well. The attitude of total trust which is necessary if a student is to learn from the instructor also contributes toward the emotional ties which ideally bind sensei and student.

The teacher is the gate through which the added dimension of the martial arts is approached. The stress on rank and hierarchy in the modern martial arts is directly proportionate to the strength of the hope that members hold for them. A sensei must by definition be a master if he or she is to serve as the conduit through which a mystical transference of knowledge is to take place. The emphasis on the student's precise, almost formulaic imitation of the techniques taught also reflects the sense that the transmission of the content of the art is achieved by almost spiritual means. This is due in part to the impact of religious ideas on the theory of modern martial arts.

This power transference/enlightenment experience is the end point of training, however (even if we assume it ever actually occurs). For most martial artists, validation of status and the group's hierarchy takes place on a more mundane level and continues in all training sessions. In a sense, physical movement within the training hall, which is minutely conditioned by the precepts of the group, takes on a symbolic dimension as a demonstration of fidelity to the community's basic principles. There are innumerable styles of karate, all of which have altered technique slightly. All claim to be effective, and each group's members believe strongly in the superiority of its style. This faith really has nothing to do with efficacy, however. In the martial arts world, the defeat of a particular stylist reflects merely on the individual's skill, not the style's worth. It is the experience of training in a group setting that makes the trainee so sure that his or her style is authentic. The sight of so many of the style's disciples leaves little doubt in the mind that the trainee is engaged in an activity that is widely judged as significant. Once convinced that the community's values and goals are authentic, the trainee can then accept the standards of the group as a way to gauge social status.

For it is in submitting to the standards of the training hall, its instructor(s) and members that the individual creates a personal identity within the system. This identity is an individual one, carved out by personal effort, yet it is an activity that is ultimately oriented toward others. Through training the individual finds a sense of self, yet it is a sense firmly rooted in group expectations and evaluations.

This is, of course, the reason behind the emphasis on adherence to group principles, to orthodoxy, to "tradition." It is not just an appeal to history or lineage to demonstrate the age and authenticity of the style in question. A trainee submits to the tyranny of the group precisely because, by faithfully imitating the physical techniques, customs, and outlooks of the school, he or she forges another link in the chain of continuity that gives the organization its corporate character. It is this group nature that is of extreme importance in the martial arts.

Thus behavior within the group is as significant for martial artists as are the ideas concerning that behavior. *Karateka* participate in a number of structured, stylized activities relating to the art. These may be viewed as ritual activities in the classic sense. These rituals are the physical expression of beliefs concerning the martial arts, and serve to link individual desires with those of the group.

We may isolate a number of significant activities in training. There are tournaments and competitions of various types, where individuals and teams vie for recognition of their fighting and performance skills. These are contests or demonstrations, and take on many of the same characteristics of athletic and artistic spectacles everywhere. Trainees also participate in seminars and workshops, and very often must take part in examination performances before judges who decide on promotion in rank. For most karateka, however, their most common experience of karate's ritual dimension is that of the regular training session. Under the supervision of an instructor, students labor at the acquisition of skill in a training hall set aside for this purpose. It is this aspect of karate training that I would like to examine here.

Training is formalized and stereotyped in terms of the structure and progression of activities. In addition, like many physical activities that approach the ritual, it is extremely rule-bound; it possesses a charter that underlies the specific physical actions. Practitioners of martial arts like karate are enmeshed in a highly symbolic cultural activity in which color, language, and motion all act to transmit specific messages about the world as interpreted in the dojo. Above all, training shares a characteristic universal to all ritual activity: the channeling of brain functions into paths outside normal experience.

The experience of participating in karate training is ideally one in which the physical and mental aspects of the person become fused, and indeed, one in which the distinction between individual and group goals becomes indistinct. The frequency with which this goal is realized is difficult to establish, however, and so serves to underscore the distinction between the ideal structure and purpose of ritual activities and the real experience of individuals engaging in them. In this light, karate training is both a ritual that expresses the aspiration of trainees as well as a vehicle that effects the realization of these aspirations, a common feature of rituals. We may additionally speculate that part of karate's attraction lies in the fact that, while "enlightenment" may be a frustratingly elusive goal for most trainees, the side effects of intense physical training and mental concentration can act to create physiological states that mimic those traditionally associated with "higher states of consciousness." Thus, while on one level it matters very much whether the calm exhibited by a karateka is a reflection of mu-shin or the effect of the body's production of endorphins, in terms of creating an altered physiological state in trainees, the results are very similar. In a maddening way characteristic of the Zen philosophy which has come to strongly influence the martial arts, the goal and the technique used to reach that goal merge and become indistinguishable.

Thus an overt point of the martial arts in general is to create the "oneness" of *mu-shin*, a condition that can be interpreted as both an accurate description of the physical experience of training itself and as mental state whose identification has been strongly influenced by the sensibility and vocabulary of Zen Buddhism. In objective terms, both the sensation and mind-set have a wide appeal for participants in the United States today.

The mind-body unity that is the goal and end point of the focus developed through karate training is not unique to this activity. As described by the researcher Csikszentmihalyi, this sensation of "flow" is common to a variety of physical and mental activities. Certainly a central concern of religions and ritual activities associated with them is the creation of a type of "optimal experience" that approximates the flow experience.

In an increasingly secular society, however, Americans no longer invest a large portion of their time in religious ritual that may generate such experiences. They do, however, continue to search for occasions of flow. Ritual structure creates an environment conducive toward the creation of this experience, and this may in part explain the attraction of karate training for individuals: it offers a highly structured and symbolic activity that facilitates the focus of psychic and physical energy to create a flow experience.

The intersection of personal experience as generated through the physical activity of training with an expanded social sense of the self is characteristic of this type of training. Students engage in study with an overwhelming concern about their personal development of skill. Their attention is initially very narrowly concentrated. It is significant that, while it is rare to hear instructors in many karate dojo call for more *ki* from their students, it is not at all uncommon to hear them plead for more *kime*, or "focus." An ongoing lesson in karate training centers around the ability to focus properly, and the important adjunct to that lesson is that one learns to focus only by expanding awareness to include other members of the training community. In the dojo, all members can be potential sources of instruction for the trainee. Once again, it is ironic to note that the mechanism whereby a karateka develops an expanded sense of self is the same mechanism whereby that individual learns not to be absorbed in self-concentration.

This is partly the significance of the philosophical contentions of martial arts masters concerning the need for true students to abandon concern with themselves entirely. In the terminology of Zen, this state is called no mind (mu-shin). In karate, trainees often recall that Funakoshi Gichin, widely viewed as the father of modern karate-do, was fond of saying that one of the significant things about the name karate is that the sound "kara" can also mean "hollow," and that the true karateka should strive to be empty of self-absorption.

So in developing the self, trainees also learn to lose a little of that self.

It is abetted through the training process itself, with its heavy emphasis on precise emulation and valuation of orthodoxy. The whole concept of mystic transmission from a master underscores the relative impotence of the individual trainee; power is obtained only through group affiliation. To persevere in training, the karateka learns that mu-shin is not merely an exotic and obscure idea, it is a living metaphor for the process of surrender necessary for group integration.

The corporate nature of martial arts training is significant. The contemporary organization of the martial arts, particularly karate, has been decisively shaped by the social templates of East Asia, and most commonly those of traditional Japan. Although transplanted to an contemporary America, the basic organizational paradigm has undergone surprisingly little erosion. An emphasis on the corporate nature of such groups, a stress on hierarchy, and the importance of superior-inferior relations endures in the martial arts to this day.

That this is so, even in the United States, may initially have been due in part to the dominance of Japanese instructors in these arts. The proliferation of non-Japanese students and schools of martial arts around the world today indicates, however, that the fact of Japanese numerical dominance may be changing. Yet it is interesting to note that the strong Japanese cultural influence still remains. The international dimension of the martial arts should prompt us to ask if there are other reasons why, if much of the organizational blueprint for these arts' organization is Japanese, this structure has endured in a non-Japanese cultural environment? In places other than Japan, would it not be easier, more "rational" and "efficient" (more Western) to study these techniques without their ritual trappings?

These questions lay bare another reason for the unique organization of martial arts training halls: one that relates to questions of the maintenance of group solidarity as well as political and economic control. The organization of modern dojo is, in fact, strikingly similar to a type of Japanese voluntary association, often associated with the performing and other arts, which has very overt economic functions: the *iemoto*. Basically, the iemoto is a voluntary association which consists of a master of some art or skill and his or her disciples. Such an organization can be small or can grow to be a vast pyramidal organization with more than a million members. Each of the master's disciples in turn forms a nucleus around which new members gather. Such branch organizations, formed around a second generation of masters, produce new disciples, who in turn become third generation masters with their own disciples, and so on.

Despite differences in the formal identification of martial arts schools, the structural organization and hierarchical emphasis of the various modern martial arts systems remains virtually the same. They are hierarchical, ranked structures which emphasize dyadic relations between individuals of different statuses.

The emphasis among martial artists on the quality of their school and their instructor is a direct result of the hierarchical tradition of transmission of martial skills. This sense of transmission of a skill from a grand master to disciples of the first generation who, in turn, pass these skills on to disciples of the next generation, and so on, is highly reminiscent of the characteristics of iemoto organization. Indeed, very often the ultimate source of an instructor's authority is the connection between himself and a recognized master of the art. These links form a sort of genealogical pedigree which validate an instructor's claim of competence.

The master/disciple system has a political (in its widest sense) dimension in that it serves to regulate access to the arts by designating only certain individuals as certified teachers. The process of granting teaching certificates is a carefully controlled one. Since pedigree is an important criterion in establishing oneself as a martial artist, and as the demand for teachers of these arts increases, the mechanisms for granting dan ranks are extremely significant. The process of formal examination before a certified instructor, and very often the charging of examination fees and the recording of promotions with head dojo in Japan standardizes and controls the trainee's process of advancement, serves as a validating system for creating new instructors, and formalizes and regulates relations between instructors. Most dojo belong to national or international organizations which regulate their operations and provide business and technical assistance.

For the modern martial arts are also big business. The control of accreditation and the perpetuation of orthodoxy is not simply a question of esthetics and skill. There is an overt politico-economic dimension present as well. In most dojo, students pay fees for training, registration with the head dojo, and for promotion. Many instructors thus support themselves as professional trainers or coaches. This is the case both in Japan and in other countries, particularly in popular arts such as judo (an Olympic sport) and karate. There is a growing martial arts industry complete with periodicals, book publishers, and equipment supply houses. The close regulation of student promotion and the granting of teaching licenses can thus be revealed as an overtly political process concerned with allocating "territories," managing resources, ensuring that markets are not oversaturated and that quality control remains high. The sense of vested interest, which is palpably financial in nature, is thus nicely buttressed by a constellation of socio-cultural elements often associated with the martial arts, which today act to regulate and control the spread of these arts, even in the United States.

In a sense, all the ideas and actions, symbols and rituals which inform action in the martial arts training hall deal with individual and group questions of purpose and place. From this perspective, it can be demonstrated that the martial arts have a social function concerned with the creation and maintenance of social identity on a number of different levels.

There is a strong corporate identity, reinforced by symbolism, ritual, and custom that creates a formally-codified system for assigning social status and rank within the organization itself. There is a very real sense of personal allegiance to the school, it's founder, and, on a most immediate level, the head instructor of a particular dojo. There is acceptance of both an ideological system which offers a rationale for engaging in such training. In addition, the absolute insistence on the transmission of skill from sensei to disciple, whatever additional political and economic implications it may have, strongly reflects the assumption of a supernatural dimension to training and so increases the American valuation of the experience.

Finally, martial artists, in addition to sharing a common ideological charter and strong sense of group identity expressed through a variety of symbolic mechanisms, are also members of a highly organized, rigidly stratified society, which aids in the management and perpetuation of the group itself.

Once again we are presented with extremely complex factors that contribute to the popularity of these arts in contemporary America. It is perhaps indicative of the unfolding development of our understanding that we are presented here with suggestions that it is the concatenation of myth, hope, the search for individual aggrandizement, the need for social connection, as well as more material considerations, that have helped condition the shape and tenor of the American martial arts experience.

8. Miyamoto Musashi and the Search for Success

In this selection, Hurst examines the interesting history of Musahi's Book of Five Rings. From an historian's perspective, the wide Western interest in this book seems at odds with historical reality and can be attributed at least in part to stereotyped ideas about Japanese society and culture, as well as a general fasination with the "mystic East." Looked at another way, it underscores how the martial arts engage the imagination of people from all over the world, and how they adopt, adapt, and reiniterpret these systems to fit their own particular needs.

From *Samurai on Wall Street* BY G. CAMERON HURST

The tremendous success of James Clavell's Shogun, both as a book and a television miniseries, demonstrated the popular appeal of the Japanese samurai to modern-day Americans. Since Clavell's book appeared, fascination with the samurai has become something of a phenomenon, as revealed in a string of popular novels in the corner bookstore and on racks at the supermarket.

Robert Shea's novel *Shike* (two volumes), describes the war between two Japanese clans, the Taira and Minamoto, in the late twelfth century and the Mongol invasions of Japan in 1274 and 1281; *The Sword of Hachiman* also treats the Taira and Minamoto drama; Jessica Amanda Salmonson's two volumes, *Tomoe Gozen* and *The Golden Naginata,* take a legendary heroine, Tomoe Gozen, from the Taira and Minamoto era and transfer her to another dimension; and Eric Van Lustbader's *The Ninja* (soon to be a movie) presents as protagonist a man skilled in the sixteenth-century Japanese an of stealth and assassination who terrorizes New York city with a series of murders. The list goes on— Trevanian's *Shibumi, Bushido Blade,* and others.

Of perhaps more significance, however, is the sudden popularity in the United States of Miyamoto Musashi, skilled swordsman and noted painter of late sixteenth- and early seventeenth-century Japan, precisely the tumultuous era described by Clavell in *Shogun.* Yoshikawa Eiji's novel, *Miyamoto Musashi,* had delighted millions of Japanese readers since its first publication in serial form in the 1930s. Recently translated and published in English, *Musashi* runs, to almost a thousand pages, rivaling *Shogun* in both length and excitement. It, too, should find avid readers, for Musashi's name was already rather well known in North. America, thanks to the rather curious ways fads arise in the United States.

Near the end of his life Musashi wrote a slight volume on military strategy called *Gorin no sho (A Book of Five Rings,* or *The Book of Five Rings), Gorin no sho* was translated by Victor Harris and published in 1974 as *A Book of Five Rings* by The Overlook Press, the publisher's name perhaps accounting for the book's initial nonimpact. Though adequately translated and attractively packaged, including reproductions of Musashi's art, *Five Rings* attracted little attention outside the martial arts community.

As Japan began to challenge America's position as the world's pre-eminent economic power, however, Musashi came off the shelf. A retired Japanese professional baseball player—actually a Korean resident of Japan—mentioned *Gorin no sho* to a New York ad man who suggested, half in jest, to some businessmen that reading Musashi's book was the key to understanding Japanese success. The rest is history. . . .

Why? How many Japanese even gave him a passing thought before he was brought to their attention by marketing hyperbole? More important, how useful is the samurai image in understanding contemporary Japan, corporate or otherwise? Who is Musashi and why are people saying these things about him?

THE REAL MUSASHI

Accurate historical information about Musashi is sparse, but it seems he was born in 1584 in the province of Mimasaka, modern-day Okayama, in the western part of Japan's central island, the son of a minor warrior best known as Shinmen Munisai Takeo. Munisai was a master of the *jitte*, a short truncheon, as well as a noted swordsman who was once praised by Shogun Ashikaga Yoshiaki as "Japan's peerless martial practitioner."

Late in his life Munisai became involved in a rather messy business which affected Musashi's career. His lord ordered him to kill the house elder, Hon'iden Gekinosuke. Although he initially protested the order, Munisai ultimately carried out the murder. Rewarded, he nevertheless secluded himself and later moved to Miyamoto village where he remained incognito. Although some feel he fled there when Musashi was about six years old, it may well be that he left the village and went to Kyushu, Bungo and then Nakatsu, where he established relationships with both the Kuroda and Hosokawa houses, most likely as a fencing instructor. He died about 1607. If his father did live this long, it would help explain how Musashi learned his swordsmanship, at such a precocious age, for we have no other record of a teacher. Musashi's own account records that he killed his first opponent in a duel at the tender age of 13.

Musashi lived a rather lonely boyhood. When his parents divorced, his mother returned to her family home near the Mimasaka border, taking Musashi with her. He later returned to spend time with his father, and since his mother's home was not far away, he could go back and forth rather easily. He appears to have been a rather rambunctious boy, and quite large for his age.

Mushashi left Miyamoto at age 16 to travel in order to develop his martial skills, a not uncommon practice reached its height during the late early seventeenth centuries in Japan. He had already had his first encounter, described in a perhaps apocryphal story, with a Shinto-ryu swordsman, named Arima Kihei. Musashi was living with his uncle. One day, while returning from a calligraphy class with other children he came across a signpost erected by Arima, saying he would fight anyone who would accept his challenge. Musashi wrote on the placard that the next day Miyamoto Bennosuke (his childhood name) would appear for a duel. That night a messenger from Arima visited the uncle's house, and Musashi's uncle tried desperately to get Musashi out of the promise, since he was just a boy. Arima was understanding, but claimed that he would lose face if he didn't go through with the duel. So if the uncle showed up for the match, Arima said, and explained the situation to everyone, he would forget the matter and not lose face. The next day the uncle went off to explain, and it seems that quite a crowd had gathered outside Arima's inn. While the uncle was explaining the situation, Musashi, carrying only his short sword and a six *shaku*[1] stick, opened the door, identified Arima and started to hit him. Arima jumped up and a struggle ensued; Musashi threw away the stick, and after grappling for

---

1. A *shaku* is slightly shorter than one foot.

a while, picked Arima up over his head and threw him to the ground. He proceeded to strike his opponent 14-15 times, until he died. The story is probably an exaggeration, but Musashi was already rather adept when he left on his quest to polish his skills in 1599.

The second phase of Musashi's life covered a period of 16 years during which he received training and engaged frequently in major duels with martial practitioners of various schools. It ends in 1615, when he participated in the Battle of Osaka Castle, the summer campaign, at age 32. He himself claims to have fought more than 60 duels during the period, never meeting defeat. He also saw action in all three important battles, all in 1600, his seventeenth year: Fushimi, Gifu, and Sekigahara, where Tokugawa Ieyasu by his victory determined Japan's future course. Among the most famous of his encounters of this period, celebrated in novel, film, and television drama, were the three fights against the Yoshioka fencing school, whose founder, Kenpo, had once dueled and lost to Musashi's father. The most famous encounter, however, occurred when Musashi was 29, at the small island of Ganryu-jima lying between northern Kyushu and western Honshu. His opponent was Sasaki Kojiro, a skilled fencer who was an instructor of Hosekawa Tadaoki, lord of Kokura in Buzen. His victory over Kojiro, using a wooden sword he had fashioned from an oar, is certainly the most dramatic moment in all the Miyamoto Musashi films and is indelibly printed on the minds of Japanese when Musashi's name is mentioned.

The third phase of Musashi's life covered roughly the next 20 years, until he was about 50. It was again a period of wandering, but he engaged in no more major duels, although he fought a few matches; in the main, he devoted his time to further mastery of technique, teaching his own students, and striving to discover the deeper meaning of military arts. It is believed that this is when he came to discover the secrets which he explained in *Gorin no sho*. Since he also must have studied Zen and become proficient in a number of cultural forms—painting, calligraphy, poetry, composition—this was obviously the most creative period of Musashi's entire career.

At age 57, Musashi went to the Hosokawa fief at Kumamoto, where he accepted a post and served until he died 5 years later, in 1645. Besides serving as a military advisor, he devoted his time during this period to poetry, painting, calligraphy, and tea; and here he wrote *Gorin no sho*, explaining the teachings of his style of swordsmanship. Not long after he arrived in Kumamopo, however, Musashi suffered a great loss when his lord Hosokawa Tadatoshi died.

Japan had changed totally by the time of Tadatoshi's death. The continual warfare of Musashi's youth was a thing of the past. In fact, Musashi had little alternative to relying on the good graces of Tadatoshi, which was probably why Musashi had accepted an appointment in Kumamoto after a lifetime as a ronin (masterless warrior). After Tadatoshi's passing, Musashi seems to have largely abandoned the world, devoting all his energies to cultural pursuits.

It was in such a frame of mind that he secluded himself in a small cave in the nearby mountains and committed his idea to writing in *Gorin no sho*. This he passed to his student Terao Nobuyuki, and thereafter it was handed down among the members of his school as a secret text. The audience for which it was intended was thus quite limited.

Thus the facts of Musashi's life are few; even the biographical data presented here are subject to deputes. It matters little, however, because Musashi is really a legendary hero in Japan. He has more in common with Robin Hood than with King John. Some people know him best as swordsman, others as an artist; but most people know of film through drama, novel, and film.

MUSASHI AS LEGEND

Less than a century after his death, Musashi was already the subject of a play, written in 1737 by Fujikawa Banzaburo and performed in Osaka. A year later the play, called *Vendetta at Ganryu Jima* (*Katakiuchi Ganryu-Jima*) was a great success in Edo (Tokyo) at Ichimura-za where the chief writer was Fujimoto Banzaburo and the main actor Bando Hikosaburo. Musashi remained a popular subject for various forms of drama, including puppet plays. One scholar has calculated that between its first performance in 1737 and one in 1907 in Tokyo's Miyatoza, *Vendetta* was performed 77 times in 170 years, or once every 26 months. In addition, many great writers of the Edo period, including Jippensha Ikku, Hiraga Baisetsu, Tsuruya Nanboku the Fourth, created their own Musashi plays.

In these dramas, however, Musashi is a one-dimensional figure, the swashbuckling swordsman of peerless ability. Such characterization was typical of an age that demanded a hero, the victory of good, and the defeat of evil. It took a modern writer, Yoshikawa Eiji to create the now familiar Musashi: the rambunctious young man off on a quest to polish, his skills as a swordsman, but also to seek the truth, to perfect himself, forsaking the woman who loves and pursues him, not yielding to the demands of the flesh as he struggles to find the "way" to conquer himself.

First published serially between 1934 and 1339 in the *Asahi* newspaper, his story later became a best selling novel (the collected works of Yoshikawa have sold in the tens of millions, with *Miyamoto Musashi* the most popular). Perhaps its greatest popularity came in the late thirties, when in a period when there was little entertainment available, people delighted in the weekly radio series in which Tokugawa Musei, the famous voice of silent screen days, read all the parts. From there it went to at least three movie versions, plays, and more television series than one can remember. Musashi is truly the King of popular culture in Japan.

The Yoshikawa novel deals only with the first 30 years of Musashi's life, when he was essentially a wandering swordsman, and adds a moral and ethical dimension that none of the early plays contained. Since we know that, by the end of his life, Musashi had mastered many of the cultural forms of the day and had seemingly arrived at some measure of "Understanding," Yoshikawa may well be presenting in fictionalized form a process through which Musashi actually passed. Truth is mixed skillfully with fiction to give us a new and more empathetic Musashi. The Musashi at the beginning of Yoshikawa's novel is an orphan—rough, rowdy, independent, stubborn, and mischievous—a Tokugawa version of a rural kid going bad, a budding juvenile delinquent for whom one nonetheless feels sympathy,

The real moral force in the story is provided by the introduction of an historical character, the famous Zen prelate Takuan, for whom the even more famous Japanese pickled radish is named. Takuan is responsible for curing Musashi's violent temper, first by hanging him in a tree for several days and then by confining him in the *donjon* (dungeon) at Lord Ikeda Terumasa's Himeji Castle for three years—with appropriate books to train his mind. When he emerges—in "The Birth of Musashi" chapter—Musashi has begun to understand what life is all about, and Takuan has thus prepared him for the "Quest for Self"' that occupies the rest of the book.

Yoshikawa includes many of the famous battles Musashi actually fought, plus a few encounters with fictional characters as well as Takuan, who re-emerges periodically to attest to Musashi's progress. In fact, the way this handful of real and fictional characters encounter one another "by chance" in Edo, Kyoto, and everywhere else in Japan is almost comic.

The legendary Musashi thus improves his swordsmanship through continuous battles against wily opponents and his character through the spiritual guidance of Takuan. To account for his cultural development, Yoshikawa inserted another historical figure of great renown to introduce Musashi to art and poetry—Hon'ami Koetsu. Koetsu meets Musashi, entertains him as a guest in Takagamine in Kyoto, and takes him along on his visits to the gay quarters where he entertains several courtiers of distinguished lineage. Together, Koetsu and friends introduce Musashi to painting, tea ceremony, calligraphy, song and dance. In the last connection, he becomes the target of the affections of Yoshino Daiyu, a famous courtesan of the day.

In real life Musashi was linked with a woman of the gay quarters. Similarly Yoshikawa attempts to unite fact and fiction by introducing Jotaro and Iori, two young waifs that Musashi picks up along the way. Although he never married and had no children of his own, we know that Musashi adopted two boys, the eldest of whom, Iori, became a famous military adviser to the Osagawara in Kyushu. Furthermore, Yoshikawa had Otsu, Jotaro, and finally Musashi meet with Lord Yagyu Munenori, the shogun's fencing teacher and one of the noted military experts of the day. In fact, Munenori must have played a large part in Yoshikawa's thinking. Takuan, for example, was a confidant of Munenori, and wrote to him a very famous treatise on swordsmanship. We have no record, however, that he or Munenori ever knew Musashi.

The climax of the story, in novel and film and even in Edo period drama, was the Ganryu-jima battle with Sasaki Kojiro. In the historical record, the two men met in the duel—there are several versions of the result and a controversy over Kojiro's age—but we do not know whether they had ever met previously. In both book and film, Kojiro patiently stalks Musashi, building suspense toward the battle we know will eventually take place. Kojiro is a skilled swordsman, perhaps even more adept than Musashi. As his character unfolds, however, we perceive that he lacks that understanding of life Mushashi has been seeking. He remains proud, even arrogant, and seeks only to polish his technique: his soul remains uncultivated. Thus Musashi's victory is not only physical, a faster sword if you will; it is also moral.

Part of Musashi's popularity is certainly due to the heroic-quality of his martial prowess—a skilled swordsman with wooden sword, staff, or blade, undefeated in more than 60 fights against a variety of opponents. Adding to that the moral qualities from the Yoshikawa Eiji version—the rigorous and continual training and discipline, the search for physical and spiritual perfection, the conquest of self—we have the strength of character, the masculinity which makes him in many ways an ideal "real man" for people, today.

In his book on "the noble failure" as cultural hero in Japan, Ivan Morris noted certain requisite qualities: courage, unflinching loyalty, selflessness, willingness to the in the face of certain defeat, and perhaps above all, sincerity and purity of motive. Virtually all the samurai in this heroic-category —Yoshitsune is the classic, but Kusunoki Masashige and, Saigo Takamori are also included—die by their own hand, in a lost cause. Although Morris does not specifically discuss this point, it seems that in a society in which personal feelings are normally subordinated to group demands and individual initiative stifled by the emphasis upon collegiality, individuals who go against the flow of history, who strike out on their own and follow that course regardless of consequence are likely to be heroic figures.

Musashi in the novel, that is the Musashi known to Japanese today, has no lord, he is an orphan, he shuns those women who try to get close to him, and he single-mindedly pursues his goal. Although he starts jut as a bully, Musashi grows over the course of the story, coming to embody the sincerity, selflessness and purity of motive of the other heroes. He certainty shares their courage, although he does not employ it to demonstrate his loyalty to lord or sovereign, nor does he go down to defeat in a blaze of glory and take his own life. He is no failed hero in that sense. Rather, he is perhaps the classic example of the Japanese individualist, without family or even friends, ultimately "doing his own thing" regardless of the views of others. Thus Musashi is a seductive personality for many who feel bound by the rigid rules of a conformist society. Yet Musashi represents the last of his kind, the wandering swordsman seeking to polish his art in a world where the demand for that skill is rapidly disappearing.

THE BOOK OF FIVE RINGS

Both of the English translations treat *Five Rings,* one of three works Musashi wrote on swordsmanship, as a classic of military strategy and not solely as a guide to understanding Japanese business prowess. What, then, accounts for its popularity in the United States? Its brevity is certainly one factor. In the Overlook edition the translation runs to 56 pages, including a number of half pages, generous margins, and 54 footnotes, some of which are quite long. The Bantam translation, a smaller book in its overall dimensions, requires 74 pages, but the translators have added a "commentary" on each chapter to make it more readily understandable and "relevant" for contemporary Western readers.

After a brief autobiographical introduction, Musashi has divided his work into five short chapters—Earth, Water, Fire, Wind, and Emptiness or Void. In the Earth chapter, he discusses his philosophy of *heiho,* referring both to swordsmanship and military strategy, but in a larger sense to his world view, derived from long years of combat and study of numerous art forms. The Water chapter deals with winning. As in Taoism and other East Asian ways of thought, water for Musashi is a crucial element that permeates everything, fluid and flexible, ultimately adaptable to any environment. In his Fire chapter, Musashi discusses fighting, especially large-scale battles. He devotes the Wind chapter to an examination of other schools, some good, some bad (not surprisingly none are "true schools" like his own). Finally, the Emptiness chapter is a very brief summary. Overall, the book is an explication of his school of fighting, known as *Ichiryu nito* ("one school, two swords"), *nito-ryu,* or *Niten-ryu* after his art name, Niten. The greater portion oft he book is devoted to very specific types of sword techniques of little interest to anyone today except a *kendo* practitioner.

What do the promoters of *Five Rings* mean when they tout this work as a "classic" or an "age-old masterpiece"? Certainly it would not be included among the great works of Japanese thought; it was also designed for a small audience. Musashi in his last years was employed by a Kyushu *daimyo* (lord); he did not write for the populace, of Edo, Kyoto, or Osaka. Furthermore, the work was primarily passed on secretly within his school. Certainly none of the great figures of the day mentions *Five Rings as* compulsory reading. When it came to military strategy everybody read Sun Tzu, not Musashi.

Another reason for *Five Rings'* failure to reach canonical status may be that it was an anachronism when it was written. Musashi was one of the last of his type, a real swordsman in an age of peace. Pax Tokugawa was one of the longest periods of protracted peace in Japan's modern history, indeed in world history. Wandering swordsmen of Musashi's ilk were targets of government regulation. While warriors were urged to practice both the arts of war and peace, the latter took precedence. The Shimabara Rebellion of 1637-38, in which Musashi participated in a noncombatant role, was the last outbreak of substantial violence. Not until the coming of Perry would the samurai again display the concern for swordsmanship common to Musashi's early days. The samurai of Tokugawa Japan was more administrator and scholar than warrior, and more likely to read Mencius than Musashi.

Musashi's nine most clearly, articulated pieces of advice have been extracted by the Bantam translation team and placed at the front of the book under the heading, "The Winning Strategy":

1. Do not harbor sinister designs.
2. Diligently pursue the path of Two-Swords-as-One.
3. Cultivate a wide range of Interests in the arts.
4. Be knowledgeable in a variety of occupations.
5. Be discreet regarding one's commercial dealings.
6. Nurture the ability to perceive the truth in all matters.
7. Perceive that which cannot be seen with the eye.
8. Do not be negligent, even in trifling matters.
9. Do not engage in useless activities.

Musashi constantly enjoins the reader to study hard, to develop an indomitable spirit, to understand timing, to be broadly based rather than narrowly technical, and to know one's self. Warning us that sleepiness and yawning are catching, that we should think big, or that "he who hesitates is lost," Musashi is hardly original or especially profound, certainly not very mystical, and not especially foreign to Americans. Only the enjoinder to practice the two-sword school seems a bit foreign to us, but modern Japanese will be no better off here either. While all the rest of the advice is sound enough, it is all too familiar from British and home-grown sources: Samuel Smiles, Benjamin Franklin, McGuffy's Reader, and the Boy Scout Manual.

Is there something more? According to Bradford Brown, head of Nihon Services Corporation and one of four Bantam translators, what on the surface appears simple hides finer meanings. When *Time* reviewed Harris's Overlook translation. Brown was already planning his own version which would lay out the subtleties for us, in "at least 200 exhaustive pages." Well, either the subtleties proved too difficult to capture, in words or were never there in the first place, since the Bantam book ended up only half that long with a few cursory comments on the background and several pages of discussion on the five chapters to help us grasp the meaning. Except for the last section on *ku* (Emptiness or Void), the reader will find little that is esoteric.

One might argue that swordsmanship is simply a metaphor for life, and thus all the specific information Musashi gives us about swordplay—and well over half the book details offensive and defensive tactics—needs to be seen in this light. As *Time* quoted Dean Robert Allio of Rensselaer Polytechnic Institute: "The message is very dear. Business needs to be approached as though one were a warrior. You can't win by dabbling or playing the role of the dilettante."

Is the message really as inscrutable as *Time* and the *Rings* advocates would have us believe? It is inscrutable only if you try too hard to apply it to the modern corporate game. *Five Rings* is undeniably the product of the mind of a man who lived through a turbulent and bloody era that demanded a highly realistic approach to life. If for some Japanese and Americans modern business competition may seem fully as turbulent and bloody as the politics of Japan's *sengoku* period, then Musashi might, by a stretch, be relevant today.

That brings us to the $64,000 question: Do the Japanese, as the two publishing houses would, have us believe, really see *Five Rings* as some sort of corporate Bible, Koran, or little Red Book to guide their business lives? Some businessmen have surely read *Five Rings* and profited from it. My answer to the general question, however, is an unambiguous no. One can find Japanese managers who will swear that Zen Buddhist meditation—by themselves and their workers—accounts for their success. Others will sing the praises of Pure Land Buddhism, Soka Gakkai. their Christian faith, hard work, or the training they received at Tokyo University or the Stanford Business School. Matsushita Electric has *PHP.* Musashi, if anything, is one very minor god in a corporate pantheon.

Five Rings can be rather hard to come by in Japanese bookstores. When I first sought it out in the late sixties, the most easily accessible versions were as sections of a collection on Japanese thought. In the most readily available one, the entire text is not reproduced, only a selection. Moreover, most of these editions have the text in the original Tokugawa language: this is not quite analogous to Americans reading *Beowulf* in the original, but increasingly fewer Japanese are able to read such difficult texts. Thus *Five Rings* was simply not the kind of book one picked up at the corner bookstore. It was a highly specialized work not too well known outside the academic and martial arts communities.

Ironically, American promotion has increased the book's readership in Japan. The first popular paperback edition, a modern translation designed for broader appeal, became available in 1960. The volume also includes the translation of another important military treatise of the day, *Heiho kadensho,* by Yagyu Tajima no Kami Munenori, the fencing instructor and primary military adviser to the Tokugawa shogunal house. The Japanese translator finds that while Musashi deals mainly with technique, Munenori is instead discussing "spiritual control" in combat situations. The translator, Okochi Shoji, gives a brief historical background and discussion of both texts. He devotes but one sentence each to their possible implications for the Japanese of today: "Can't we say that *The Book of Five Rings* has somewhat suggestive and attractive elements for today's competitive society?"

Read for the right reasons, the reasons for which Musashi presumably wrote the book, it is a useful tome. Historically, it is also an important expression of an age. But Japanese companies in great numbers do not put all their trainees to work mastering this text. Indeed, looking at *Five Rings as* a text, and at the career of Miyamoto Musashi, one can see reasons why the book might not be a good guide or Musashi an especially good model for Japanese companies to follow.

First, Musashi has virtually nothing to say about those human traits which we associate with Japanese companies and their workers: loyalty, harmony, group cohesiveness, dependence, mutual support, and the like. For all but the last years of his life, Musashi was a ronin, a masterless samurai whose only loyalty was to himself. His parents died when he was young, and he himself never married (although he did adopt two sons). Thus he spent little of his life in the company of others to whom he was connected by moral and ethical ties. He was outside the web of *giri* and *ninjo* or duty and human emotion, which provide the audience interest in virtually all Tokugawa and modern drama. He is the *"ippiki okami"* of samurai drama fame,' the "lone wolf" whose very estrangement from the larger society makes him at once attractive, but at the same time a poor role model.

Second, Musashi is perhaps the most independent and individualistic thinker in the Japanese samurai tradition. As he says himself: "I have lived without following any particular Way. Thus with the virtue of strategy I practice many arts and abilities —all things with no teacher." He is headstrong, stubborn, and independent, a very poor ideal type for corporate conformity and loyalty. The moral values he symbolizes in the Yoshikawa Eiji version are noble—certainly it is this aspect of Musashi's character that accounts for the appeal of the radio serials in the late 1930s —and the sort of ideals Japanese managers would like their workers to possess. Nevertheless the highly individualistic way in which Musashi attained those ideals appears counter to the corporatism of Japanese business. One might even argue that Musashi's advice ought to appeal less to Japanese than to Americans. After all, it is the latter who traditionally value individualism, personal initiative, and conflict that leads to total victory. Conciliation and compromise are not high among, our cultural ideals. Perhaps *Five Rings* tells us more about its American than its Japanese reader.

THE SAMURAI IMAGE: IS IT VALID TODAY?

What about the image of the samurai in contemporary Japan? There is in the American promotion for *Five Rings* the explicit assumption that the Japanese, or at least businessmen in Japan, are modern-day samurai in suits; thus to compete with them we must become Wall Street warriors as well. While it would be impossible to deny that there are elements of the Japanese character which are quite similar to, and perhaps even derivative of the samurai mentality of an earlier era, most of the writing in contemporary Japan does not reflect much consciousness of this heritage, with the exception of books like *The Modern Samurai Society*.

In perusing the major opinion journals, one is struck by the fact that Japanese are trying to come to grips with the reverse of the problem faced by Americans: while we are fretting over America's economic decline, the Japanese are trying to explain and understand their success. There is, to be sure, a good deal of self-congratulatory literature; and not surprisingly, books like Ezra Vogel's *Japan As Number One* have enjoyed remarkable success (far greater than *Five Rings*). Others have voiced warnings that Japan should not become complacent over success. Still others worry about the tremendous discrepancy between Japan's great wealth and virtual impotence in world politics. Many writers have been caught up in. the *tokushuron,* or the theory of Japan's "special characteristics," which is represented in the U.S. by *Five Rings* translations and others who advocate the "search for secrets" approach to doing business with Japan.

Reviewing recent Japanese literature, there appears to be little explicit attention devoted to Japan's samurai heritage. I am struck, however, by the number of works that de-emphasize or refute such a heritage, although it could be argued that the cultural assumption of a samurai heritage is always implicit. The three recently published articles discussed below seem to me to be representative of Japanese thinking about themselves.

Sakaiya Taichi, in an article entitled "Debunking the Myth of Loyalty," claims that the Japanese have historically been notoriously disloyal and are by no means the "martial race" some assume. Sakaiya says that many other peoples, called upon to make sacrifices for the military over the generations, "are, from the sovereign to the ordinary citizen, imbued to the marrow with a war ideology and well-defined attitudes toward war. The Japanese never were and are not now, and this may well be due to the fact that they have never experienced all-out war on their own soil against an alien people." In the Tokugawa period, when Japan was totally dominated by the samurai class but also almost totally at peace, Sakaiya claims "the Japanese, who had always lacked a war ideology and well-defined attitudes toward war, thus passed 250 years in a society that had disarmed to the point of having no army, and in the end lost all conception of military matters. Thus far from being a 'martial race,' 'the Japanese are a peaceable, agricultural people ignorant of military matters."

To prove his point, Sakaiya mentions that the shogun at the arrival of Perry in 1853 had more than 100,000 retainers. "That Japan, with this number of armed men," he says, "should ignore public opinion, which was overwhelmingly in favor of expulsion of foreigners, and surrender to the 600 men of Matthew Perry's squadron surely deserves mention in the Guinness Book of Records."

Loyalty was conspicuously lacking among Japanese warriors prior to

Hideyoshi at the very end of the sixteenth century. The samurai, Sakaiya says, was essentially playing "for the team." "If a baseball player is traded to another team, he is expected to give his all to his new team and to give no thought to 'yesterday's friend." Like the baseball player, the samurai was not bound by "any ethical premise that one cannot serve two masters." In fact, he did it all the time. The "loyalty" that is bandied about so much today — the personal version of this, *giri-ninjo*, he claims, "has been placed on an offensively high pedestal"—is thus not some hereditary national characteristic bred from a martial spirit of the samurai age, but rather lies in the Japanese "system of lifetime employment and the seniority based wage structure that supports it." Traditionally, loyalty was indeed a virtue, especially from the viewpoint of the lord; but Sakaiya reminds us that "however a certain quality is considered desirable is no guarantee that it actually prevails."

Amaya Naohiro of the Ministry of International Trade and Industry, in an article entitled "Grumblings of a Shop Clerk of Japan, A Tradesman Country," feels that the "Japanese people...must reflect deeply and widely on the question of whether the way of life for Japan is that of a 'tradesman' or that of a samurai..." He likens international society to a "semi-jungle." Japan, he warns, "is something like a plump rabbit living in this jungle. We must not harbor such an illusion as to think that the bears and the wolves will show kind consideration, feeling pity for the poor rabbit, which has neither claws nor fangs. For the rabbit to survive and multiply in the jungle, and for the tradesmen citizens to prosper in samurai society, they need very outstanding intelligence-gathering ability, planning ability, intuition, diplomatic ability, and even the art of flattery, at times."

Amaya feels that the Japanese in the postwar world have emulated the merchant class of Tokugawa times. Although the samurai supposedly controlled society by virtue of sitting atop the Confucian social order, it was in fact a world determined primarily by the economic power and cultural aspirations of the merchant. In an international society dominated by samurai—powerful countries which possess large-scale military capability, including nuclear weapons—Japan has skillfully manipulated itself into a powerful position by employing the same techniques as the Tokugawa merchant. He is well aware that many Japanese neither approve of this approach, nor wish to continue it, but he feels that a shift to a samurai society will be costly for Japan. Becoming a samurai will mean adopting an attitude of "pretending not to mind," sitting back when starving in the manner of a Tokugawa' samurai, accepting things as they come. Furthermore, Japan would not only have to wear two swords, or rearm, but it would have to use them. Perhaps most important, Japan will have to abandon its three nuclear principles. He concludes that, for the time being, Japan will remain a merchant society.

Last spring's *Chuo* Koron, on management, devotes a long section to "train-

ing the mind";' no fewer than 10 articles "describe ways of improving or training a creative mind to produce fresh ideas. Some are essays by professors,
business executives, critics and management specialists; other articles are
composites of roundtable discussions or interviews with groups of executives.
A rather wide range of important opinion is represented: not one person even
remotely alluded to the *Book of Five Rings* or ideas associated with it.

One article on "study groups" was a discussion among seven executives
from the Experimental Group VSOP (Very Special One-Time Performance)
to IBC (International Businessmen's Club), and including such organizations as The Society for the Study of the "Techniques of Intellectual
Production" and Japanese Changes (Japanizu *Chenjizu*), one of whose activities last year included psychological study employing psychodrama. There
may indeed be something very Japanese going on here, but there was no
Five Rings Philosophical Study Group. Indeed, much of this article
described-efforts to reduce stress, soften up, and become more human.. The
models were predominantly based upon contemporary psychological developments which appear distinctly non-Japanese.

Some spoke of toughness—"action seminar," "all-night discussion," and
survival *(sabaiburu)*, but others, like Mr. Aoki of the Human Harbor Teiki
Salon group, are unabashedly interested in fostering a spirit of enjoyment:
"I wish *sarariman* would understand intellectual pleasures, allow themselves
a little more elbow room. A spirit of pleasure gives rise to a kind of softness,
and isn't that where human durability comes from?"

Morita Masaaki of Sony, as though he had been asked to comment on
America's "search for secrets" literature, was quoted in *Chuo Koron:* "We talk about
'Japanese management;' but I realty don't believe we have some kind of Bible or
Golden Rule. On the one hand we Japanese have an indecisiveness about us,
so that after the Second World War, though we had become that caught up in militarism, we completely changed. With a totally casual attitude, we all became
friendly with Americans. It's just that we Japanese have a character that allows
us to change completely with the conditions; so when foreign managers say
'Aha! That's Japanese style management!' Japanese managers shift and go in a
completely different direction. And that. I think, is how Japanese survive."

Japanese management practices and success can only be explained as part
of a larger social context. Japanese companies are not successful because
they have added some mystical ingredient unavailable to or undiscovered by
U.S-corporations and business schools. Nor have they turned their workers
into modern-day Musashi. What they have done is to utilize Japan's only raw
material, if you will, human capital, and organize it effectively.

Japan's child-rearing practices, schooling, indeed the entire Japanese
socialization process, is designed to promote social harmony. The ideals of
the Tokugawa Neo-Confucianists are still alive here: loyalty to group filial
piety, dedication, hard work, and frugality. Whether white-collar or blue,

Japanese companies begin with workers conditioned to such ideals. Certain firms, especially large ones like Toyota and other automotive firms with which American companies compete, offer lifetime employment, a seniority system, and early retirement—all of which function to ensure loyalty to the firm and provide incentive to produce. Add to the formula a number of fringe benefits, such as low-cost housing; vacation resorts; facilities for cultural, educational, and sports activities; and liberal expense accounts for managers, and it is not surprising that Japanese firms secure a high degree of worker loyalty. Finally, when you. consider that Japanese companies enjoy relatively cooperative rather than adversarial relations with the government, face low levels of demands from organized, labor and stockholders, and value long-range planning over short-term-profits, it should not be surprising that Japanese firms compete effectively at the international level.

Many Japanese and Americans feel that the Japanese values of community, cooperation, and conciliation leading to social harmony result in greater and more efficient productivity than the American system, which values individualism, competition, and adversarial labor-management relations. If one seeks a better understanding of the social context upon which Japanese business rests, Musashi is not an especially good guide. Instead, read anything and everything by Ronald Dore, Robert Cole; Thomas Rohlen, and Nakana Chie. Or study Japanese.

The "search for secrets" literature, books like *Five Rings* and *Theory Z,* and, to an even greater extent, *Japan as Number One,* plays upon American apprehensions about the viability of the U.S. system and suggests that there is much to learn from Japan. While I agree that American ethnocentrism is both dangerous and impractical, we should not go too far and attribute too much success to the Japanese and their economic growth. The Japanese, like the Americans, are far from perfect. They are not all Musashis, nor is the Japanese character alone responsible for Japan's economic success today.

One should not underestimate, for instance, the role the United States has played in Japan's development, since by virtue of American defense forces, Japan has been able to devote its national energies and resources to that single goal for almost 40 years. Thanks to the "Peace Constitution," Japan has not only been spared the enormous expense of developing an adequate defense structure, but she has also been virtually a nonparticipant in all the major international political decisions and crises of that period until the "oil shock" of 1973-1975. When else can one remember that the second most important economic power in the world was virtually impotent in international affairs? Japan's international position is one of virtual anonymity, even invisibility. It also cannot continue indefinitely.

There are other factors, too. Penelope Hartland Thunberg writing in the *Seattle Times* (May 5, 1982), suggested that the real key to Japan's export success is a grossly undervalued yen, concluding that "there is nothing wrong with American exporters that a yen at 175 to the dollar would not cure." Such reasoning may be just another link in the "search for secrets" chain, but it has the advantage of emphasizing a factor that has nothing to do with "character."

Perhaps the best antidote to fanciful speculation on Japan's success is any reading of contemporary Japanese literature: there is serious concern with Japan's future, and the answers proffered by various analysts by no means reflect a consensus. Moreover, the affluent society has come but recently to Japan; and only now is the first generation in memory to grow up in relative luxury. How the Japanese will deal with continued affluence remains to be seen.

Besides, Yankee ingenuity must still exist. If a country beset be economic insecurity, recession, and self-doubt can successfully market a book about a wandering Japanese swordsman, dead for almost 350 years, as the key to a winning business strategy, there is cause for optimism. Recently, Morita Masaaki, the Chairman of Sony's Board of Directors, echoing a commonly voiced concern in Japan, asked "What has happened to your frontier sprit? Where has the heroic figure of John Wayne, who opened up that country, paying great sacrifices, disappeared?... We Japanese...feel like telling (the Americans) to wake up and shape up" Even now the Japanese are facing the erosion of their traditional values as a society of surplus spreads its degenerative seeds. Perhaps someday soon, we Americans may be asking: "What has happened to your samurai spirit? Where has Miyamoto Musashi, who trained his character so assiduously, disappeared?"

9. THREE MARTIAL VIRTUES

Nicklaus Suino is an accomplished swordsman in the modern discipline of iaido *who has benefited from extensive training in Japan. His writing is among the most lucid commentaries on the technical and spiritual dimensions of modern* budo. *Here he discusses the virtues of strength, courage, and loyalty in the context of modern martial arts training.*

From *Arts of Serenity, Arts of Strength*
BY NICKLAUS SUINO

> Perceiving what is right, and not doing it, argues lack of courage　—CONFUCIUS

STRENGTH

There are three major types of strength in *budo*: physical strength, strength in technique, and strength of character. The power of the body is the most basic type, since it is easiest to develop and all of us have some strength to begin with. Technique is more difficult to develop because it involves overcoming natural responses and, through training, replacing them, with reasoned ones. Strength of character is the most important of these three qualities, but budo is based on the idea that the way to improve character is mainly through hard work in the other two areas.

A long period of arduous physical training (measured in decades, not weeks) is necessary to develop mastery of technique, and to affect personality. Though great masters such as Yamaoka Tesshu and Ueshiba Morihei said that a unified spirit was the single most important quality for a martial artist, both men, and many other acknowledged masters, spent thirty or forty years in extraordinarily hard physical practice before reaching that state known as "enlightenment."

The martial artist must be physically strong because all technique is based on movement of the body. In order to persevere through the daily hours of practice, one must have endurance; to wield the sword properly, one must have strong arms; to kick well, the leg muscles must be able to easily lift the leg repeatedly into the air. Through strength training, one also develops coordination.

Strong technique is important in self-defense because we always run the risk of meeting an opponent stronger than ourselves and because our skills, especially those based on muscular strength, lose effectiveness as we grow older. Technique is also important because we gain strength of character through the very process of studying and improving our skills. Personality and technical ability, in fact, are inseparable, and by practicing technique we learn about ourselves. The knowledge and humility that come through lengthy practice are crucial aspects of character development.

A strong character is better than a weak one, of course. We need character because training is sometimes difficult and frustrating. We need it also because the skills we learn can make us overconfident, and because right action requires a strong will. Strength in this area is valuable, both to us and to society, because it allows us to follow through on our intentions.

The way of the martial arts is to build strength through daily practice. Start within the limits of your capabilities, gradually increasing your own demands on yourself, and practicing every day. Study those more advanced than you to find out what you need to do to improve, and read about past masters for inspiration.

This method applies to each of the three areas described above.

Physical strength can be increased in isolation, through a program of calisthenics or weight lifting, or it can be increased in conjunction with the development of technique. The way to develop them together is simply to practice each technique many times, attempting to improve gradually, while increasing the number of repetitions to fill the time available. Few students of the martial arts become experts only by attending classes, because there is not enough practice time within class hours. Most teachers utilize their class time for valuable lessons on skills and principles, and cannot include sufficient practice time, so it is the students' responsibility to seek out such time for themselves.

It is a mistake to want or to expect expertise overnight. Trying to reach too a lofty goal at once leads to failure, because neither the body nor the mind are prepared for the effort. In traditional martial arts, we can learn to move mountains, but we follow the method of moving them bit by bit, in amounts we can carry safely.

Developing strength of character is a natural result of correct training, but most of us need to pay special attention to right action, since not all of us were taught to choose correctly every time. In training, part of right action means admitting that some of our techniques are not as good as others, and taking the time to work on them until they improve. It also means being truthful about the results of our techniques and realizing that, although they may work in certain practice situations, they may not be as marvelous as we sometimes believe they are, and thus they need even more work. Failing to be self-critical in this way can be disastrous.

There is an alarming trend in the training sessions at some aikido schools toward tailoring attacks to the defensive techniques being taught. Attacks are mounted from weak or off-balance positions and attackers fall as if they had really been thrown. Instead of practicing and refining their techniques to be effective against truly strong attacks, students learn only to ward off weak, staged attacks, and thus can never improve. This travesty of martial arts instruction is justified by the assertion of some instructors that aikido is supposed to be harmonious, but this approach bankrupts the art of its value as a teaching tool. It also places students in serious danger of having their skills fail them when confronted with a real self-defense situation. Real technique is technique that works, and though we try to practice safely, we must never totally remove the martial underpinnings of our arts. If a proven technique does not work for us, we must deepen our study of it until it does. Teachers at these schools do not seem to realize that, though self-criticism can be uncomfortable, the very process of overcoming our weaknesses is what makes us stronger—in body, in technique, and in character.

Outside of training, we need to consciously choose to do that which is honorable, necessary, or right. When given an opportunity to cheat, we must refuse it, knowing that cheating can become a habit. When faced with an unpleasant task, we must think through to the importance of getting it done, and overcome our reluctance to complete it.

The higher one rises through the ranks of martial artists, the more important this last characteristic becomes. Because the path of martial arts is so difficult, newer students often try to find ways of making it easier, and those ways include shirking their duties, Waning others for problems, and self-delusion. It falls to the senior students to correct their juniors, and almost nobody enjoys such work. Still, the necessity for doing is clear, since a dojo would become chaotic and dangerous without this kind of people management. The best students get the job done. By doing the necessary it unpleasant tasks, they learn about the rewards of correct action, some of which are greater control, a clearer conscience, and a better perception of truth.

There are many pitfalls on the path to becoming stronger. At the first sign of strength in themselves, my students experience an explosion of ego. They assume that since they are stronger than they once were, they are stronger than everybody, and this delusion can turn them into bullies. At the least, these students will find themselves stagnating until they can fit their sense of themselves to fit their new abilities. At worst, they will become such bullies that they have to be removed from the dojo.

Inflated egos are a problem for teachers of the martial as well. For those in positions of leadership, many of ordinary avenues for feedback are removed. Most students do not dare to attack their teachers with their effort, and teachers can set up practice situations to themselves the advantage. Being the biggest fish in a small pond is rewarding, but all of us in the martial arts remember how large the pond really is, and how centuries of work by previous generations of teachers went into preparing the way for us.

Those martial artists who spend enough time and effort developing themselves will find that they have improved their strength in each of the three areas. It usually turns out, however, that the goal of mastery does not look quite the same from higher up the ladder as it did from the bottom rung. There is, in fact, always as much more ladder above as there is below, since strength is a relative term, and one must learn to accept the fact that perfection is an elusive goal. One may work hard to overcome certain weaknesses, and find that progress has been made, but one will also find that constant work is required to maintain those gains. New problems often arise to replace those that have been conquered. The increased responsibility that comes with higher rank often vexes students, who find that they have to balance the problems of the dojo and its members with matters related to their own training.

Long experience in martial arts practice will show us that our only real competition is with ourselves, but some students cannot overcome the desire to compete against others. They may become strong and skilled, but find that others are still stronger and better. Instead of letting this discourage them, successful martial artists will learn to use this fact to motivate themselves to continue practicing and improving. After enough years, if they practice hard, have a good teacher, and are lucky, their techniques will improve enough that they will work even against larger and stronger opponents. This kind of success helps one see through the keyhole of the door leading to the real meaning of budo.

Because success with technique helps motivate students to further pursue good technique, they should become more effective in a range of skills over time. Ironically, however, even the goal of perfecting technique can impose barriers to progress; those who fixate on one technique or one level of difficulty will stop progressing, while those who learn to seek out new methods and continually improve themselves will continue to grow.

Past masters tell us that, eventually, for a few of the best and most dedicated students, the pursuit of technique will become unnecessary, and they will learn to triumph using force of will. Ueshiba was said to have reached this stage near the end of his life, though he never quit practicing. Yamaoka was supposed to have been unbeatable after several decades of practice, and he attributed this to a "unity of spirit."

These days, in fact, many claim to have come near to this state, or to have reached it, As nice as it would be to believe that many martial artists are reaching enlightenment, I personally remain skeptical. My experiences training with many of the best and most renowned masters around the world lead me to believe that even the most fantastic feats these men and women perform are still just techniques, albeit remarkably well executed, and not "pure spirit."

What this means for the future of our practice is twofold. One, we must be very careful about accepting claims of greatness by the teachers we meet, and two, whenever we begin to think we have reached perfection in a technique, we must remember how much longer and harder other living masters must have worked, and that, if they haven't liberated themselves from physical reality after all their years of toil, that we probably haven't either.

After many years of training, however, it is still possible to believe in the possibility of greatness and the nobility of staying on the path toward it. The fantastic skills of the greatest masters are worthwhile goals in themselves, and studying to reach their level is made even more exciting by the possibility that something transcendent might lie just past our next thousand repetitions. We must constantly challenge ourselves to improve, every minute of every training day. If we honestly evaluate our strength, technique, and character, and improve each of them by a small increment every day, we will sooner or later certainly accomplish something worthwhile.

COURAGE

Courage is the cornerstone of the martial artist's character. Without it, he or she will never undertake all the training needed to become a great technician, or develop great moral strength. It is not a common quality, but it can be developed with the right kind of training regimen.

The most obvious sort of bravery found in martial arts is that needed to face an opponent's punch, kick, throw, or sword cut, but a much broader view is needed to understand the entire role of courage in budo. It takes many forms, but always has the purpose of keeping students on the path of right action, or getting them back on it if they have strayed.

For many, courage is needed just to enter into martial arts at all. Going into a strange school and admitting that one is ignorant requires a type of bravery. There is also courage in the act of placing one's own welfare in the hands of another, such as a teacher or another student. Teachers of the martial arts need courage to take the financial risks of opening a school, and of exposing themselves to the judgments of their students and other teachers.

But these are examples of the minor kinds of courage that we expect from the martial artist. Real courage, the kind that must be cultivated through training, is inseparable from right action, and nearly always contains a strong element of self-sacrifice. In feudal times, a samurai was expected to give up his life for his lord without a moment's thought. Nowadays, we must think for ourselves, but when there is action to be taken, we must still take it with the greatest commitment.

The threat of death shines a bright light on courageous people, and one can read many stories of great warriors who calmly faced their own impending deaths. While these stories do show the result of a long period of hard training, the real sources of courage are the countless small challenges of everyday training. Without facing these smaller problems directly, we cannot learn to handle the larger ones. Just as in cultivating strength, we must learn to develop ourselves gradually, we must build up to extraordinary levels of courage by starting with ordinary ones.

With physical courage this is easy to understand. It would be unreasonable and dangerous to try to defeat a national judo champion on our first day on the mat, and any sensible student would feel fearful at the prospect of trying to doing so. Our entire first year would be better spent learning how to fall safely, how to maintain balance, and how to overcome the fear of being thrown. After two or three years, if we are talented, we might profit from a match with the national champion, but we could not reasonably hope to pose any kind of challenge to him for several more years. The quality we would demonstrate by trying to beat a champion judoist on our first day in the dojo is not courage, but stupidity. In this case, the amount of courage we possess is inseparable from the amount of time we have spent in training. The usefulness of the relationship between the two is clear: the greater courage needed to calmly face more difficult challenges comes through extended training.

Stories of warriors giving up their lives for their lords may be helpful, though, to understand when self-sacrifice actually is courageous. The principle behind those historical loyalties was that the action of the warrior helped to further the good of the community. A leader, who probably had a broader view of the situation, would tell the warrior what was needed to win a battle, and the warrior would obey because victory would help all of those with whom he identified. The possibility of his death was considered a necessary risk to support the overall good, and, should he actually be killed, his family would rejoice at his contribution even as they grieved for their loss.

In today's society, people identify so little with their families and their employers that they can rarely be counted on to take action that will help the larger cause. There are many reasons for this, mostly social and economic, but a population more willing to "do the right thing," even at some personal risk, would change our country for the better. The question of whether there is a cause worth nobly serving in this country we will leave for another discussion.

In the dojo, where these social and economic factors are not in play, what constitutes an act of courage is much clearer. Not flinching when facing a punch is a basic and irrefutable courage that must be learned by every karate student. Having the fortitude to stand up and be thrown again and again until the technique no longer inspires fear is essential. Confronting a troublemaker and enforcing the school rules is necessary to the smooth running of the dojo community, and requires bravery.

All these examples of courage arise out of an understanding that there is some purpose greater than the immediate threat. One learns not to flinch at a punch because an opponent would recognize weakness in it and follow up the attack with other, more effective, punches. One gets up many times to be thrown because that is what is required to learn how to avoid being thrown in the future. The dojo member who disciplines his junior does so because he values a safe, positive training environment more than he fears the junior's displeasure.

Seeing the larger picture helps to diminish the emotional relevance of the minor discomforts. Over time, something as intimidating as a punch recedes in impact to its true value as a tiny element of a complete training life, and we can then deal with it calmly. This learning process is a vital part of character development in the martial arts. In training, we expose our students to fear-inspiring events, starting with the very small and the physical, and gradually raise the stakes, introducing more complex events, and encounters that inspire fear on an emotional or moral plane. These events cause fearful reactions at first, but little by little students come to understand their relative importance, and to handle them with calm and discipline.

The assumption we make, of course, is that learning to handle specific fears will eventually lead to a general equanimity, and it often does. Even the best teacher, however, can only take a student so far, and few students ever seem to overcome all fear, as legends lead us to believe some past masters did.

In fact, the idea that one can lead a satisfying life without fear is questionable, since fear may often be a strength associated with caring. Understanding this, our goal is not to make people into killing or dying machines. Though we do want to teach students to overcome their fear of personal, physical risk, we would be doing them no favors if we taught them not to care about their loved ones or their friends.

I can say from personal experience that two decades of hard practice does reduce the fear of danger, but it does not produce the kind of iron-headedness that one would expect from a robot warrior. One learns, instead, to put dangers in their proper perspective, to care deeply about important things and to take action to protect those things, whether that action causes fear or not, Adopting a broad perspective and doing what is right is real courage.

Right action very often does involve giving up something personal for a greater good; the great martial artist is ready and willing to do so.

LOYALTY

Loyalty is the glue that connects the martial artist to his school, his family, and to all of society. We have already seen that courage with no good cause is not courage at all, and since all good causes are related to issues larger than ourselves, we must have a sense of our connection to them. If we recognize and accept that connection, either overtly or intuitively, we will develop loyalty.

The dojo is an excellent place to foster the development of loyalty. Many students enter a dojo for very personal reasons, such as a desire to learn self-defense or to become more fit, but those who end up staying often do so because they feel a sense of family there. That sense of belonging is exactly what we hope will develop in students, since it will make it easier for them to follow the orders of their seniors and help them through the times when they are frustrated with their training. Students who love and respect their teachers make the best training partners because they will execute techniques willingly, with a spirit of enthusiasm, whenever they are asked to do so. Viewed from the outside, this devotion can seem misguided, even dangerous, and there are probably situations in which it is. An unscrupulous teacher might well be able to influence students to do something bad or illegal, but we must be careful not to assume an unhealthy relationship exists just because a teacher expects extreme devotion from his students.

There are times when teachers will throw their students about like rag dolls, and a non-martial artist might well wonder why students allow their *sensei* to treat him so badly. What such an observer would not realize, however, is that the willingness of students to commit fully to the interaction allows them to experience first hand the most powerful techniques of the teacher. At the extreme boundaries of human perception and physical reaction time lies a close approximation of a life and death battle, with high stakes and with great emotional awards. If the teacher is really talented and, together with the student, enters into the exercise with positive intent and commitment, there is nothing more rewarding than this kind of training experience. It can be almost spiritual in its intensity, and because of the sheer joy of experiencing it, the student will be even more loyal once he has been shown these outer boundaries of skill.

Furthermore, experiencing the teacher at his best gives students something to aim at. They will realize how extreme the limits of skill are, and will see how much their own skills must be developed to reach those limits. This realization produces another kind of loyalty, since the teacher is the best guide for the student intent on following the path of budo, and once a student is committed to becoming great, he or she will stay with the teacher for a very long time.

Leading students to the point of such awareness is no easy task, however. In the first months or years of budo training, students not aware that there can be any such reward from the experience of great technique. To them, training can seem to be made up only of endless, repetitive drilling and physical toil. Great techniques performed in their presence may seem awesome, and they may have a desire to be able to perform them, but they will not necessarily experience the broadening of perspective that more advanced students will. Beginning students must take the rewards of martial arts training as matters of faith, and they will persevere through the difficult first period of training only in proportion to how well they can imagine what may lie in the future, their sense of belonging to the group, and how much they enjoy training for other reasons.

Loyalty opens the way for great possibilities in training, and as we have seen, it can also be abused. For this reason, it is important for beginning students of the martial arts to shop carefully for a teacher. I stated earlier that you would not be wasting your time even if you spent a year or two looking for a good teacher, and it bears repeating here. A student should visit many schools, and ask others about their experiences with their teachers.

Once students choose a school, however, they must commit fully to the training, following the orders of the instructor and doing their best to perform perfectly the techniques they are taught, without asking a lot of questions. The techniques of the martial arts cannot be transmitted through words alone, nor can they be experienced in a few moments of training, so students must allow themselves enough time in practice to have a chance at seeing what budo is really all about. No one who gives up after a few months can claim to have really understood, much less grasped the essence of martial arts. Loyalty, in the beginning, consists of little more than believing that the future holds something worthwhile, and following the rules of the school.

Intermediate students of the martial arts should begin to feel that sense of belonging described earlier. Loyalty, for them, will mean wanting not to let down their friends and training partners. They should have had enough rewarding experiences in the dojo that their trust in the teacher is no longer based on faith, but on experience. They should realize now that it is possible for them to become much better by working hard to follow the advice of seniors. Whether or not they are willing to do the necessary work will determine whether they advance past this stage, or stagnate and eventually quit.

Advanced students of budo, who are usually assisting teachers in the running of the school, or at least helping teach some classes, must have some understanding of the meaning of reciprocity, which is practical behavior based on loyalty. They should realize that, although they owe much of their success to their own hard training, they could not have reached the same point without the teacher. This realization should be reflected in relations with juniors, who will look up to them in much the same way as they look up to the teacher. Their actions are examples to others, and they should be aware that weaknesses in their comportment will diminish the loyalty of juniors. Their relationship to the head teacher is a model for relationships between themselves and juniors, so their loyalty now becomes a very practical means of enforcing discipline within the lower ranks. What began as mere faith is now a useful principle that the senior students understand because they experience its effects firsthand in everyday training.

Some mention should be made at this point of the fact that advanced students must often leave their home dojo to complete their development. A natural part of the close relationship between teacher and student is that some students will grow and eventually become relatively close to the teacher in ability. There will probably always be a difference in the depth of their understanding, since the most advanced ten percent of knowledge in martial arts is far more difficult to achieve than the first ninety percent, but just as children nearing adulthood must challenge their parents and seek their own role in the world, so must students of the martial arts eventually become complete individuals by seeking independence.

While this separation might seem to be a severing of the ties of loyalty, and in some cases may end up being so, it is a necessary step in the maturation of students. By testing their abilities in a larger arena, students will come to have a better appreciation of what their teachers have gone through before them, and while their abilities sharpen through contact with other martial artists, they will come to have a new respect for their teachers for having endured some of the difficulties they now face. As long as the students remember that nothing in their martial arts careers would have been possible without the guidance of their teachers, they will understand their proper place in the continuing succession of martial artists.

10. THE OXHERDER'S JOURNAL

This selection, an exercise in historical fiction, attempts to elucidate some of the important qualities of training in the modern Japanese martial arts (budo). It focuses on the experience of three martial artists, individuals not as well known in the West as some others, whose experience helps explore the significance of the qualities of isshin *(single-heartedness),* mushin *(no-mind), and* zanshin *(awareness).*

From *Herding the Ox* by JOHN DONOHUE

I am drawn to the dojo again and again. I gaze through the steamy glass of storefront schools with the same wide-eyed wonder and desire of a child ogling a toy display at Christmas. In fact, what began for me as an essentially intellectual enterprise—the academic study of a particular aspect of Japanese culture—has changed into something more. The almost magnetic pull of the modern martial arts is, I believe, an attraction which far transcends their ostensible value as either exercise or systems of self defense. I am not alone in this feeling or in this suspicion, for while there are literally millions of martial arts practitioners in the world, only a tiny fragment ever attain the proficiency of champions or exhibit the psychological predisposition of the natural fighter. For the most part, *budoka* labor at their training—and anyone who studies budo will tell you that it is mostly hard work—without the ruthless determination of the competitor or the grim focus of the warrior. Elements of fear, aggression, and competition are present, of course, but they are not the sole motivation for study. Martial artists, I have come to believe, are engaged in something that is complex, significant, and fully human—something that transcends the narrow (though important) bounds of the arena and spills over into life in its fullest sense.

Martial arts are popularly understood simply as methods of fighting that are weaponless or utilize the archaic arsenal of a foreign culture's bygone age. When people think of the martial arts they envision the seemingly effortless grace of judo flips or the destructive impact of the karate chop. Certainly the promise of heightened defensive and offensive powers is part of the attraction the martial arts hold for people today—witness the seemingly endless series of martial arts movies. Anyone who perseveres in their study of these arts, however, must certainly be seeking something more. The "something more" they find is as multidimensional as the arts themselves and as varied as the individuals who study them. Some indication of the broad dimensions of meaning people find in dojo can be gleaned simply from the way martial artists talk about what they do.

As we have mentioned, budoka describe their activities in many different ways, and these descriptions convey something of the wide spectrum of functions the martial arts assume for people. Individuals may "study" an art—a word that reveals the intellectual predispositions of the Western mind as well as the sentiment that the martial arts are something worthy of serious (which to the West means intellectual) consideration. Other budoka "play," a usage that reflects, I suspect, the translation of the Japanese word concerning activities surrounding things as varied as cooking, using mystical instruments, and engaging in sports. Judoka, for instance, always sat that they are playing judo. This reflects judo's strong sport identity in the modern world (it has been an Olympic event since 1964). I also think it has a deeper significance: its use is an implicit recognition of one of the central tenets of the art—the expression of *ju*, or gentleness, through the pursuit of mutual benefit and welfare. The use of "play" is a tacit acknowledgment by judo students that very few of them will ever attain the skills or statuses of champions. They play, in short, for sheer enjoyment of the beauty of the art.

A final often-heard description is that of "training." This can reflect as variety of orientations. Competitors train. The use of the this word conveys a seriousness of purpose which is found among budoka who are contest oriented, or whose particular style is heavily concerned with self-defense and combat. This is a particularly grim approach, and one in which the true meaning of budo can be obscured if great care is not taken. To focus only on contest is to be fixated on winning and losing, to define oneself solely on the basis of a fleeting moment. It is, of course, a highly human sort of thing to do, since we are by nature goal oriented, but there is little of a martial "way" in this sort of study. In, the relentless pursuit of victory we run the risk of not preparing for the inevitable event in human life—defeat. We make the art a means to an end (and a very limited end a that), rather than a thing to be savored and enjoyed for its own sake.

This is not to say that the pursuit of the martial arts is not a serious thing, for it most certainly is. Nor do I mean to say that competition has no place in budo. I merely caution aspiring martial artists (as I must constantly caution myself) to be fully aware of the nature of the activity being engaged in and not to lose either perspective or the capacity for self-criticism. As a mater of fact, most traditionally-oriented martial arts will always refer to martial arts activity as training. The traditional use of the term, however, implies a much more comprehensive meaning than the one used above. This has important implications for our emphasis on the spiritual dimension of the martial arts.

Training encompasses study, in the sense that we reflect lessons passed on to us from our teachers. The study *of* budo is a gateway into Japanese history and society. It is a cultural activity in the broadest sense—we learn of the thoughts, insights, and lessons of past masters and apply them to our lives today. Budo is not just an intellectual enterprise, however. We are also engaged in a type of physical activity which is often conditioned by specific rules and methods of execution tacitly accepted by other trainees to obtain a variety of physical and psychological benefits. A ritualized, rule-bound type of activity which offers enjoyment on a number of levels is of course, a type of sport, and sports are played.

Ultimately, we are doing all these things, and something more. We are, as a *kendo* sensei told me, training, not for contest, not for promotion, but for life. The lessons learned on the hard wood floor or the padded surface of the dojo, are ones that transcend technique, that go beyond categorizations of people into groups of winners and losers. These lessons are about fine-tuning the body, clearing the mind; about uniting these two often warring aspects of the person in such a way as to combat the sense of fragmentation and purposelessness so common in society today. They are about joining together with other people in an often intense and violent activity which in the end brings people together, not drives them apart. And, finally, these lessons are about exploring the boundaries and possibilities of being fully human.

One of the ways in which the student's imagination is engaged in the process of learning something about the more complex aspect of martial ways is through the apocryphal stories told regarding masters of the arts. These stories may or may not be true in the historical sense. On a certain level, their veracity is not even important. What matters is that these stories are told and retold by martial artists and are believed to hold some sort of significance and impart some sort of lesson. In a sense they are the myths of the martial arts world—significant tales that are passed on by generations of believers. Very often the lessons contained in such "martial myths" are complex ones: they reveal themselves gradually over time and one's understanding of them evolves with the progress made in the arts themselves.

In light of the emphasis on moral action I am advocating, I would like to examine some myths and subject them to an interpretation that is somewhat unique. I should caution the reader that my interpretation is not the only way these myths can be understood; it is rather an exploration of one facet of the very complex phenomenon of the martial ways.

ISSHIN

In the recesses of an abandoned granary the strong light of the countryside was swallowed up in shadow. It was cool in there, a coldness like newly turned earth before the Spring gets to work on it. Maybe it was the dark or the dampness or the frigid feeling like something ancient and waiting, but the murderer fled there like someone heading home.

The boy was terrified of course. He had been gathering small sticks and bits of straw for his mother's fire, wandering along the lesser used paths outside the village. Sound caries far in the country, and he had sensed the thudding of feet long before the man shot into view around a bend. The thing was done in an instant, the boy pinned and dragged along with the fleeing man. He was dense and large and dirty. The battered hilt of a short sword was stuck in his sash. His breath came in great gulps as he stumbled down the path, shooting hurried glances over his shoulder. He had thick, strong fingers with dirty, broken nails. They grasped the boy cruelly, and when the boy cried out, the man cuffed him with a quick harshness that shocked the child into silence.

In the intuitive way children have, the boy knew he was in the presence of evil.

The pursuers ran them to ground in the granary. There was a crowd of farmers, the potter, the local blacksmith—men who knew all the local ways someone could try to escape. They all knew the boy, too. Once the murderer and his hostage disappeared into the building the crowd paused, momentarily at a loss.

"Anyone comes any closer, I'll cut his throat." It was a raspy, matter of fact voice. The man edged a bit nearer the doorway, his blade held across the boy's neck. Everyone in the crowd had been raised in the country. They had seen how easy it was to slit an animal's throat many times—seen how fragile life's container was. None of them had any doubt that the man would do what he said. None of them thought there was any way to prevent him.

"We should send for the constable," the potter whispered.

"Idiot," the blacksmith countered." It'll take hours. By that time, he'll be long gone. And once he's gone . . ." he drew a finger across his throat, "He doesn't need the boy."

The discussion dissolved into futile suggestions, sounds of despair. A crowd gathered, intent that the murderer should not escape, but intent on saving the boy, and equally perplexed about how to go about doing it.

A small group of men came into view down the road. They had obviously been traveling: their sandals were dirty and their robes had been hitched up to avoid the mud. The crowd slowly grew silent as they approached, eyeing each other warily: these were *samurai*. Their clothes, their distinctive top-knot hairstyle, but most of all, the *daisho*—the short and long sword of the warrior—they each carried gave them a fierce, predatory look.

The crowd sank to the ground and bowed deeply, a new element of anxiety adding to their consternation. Samurai were notoriously unpredictable. In the hierarchy of things, farmers were said to be the backbone of the country, but the real power lay in the hands of the men with swords. Warriors ate the rice the farmers grew, but often treated them like the dirt they spent their lives working.

The oldest man present approached the swordsmen and, with a great deal of bowing and apologies, explained the situation. The swordsman began to murmur, loosening their blades and spreading out for action. They seemed excited by the prospect of fighting, the chance to bring a murderer to justice, and the potential it all had for their reputations as warriors. The villagers grew more agitated. Could it be possible that the samurai failed to see the real problem? It wasn't that they had a murderer trapped here; it was that a boy from their village was being held hostage.

The village elder began to stammer, trying to figure out a way to stop what seemed like an inevitable blood bath.

"Wait." The oldest swordsman was smaller than the others. He had an impassive face with deep lines cut by seasons of squinting in the sun of countless battlefields. Compared to his burlier companions he seamed almost frail, although he had the thick, over-developed forearms of a swordsman. The others deferred to him, however.

For the first time, the village elder spoke directly to the leader, bypassing the conventional go-between. It was a risk, since the swordsman could take great offense, but what was he to do? Remain silent and have to explain to the boy's parents that, yes the boy died, but the social niceties were never violated?

The swordsman listened again to the elder's explanation, standing there quietly, not interrupting, and asking only a few questions when the elder was done. How was the man armed? How long had he been fleeing? How big was the boy?

The *bushi* sighed to himself, rubbing his chin as he tried to think of a way to solve the problem. A frontal assault was out—while there was no question his disciples would cut the man down, the boy would most certainly the as well.

He sighed again. Such a waste of life. He had seen a great deal of blood spilled in his time. In a way, he had spent his life studying the most efficient ways of doing just that, traveling with his disciples across the country, looking to perfect his skills. But he hated to see innocent life lost and, in a strange way, felt that saving the occasional innocent might somehow make up for the long roll of men he had dispatched.

The problem here was that he could see no way of saving the boy. So he squatted down and waited.

His students hated this about him. They were young and full of energy. They itched to use their skills. The master constantly reminded them, however, that waiting was a skill as well. So they all waited, the warriors and the people in the crowd, while the sun crept across the sky and the shadows began to lengthen.

"Hey out there. I want water. Food. Bring it to me." From the shadows the boy squealed briefly in pain as the murderer punctuated his demands.

The villagers looked at the master for guidance. They were all a bit afraid to approach the granary—after all, there was no reason to make things worse or tempt fate. At the same time, if one of the hot-blooded young swordsmen were picked, there was no telling what might happen.

The master stood up, stretching his back. "Ahh. . ."

"I will go," came a voice from the crowd. A monk, drawn to the commotion, had been sitting there for some time. The master looked at the monk as if seeing him for the first time—the shaved head and saffron robe of office symbols of this man's total devotion to compassion and his complete removal from the concerns of the world. The perfect emissary.

It took some time to assemble the food and water—more time than you would think to find a water gourd and some rice balls. The boy's whimpering could sometimes be heard by the crowd. Eventually the monk emerged and slowly approached the granary. He walked a bit unsteadily, as if afraid to do what he was sent to do. He wobbled along the weedy path to the door, eventually ending up on its right hand side. The murderer had eyed his approach with contempt but moved cautiously into the middle of the door to keep an eye on the monk.

"That's far enough." The monk was unarmed, but a lifetime of caution told the murderer to keep him at least an arm's length away. He still held on to the boy with one hand and his sword with the other.

"I am unarmed," the monk said. Despite his wobbly approach his voice seamed calm and quiet. But who could feel threatened by a monk? "Here is food," he said, holding out two rice balls. The murderer began to reach out, hunger driving away some caution. "Here. I will come no nearer." The monk gently tossed the ball of rice. The man relaxed his grip on the short sword—it was attached to his wrist by a cord—and caught the ball. Without pause, the monk tossed the other one in the same gentle manner.

The murderer fumbled for a split second to manage the boy, the rice ball he held, and the one tossed to him. In a flash, the man the killer thought was a monk was on him. A crashing blow, a twist of the arm, and the killer's feet were swept out from under him.

"Tie him up," the master said to his disciples as they rushed the granary. Then, walking back down the path to the crowd, he said, "Thank you for the loan of your garment, monk. Whatever you may believe, for today at least there is a little less suffering in the world."

The master walked through the crowd, ruefully rubbing his newly shaven head and wondering how long it would take to grow a topknot back.

As human beings, the world of the senses offers us great joy and great danger. Buddhists speak of the problem of *maya* (illusion) as an impediment to enlightenment. It is not only that the senses can deceive us; the problem is often that we set too great a store by appearances.

The vignette I have presented above is a famous one in the martial arts—it was even used by Akira Kurasowa as the opening scene of *The Seven Samurai*. The way it is generally interpreted is as a demonstration of how the incredible skill of a martial artist can be put to use righting wrongs or helping the innocent. In a sense, this is true. I think it is even more importantly an exploration of how the martial artist's obligation to society—for with great skill comes great responsibility—can impel him or her to transcend a concern with appearances and illusions.

Notice in the story that the essential trick that is being played on the murderer is one that surrounds perception. In this case, the master swordsman disguises himself as a Buddhist monk—a peaceful, unthreatening, somewhat inept person—to effect the boy's rescue. The outer badges of a monk's identity—a shaven head, a distinctive type of clothing—delude the killer into permitting the master to get within range. The murderer is by definition deluded, since his mind has been clouded by rage, and the master knows this and uses it against him.

The importance of symbolic trappings in this story has something else to tell us, however. We have to remember that the country where this story took place, feudal Japan, was a deeply class-conscious one. Like many societies of this type, class distinctions were expressed in terms of dress, hairstyle, manners, and even language. Even today, it is possible to listen to two Japanese people speaking and guess, merely from the level of polite language each uses, which speaker has a higher social status.

In feudal Japan, members of the warrior, farmer, and merchant classes were easily identified. They dressed differently (a variety of sumptuary laws even specified what type of fabrics *non*-samurai were allowed to wear). Their hairstyles were distinct, as well. The men of the warrior class had the top of their heads shaved and grew a topknot that was combed forward. At around age five, samurai boys were symbolically initiated into their warrior status in a ceremony where they stood on *a. go* board (symbolizing strategy) and presented with a toy sword. Their heads were also shaved in the manner described above. So from a very early age, warriors were aware of how the way they looked was related to who they really were.

The fact that Buddhist monks shaved their heads was a real symbol of their renunciation of the world and its social order. Samurai sometimes entered the monkhood, but usually when they were old men and their utility as warriors was done. In any other situation, to lose your top-knot was a source of real humiliation.

But here we are presented with a story where a master swordsman—a man whose entire life was devoted to refining the arts that helped define the samurai as a class—voluntarily shaves his head to do a good deed. It may not seem terribly significant to readers today, but this was an unheard of thing. This was a society where the warrior class took for granted their superiority and viewed all other people as essentially existing to service the needs of the upper class. This kind of world view breeds a certain callousness. In fact, any samurai, anywhere, who felt that they had even been insulted by a lower-class person, had the legal right to kill that person on the spot and walk away, no questions asked. The gulf between warriors and others was that wide.

The lesson, although centuries old, is relevant for martial artists today. You only have to observe the many subtle ways in which rank and status are indicated in dojo to understand that questions of pride and humility are enduring ones, and that even today we create illusory chasms between ourselves and others. The hunger for rank and advancement on the part of novices is a common phenomenon in many training halls. The white belt stumbles onto the floor, gazing with envious eyes at the yudansha. They wear *hakama*. Or *obi*, somber, dark as night, heavy with mystery. They are, to the uninitiated, the embodiment of skill and arcane knowledge that is part of the allure of the arts. They are different, more experienced, more skilled. It is quite common for all involved to believe that they are somehow superior.

Here the danger of illusion is as real for the trainee as it was for the murderer in the story. In the environment of the training hall, it is easy for the more advanced student to let things get to his or her head. It is easy to forget that the trainee is always, in some ways, a novice, and needs to approach training (and relations with others) with that in mind. Many of us can remember coming across individuals who, although skilled, were tremendously self-satisfied about the fact (as if all skill is not relative); seniors who were more interested in impressing others with their competence than with helping their juniors gain some insight into the art.

In judo dojo, for instance, a central concern for all lower ranks (whether they admit it or not) is to try to identify which yudansha will help beginners to learn and which will merely use *randori* as a way to pound home the fact that a black belt can make a lower rank fall down in a number of different ways. In good dojo, the sensei usually monitors this situation and is not averse to stepping in to teach the senior student a little humility. This is, in fact, an important lesson that needs to be imparted. After working so long and so hard to gain a certain level of skill, students indulge in the quite understandable feeling that they have accomplished something admirable. They have, of course, but they are not done learning. Above all, they run the risk of thinking about themselves more than they think about the art. In such a situation, they lose the focus and seriousness that the martial arts demand. By celebrating their own accomplishments, by forgetting the more complex goals of training, and, above all, by forgetting their obligation to others, they lose the quality of single-heartedness, or isshin, that is so important in martial arts training. They are not a violent type of criminal like the man in the story, but the same flaw that makes them arrogant causes them to lose their capacity to become actors in a positive moral sense in the human community

The swordsman in the story is obviously someone who has transcended the conceit that comes with accomplishment. He is devoted to his art, not to himself. His sincere pursuit of the way, despite the discomfort and danger it brings him, is an example of the quality of isshin. This man was a master swordsman. His skill was so great that he had attracted a body of students who followed him around. His confidence was so strong that he traveled the country seeking out opponents to vanquish. He may have traveled through the countryside, but in social terms he barely touched the ground as far as local farmers were concerned. Yet he pauses in his journey and voluntarily submits to a type of humiliation in order to save the life of a total stranger— and a lower class stranger at that—when it would have been a great deal more convenient to let the local authorities try to solve what was really a parochial and rather squalid situation that could do little for his reputation as a fighter.

Why?

I believe that this is the crux of the story. Disarming an armed man is an impressive feat. The power of the art in subduing a madman pales, however, next to the force it exerts on the master. For by virtue of his pursuit of the way, he is compelled to transcend the limitations of his own pride and concern for public opinion, and to do what is right. His sincere pursuit of the way, despite the discomfort and danger it brings him, is an example of the quality of isshin—single heartedness—that is a central part of training in a martial way, and of the moral dimension implicit in walking this path.

MUSHIN

Late at night, he burned.

Katsuyoshi was a proud man, and even in sleep he could not flee from shame. He would train, grunting and straining through the humid days, his staff sweeping in flashing arcs, reversing, thrusting, until his surroundings dimmed in the gray-blue onset of twilight and his shoulders were cooled with the falling of dew. Then he would sit, calming his breathing, his heart slowly thudding into a slower tempo.

He would review the lessons of the day in the tidal wash of pulse and breath. He felt the tension in his legs and arms burn away. In time, the night whirring of insects grew and grew in volume, magnified as the light died, and drove conscious thought from his mind. Sometimes, as he felt himself drifting away, it was almost as if the match had never taken place. He felt something almost like the peace of former years.

Then he would close his eyes and, in a horrible flash, relive the moment— the stutter in his step, the flawed attack. His opponent's wooden swords trapped his staff. He was checked, thrown off balance and, in a flash, was confronted with the blurring slash of the *bokken* that ended a hair's breadth from his neck. Defeat.

It was an experience no less bitter in his dreams.

Gonosuke Katsuyoshi had driven himself from a very young age to master the arts of the warrior. As a child, he had been beaten and humiliated by older boys. It was an incident whose cause even Katsuyoshi had forgotten— like many things of childhood, the precise details seemed to fade with the passing years. What never left him, though, was the shame he felt as he lay, bruised and beaten, in the dirt of the crossroads, nor the resolve he had limped home with: to someday be a warrior that all men feared.

He grew into a prideful young man who, despite his unimpressive physical presence, had an uncanny gift for the art of the sword. With a weapon in his hand, he seemed to swell, growing more confident and menacing in appearance. He trained with a devotion and barely contained ferocity that was fueled, even as an adult, by the emotions of hurt and shame and fear he had experienced so very vividly as a child.

He mastered the techniques and strategy of the Tenshin Shoden Katori Shinto Ryu. Then the Kashima Ryu. He wielded the kata*na*, the *naginata,* and the *yari,* coming to know their qualities and uses with an almost instinctual transference that seemed to occur merely by holding the weapons in his hand.

But his teachers, while impressed by his skill, remained unsatisfied with other areas of his development. Sitting together sipping tea, they appeared stolid and unperceptive: thick men in well-worn *keikogi*. Their eyes told a different story, however. They glittered with alertness and could fix a trainee with a piercing glance. They appreciated Katsuyoshi's achievements, but saw them as somehow incomplete. They challenged him to explore other arts, other weapons, in the hopes that a new perspective or new frustrations would generate something within him that mere technical mastery seemed not to have done. Eventually, despairing of their prodigy, his masters had encouraged him to become a *mushashugyosha*, an itinerant warrior who wandered the land in search of new venues in which to conquer (or be conquered). Some day, the group *of* sensei hoped, Katsuyoshi would discover that even his immense talent could be defeated, and that this experience would temper his spirit and introduce him to the critical element currently lacking in his mastery: humility.

He had wandered throughout the seemingly endless chain of hills, threading different forest roads to the bright clearings of towns. He churned the length of central Japan, seeking out new masters and dojo to test his skills. He grew so proud that he once more picked up the staff, that most simple of weapons, so confident in his skill that he would face a swordsman with nothing but a shaft *kashiwa* oak. He left a trail of opponents in his wake, and each humbled challenger lying panting on the ground helped ease the memory of a little boy lying bleeding in a dusty road two decades ago.

Then he met Musashi.

He was a scruffy looking character, ill-kempt and slightly bug-eyed. He walked, however, with a swagger that seemed somehow familiar to Katsuyoshi—and any observer with the nerve could have told him that was because both these warriors had the same look of defiant arrogance. Once they had been introduced, it was inevitable that a match would be arranged.

It was held early one morning in a clearing by a narrow river. Tendrils of mist still steamed up from the water's surface as Katsuyoshi waited for his opponent to appear. They had agreed on dawn for the match, but here in the narrow mountain valley the sky had lightened long before the sun peered over the eastern rim of hills. Katsuyoshi wondered whether Musashi had forgotten; even allowing for a misunderstanding of what dawn meant, surely he would want to examine the field? Many a warrior had been defeated by things other than technique, and the secret transmissions of many sword ryu dealt with admonitions to examine your surroundings carefully, and to use these things—the slope of the land, the angle of the sun—in your strategy.

Musashi came boiling into the clearing and, without any but the most minimal preliminaries, tied up his sleeves, handed his swords to a companion, and drew a pair of wooden swords from a bag.

"Bokken?" Katsuyoshi asked.

Musashi nodded nonchalantly and shrugged at the staff his opponent held. "Your wood against mine."

Katsuyoshi regretted the choice. Sometimes, just the confidence he displayed by daring to go against a live blade with an oak staff was enough to shake an opponent. Besides, carefully used, it was possible for a wooden *bo* to actually shatter the steel of a kata*na*. It was hard to tell whether Musashi's choice was a reflection of his confidence, his cunning, or even both. Katsuyoshi felt a small thrill of anticipation: this would be an interesting match.

And so it was. There were few spectators, and those that were present were silent. Except for the murmur of the river and the distant chirping of birds, the only sounds that could be heard were the swish of the swordsmen's hakama, the rush of their breath, and the sharp clacking of their weapons as each man furiously sought the critical opening that would decide the encounter.

It was not totally unheard of for a swordsman to use two swords at once, but Katsuyoshi was startled with the skill Musashi displayed, wielding them, now in tandem, now in separate movements, so that his opponent was continually on guard. It became gradually apparent to both men that the flow and celerity of technique being displayed that day was of a higher order. The few senior *kenshi* watched with narrowed, appreciative eyes.

Some of the apprehension Katsuyoshi felt early in the match began to fade, however. The bo's greater length helped in keeping a swordsman at bay; it could slash like a *naginata* or thrust like a *yari*. He had some close calls early in the match—Musashi's quickness was extraordinary and he would shoot into any opening with the gliding, focused step of a master swordsman—but Katsuyoshi managed, through clever reversals and sweeps, to avoid his opponent's counters.

It was in attempting another maneuver of this sort that he was defeated. As Katsuyoshi thrusted, Musashi slid in along the length of the bo. Katsuyoshi began to adjust, preparing for a diagonal strike down across Musashi's shoulder—the cut known as *kesa-giri*. By retracting the bo in his movement, he was forced to readjust his grip. Musashi darted a feint to Katsuyoshi's hand. Katsuyoshi jerked his arm out of the way and attempted to regain the momentum of the attack, but the stutter in technique was telling. The strike was not as decisive as it should have been; Musashi caught the shaft in the crossed-sword block known as *juji-dome*, forced the staff down and pivoted around to bring his bokken slicing in an arc that stopped just short of his opponent's neck. Katsuyoshi was frantically trying to regain his balance, and even though Musashi had spun into his *shikaku*—the blind spot just outside the range of his peripheral vision—Katsuyoshi's senses were strung to an almost unbearable tension and he could clearly hear the soft moan of Musashi's sword as it cut toward him.

He half expected the explosion of the finishing blow: Musashi had killed men in matches of this type before, even using a bokken. But it never came. The bug-eyed swordsman seemed content with his victory as it was.

Katsuyoshi, knelt, breathing heavily, and bowed to Musashi. *"Maitta."* The phrase was so hateful to say—I am beaten—that it had a tight, croaking sound in the stillness of the morning.

Musashi merely nodded, striding over to place his weapons in their bag. He turned as he was adjusting his daisho in his sash. It was usual for the victor, in a position of superior status, to bring the meeting to a close. Katsuyoshi sat, his ears burning in shame, at a complete loss. It was well-known that Musashi accepted no disciples. Deep down, Katsuyoshi still believed he could best the bug-eyed swordsman and his pride kept him from begging to become Musashi's disciple. He did not want to learn from this man; he wanted to destroy him.

Musashi's head popped up as these thoughts shot through Katsuyoshi's head. Standing there, looming above him, Musashi looked directly at his opponent with narrowed eyes and said. "No. Do not even think of it. There is no point in another duel. I would kill you then. To have a weapon be inadequate is one thing. When man and weapon are inadequate is quite another."

With these cutting words, he strode off. The witnesses trailed after him, like so many grave ducks. Katsuyoshi rose to his feet, and although he felt the warmth of the sun as it edged over the rim of the hills, his heart was cold within him.

He left that town as quickly as possible, trying not to be conscious of the knowing glances and soft comments made as he hurried down the road. There was nothing left for him here. His sensei had set him on a path that now seemed to have no real point to it. He wandered south. Passers-by saw a silent figure, carrying the well-used weapons and predatory look that usually spelled trouble in local dojo. But Katsuyoshi never paused in his wanderings. He stared into the distance with the look of a man who was searching for something that, deep down, he felt would never be found. He sat in a boat taking him to Kyushu, a gray man in a gray rain, tossed about by the waves that seemed to him to be much like life itself: shifting, changing shape, incapable of being tamed. On shore, he wandered up into the hills, his staff in hand. It served as a goad to travel; a reminder of his humiliation.

Perhaps in the heights, he thought, he could see clearer. He labored up, only to find the slopes of Homanzan shrouded in fog. The trees, black and silent in the dimness, dripped water onto the ruins of temples. The buildings slouched on slopes, decayed and canted, the victims, not of catastrophe, but of neglect. They were empty mouths gaping into the uncaring night.

Finally, his flight came to an end, not because he had arrived, but because he no longer felt that a destination actually existed. He was empty. Of ambition. Of energy. Alone on the fog-bound hillside, he gazed into the twilight, staring sightlessly at the decayed temple statues known as *jizo*. They stared back.

Eventually, he slept.

Once again, in his dreams, he fought. In a mountain dell, studded with rocks and the dead branches of trees, a young fighter—a boy—attacked. He was silent in assault, smiling faintly, his black eyes glittering with a type of amusement. Again and again, Katsuyoshi attempted to bring his staff to bear, only to have his attacks thwarted.

He burned.

But try as he might, there was no defeating this maddening boy. In the close quarters of the ravine, the staff was too long, his attempts too clumsy. His growing fury choked him until, with a check and a sudden twist of his opponent's hips, Katsuyoshi was thrown down.

The boy pinned one of Katsuyoshi's hands, still gripping the staff, to the ground. The victor stood, gazing down, the point of his sword in the defeated man's face.

"Katsuyoshi." he said, "you must learn to let go."

The sword arced up and then down toward Katsuyoshi's pinned forearm. The blade rang as it sliced through arm and staff.

The sound, still ringing in his head, woke him from his dream.

Letting go. A strange dream. A stranger message. He sat, gazing at his hand, running it over the staff, until the night grew grayer by degrees and morning came.

He was by nature a practical man—a lifetime in the martial arts had shaped him in that regard. But here, on the mountain, where the ghosts of worshipers seemed to slip in and out of the fog-bound ruins of the mountain temples, it was all too easy to believe in a more complicated reality filled with portents in dreams. The very air seemed to lend credence to the tales of the *yamabushi*, the magic monks of the remote hills, renowned masters of the darker aspects of the martial arts. Or of the mythical beings known as *tengu*, who on occasion appeared to supplicants to reveal their combat secrets. In a place where the fog dappled forms and obscured the hard edges of shapes, it seemed to Katsuyoshi that his dream was something more than it appeared.

Letting go. "What was the message here? He couldn't completely shake the effects of his training, so he tended to think in largely martial terms. Was he supposed to use only one hand? Would that have saved him from the awful ringing of the katana as it sliced through his arm? But the staff was too long to manage that way.

One handed. By letting go, the dream seemed to say, he would avoid defeat and the awful maiming that would ruin him as a warrior. But how could he do so? He relived his duel with Musashi, the way in which the nature of the bo—its length usually such an advantage in a duel—had worked against him. Musashi, he now realized, had used his reliance on the staff's length to defeat him. It was in the stuttering moment where he had needed to realign his hold on the shaft that Musashi had driven his attack home.

Length . . . Letting go. . . .

Katsuyoshi descended from the hills with a new weapon. A shaft of oak shorter than the 60, it retained some of its advantages in reach but, because it stretched only to his shoulders, it was far more manageable. They *jo,* as Katsuyoshi termed it, was quicker to use in reversals, could be deftly shortened and extended. It would be managed with one hand as the fighter adjusted to shifting lines of attack and defense. It permitted him to let go.

He now churned up the turnpikes of central Japan with a new purpose, Bushi wise enough to read the balance in his gait and the look in his eye avoided him. What was unusual for Katsuyoshi, however, was that the implicit challenges of less seasoned, more foolish, swordsmen were totally ignored. The man who had in times past sought out all comers as a way of proving himself over and over again seemed, like his weapon, to have been subtly altered.

He and Musashi met after the seasons had wheeled them into the cusp between autumn and the dark grip of winter. The stubble of the field in which they met had been trampled down by the press of weather. Their breath smoked in the cold dawn, the clouds of vapor lit up by the rising sun, emanations of *ki* that billowed out, flashed golden, and were torn apart by the chill wind.

The clash was colder, crisper, harder than their last match. Musashi's force was almost overwhelming, his eyes bugging hungrily as he slashed and whirled at Katsuyoshi. It was, in many ways, more terrifying than the dream that had haunted Katsuyoshi all those months ago.

And yet he was possessed of a type of calm. An observer would almost say he looked remote, except for the fact that the high level of weapons play demanded a vital connection with the here and now. With the jo in his hands, Katsuyoshi met Musashi's attacks, gave way and advanced, with a cold focus that made even the Two Sword Man take notice.

This time, it was Musashi who ended up in the dirt. He lay there, breathing heavily and waiting for the final blow from the new weapon that Katsuyoshi wielded so effectively. The cold, brittle earth held him up, as if to offer him to his opponent.

But there was no strike. Katsuyoshi backed away carefully, bowed, and walked quietly away like a man in a dream. He gave Musashi only a fleeting thought—"Now, perhaps, he will know what it is to burn."

Then Katsuyoshi set out for home. He needed to present himself to his sensei. To tell them he had learned that, for all those years, when he had grasped his weapons so tightly, so intent on winning, on proving himself, he had in fact been overlooking the most essential lesson: letting go.

There is a significant challenge for human beings in the act of fighting. As biological organisms with the essential purpose of surviving and reproducing, the ability to respond to aggression, or display it ourselves, runs very deep. All living things share this propensity. Yet for people, the whole thing is even more complicated than merely just fighting for survival—killing or being killed. As members of the species *homo sapiens*—"wise" or "knowing" man— we bring a consciousness of the import of our actions to each struggle. In other words, in addition to being involved in a struggle for survival, we have the capacity for knowing what its implications are. And for worrying about it.

Certainly this was one of the things that attracted the feudal samurai to the study of Zen Buddhism. Much of Zen seemed to be oriented around combating that sort of reflective consciousness. Through the process of meditation, pupils of Zen learn to let conscious thought "bubble off" and free the individual to experience the here and now with little or no interference from the conscious mind. Certainly one of the things that attracted swordsmen like Yagyu Munenori to Zen was the idea that, by doing away with the sort of worry and thought that defines human beings as sapient, warriors could improve their reflex action and, consequently, their ability to survive.

A real test of an individual's accomplishment in any area is to require him or her to perform in moments of great stress. The notion that you can truly measure someone's character through the way they act in the crucible of extraordinary events is a widely accepted one. It is also one of the reasons why human beings are so interested in stories of heroism—the courage of a soldier on a battlefield, the daring act of rescue, the mother's tenacious defense of her young. For the warriors of Japan, the true test of their progress in Zen was considered to be the way in which they faced the ultimate challenge of life and death embodied in combat.

A great deal has been made of the seemingly suicidal dimension of the warrior's code known as *bushido*. The morbid fascination of Westerners with the act of ritual suicide properly known as *seppuku*. (but often coarsely termed *hara kiri*, "belly cutting") or the willingness of Japanese fighters to the for seemingly pointless reasons (fueled by Pacific War veterans' remembrance of the appalling futility of *"banzai* charges") masks the essential reason why Japanese fighters were adamant in their insistence that the warrior must be able to transcend a concern with living in order to reach full fighting potential.

Part of this ideal was, of course, shaped by political reasons. Any army has to indoctrinate its soldiers in an ideology that celebrates the performance of duty under hazardous conditions. It also has to convince the individual fighter that there is something more important than his life—honor, duty, country to cite an American example. And, of course, considerations of these type were part and parcel of the Japanese fighting man's beliefs.

In addition to these more pragmatic considerations, however, the Japanese martial tradition is relatively unique in its incorporation of more philosophically elevated concepts. In this case, Buddhism's conviction that life as we generally perceive it is a type of illusion, and Zen's insistence that the individual could come to enlightenment through the abandonment of a mind-set that made distinctions between the self and other, between subject and object, encouraged Japanese warriors to develop an ideology that encouraged a disregard for death. In this instance, warriors were encouraged not to fear death, not just because it was militarily functional, but because such a mind set, exhibited at critical moments on the battlefield, was dramatic proof the extent to which the individual had internalized the lessons of Zen.

In more civil times, the Japanese acknowledged that the crucible of combat was not a practical way to evaluate enlightenment. Yet, they felt, the combative aspect of the martial arts was so vitally important that it should be preserved in some way. The martial tradition, they felt, was ultimately of value due to its ability to train the human body *and* the spirit. This is, of course, what lies behind the emphasis in the term commonly used for the modern martial arts—budo (martial ways).

The masters who adapted martial systems to fit the needs of contemporary trainees were nonetheless aware that they could rob budo of some of its intrinsic worth by eliminating the combat experience. If, as Japanese thinkers maintained, budo was a type of *seishin tanren* (spiritual forging), then surely a forge with all the heat bled out of it would be of little use to further generations of martial artists.

Traditionally, Japanese martial systems had utilized structured training through a fixed sequence of actions embodied in kata. The predictability of kata permitted a refinement of technique and created a safety cushion for training with bladed weapons. Yet, during the feudal era, these trainees would also be truly tested outside the precincts of the dojo in the lethal environment of the battlefield.

With the pacification of Japan in the seventeenth century, opportunities for true combat testing dwindled. Individual warriors could engage in single duels, as was the case with Katsuyoshi and Musashi, but these activities became increasingly difficult to arrange and were eventually banned by law.

Yet the masters were wary of doing away with all combat. Some martial arts schools, it is true, emphasized training exclusively through forms, but many senior sensei decried this as "flowering fighting." If you were teaching someone to fight (even in theory), they maintained, you still needed them to fight.

This led to the institutionalization of various types of free fighting in the modern martial arts forms. Swordsmen had long used wooden training weapons to minimize injuries, and continued to create innovative mock swords that could be used in sparring. The various types of *shinai* used today by *kendoka*, some *aikidoka*, and others, represent good examples of non-lethal weapons that can aid in keeping all the heat (but little of the blood) in contemporary training.

But by eliminating one type of danger, the masters inadvertently introduced another. Non-lethal encounters are, of course, contests. Contests have winners and losers. In the thrill of victory, the rush of pleasure in winning a tournament match, there is a danger of enlarging, not diminishing, the ego. A martial artist infatuated with competition must be on guard not to lose sight of the ultimate purpose of the martial ways.

Katsuyoshi's experience is a case in point. Here is a brilliant martial artist who has mastered the technical aspects of his craft, who has beaten countless opponents, and who has missed the point entirely. For this man, the martial way had ceased to be a path to spiritual development and instead had deteriorated into a means of personal aggrandizement.

So his sensei sent him out into the world, hoping that he would suffer defeat and, in the heat of that crucible, have his spirit strengthened.

That process of spiritual forging was an extraordinarily painful process for a proud man like Katsuyoshi. It led him to depression and despair, isolation and doubt. Yet for some reason (perhaps just the habit of training and the need, in all this confusion, to hold onto something familiar), he continued to seek an answer through his training.

An eventually, of course, he found it. We may assume that his teachers saw the potential for enlightenment slumbering deep within him. Yet when it comes, enlightenment arrives in an unexpected way and bearing a confusing message.

For Katsuyoshi's enlightenment comes in a dream. Today, many students of the mind look for insights and messages in dreams that remain hidden from us by the light of day. People of Katsuyoshi's time believed significant dream experiences to have a supernatural origin, and he eventually named his system of fighting with the jo Shindo Muso Ryu—the martial tradition of the spirit way dream.

Certainly part of this dream had a technical component that led to the creation of they jo. But, we may ask, what else was transmitted? What would have allowed a once-proud warrior, publicly humiliated with his reputation in tatters, to once again confront Musashi with a new, untried system of fighting?

In essence, he had learned to heed the advice of the Spirit Boy in his dream. He had let go. Of pride. Of concern for his reputation. Of the fear of losing. Katsuyoshi had ceased to be haunted by the dream of defeat and became so focused on pursuing total excellence with his new art that he had achieved the state so valued by Zen masters and martial artists alike—mushin.

The lesson here for contemporary budoka—particularly those active in competitive arts—is to be aware of the spiritual danger inherent in this sort of activity. I am not implying that sparring and various types of matches should be abandoned. I believe that the masters who insisted on their development had some very good reasons for doing so. I am maintaining, however, that, human nature being what it is, there is a real risk that too much of a psychic investment in competition may be ultimately harmful for a sincere pursuit of the martial ways.

The trainee should always be aware that any contest is merely a means to an end. If we vie with one another to test our skills in the heat of a ritual type of combat, it is because we are seeking to test just how well we have internalized the precepts of our arts. We are not (or should not be) there solely for the psychic gratification of winning. In any real sense this would be foolish. No individual wins all the time. We have good days and bad days. Certainly as we age, speed and strength decline. To appreciate sparring only when we win is to effectively rob ourselves of enjoying many of our free fighting experiences.

It is true that the martial artist competing in tournaments will observe many students who have forgotten this lesson. The kendo student intent on perfecting technique and pursuing an accurate vision of the art will not always be the most successful of tournament players. She will come across highly competitive kendoka who specialize in scoring at all costs, often at the expense of classical technique. Generally speaking, senior kendo sensei are quite sensitive to matters of tradition and technique, but in the speed and heat of contests, the sound of an accurate hit alone (since the shinai often moves too quickly for the eye to follow) can result in a point. Tournament players know this, and so work to truncate their techniques for maximum speed and tournament effectiveness. In doing so, of course, they move their kendo further and further away from its martial roots, and, should they persevere in their studies, lay the groundwork for a spiritual crisis in later years.

The ethical lesson in Katsuyoshi's tale, then, and in the quality of mushin, is to exert care lest our pursuit of the martial arts becomes just another way of feeding the ego instead of a way of conquering it. To follow the martial path correctly (that is, ethically) we need to constantly keep in mind the real purpose of training.

I am reminded of a group *of* kendo trainees I was with who were discussing their recent meeting with a Japanese national champion They were all active competitors who were mesmerized by the speed and skill of the champion. What, they asked, was the secret of his training?

There is no secret, he told them. You just need to remember to strive always to make your kendo beautiful. Not fast. Not flashy. Only beauty matters. Everything else will follow.

That man was a champion, not because he grasped his shinai tightly, but because he was so focused on the perfection of the art that he had learned to let go.

ZANSHIN

Sound. Stillness. Each with a message.

In the hush of the garden, the remote hum of the city was kept at bay. The dry rasp of calloused feet on the wood floor, the faint rustle of the hakama were magnified. The bamboo shafts rattled briefly as Shiro set himself in the ritual that was *kyudo*. The tidal wash of breathing began as he settled into the focus of his art. The bow, arching above his head, and the target became linked.

Thrummm. The arrow sped on its way. The pattern begins again. *Thrummm.* Again. *Thrummm.*

Thud! The rhythm of the sound pulls him back ten years. The sounds are harsher, but as regular. *Thud!* The hiss of breath, the moment where time seems to stop as the interplay of speed and technique and balance are measured in the blink of an eye. Then the sound—*thud!*—As bone and muscle crash into the mat. He is back in the Kodokan.

No solitary ritual there, no measured ceremony of placement. An elegance, yes, but an elegance of a different order. The nervous shuffle and sweep of feet as fighters waited for a chance on the mat. The tight, coiling moves as players rehearsed technique. The bright eyes watching, measuring, probing for weaknesses. The sweat. The bone-crushing slam to the mat. The lethal darting for the choke hold.

The joy of the champion.

Shida Shiro, it was said, was born to study *jujutsu*. In late nineteenth century Japan, hundreds of schools of unarmed combat flourished as the nation entered the modern era, determined to both preserve its past and enter its rightful place in the world as a progressive leader. Jujutsu dojo were flooded with trainees and, in the heat of competition between students and between schools, a vicious type of selection went on where only the quickest and hardiest could endure.

Shiro was naturally quick. He had an almost reflexive ability to respond to his opponent's moves. Although never huge, he thickened over the course of the years, seeming to grow a protective layer of muscle to cushion the falls, fight off the twisting of his joints, and give him that extra edge that spelled the difference between defeat and victory.

As a youth, he had his share of humiliations. His step-father, Saigo Tanomo, was not a gentle man. He had a ruthless drive within him to elevate his jujutsu to the pinnacle of the martial arts world. He saw within Shiro the raw material to effect this, and he pushed the boy mercilessly

And so Shiro grew, almost unthinking, into a champion. He was pushed along by the drive of his elder's ambition, helpless in the pull of his duty as a son. Nor was the relationship entirely one-sided. His step-father, custodian of the secret technique of *oshiki-uchi*, had armed Shiro with a combination of finesse and fury, making him the jewel of the dojo.

In his skill and youth, Shiro tended to disregard his opponents. He took them seriously, of course—in his father's dojo every bout was to be treated as if it were *shinken shobu*, a match with real swords, a fight to the death—but gave little thought to the bodies he left groaning on the mat. Shiro trained himself into a type of weapon and, like a weapon, he was capable of no real thought about his targets.

Yet deep within Shiro there was something that yearned for more than the single-minded pursuit of his father's jujutsu. He would have been hard pressed to give name to it and, indeed, was only fleetingly aware of it on any conscious level. Sometimes in the quiet night after the flush of victory had faded, while his step-father slept, Shiro wondered...

Then, he met Professor Kano. Kano Jigoro Sensei was gaining a name for himself as both an educator in the new style as well as someone deeply concerned with preserving what was worthy in Japan's old culture. Kano the educator and Kano the custodian of culture met in his work with jujutsu. The Professor had studied a number of different ryu. He was not a brilliant competitor like Shiro, but he was persistent, methodical. He trained intensely. It was said you could tell when Kano was coming before you laid eyes on him because of the smell of the liniment he freely spread all over his bruised body.

But in that compact, battered form, there lived a mind of deep complexity and razor sharpness. Kano studied jujutsu in a way never done before. He learned the techniques. He analyzed them. He attempted to distill the essence of any movement, to purify it, and make it plain.

Not for the Professor was the mystery of traditional jujutsu. As a cultural treasure, he believed the art should be celebrated and explained, not hoarded away and revealed only to an elite few. Above all, Kano was deeply concerned that the practice of martial arts should have an ethical purpose. Jujutsu, he felt, should be practiced as judo, a "way" that lent depth and meaning to each trainee's life in and out of the dojo.

When Professor Kano was received at Shiro's dojo with barely concealed hostility, the young man watched his reactions carefully. If Kano noticed the subtle insults directed his way, he gave no indication. He quietly and respectfully told Shiro's father that he had been told of the excellence of the jujutsu practiced here and of the remarkable ability of Shiro. He asked only the opportunity to watch the training and to discuss the techniques.

Saigo was not immune to flattery, and Kano was invited to stay. He watched intently, sitting motionless off the mat. Shiro felt the power of Kano's gaze, the sword-like sharpness of his scrutiny.

After training, Kano and Saigo had a brief discussion of some technical points that the Professor raised. Saigo rarely discussed anything about his art, preferring students to learn through hard knocks, but Kano managed to drag the old man into a brief conversation.

"Saigo Sensei," the Professor concluded, "I am inviting the most skilled students of jujutsu to my school to help preserve this art for future generations. Would you permit Shiro to come and demonstrate his remarkable technique?" Only the best fighters in Tokyo would be invited, he continued, and it would be an honor if he could include Saigo's star pupil.

Shiro held his breath. Eventually, the persuasive Professor won out over the gruff Saigo.

And so, Shiro entered the Kodokan.

Here the vague unease Shiro felt in the quiet of night was put to rest. Under Kano's tutelage, the new judoka were encouraged to think about their art. How is this throw done differently by the different ryu? When you stripped away its variations, what was the essence of the technique? What principles does it reveal about movement, human action, purpose?

Kano pinned his students to the mat in more ways than one. His focus was never on winning a match, but on uncovering fundamental principles through action. It was perplexing to Shiro and his fellow students how such a bookish fellow could be fixated so much on principles and yet so skilled on the mat at the same time. It was not unusual for Kano to break off in the middle of a contest and deliver a long, complex, but perfectly lucid discussion of how the contestants had illustrated some interesting points, and how these points could be understood through assiduous training in the following techniques . . . Then Kano would resume his actions. In later years, senior judoka would assert that Kano, for all his erudition, was almost impossible to throw down. It was, one pupil asserted, like fighting with an empty jacket—when you tried to execute a technique, there was nothing there.

Principles were in the air of the Kodokan. Kano insisted that it was not enough to be a skilled fighter. To fully practice budo, one needed to devote oneself to overarching principles that were equally applicable in the dojo and the world outside. He insisted that his students be gentlemen. They were, to be sure, hard fighting and overly athletic gentlemen, but they were gentlemen nonetheless.

For Shiro, this was a new way of looking at things. He embraced Kano's concept of judo wholeheartedly and found the ethical and philosophical aspects of the Kodokan as valuable as the tremendously punishing training that was its counterpart. In elevating the art from a type of *jutsu* to a *do*, Shiro had found an answer to many of his nameless problems.

But like many types of enlightenment, this one was not without its painful side. For, in embracing Kano, Shiro had effectively rejected his step-father. At first, he had dutifully attempted to divide his time equally between Saigo's and Kano's training halls. He hoped in this way to hide his growing attachment to his new teacher. What was harder to obscure was the development of his technique. Under Kano's tutelage Shiro seemed to blossom, developing a poise and skill that was only matched by a growing sense of humanity. In Saigo's rough and tumble dojo, the technique was welcome: The humanity, however, was decidedly out of place.

Eventually, Shiro came to spend more and more time under the watchful eye of Professor Kano. A sense of duty prevented him from totally abandoning his step-father, but it was clear to all observers where Shiro's real heart rested.

Deep in his heart, Shiro knew he would have to decide. On the increasingly rare occasions when he trained at his step-father's school, he felt the smoldering gaze of Saigo burning just out of sight. Even at the Kodokan, where Shiro came to play an increasingly prominent role as an instructor, he was not immune from a similar scrutiny. Kano would watch from the side of the *tatami*, his eyes keen in an otherwise placid face. Both sensei watched their pupil to see which way he would follow.

It came to a head on a steamy summer day in an exhibition hall where the air was as thick and humid as the Tokyo afternoon. Months before, many of the old jujutsu masters had grown alarmed at the growing prestige of the Kodokan. The upstart Kano had shrewdly attracted not only extremely able pupils like Shiro, but a number of influential patrons who were advocating that Kano's new system of judo become part of the training regimen of the Metropolitan Police. At this, the jujutsu sensei exploded in indignation. Finally, it was agreed upon by all concerned that, in the interest of patriotism, a contest should be held. Not to decide whether a form of unarmed combat should be taught, but, rather, which form should be used.

The jujutsu sensei sat around tables, sipping *sake*, blunt men who had faced each other in contests over the years. United in their enmity, they grouped together and plotted their strategy. Ultimately, the question was asked.

"Saigo, will Shiro fight for you or the bookworm?"

It was a dangerous question to ask of a man never known for his patience and now not in the best of moods. His reply was remarkably tame: "The excellence of my dojo does not hinge on any one man. Shiro will do what he will. My students will beat Kano."

The tournament, when it came, was an exposition of some of the best practitioners of unarmed grappling Japan had ever seen. They lined up to salute the referees at the beginning of the meet, their uniforms as varied as the styles they represented; gray and striped hakama, *keikogi* of every conceivable style and color. And, conspicuous in their simplicity, Kano's students bowed to the judges in the whitest and black belts he had awarded them. Shiro stood with them.

The hall was a cavernous affair, and the spectators were buzzing with anticipation. Once the tournament began, however, the hall grew silent. The only sounds were from the fighters on the mats': the shuffle of feet, the rasping of breath, the slam of bodies falling, the croak of submission, and the calls of the judges.

As the day wore on, the tension mounted. Clearly, Kano's students were not invincible, but they more than held their own against the challenges Japan's jujutsu sensei could throw at them. And it was clear that Shiro was among the best contestants there. Experts watched with narrowed eyes as he moved through match after match, eliminating the weaker contestants. They nodded in silent satisfaction at his skill.

And at the end, it came down to a contest between Shiro and a cropped headed bull of a man, a student of Saigo's, renowned for not only emerging victorious in a string of contests, but for maiming his opponents in the process. The hall had dimmed as the summer sky darkened with the promise of rain. Thunder rumbled ominously in the distance. Lightening flickered on the two fighter's faces as they jerked into the ritual bow before the match began.

The struggle was so rapid, so fluid, that only the most advanced practitioners among the spectators could really follow every nuance. The men feinted, adjusted, jockeyed for dominance in a superheated dance that few in the audience had ever seen before.

Saigo, on the sidelines, grunted and hissed with every move, following the fortunes of his new protégé and his stepson with furious attention. Kano sat, impassive, only his eyes alive to the drama unfolding before him.

Shiro stumbled under a furious attack. A collective gasp rose up as the crowd anticipated a finishing throw. But with the cat-like agility he was known for, Shiro escaped. His opponent, unbalanced by his anticipation of a winning move, backed off for a split second to adjust for a new line of attack. In that split second, Shiro flashed onto the offensive. Using oshiki-uchi, he slammed his opponent into the mat and choked him into submission. The hall exploded. Kano stood and across the room his eyes locked onto those of Saigo. The bigger man glanced at Shiro, standing with head bowed, panting, almost disconnected from the tumult around him. An impartial observer would almost say he looked appalled at what he had done. Finally, Saigo turned, stiffly bowed to Kano, and left the hall.

After the closing ceremony, the Kodokan members circled Kano in a jubilant ring. Only Shiro seemed less than elated.

Kano looked him in the eye. Their relationship had become so close that no question needed to be asked. "Sensei," he stammered, "it was *his* technique I used. His."

"Shiro," Kano murmured, "the point is not where we get our gifts, it is what we do with them."

Outside, the rain fell in torrents.

After that day, Shiro could never approach the Kodokan without the feeling that, in using the technique he had mastered in his stepfather's dojo to win the day for Kano, he had betrayed both men. He had rejected Saigo's ryu for the allure of the Professor's martial way, yet had used Saigo's special technique. He had embraced Kano's system, feeling it superior in every way, yet had, seemingly, abandoned its precepts in the heat of the tournament.

Gripped by a sense of guilt and powerless to break its hold through rationalization, Shiro merely went through the motions of training in judo. Finally, unable to bear the conflict within him, and unwilling to give Kano anything but his best, Shiro went to the Professor and announced his intentions to quit judo for good.

Kano silently motioned for the young man to sit beside him and spoke carefully and slowly. "Shiro, you are an honorable man. I could argue that you, in fact, acted in the best interest of the martial arts by using all your skills—*all of them*—in the service of a greater good. Because I truly believe that judo is a superior way of studying the martial arts of our nation. Your victory will permit us to bring many benefits to the people of this country through training in our art."

Shiro started to speak, but Kano held up his hand. "It is a measure of your goodness that you feel the conflicts you feel. I hope you can find a way to live with yourself. If, however, the burden becomes too great, remember that there are many do, many ways to follow in this world.

"I once told you that we are all given gifts, but the most important thing is how we use those gifts. I will now tell you that there are many virtuous ways to use our talents. In some ways it grieves me to say it, but judo is not the only way for you. Choose the path you will." Sighing, Kano got up and walked toward the door. "The students need me now."

He paused briefly and, looking for a last time at his pupil, Kano said, "Remember, you will always be my student as long as you follow the way, no matter what form it takes."

Saigo Shiro left Tokyo, unable to reconcile the pull of his two fathers. He moved to Nagasaki, eventually becoming a journalist. As if the memories of judo were too painful, Shiro abandoned the art and instead immersed himself in the solitary art of archery. Stripped of the distraction of competition and opponent, Shiro seemed to find solace in kyujutsu.

But on some quiet days the rhythm of the bow and the thudding impact of the shaft pulled him back. Almost unbidden, he relived his choices. He reviewed his life's trajectory with all the intensity once displayed on the judo mat and with all the cold dispassion of a master archer watching the arrow's flight. On warm quiet evenings, the measured punctuation of kyujutsu's ritual swept him into painful reverie, until he was no longer sure whether what he heard was the thud of the arrow, the sound from that fateful contest reverberating over the years, or merely the beating of his own heart.

Like judo, life is a game of balance, of awareness, and of sensitivity to others. In this art, like many others, the concept *of* zanshin is stressed. Literally "remaining mind," this term is often translated as "awareness." But it is awareness of a particular type. It involves the ability to be focused on a technique but not to lose sight of the greater picture. In judo, you can demonstrate zanshin by maintaining your composure even as you fall, controlling that fall through the art of *ukemi,* and remaining alive to the possibility of countering your opponent's move. In *kendo,* trainees are encouraged to display zanshin of a slightly different type by maintaining perfect posture and follow through after a technique and remaining aware of the movements of opponents.

In both cases, trainees are encouraged not to lose themselves in the moment. Focus on actions, yes. Commit fully, of course. Yet, at the same time, the sensei seem to be calling for a heightened awareness of a greater sphere of interaction: the relation of the technique and the moment to the wider context of the contest. When we extend the notion of zanshin out beyond the confines of the dojo, we are warning against all types of self-absorption and advocating an awareness of and sensitivity to the larger context in which we all live our lives.

Shiro's tale is one that shows a master competitor and a martial artist coming alive to the full potentiality of the way. At the same time, he is an individual enmeshed, as are we all, in a complex series of relationships, loyalties and conflicts. For our purposes, the interesting thing about this story is not the recounting of his prowess, but rather the examination of how an extremely well-developed type *of* zanshin led him to a particular series of actions.

The struggle Shiro experienced may seem somewhat minimal to us today. The Japanese, however, have an extreme sensibility to the nuances of human relations, especially those between superiors and subordinates. The concepts of on, the deep obligation that a child owes to his or her parents, and of *giri,* the sense of duty that such obligation entails, are extremely powerful. They are rendered even more compelling by the realization that, in real terms, children can never fully repay their parents, and that the process of growing up inevitably makes demands on an individual that can cause conflict with the notion of giri.

Such is the case with Shiro. A gifted youth with tremendous potential, he is trained by his step-father in the art of jujutsu. Saigo's rationale for doing so may be debated. It could have been for adult self-gratification through the triumphs of a child (familiar to anyone who has come into contact with a particular type of Little League parent) or a genuine attempt to give Shiro something of lasting value, however gruff the giver's demeanor. But this question is insoluble and beside the point. The fact of the matter is that Saigo's training created a tremendous obligation on Shiro's part to honor his mentor.

When Kano enters the scene, the stage is set for an intense type of conflict. Kano Jigoro was erudite, cosmopolitan, highly intelligent—a gentleman in the truest sense. He brought an added dimension to his study of the grappling arts: the conviction that they were structured by an underlying logic, and that the exploration of that elegant logic could be used as a way for cultivating the human spirit. The young athlete Shiro responded to this vision, to Kano's revelation of new and undreamed of horizons. For a time Shiro may have deluded himself into thinking he was only polishing technique by studying with another style of fighting (not an uncommon practice), but ultimately, the vision Kano had for his Kodokan completely seduced the young trainee. And this vision continues to do the same thing for countless trainees today.

But for Shiro, this new and heartfelt allegiance *to* judo created a terrible dilemma. It was made all the more difficult by the very public struggle between the Kodokan and other jujutsu schools for preeminence. The moral courage Shiro must have possessed to stand that day in the simple white *gi* of the judoka, signaling to all his complete break with his step-father, was enormous. He had, in fact, reached that inevitable day when a grown child chooses his own course of action, often hurting a parent in the process.

But for Shiro the intolerable thing was not his mere choosing of Kano over Saigo; it was in the double offense he had committed in using his stepfather's own technique against him. For Shiro, it must have seemed hypocritical. Here he was, making a public display of fidelity to Kano and indicating that he thought the Professor's system was superior, and yet using the techniques of another style—his stepfather's—to prove this dominance.

You could rationalize the action away, of course. The heat of the contest. A sudden reflexive action, not a conscious thought. Kano's system really a synthesis of many styles, no real betrayal in using this technique. Kano probably attempted something of that type as is indicated in the story. But for Shiro, this seemed an almost overwhelming violation of the respect he owed his step-father.

And, as always with the Japanese, the question was how to make amends for this violation.

We know Shiro's solution. In many ways, abandoning judo would not take back the hurt of his actions. It would, however, ensure that nothing of that type could ever happen again. And, as far as we know, Shiro never went back to *a* judo dojo again.

Imagine the sacrifice that must have entailed. Many of us training in the martial arts have developed a real attachment to them. There is something about them—the physical activity, the mental challenge, the spiritual gratification, the shared purpose—we crave. To give them up would be almost unthinkable; a painful process at best.

How much more wrenching must Shiro's decision have been? He was not just an enthusiastic trainee. He was one of the greatest grapplers in Japan. Ahead of him stretched a bright future. As Kano's premier student and chief instructor, Shiro's fame and fortune would grow with that of the Kodokan. A man blessed in being able to follow his avocation and to gain security and respect through his performance, he threw it all away.

But, as another thinker once asked, what does it avail someone to gain a fortune and lose the soul? For Shiro, the only honorable choice was to forsake the art he loved, to sacrifice an aspect of his personal happiness for something even more important. Obligation and duty sound like such harsh things, but the very strength of the words underscores their importance.

For, whether we like it or not (and Shiro's story indicates that there may well be times when we do not) we are bound in a whole host of ties and relations to other human beings. Our actions impact not only on ourselves, but on a wide network of people. And because this is the case, we need to scrutinize the tenor of our actions, to impose the harsh, critical gaze of the sensei on what we do, in the dojo and out. And when we find that what we do, however convenient or pleasurable, does not quite measure up to the highest standards, we have on obligation to change our behavior, no matter how distasteful that may be.

Shiro's story, in many ways, is a case study of heroism. Not because he achieved greatness in judo, but because, having reached that pinnacle, he was willing to abandon it in pursuit of a higher standard of behavior.

Zanshin.

11. THE MARTIAL SPIRIT

Herman Kauz is a highly accomplished writer and instructor of the martial arts. He here discusses some salient issues related to martial arts philosophy and training. His down to earth explanations provide the reader with lucid and immediately understandable descriptions of the complex experience of following the martial path.

From *The Martial Spirit* BY HERMAN KAUZ

PHILOSOPHY: ITS RELEVANCE AND APPLICATION

In the East, it is not unusual for people to think of the study of a martial art as training for living life. However, martial arts are not unique in affording this kind of training. Dancing, painting and calligraphy, the playing of musical instruments and almost any activity that is pursued in a serious and disciplined way qualified as a means of working toward self-perfection or self-realization. Over the centuries, teachers of all of these disciplines have embraced various aspects of the philosophical systems of China and Japan that seemed to give theoretical coherence to their training. We should remember, however, that these disciplines stress practice and not theory. An illustration of this bent and of the blending of martial action with spiritual development comes to us from the early history of Zen Buddhism and of Chinese boxing. Tradition has it that the legendary Buddhist monk Ta Mo or Bodhidharma on coming to China from India found the monks at the Shaolin Temple in poor physical condition. He felt that this lack prevented them from achieving their full potential in meditation and spiritual growth. In order to strengthen their bodies and ultimately their minds, he instituted a series of martial exercises which he had learned in his youth. This constituted the beginning of Shaolin Temple Kung Fu, a style that became renowned as a fighting art throughout China.

Philosophical Ideas in Martial Arts

At any rate, relevant ideas from Taoism, Buddhism and Confucianism were incorporated into the philosophy of the martial arts as they developed through the centuries. Of course, these ideas found their way into, and in another sense underlay, everything that was done in the Eastern societies. However, teachers of disciplines such as the martial arts usually attempted to originate training methods that would, enable their students to directly apprehend the content or spirit of some of these philosophical concepts. Their intention was to help students understand important truths intuitively, to develop their insight, rather than to have contact with these ideas only intellectually.

Although the emphasis in martial arts is usually on practice rather than philosophical speculation, teachers will sometimes speak of philosophical concepts which underlie their instruction. Also, an examination of the administrative or hierarchical structure and the teaching method of a school readily reveals the presence of various elements of Asian philosophical doctrine. Of course, one art might stress certain ideas more than might another. For example, a martial art like tai chi chuan may place more weight on certain Taoist concepts than might a harder style of boxing. In general, the following six ideas will be present in varying degrees:

Respect for life and Nature. A belief that we are part of Nature and should attempt to live in harmony with it rather than manipulate it to serve our ends alone. In addition, we should learn to cultivate and preserve life and avoid its destruction. More specifically, in training we are taught to avoid injuring our opponent. We are asked to be gentle and helpful to those weaker than ourselves. If we are forced to use our art to defend ourselves or those around us, we should do so with utmost restraint. Our intention should always be to avoid injuring an attacker if a less extreme method of defense will safely turn aside his attack. Unfortunately, such discretion demands a high degree of skill as well as an unusual concern for the welfare of others. If threatened with injury or worse, even a trained martial artist will seldom employ halfway measures to meet an attack once it has actually been launched. Thus, every effort must be made to avoid an attack before it is expressed physically.

Wu wei or non-action. The idea that the various systems in Nature are interdependent and that the world will function best if we refrain from disturbing one part or another in order to improve the whole. This concept is clearly related to the foregoing one. Action that interferes with Nature's function-ing is to be avoided at the risk of incurring disaster. However, action taken in accordance with Nature's course is justified and necessary. In martial arts, this concept might take the form of helping the body to relax by using cer-tain exercises designed to better enable its natural functioning to proceed unimpeded by tension. This might be reflected in training by not resisting an opponent's attack. The use of this tactic theoretically results in the at-tacker losing his balance because he has overextended in the direction of a target he mistakenly thought was solid. In this way, we use the opponent's strength to defeat him; or it might be said that by attacking he defeats him-self. Finally, many of us suffer from a tendency to overdo or to overcommit our strength in order to accomplish some end. Strictures relating to *wu wei* usually concern themselves with this fault.

Moderation and balance. An avoidance of over- or underextension in any direction. Attempting in whatever we do, to go far enough, but also not to go too far. As with wu wei, this concept in martial arts might take the form of avoiding the use of an excessive degree of strength or energy in order to accomplish an attacking or defending maneuver. But it also demands the employment of sufficient energy to achieve a desired result.

Education for training character. The idea that the subject matter a student studies and the method by which he is taught are employed primarily to develop his character. The intention of the teacher is first and foremost to turn out superior persons who would be considered "good" or "worthy" in their particular culture. Knowledge of subject matter would be important as well, but would be secondary. In martial arts, many teachers look upon their calling as a method through which they help students bring about beneficial change in themselves. Often such change is thought to take the form of learning to withstand adversity, of not giving in when things are going badly. However, such stoicism is combined with other traits, such as helping the weak, mentioned above in an effort to produce strong but gentle persons. These teachers are not concerned primarily with training fighters, although their students usually demonstrate considerable ability in this area.

Filial piety and conformity to the social order. The filial piety learned in a fam-ily in which children respect and obey their parents, and younger brothers those who are older, is carried over into society in the form of respect for authority and, above all, proper conduct or propriety. This is not a one-way street, however, since those in a superior position also have their obligations to those below them. This pattern in martial arts lends itself to a hierarchi-cal structure in which the teacher stands at the top of a pyramid with senior students on the level below him and beginners at the bottom. A teacher receives the respect and loyalty of his students, in effect taking the role of the father in the "family" formed by the martial arts school. Senior students assume the role of older brothers.

In addition, certain rules of etiquette are strictly observed within the training hall. For example, students might be asked to demonstrate respect for their training by bowing to the practice area as they arrive and when they leave. They might be required to sit in a particular way. Interaction with fellow students and with the teacher might have to follow a prescribed pattern.

Behavior outside the training hall might also be scrutinized to some degree. For instance, unseemly student conduct outside the school, if brought to the teacher's attention, might result in the erring person's expulsion.

Transcendental spirit and enlightenment. The concern here is with spiritual development. Generally speaking, for Chinese philosophers this does not necessitate a retreat from the world. Rather, the external environment, which we experience each day, provides a means to gain insight into the working of the world and man's place in the scheme of things. Another consideration, or perhaps a way of describing this insight, is enlightenment. Esoteric training methods have been used for centuries to help students penetrate beyond the surface appearance of things and events. Various forms of meditation are perhaps the most important of these methods. The martial arts can be taught with primary emphasis on their meditative character. Those martial arts teachers with the requisite skill in this area do what they can to help students penetrate their self-created veil of illusion about themselves and the world.

These thumbnail sketches of philosophical ideas which appear to be present in martial arts training are not exhaustive. They constitute the major emphasis, but they are interwoven with other minor threads of custom and manners which form the variety and richness of the cultures that produced the martial arts. Consistency of ideas may be absent, as, for example, when transcendental Taoist concepts appear to clash with this-worldly Confucianist ones. Yet a culture appears to have little difficulty in reconciling such apparently divergent ideas. The harmonizing, in the overall culture, of opposing philosophies is not uncommon. But in the East, one often finds such harmonizing occurring in the mind of one individual—an operation that appears difficult and even undesirable to Western thinkers trained to regard opposing ideas as mutually exclusive. Thus, a Japanese may observe Shinto, Buddhist and Christian rites without feeling that to embrace one viewpoint precludes the acceptance of portions of another. Perhaps the feeling about this facet of thought is that differing points of view ultimately lead to the same end.

Some of these underlying philosophical ideas are visible in brief descriptions of school procedures. It might be useful to round out those descriptions with a more detailed picture of the teaching method at a school of martial arts in which elements of Zen Buddhism are present. If we accept the premise that the teacher's intention at such a school is to help his students see themselves and life generally more clearly, we nevertheless may feel that his methods are unnecessarily stern. If our background is of a kind that excludes acquaintance with such methods, we might even regard them as dehumanizing. However, one of the underlying ideas in this kind of training is that if a student is to grow in his understanding of life he must become aware of aspects of himself that seldom come to conscious attention. To get the student to see beyond the surface of things, physical and mental shocks are employed. The teacher's approach can be characterized as an attempt to put students into a position where the usual manner of viewing life becomes subject to self-examination.

Put another way, the dominance of the ego over the student's life is questioned. By "ego" is meant the mental symbol we use to identify ourselves in our thinking. As we live our daily lives, we usually hold certain ideas about ourselves based on memory, forgetting that these ideas are just symbols and not our real nature. We are changing constantly. We are different from what we were five years ago or one year ago. Yet we approach most situations thinking of ourselves as having distinct and fixed qualities of mind and character. We even have fixed ideas about our physical appearance, although these ideas are more likely to change if we attach a fair degree of credence to what we see when we stand before a mirror. Becoming conscious of possessing certain physical and non-physical characteristics seems to occur to most of us at some particular time in our lives. When it happens, we tend to become locked into that cluster of ideas and find it difficult to free ourselves.

The various qualities we think we have, or display, are determined by the memory of our actions in past situations combined with, or tempered by, wishful or fanciful beliefs about ourselves. Unfortunately, both methods of arriving at an idea of our nature are fallible and lead to an inaccurate assessment. Memory is almost always selective. What we recall about a situation usually depends upon what we expected to see at the time and what we chose to remember. Thus, when we think we behaved in a certain way last month or last year, we are usually being selective and interpretative. Our memory of our actions in some past event and our idea of our character or personality based on these actions cannot but be distorted. This distortion is effected both by our limited ability to see and understand what happened at the time it happened and by the action of memory, after the event, which ignores aspects we believe unimportant or blocks out those that are threatening. The second major factor in the construction of our image of ourselves—the wish or desire to display certain characteristics—does have the power to make a change in us. But for this method to make a real difference in our nature, it must be pursued systematically and intensively over time. Merely wishing for some change in ourselves and even believing that the change has occurred is not enough to transform us to any appreciable degree. And it can lead us to believe we possess qualities we lack or that we are something we are not.

It becomes apparent that our image of ourselves is probably not what we are. Moreover, as time goes by, this image often becomes frozen and no longer changes as we change. As we interact with others, we carry this congealed idea of ourselves into each situation. What is happening must some-how conveniently fit this image or the image must be able to fit into what happens. As a consequence, we become unable to react to each situation as if it were fresh and new, which it is. We attempt to make it immediately into something we may have previously encountered and responded to with some degree of success. On the other hand, we may respond to it negative-ly, believing it resembles other situations in which we have failed or per-formed inadequately. Either manner of relating to life leaves little room for spontaneity or for being open enough to see what is really happening. It contributes to inflexibility of mind and a reluctance to try something new.

Thinking of ourselves in this way also has the effect of separating us from other persons, other living things and apparently inanimate objects. We con-sider ourselves, often proudly, as basically different from everyone else and as unique individuals. Although each of us is unique, we are much more the same than we are different. Our differences should not be permitted to alienate us from others or to result in a feeling of aloneness. Unfortunately, there is no doubt that many people in today's urban environment ex-perience an inability to relate adequately to others, and often suffer a sense of estrangement from the rest of life.

A teacher of martial arts who holds such views about the way most people's minds work, and who believes this state of affairs is unhealthy, will begin to help the student to see himself in a different way. To accomplish this he will probably subject the student's ego to constant attack. This offensive proceeds as soon as the beginner enters a class comprised mainly of more experienced students. It is clear that he has placed himself in an inferior position in rela-tion to these more skillful practitioners. He quickly realizes he really knows little about the art he has begun to study. If he has read about it and is able to verbally manipulate the abstractions he feels are involved, his fellow stu-dents will give him credit for this only if his ability in the particular art matches his words. In their training, they have become aware that a thought or an idea of a technique merely represents the technique and is not the technique itself. They may not be able to verbalize this concept, but experi-ence has taught them to mistrust words when they begin to be substitutes for action. Unfortunately, the beginner can seldom match word and deed. The consequence is that if he does not keep his pseudo-knowledge to himself, his fellows think of him as only a talker. This situation is especially true of arts in which the competitive element is strong, such as judo and karate. At any rate, intellectualizing about the art being studied is discouraged, and in this atmosphere the beginning student finds he must turn his energies in another direction.

The road along which beginners are guided is one marked by hard practice and discipline. They receive few opportunities to grasp intellectual handles with which to rationalize their training. Mentally comprehending the subject matter is only the first step on the way to learning. The general overriding concept is that the student must internalize what is being taught and must gradually make it part of himself. To that end he is encouraged to perform repetitious movements either alone or with a partner. As is usual with an attempt to learn something new, he feels inadequate. At first, try as he will, he cannot perform the required movements with the correctness, smoothness, relaxation and seeming total absorption that more advanced students or his teacher demonstrate. Any attempt by the beginner to avoid giving his all to his training is discouraged. Depending upon the art, this discouragement might take the form of especially rigorous treatment at the hands of senior students or the teacher. Attempts to compensate for inadequate performance by recourse to some sort of dialogue is usually treated similarly.

Of course, this method of training presupposes that the beginner has decided to accept the discipline required by his study of the art. The student must have faith in his teacher. Looked at in the opposite way, the teacher cannot accept a student's refusal to do things in the prescribed way without severe injury to his whole endeavor. A teacher will usually regard an argumentative student as a person who cannot or will not give up his idea of himself as a certain kind of individual. If matters deteriorate to such a point that a confrontation between student and teacher occurs, the student is usually expelled. If he is permitted to remain, senior students or the teacher help him to understand his error by subjecting him to unusually severe training. This severity is not considered by those administering it as constituting punishment or as an outlet for sadism. Nor should the erring student consider it in that light.

Training for even the most willing student is rigorous and, viewed from a certain perspective, might be termed sadistic. Also, viewed from this perspective it might be thought that anyone who willingly submits to such treatment has more than the usual amount of masochism in his makeup. But more is at stake here than the everyday relationships of people. The rigorous training is not an end in itself. It is designed to enable the student to experience aspects of himself that usually remain hidden, or that he was unable to see because his prevailing idea of himself obscured his views. He is often pushed beyond the limits he would have chosen for himself, finding that he can go far past the point of apparent physical endurance. He learns about his capabilities under this and related kinds of pressures. Usually he begins to see that he is not what he thought he was, and that what he remembers of himself may well have been inaccurate. Ultimately he discovers that he functions from a different base than the idea he has of himself, or his ego. He will begin to find that he can approach a situation more openly, allowing it to develop and reacting spontaneously as the necessity for action presents itself.

Combined with the training methods described in Chapters III and IV, the foregoing approach helps move students toward self-realization. At this point the reader might well ask what is meant by the term "self-realization."

Perhaps as a general definition we can say that the person who engages in serious martial arts training for a few years will be helped to more fully realize his potential as a human being. Certainly he will know more clearly who he is. (He will also learn to see his training partners with additional clarity.) He will become aware of the strengths and weaknesses of his character. He will learn that sustained application of energy over a long period is the way to get a job done that seems hopeless of accomplishment at first encounter. Thus, he will gain the strength and discipline necessary to further develop aspects of himself which he believes are beneficial and to restrain those he decides are detrimental to his well-being. Finally, he will learn not to give up even when he appears to be in a losing position. Such lessons are invaluable for living life.

INDIVIDUAL DIFFERENCES IN STUDENTS

Of course, students who engage in martial arts training will respond to it in a variety of ways. Differences in personality and outlook cannot but make themselves felt. Most teachers will recognize and make some allowance for individual differences, but deviation from the requirements of the rather severe training cannot be tolerated. If the training is changed to make it more attractive or more palatable for some students, it would become less valuable for others.

It may be of value to dwell at greater length on the matter of individual differences and their handling in martial arts. We all recognize that human beings are similar in their mortality and in their need for those basic elements like food and shelter that keep them alive. In addition, human beings are creatures who seem to function best as members of society, rather than existing alone. This may be true because cooperation between people appears to result in greater economic benefits to everyone concerned, if it is not actually essential to survival. Even if this were not true, there is little question that most of us need interaction with our fellows if our lives are to have meaning or in some sense be moderately satisfying. It is in social interplay that our character traits, however they are formed, are most clearly seen and, in general, their consequences most strongly felt. Perhaps this is so because comparisons between people are most easily made in this area. Although it is highly unusual to encounter a person who exactly fits a particular classification, we usually place people in personality categories which seem broadly to describe them. Thus, we are able to say, for example, that some persons seek to dominate their fellows and some are willing to be led; some seek the limelight and others are retiring; some are forward-looking and others live with little regard for the future; some can make quick decisions and others seem unable to decide anything at all.

It becomes fairly obvious, then, that students who come to martial arts schools to begin training will differ from one another in their mental and physical attributes and capabilities. Their reaction to the training they undergo and its impact upon them will vary depending upon the kind of person they are and, consequently, on their attitude toward it as they practice. Unfortunately, a sizeable number of beginners will give the training little chance to affect them or really get to know what it involves because they will drop out after a few practice sessions or lessons. Some of the students who continue training will be afraid of suffering physical injury. A few will resent their teacher's criticism. Others will enjoy one aspect of training but intensely dislike another. A small number might enjoy bullying or hurting those weaker than themselves. Many other differences between students will also appear. However, the training they undergo is designed for a fairly wide range of personality types and should not exclude anyone falling into the broad category considered "normal" in our society. If a student is unable to overcome his negative feelings about the training, he will leave. It will not be changed to accommodate him.

Those with various reservations about their training who continue to practice despite their problems will find their thinking and attitudes changing. Perhaps they are overcoming some of their fears, or discovering some of what it is their teacher is trying to do. As time goes by, they will experience the impact of the beneficial effects of the various aspects of training described in the foregoing chapters. At any rate, the direction of the change is usually toward the positive. Thus, this kind of training can be of value to almost every type of person who engages in it for a reasonable length of time. Just as almost everyone, no matter what psychological type he may be, can do physical exercise with consequent improvement in health, the various outcomes of martial arts training, summed up as self-realization, can also be of universal benefit.

Those who have had contact with someone who has studied one of the martial arts may disagree with the idea that such training can make one a "better" person. The person they know may not, in their estimation, exhibit exemplary traits. He may even be a ruffian, or enjoy fighting, or demonstrate some character defect. Depending upon the observer's moral convictions, the person being judged may seem to have a somewhat low standard of conduct in his relationships. We must remember, however, that martial arts training varies in content and method from teacher to teacher. The kind of training designed to move students toward self-realization is found less often than training that aims at the acquisition of skill with little regard to other considerations. Even where emphasis is on self-realization, there is no guarantee that the training will, after a given number of years, produce a certain kind of man. If we are to make a valid assessment of the effect of martial arts training on a particular person's character or mental state, we must first know what kind of person he is. More to the point, we must have knowledge of the kind of person he was before he began his training. Only with this information can we attempt to determine how his training has affected him.

A related point concerns the average person's misconceptions about the outcome of training for self-realization. Such training does not appear to confer god-like qualities upon anyone. The term "enlightenment," sometimes used to describe the result of certain kinds of training, is fairly nebulous. Not all cultures define the term in the same way. In my experience it has come to mean the growth of insight, of the ability to see oneself and others and the world more clearly. This process appears to be endless. Moreover, we should not expect to know everything in some final and ultimate way. Achieving such complete knowledge is probably not possible for us, given our imperfect and fallible understanding. We must also remember that human beings are human beings, with a wide range of characteristics, from those that we would associate with animals to those thought to be possessed by saints. We must learn to accept this range of qualities within ourselves. Those who wish to limit their acknowledgment of the qualities they possess only to an inclination to help others or "do good," should not be upset or shattered if they find themselves acting in stressful situations in a way they consider inappropriate or inconsistent with their intended direction. Nor should any of us fall apart mentally if we experience desires which we consider repulsive in human beings. Our thinking about ourselves should be broad enough to accept ourselves as we are.

DIFFICULTY OF MEETING IDEALS

However, let us suppose that we have decided that in order to live life as well as we can we must meet certain standards in all that we do. Those of us who are not too hard on ourselves might expect periodic lapses from the pursuit of or adherence to these standards. In defense of our inability to live fully in accordance with a selected set of moral and ethical considerations, we might decide that such lapses neither negate these considerations nor are inconsistent with our professed leanings. Trying to deal with the reality of our far from perfect adherence to our abstract ideals, we might settle on the usefulness of holding to some middle course in all we do. We would then attempt not to overdo or go to an extreme in any area of life, but would do whatever we undertake in moderation.

The decision to act in moderation may also come from dissatisfaction with the aftermath of overindulgence in pleasurable activity. If such overindulgence regularly brings some degree of pain in its wake, the thoughtful person might decide to exercise some control over the activity. He may attempt to reach the point where the degree or duration of pleasure is somewhat reduced, but resultant pain is minimized or absent. Another example of behavior that might be considered extreme occurs among those of us who work ourselves too hard or discipline ourselves too harshly. At some point, an assessment of our lives might reveal we have gone much too far in the use of a method that seemed to promise an effective and perhaps quick avenue to a desired goal. When we reach our goal, we may decide the reality falls short of our anticipation. But whether or not this occurs, we may discover we have begun to maintain an overly rigid approach to life. In other words, the somewhat extreme means of reaching our goal, which we may have considered only temporary, has become part of us and is making our lives less wholesome than we might wish.

The foregoing experiences can bring us to the conclusion that our lives might proceed more satisfactorily if we attempt to avoid excesses or extremes. We are then faced with the question of what constitutes extreme behavior. We know we must expend enough effort over a long enough period to do what needs doing. But how much effort is too little and how much is too much? At which point in the pursuit of some goal do we decide we are going too far? Except through the uncertain and sometimes dangerous process of trial and error, how do we calculate a middle way?

A partial answer would seem to lie in the development of sensitivity to ourselves, to others and to the various forces in play in a particular situation. Perhaps the correct word for this quality is awareness, the constant attempt to have our antenna up and functioning fully. If we are confronted with a state of affairs which calls for some response or for action on our part, we want as far as possible to perform in a way that will benefit everyone, or, at the least, to do as little harm as possible. To do this, it is helpful to know ourselves and the persons we are concerned with as well as we can and, in general, to know as much as possible about the situation in question. This information will come to us in a variety of ways, not the least among them the exercise of our intuition.

Attempting to steer a middle course in our actions requires another quality. This is good judgment. After getting the maximum information a situation affords, we must be able to determine the most suitable way of proceeding. Such a determination calls for the exercise of reason, but it also requires a feel or sense of the reality of a state of affairs. Experience in living is one way to develop good judgment. Unfortunately, however, many grow older with little appreciable increase in their possession of this quality.

The employment of awareness as well as good judgment is, however, not enough. Another important component of choosing and then holding to a middle way is control, or the ability to direct and regulate our behavior. Even if we are able to ascertain the correct course in some situation, we must be determined enough to follow that course. When it becomes clear that we have not expended sufficient energy to accomplish our ends, we must be strong and persistent enough to press on until the matter is successfully concluded. If our assessment of a particular situation calls for withdrawal, we must possess enough resoluteness to be able to pull away.

The exercise of control is not always easy. If, for example, we sense that all is not as it should be in our relations with another person, we might decide that it would be in our best interests to sever this connection. Whatever degree of awareness and good judgment we possess will have entered into such a decision. Let us also assume that we have included in our calculation the information that comes into our consciousness from the more intuitive portion of our mind. Moreover, our judgment will have been made with all the strength of our reasoning power we can bring to bear. Some might argue that the employment of reason is difficult here because we are often unable to distinguish clearly our motives in pursuing a particular relationship and, in addition, miscalculate the strength of these motives. Let us grant, however, that we are clear about our motives and have given other relevant factors their correct weight in our analysis. We have made the decision that, difficult as it may be, we must withdraw from the relationship. At this point, it is necessary for other elements in our makeup to come into play. If these elements lack sufficient strength, we will find ourselves unable to act on our decision.

If the first part of this process—gathering information, logically analyzing the problem and coming to a decision—is difficult, the second part is no less so.

It seems to most of us that the situations we meet in life, or the state our lives are in, just happen or that we somehow drift into them. We fail to realize that in all likelihood we are responsible for our lives and for what happens to us. Possibly, from a combination of conscious and unconscious motives, we have chosen these situations for ourselves. In order for some part of our nature to better express itself or to develop, we may set ourselves a particular problem. Whether or not we share this view, it seems unarguable that our capacity to work through a problem with the likelihood of achieving a favorable solution increases according to the measure in which we possess the various abilities discussed above. It would seem too that the experience gained from the process of seeking the solution to a problem is of a different quality, or of an enhanced degree of refinement, if the problem is undertaken with the help of these abilities in considerable measure.

Unfortunately, however, individuals who have developed these various abilities to any appreciable extent are not numerous. Awareness, insight, judgment and determination, important elements in holding to an attractive philosophy of life, do not grow in us simply by our hearing of them or thinking them desirable. Intellectually acknowledging their worth is merely the first step in making them part of ourselves. Our behavior in situations is the result of the way we are, not of the way we might wish to be. If we have not internalized those abilities or attributes that allow us to relate to life in a particular manner, our philosophy usually fails to meet the test of untoward events. Thus, we find ourselves time and again taking an extreme position or reacting in an unsatisfactory way. These failures often come when we face a crisis. Some mishap—suffering an accident, the injury of a loved one, or a financial setback—that evokes a strong emotional response frequently shows us that the particular philosophical approach we may have thought during some peaceful moment was ideally suited to our lives does not hold up in times of stress.

The question is then—how can we internalize a particular philosophy? More specifically, how can we develop in ourselves qualities we believe desirable? Personal experience and observation of others seem to indicate very strongly that desirable traits are not easily secured. Many persons thought to be possessed of wisdom, who have written about or taught methods of attaining certain abilities, have advocated some form of mental and physical discipline. Beyond question, the martial arts have been and can be used in this way.

In undertaking such a training method, it becomes not so much a matter of striving to incorporate a certain philosophical outlook in ourselves or of attempting to make desirable qualities of mind a part of us. Rather, training of this nature seems to bring a particular approach to life in its wake, almost as a side effect. As we proceed, our teacher does not say, "Our practice this week will make us more aware of ourselves and others or develop in us better judgment or more determination." Instead, we simply engage in our daily practice, giving whatever we do full attention. Through this method we affect both our body and our mind.

As we do individual exercises and practice together over the years, certain changes occur in the way we move, in the way we hold ourselves and ultimately in the way we think and feel. In essence, a kind of physical and mental calming and settling takes place. From the physical standpoint, we are taught to move from the lower part of our body, bringing the legs and hips into every movement. Related to and reinforcing this emphasis is the attempt, in some martial arts, to develop the *tan tien*. Where the tan tien receives special attention, we gradually learn to keep our energy in this lower abdominal area and to direct this energy onto a target when we choose. In addition, all martial arts students are taught to keep their muscles relaxed when not engaged in some action and to use the body and its energy as efficiently as possible. As a consequence, the physical appearance of students with some years of training is usually one of relaxed alertness stemming from the absence of tension and their centered and coordinated way of moving. Contrary to their placid appearance, such persons can move with quickness and certainty in response to a sudden threat. Faced with a physical emergency, a person trained in this way does not have to take the time to think or turn over in his mind a particular answer to some danger. He acts automatically, and usually correctly, bringing his highly developed skills into play.

As pointed out in the foregoing chapters, martial arts training is designed to elicit from every student a total mental and physical commitment and involvement. Thus, as their bodies become relaxed and settled, their minds also, in a manner of speaking, begin to change in this direction. The various aspects of training designed specifically to work upon the mind have their effect. The result, after the passing of some years, is a change toward greater calmness and serenity. Yet mental alertness and awareness are also present. Also, we may use our minds differently than in the past, perhaps allowing the intuitive portion more play and thus getting into closer touch with what we are and what our relations are to the rest of life.

In addition, we will come to know that there is no substitute for our own experience in finding what life is about and deciding how to live it. Over the years, martial arts training provides this essential experience. Moreover, it promotes the growth of awareness which enables us to fathom the content of the experience encountered both inside and outside the training hall. We begin to see that we need not rely upon others to tell us what we are and what we should be thinking or feeling. When we are confronted with the ideas of others in these realms, we are not reduced to weighing conflicting statements on a balance, with truth being on the side where the largest accumulation occurs. Rather, we can test the validity of another's ideas against our own experience and can accept or reject them from this solid ground.

As we live from day to day, all of us face problems of varying magnitude. We do our best, with the equipment we have, to solve them in the most appropriate way. Our training may be said to have added to this equipment or strengthened it by sharpening or enhancing certain desirable qualities of mind. Perhaps the most noteworthy change is the rise of a kind of feeling or sense of how far to go in certain directions. We may also, because of this sense, automatically reject some possibilities. Where the application of effort, persistence and determination are deemed necessary, we find these qualities to have formed in us. It is as if a kind of regulator grows in our system that works to keep us from going too far, exercises restraint, but allows us to react appropriately when quick or sustained effort becomes necessary. Action taken from this particular ground is felt to be right and is generally not subject to reservation. When faced with a crisis, we need not review our philosophical outlook, if we consciously have one, searching for the correct course of action based on abstractions which we probably have not internalized. Thus, we can act in a more unified way, perhaps even spontaneously. Nor need we force ourselves, where this is even possible, to take action which seems logical but which we somehow sense is inappropriate. Above all, we find that our judgment or decision is usually sound and seems to stand the test of time.

We must remember, however, that no matter what training he undergoes no human being fully possesses these attributes. For most of us it is a question of slow and halting progress on this path, with death cutting short our movement before we have advanced very far. Yet even to have advanced a little way along this road is preferable to not having started at all.

12. PORTRAIT OF THE TRADITIONAL MARTIAL ARTS TEACHER

Dr. David Jones is a professor of anthropology at the University of Central Florida who has also received extensive training in a variety of martial arts in the Chinese and Japanese traditions. As a trained observer of human nature and a gifted teacher in his own right, Jones analyzes the personalities and approaches of his martial arts teachers and presents a portrait of the martial arts teacher that is bound to strike many readers as unerringly accurate and familiar.

In this paper, I will attempt to draw a portrait of the traditional teacher of the Asian martial arts. I stress "traditional" as opposed to the typically young fly-by-night instructor who, for a profit, dishes out a watered down Kung-Fu, or Ninja-Fu, or whatever "Fu" happens to be in vogue at the time. A comparison of the Americanized and sanitized "fast food" approach to the Asian martial arts with the traditional Asian approach would be an interesting study. However, the teachers I intend to describe are part of traditions of learning. They are individuals who are transmitting, in a traditional manner, a traditional martial arts style with known ancient roots.

In what follows, I will use the term "martial arts" in a general sense without the fine distinction that is sometimes made, particularly with reference to Japanese martial arts, between a "martial Way," and a "martial art". Further, I will use the term "teacher" to mean a traditional teacher of the Asian martial arts.

My observations are not drawn from a study of the literature on the subject, but from my own experience. I do find, however, that my observations are echoed in the relevant literature.

I have been involved with the martial arts for seventeen years. From March 1988 to March 1989, I resided in Japan as a Fulbright Visiting Lecturer. During that time I practiced three traditional Japanese martial arts, and was ranked to the level of shodan, or "first degree blackbelt" in two of them. Specifically, I am a sandan, "third degree blackbelt," in Ueshiba Ryu Aikido, being appointed to that rank by Saotome Shihan, Headmaster of the Aikido Schools of Ueshiba, and a nidan, "second degree blackbelt," in Sakugawa Koshiki Shorinji-ryu Karatedo, having been promoted by Mr. Thomas Cauley, seventh degree blackbelt and Director in America of Shorinji-ryu.

While in Japan, I studied Kyudo, "traditional Japanese archery," under Asakuma Shihan, three times All-Japan Women's Kyudo Champion and was promoted to the rank of "first degree blackbelt." I also practiced Shindo Muso Ryu Jodo under the instruction of Ogata Sensei, a seventh degree blackbelt, and was promoted to "first degree blackbelt" before a testing panel headed by Otofuji Shihan, Headmaster of Jodo.

I am also an instructor in Old Yang Style Taichichuan, having been taught this art by Sifu Chan Poi of Canton, Grandmaster of Wah Lum Praying Mantis Kung Fu. While studying with Sifu Chan I had ample opportunity to observe many Kung Fu masters from Hong Kong and south China who paid lengthy visits to Sifu Chan.

Through the years as I practiced the martial arts both here and abroad, I gradually came to my conclusions about the common personality traits that seemed to describe the traditional martial arts teacher. My description will be impressionistic, and, if my observations prove to be anywhere close to the mark, hopefully suggestive of further more rigorous study.

I was directed by the following observations as I built my portrait of the typical martial arts teacher. Every observation I will make about the shared character traits of the teachers will be evident in all the teachers, or will be true of a majority of them. Further, I will offer comment only on those aspects of the teachers' profile which the teachers seem to possess in some uncharacteristically potent fashion. For example, I would assume that most individuals seek social approval for their actions. Therefore, I will not mention such a trait unless the teachers seem, in my opinion, to be differentiated from their fellows and social context by an unusually dynamic demonstration of the trait in question. Also, sometimes the traits I point out may appear to overlap, as, for example, in my observation that the teachers are honest, and innocent. However, though innocence is honest, honesty may not be innocent. In this paper I do not have sufficient time to delve into semantic shadings.

To begin, the martial arts teacher is a powerhouse, an individual of more than average presence, energy, and charisma. The high energy levels of the teacher is a sword that can cut two ways. It can inspire the student, and even seem to be capable of being transmitted from the teacher to the student. However, in certain students, the teachers' fire can drive and push the student with a force that they cannot tolerate. It is not uncommon in interviewing martial arts students to hear about certain students who were "burned out" by a teacher.

The teachers are people who "think big." They typically have an organizational and conceptual scope that extends far beyond their individual locales. The organizations which they represent have links around the world; the truths they teach are believed by them and their students to be universal, and the implications of their actions are cosmic. They are most definitely proponents of "the big picture."

One of the prejudices I had to overcome in dealing with the teachers was the attitude that humor was not part of the deadly serious warriors' Way of Life. Though I highly prize humor, I equate it with triviality, and therefore not appropriate for the weighty themes found in the more subtle levels of the martial arts life style. The teachers showed me that my view was in error.

All the teachers love laughter, and one of their constant themes is that we should not take ourselves too seriously. The humor of the teachers is rarely merely clever. It generally possess some teaching content. Their style tends toward the broad, boisterous, and satirical type of humor. They also tend to be very physical, using body movements, exaggerated facial expression, and mimicry. Though the teachers can be very funny in a one-on-one situation, the overall impression I received was that their style of humor is most effective before groups.

The teachers are authoritarians exerting absolute authority over those around them. There is no democratic relationship with a teacher. It is not surprising that this would be part of the teachers' personality. Each believes that they have access to a very special and very potent power, method, or domain. The student is clearly outside this special knowledge and seeking access to the teachers' world. It seems therefore obvious that the teacher should speak and the student should listen. However, since the lessons of the teacher are about life, death, and destiny, the "listening" role of the student is amplified. The student is expected to listen and respond with their entire being. Since the stakes are so high, the lessons so grand, and the students so ignorant, the teachers behavior often resonates with this authoritarian and domineering aspect.

Symbols of their unique authority abound in the formal teaching environment. They can wear certain items of clothing and certain colors, face in certain directions and occupy certain parts of the training hall that are barred to the student.

It is also true that this dominating behavior is very often carried out with a soft touch. One teacher even pointed directly to an old Chinese saying that stated that the correct way to rule a kingdom was similar to the correct way to cook small fish: "Proceed lightly, but thoroughly."

The teachers are unpredictable, clowns one minute, rigid dictators the next; one day your friend, the next day a stranger; one day kind and gentle, the next, rough and abrasive. During a particularly accessible mood, one teacher told me that the unpredictability of the teacher is conscious, a kind of teaching ploy.

"If everyday I am the same," he said, "the students might go to sleep. No! One time I might be mean, and the next day I give you candy."

He continued to explain that the teacher is supposed to represent a model of life, which by its nature is unpredictable. A warrior, a student of life, must have a teacher who presents the lessons in the context of reality, a reality in which one day it storms and the next day the sun shines. The student should be ready to learn and respond regardless of the weather.

Naturally, it might also be the case that the teachers are simply using an aspect of their special position and their volatile energy to their best advantage as teachers.

It is fascinating to me that the teachers, those most complex of individuals, also tend to radiate a child-like innocence, sometimes bordering on naivety. Although very intelligent people, at times they all seem to be charmingly out-of-step with what their students perceive to be the real social situation. The tremendous authority of the teacher often leads the discerning student to wonder who in fact is really out-of-step, themselves, or the teacher.

When an otherwise authoritarian and charismatic teacher suddenly reacts to a situation in what appears to the observer to be a naive fashion, it causes the student to focus more intently on the situation. The spectacle of the wise teacher suddenly acting like a child frames and highlights the moment. It is also true that the birds that fly the highest often have the most difficulty in making a precise landing, in deftly returning to earth. Perhaps the broad perspective of the teacher causes them difficulty at times in focusing on the moment. Maybe their behavior suggests that the child-like mind is not one that is narrow and limited in its perspective range, but rather one that is very broad and inclusive.

All the teachers complain on occasion of the burden of being who and what they are. Once I was interviewing a high ranking Karate master who has been trained in Karate-do in a Zen temple in northern Japan. He said that on the day he graduated and was given a diploma to be a free-teacher of his Karate style, the head monk told him;

"I pity you! If you find one true and good student in your entire life, you must write to me immediately, and I will erect a statue in your honor!"

Another teacher, making reference to his students understanding of who and what he was said, "They treat my blood like water"; and another teacher said of his role as a teacher, "I wouldn't wish this life on a dog."

The teachers are all very charming and charismatic personalities, as I have mentioned, excellent at relating to people, and able to be surrounded by adoring students whenever they wish. However, I have noticed that they generally have few, if any, close friends, and that they express at a fairly constant rate their feelings of aloneness and isolation.

The quality of aloofness, so typical of the teacher, is perhaps a result of their need for companionship, coupled with their need to remain free of personal entanglements with the students who always surround them.

This aloofness is often romanticized, and rationalized by the students in likening the teacher to a mountain peak. Mountain images are, of course, found throughout the tales and myths of the teachers and of those who possess some putative higher knowledge. A convenient and universal metaphor, the mountain is beyond us, the mountain is singular and vast, the mountain directs our eyes upward, the mountain is unmovable, and the mountain is aloof and alone.

I have heard each of the teachers state from time to time that they wished to abandon their special positions because they felt unequal to the task of continuing, or because they felt they had failed in their work. Usually this kind of statement is associated with complaints about being overworked, or about the lack of understanding or commitment on the parts of their students.

Two of the major virtues promoted by the teachers, and possessed by them in abundance, are patience and persistence. Further, they all agree that a sense of urgency or haste is fatal to the attempt to internalize the larger lessons they have to teach, and it is these larger lessons, they insist, which hold the secrets of their knowledge and power. One teacher said of his Master, "It was principle, not technique that made my master great."

A typical tale that reflects the dual themes of patience as a virtue and haste as a vice, recounts the story of a young man who came to a famous sword teacher and asked, "How long will it take me to become a great swordsman?" The master replied, "Thirty years." The student continued, "But what if I try very, very hard and learn very, very quickly?" The teacher said, "Then it will take you fifty years."

The analogy of the parent-child bond is common in the relationships of teacher and students. They are the wise and loving parent possessed of unruly and often ungrateful children. Sometimes the parental image is indicated by the title or term of address directed by the student to the teacher. The Chinese term *sifu*, and the Japanese term sensei, mean "teacher", but they also carry the connotation of "father," or "senior male," or "one who has gone before."

The teachers see themselves as loving parents and like most parents, feel they have a right and a duty to advise and offer direction in all aspects of their children's lives. Nothing escapes them . . . diet, choice of occupation and potential spouse, social life . . . all may come up for strenuous comment by the teacher. But the teachers are frustrated parents(or just perhaps typical parents) because their students rarely conform to their wise counsel. I once heard one of the least authoritarian of the teachers exclaim in frustration, "Where is the student who will say 'yes' to me!"

Most people, to varying degrees, attempt to think before they speak. One of the traits I have noticed with the teachers is the way they seem to allow little lapse-time between their thoughts and speech, or it seems to be this way. Rather than examining a thought or idea before speaking, they often seem to blurt it out with little of the customary self-monitoring enforced by most of us. This makes them appear at times tactless, rude, contradictory and childish. Once when a student pointed out to a teacher that he had contradicted himself on a point he had made the day before, the teacher replied in his characteristically highly energetic fashion, "This is not yesterday, this is today." Another teacher, in a similar situation said, "Fortunately, now is now."

Once you come to accept this aspect of the teachers' behavior, you can come to accept their words as a kind of gift from a person who is inviting you directly into their mental processes without the plethora of screening devices we all come to accept as normal. This "thinking-out-loud" aspect of the teachers behavior presents a spontaneity of thought and speech that is stimulating, confusing, refreshing, and often whimsical.

The teachers are honest. Before my experience with the teachers, I felt that honesty was a desired trait in interpersonal relationships. I still do, but the teachers have shown me that there is a level of honesty that is well-nigh unbearable. I do not mean that candid statement being directed from a teacher to a student, but rather honesty in the sense of a pervasive lack of will to, or ability to, hide feelings that common decency would indicate should be hidden. Absolute, stark honesty from one individual to another is a breath-taking and powerful experience.

On one occasion, I was passing an afternoon with a teacher, observing the interactions of the students with him, and each other. The teacher was watching one middle-level student practicing in a corner of the practice hall. Suddenly, the teacher began to laugh uproariously. He pointed to the young man and said, "You look like a camel, just like a camel. What are you doing, practicing Camel Style Kung Fu?" The teacher began to mimic the boy's mannerisms and style of movement with brutal and ferocious accuracy. All the students laughed, it was just about impossible not to given the comedic skill that the teacher showed in his performance. The young man who was the target of the teacher's attention became flushed, and tears came to his eyes as he turned and stormed out of the room. The laugher stopped and was followed by an embarrassed silence. The teacher, speaking to no one in particular, said," Don't worry, he'll be alright."

As a few students in the room gathered together to discuss what had just happened, I left to sit outside under a tree next to the practice hall. I had been sitting for a few minutes, writing in my notebook when the teacher appeared from behind a cook shed with the young man who had left in tears. The teacher and the boy came over to where I was sitting and the teacher, with his hand on the boy's shoulder, said,

"Don't worry, he's alright now. I tell him that he really does look like camel when he does his Kung Fu wrong. He understands now. He can't run away and cry when someone hurts his feelings. I told him, What if in olden times on the battlefield some enemy says to you, 'Hey, you're fat and ugly', would you run away and cry? I told him the truth and next time he won't run away and cry. I cut him but there's no blood, no arms laying around on the ground anywhere, no heads rolling around on the ground."

All the teachers feel connected to a long and illustrious past through their relationship with their teachers. These master mentors are always revered and used as a source of the contemporary teachers authority. All the teachers, for example, keep pictures of their teachers where they work, teach, or live. The old masters are the model for the teachers from the least significant aspects of their behavior to the most significant. The teacher routinely claim that they are pale versions of their teachers. I have never met a teacher in any tradition that claimed to be better than his teacher. Further, the teachers can generally trace a lineage of teachers, of which they now stand as the most recent addition, reaching back many generations, sometimes thousands of years, and sometimes back to a god-like original source.

The teachers are men and women with a mission. They seem themselves as destined to play out their part in an ancient and continuing plan. They do not see what they do as merely a job, a way of making a living. It is far more grand than that. This powerful sense of purpose provides a keel and a rudder in an often lonely and tumultuous life. The teachers have the attraction of a Don Quixote. They may never win, but they cannot allow themselves to stop trying due to their sense of mission and destiny. It is an internal font of courage. It is the lodestone that draws them onwards and orients their course.

I find that I often use the word "disarming" when I am describing the teachers. One of the ways they disarm is by their spontaneous acts of sometimes surprisingly impressive generosity. Each of the teachers has given me money, clothing, art objects, religious paraphernalia, food, and most importantly, their time. Further, in interviews and conversations with their students, I have heard numerous tales in which the teacher secretly paid a hospital bill, rent, or debt, arranged for employment, or facilitated travel to some distant point. However, their generosity also serves as a means of ensuring a deep relationship.

For example, it is the custom in traditional Japanese martial arts, that blackbelts do not pay for instruction. Before students come to understand the nature of this "gift," they look forward to a time when they may study and learn for free. Once when a teacher of a Japanese martial art was talking about the payments of the students, he said:

"Some teachers are interested in your money. I am interested in your loyalty and attention. I run a much harder deal than most teachers."

The teachers are marked by an unmistakable originality and creativity. They are inner directed beings. The most common crucial question asked of the teacher and asked in many forms, is "What should I do?" The value of the teachers active and original minds under these circumstances is that their creative, and often totally unexpected responses can break the patterns of thought that often blind the student to the solutions of their problems.

It is often the case that the teachers' response to a question of this type is not that original. For example, the answer to a particular students question may be that he or she should persevere and not give up. This, by the way, is the major teacher response to most questions. When delivered to a distraught student in the words I have just used, the message falls as a dead weight. However, when the teachers deliver this response with their power, authority, and originality filtering through a parable perhaps drawn from the history of their particular martial arts style, the effect can be dramatic enough to alter an individual's life course. I have seen this happen many times.

The teacher must be the center of attention in any group. They are teachers and showmen, and their entire life style might be seen as a mechanism to capture the attention of their audience. Very often the ritual procedures surrounding the student/teacher relationship assures this. I

think that the teachers genuinely enjoy being the "life of the party." If you enjoy occasionally sitting back and enjoying a good show, full of energy, originality, and entertainment and educational insight, the teachers can always be counted on to provide it.

I discovered an interesting aspect of the teachers' behavior by chance while interviewing students. Many said that they had come to a class with a particular question on their mind, and that, at some point during the class, the teacher would begin to speak directly to the student's unasked question. When I asked for examples I found that these questions were often very specific. In one case, for example, a student was wondering about taking a trip far to the south. That night the teacher began describe the value of occasional making an unplanned trip. The students often found answers to their questions in the rambling monologues so characteristic of all the teachers.

The emotional environment of the student/teacher relationship is very hot and intense. The teacher is often surrounded by students vying with each other for his or her favor. This personal and political tension seems to characterize the inner circle of the teachers' group. I also found that the teacher would seek to generate this emotional storm if, for some reason, it showed signs of abating on its own. In commenting on this stirring of the pot, one teacher said, "It takes fire to make a fine sword, does it not?" and another said, "I am the master of this storm." The teachers seem to agree that the hot emotional climate surrounding the teacher, and indeed the stimulation of this environment is part of the testing ground for the student of the martial arts.

An aura of potential danger hovers around the teachers. This sense of danger takes on various guises. There is the constant awareness of the physical mastery the teachers have over the students, coupled with the potential for psychological, and perhaps, spiritual attack. This potential field of danger is always subtle and hidden. It is never presented as a part of the teachers' public persona, quite the contrary. However, the teachers are never to be taken as safe and passive. They are forces to be reckoned with.

For most people, the human being is contained within a layer of flesh. The individual is usually considered to be somehow the product of the joint action of genetic inheritance, and social, cultural and idiosyncratic conditioning and learning. And, though lip service is often paid to the belief that there is a soul or spirit associated with the human being, as likely as not such a dimension is not very important in the day to day encounters people have with one another.

I have found the teachers to be very astute in their understanding of the social, cultural, psychological, historical, and environmental aspects of the human situation. However, for the teachers, some of the most important pieces of information they use in their interactions with others come from dimensions not normally acknowledged by the majority of students. The two most common extra-dimensions granted to the student by the teacher include what might be called "aura," and also the belief in the existence of spirits associated with the student. "Aura" refers to a perceived light/energy surrounding the individual. Most teachers claim to be able to see or perceive this phenomena. A third unique access to the students may be through what the teachers believe to be past lives of the students, lives which the teachers can see, or read, or experience . . . the language varies. Part of the teachers' allure is that the student can sense that the teachers sees them as a larger, richer, and more complex entity than they are seen by their family and friends.

The teachers do not reveal all. There is a facet of their personality which strongly suggests hidden knowledge, or as-yet unrevealed information. Each has a repertoire of looks, gazes, body movements, facial expressions and hand gestures which communicates that there is much to be known about some issue which at the moment the student is not capable of understanding.

Teachers engage their students in mind-games and mini-psycho-dramas in which the teachers play out elaborate deceptions for educational ends. These false settings can be very complicated with props and supporting actors included for more potent effect.

One of the many lingering benefits to this facet of the teachers behavior is that it makes students very aware of the "game" aspect of social relationship, and of their learning import. It provides the students in a lesson in "not dozing off" as life unfolds. Their appreciation of the

larger pattern of social involvement is sharpened. The games of the teachers also serve as a warning as to how easy it is for another to manipulate you if you do not pay attention to what is happening at all times. At least, these are some of the reasons, according to the teachers, that they utilize the games they play with their students.

The teachers are robust and vital personalities. Possessing good physical health, they revel in the joys of the flesh. They are not people who are afraid to satisfy themselves. They dare to do it. The people around the teachers often seem, by comparison, squeezed and timid. The teachers enjoy sex, good food, music, laughter, and socializing. They greatly enjoy travel, meeting new people, and novel experiences of all kinds.

With regard to the basic profile of the teachers, I found that they are individuals with tremendous personal energy and magnetism who are characterized by the vitality of their physical, emotional, and intellectual life, by the broad scope of their thinking, their innocence, and generosity; and by their honesty and sense of humor. They seem to be motivated in the main by their dedication to their mentors and to the mission of transmitting and maintaining their mentors' Way. Their students see them at times as domineering and unpredictable, emotionally volatile, possibly dangerous, and in possession of secret and mysterious knowledge. At the same time, the student will feel related to the teacher in a quasi-kin mode, and grateful for the teachers' attention. This attention will be experienced by the quality of the teachers' instruction, by the seemingly uncanny ability of the teacher to anticipate the student's questions and personal dilemmas and by the many mini-dramas generated by the teachers in the learning environment. However, despite the respect granted to the teachers by their students, the teachers often feel exhausted, unfairly burdened, isolated, frustrated, and defeated in their attempts to carry out their mission of education and service.

It is also important to understand that the teachers are not perfect specimens of exemplary human behavior. Several of the teachers have violent tempers which erupt with swiftness and unnerving intensity. The teachers I have known can be venal and self-serving at times. Occasionally their control of their more passive students struck me as verging into an unhealthy dominance/submission relationship. The teachers I have discussed today, however, are examples of people who, though not necessarily paragons of virtue, overwhelmingly used their skills and abilities for the betterment of their students. One of the facets of their personalities that I found most refreshing was that none of them ever claimed to be perfect. One teacher said, "Perfection is reserved for the gods," and another said, "Everyone has an asshole."

Finally, I would like to offer my observations of the broadly conceived instructional approaches shared by the teachers. They are teachers who use every possible opportunity to advance tuition. The student comes to feel that when in the vicinity of a teacher, every act is a lesson of some sort. The teachers will also use the quirks and foibles of their own personalities as teaching aids. Teachers teach constantly.

They tend to absorb students into an attitude of mutual obligation in the learning process. In a myriad of ways the teachers communicate that they are under obligation to effectively teach, and the students are under obligation to effectively learn.

The teachers constantly challenge their students in their complacency by presenting to them novel, unconventional, and sometimes potentially threatening ideas, and behavior models. The approach of the teachers is also typically emotional. The image of the cool and detached professor in the Western style is not part of the teachers' method. They promote a hot emotional learning environment. They feel that passion, sentimentality, commitment, spirit and excitement must be present for real education to take place.

The teachers are also prone to lead their students on an emotional and intellectual roller-coaster ride; they raise the students very high and then bring them down sharply. This "up again/down again" aspect of the teachers approach is thought by them to create humility, resilience, and a realistic outlook on life in their students.

A sense of mystery is another common aspect of the teachers' method. The feeling of mystery and the suggestion of hidden knowledge serves many purposes. Mysteries can be doled out in graded levels, which provide a system of rewards for the serious and persistent students, and they also can be a constant lesson to the student that there is more to any situation than is immediately apparent.

The teachers prefer a method of teaching in which the students are encouraged to find their own way of dealing with a series of problems, problems artfully and systematically presented by the teacher. A common term for high level learning in Asia is translated as a "Way. "A "Way" is not a goal, not an end but rather the means to some end, a method of attaining whatever you set your sights upon. Students are always in fact in their own Way, and the teachers simply help each student to refine the effectiveness of this personal approach.

The emphasis of the teachers method is in the here and now situation. Their lessons always aim in the final analysis to help the student with the wherewithal to clearly see their current situations and to act efficiently in that situation. The martial arts provide the concept in the metaphor of deadly combat in which death awaits those who do not clearly comprehend their present predicament and who do not possess the technique to deal with it.

It can also be said that the teachers do not operate democratically with their students. They are most definitely and absolutely in charge. The teachers, in fact, often have very negative attitudes about teachers who attempt some egalitarian method of interaction with their students. They feel that because the teacher represents life to the students, the student is cheated at a most profound level by an illusion of equality with the teacher. Life does not deal leniently with the ignorant. The student practices life situations with the teacher who plays the part of the total potential life context of the student. As one teacher said, "I teach abstract art."

One of the more surprising assumptions of the teachers, at least from a Western perspective, is that words are not to be overly depended upon in teaching, or in assessing the level of the students' understanding. The teachers assume that a lesson is learned to the degree to which it can be applied in a variety of novel situations. Therefore, they are little interested in a students' telling them about something, the teacher wants to see it happen. "Talk is cheap," can be seen as a major dictum of the teachers.

The "will-to-perform" is another aspect of the student personality that the teachers aim to stimulate and develop. Even if the student knows what to do in a given problem situation, if they do not have the ability to move, or act, their mere understanding is useless. Therefore, one of the continual acts of the teacher is to create situations where the will-to-perform can be exercised by the students. The constant round of testing and challenges found in martial arts training hall is intended to serve this function.

As mentioned earlier, teachers tend to see their students not as limited body units that show up simply to "work out" for an hour or so, but as vast entities composed of many dimensions. This awareness permeates the teaching situation in a hundred different ways. Teachers will often instruct students to perform certain exercises the purpose of which is not understood by the student.

The teachers assume that some extraordinary, or perfectly ordinary, life-energy exists, called *ch'i*(Chinese) or *ki* (Japanese), for example, and that everything depends on stimulating this energy to more efficient functioning through the vehicle of the students mind, body, and spirit. According to the teachers, any physical, mental, or spiritual act is relatively weak without the energizing of this special type of energy.

In this paper, I have attempted to present a broad profile of the traditional martial arts teacher, a profile that touches upon the personality traits, teaching methods, and assumptions about students that they all seem to share. The teacher is the students' model, and this is particularly true of the traditional martial arts teacher. "What am I supposed to do? How am I to behave?" The teacher stands before the student for the answers to be gained.

The justly famous physical prowess of the traditional martial arts teacher is, I feel, only part of the message that the teacher sends. In part, I tend to feel it is the least important message of the traditional martial arts. . . . "Candy to get the attention of children," as one teacher put it. Watching the teacher kick, punch, block, throw, and perform the traditional forms, *kata*, or *poomsei* of a particular martial arts style is the most obvious aspect of the observation of the teacher, but is that the real point? Once during a break in an intensive seminar in a traditional Japanese martial arts, the teacher was asked by an intense young man about which kind of kick was most likely to make a man's heart stop beating. The teacher looked shocked, turned away, and said in despair, "What kind of a man does he think I am?" A common observation in Asia is to warn against those who mistake the finger pointing to the moon for the moon itself. The personality portrait of the teacher that I have drawn might be seen as one of the major lessons that the martial arts of Asia have been communicating for generations. In China it is said:

Thanks the gods for creating you.

Thank your parents for rearing you.

Thank your teachers for everything else.

13. EATING BITTER: WUSHU IN CHINA

Mark Salzman's book on his experience in modern China, and particularly his account of learning wushu *under the tutelage of a well-known master, has the charm of personal experience in the contemporary world combined with the esoteric promise of remarkable skill. As such, it has the appeal of something that is broadly familiar to many martial arts students all over the world.*

From *Iron and Silk* BY MARK SALZMAN

Early one Saturday morning in March one of my doctor students knocked at my door. A cold, steady drizzle that had been falling since January had convinced me to stay in bed as long as possible, but at ten past seven a terrific pounding and the voice of Dr. Nie calling my name woke me from a dream. I remember the dream clearly. A team of cadres from the Public Security Bureau had tied me by my feet to a giant ferris wheel, so that each time it completed a circle my head scraped along the ground. Once awake, I thought I might keep silent and pretend to be out, as I was in no mood to smile and answer grammar questions at that hour. Then I heard Old Sheep telling Dr. Nie that I hadn't gotten up yet, so he should just knock louder. When the pounding became unbearable I got up. I didn't bother putting clothes on over my several layers of woolen underwear, and tried to look as much like hell as I could manage, but this only seemed to amuse him. "Follow me," he said, and started down the stairs. My annoyance grew as he yelled from the front door for me to hurry. I told him that I had something to do. That was all right, he didn't mind, and he laughed—let's go! I said I was expecting a visitor any minute now, so I couldn't leave the house; he said it didn't matter, and laughed—let's go! I said I didn't feel well, maybe we could go out and play another day; he said we could do that, too, and laughed—hurry up! I put on some clothes, went down-stairs and pleaded-with him to leave me alone, but he grabbed my arm and pulled me out of the house. "Do you have grammar questions this morning, Dr. Nie?" I asked. "Thank you," he answered, and led me out of the college gate.

I was in a poor mood as we wandered through the streets, splashing up coal dust mixed with rain, at seven-fifteen in the morning. I could only hope that this would be a half-day outing instead of the full-day English-speaking marathons our students loved so well. At least it was winter; if it had been warmer out, I would have been obliged to spend several hours in a rented rowboat at Martyrs' Park eating dried melon seeds and enjoying "free talk" with no hope of inter-ruption or distraction. "Free talk" involved relentless, vigorous conversation of absolutely no import that drove me to near-madness. Floating helplessly in the middle of a dirty pond only made it worse. "Where are we going?" I asked. "A surprise," he answered and I shuddered to imagine what it could be.

Twenty minutes later we came to the gate of the Provincial Sports Unit, a large complex for the Hunan athletes. Each province in China has such a unit, where the best athletes live and train. They receive their education there, too, but an abbreviated one. They are the closest thing to professional athletes China has, and they spend most of their time training.

I remembered that Dr. Nie specialized in athletic medicine and performed surgery on the more serious cases that arose in this unit. He led me to a large five-story cement building, which had a training space on its uppermost floor, judging from the arrangement of its windows. We climbed the filthy, unlit staircase and Dr. Nie paused in front of two large wooden doors to savor the moment. He turned and smiled at me, indicating that I should listen. I heard through the doors a cacophony of cracks, whooshes and thuds. Just as it began to dawn on me what might be going on, he swung open the doors to reveal a dingy, cavernous room with bare cement walls and a dull red carpet on the floor.

Ten or eleven young men and women in battered sweat-suits stood around against the walls, watching silently as three of their colleagues engaged in furious armed combat. Two of the men had six-foot wooden poles, and were teamed up to defeat the third, who wielded a three-section staff—three short poles connected by chains. Even in the movies, with the assistance of trick photography and trampolines, I had never seen anything to match this fight. I felt my stomach tighten, thinking one of the fighters would surely be brained by the poles, which swung by so fast I could barely see them. Suddenly, in perfect unison, the two with the long poles froze in position, poised for the last attack. The other athletes tensed, and all was quiet for a full second. Then several of them shrieked, and the fighters seemed to go mad, rushing into their final clash. The man with the three-section staff leapt into the air, rolled over the back of one of his opponents, and took an overhead swing at them both. They moved out of the way just in time and the weapon crashed to the ground, inches from their feet, with such force that the whole carpet shook and the air filled with dust. Without stopping, the three spun and froze again in an atti-tude of readiness, held it, then doubled over to breathe. The assistant trainer, a frail-looking woman in her thirties, walked over to them and barked a few words of criticism on the routine, then told them to get out of the way for the next group. The three fighters, who looked more like panthers than humans, loped off to one side. Immediately, two young women marched to the center of the room. Theirs was to be an unarmed battle.

They stood about an arm's length from one another, staring straight ahead.

The trainer gave a yell and the two women turned their heads to exchange a deadly glance before exploding into action. One of the women was fairly tall with long hair put up in a bun; the other was short, with thick shoulder-length hair that hung loose around her face. The tall woman began the attack, lashing out with a back-fist. The short woman leaned back so that it just grazed her throat, spinning around and jumping into the air as she did so, so that her right leg swung in an arc that ended full-force on the chest of the tall woman. Both crashed to the ground and lay still. Then, as if they had springs underneath them, they bounced up into the air and continued to fight. What struck me most about these women was their power; they hit with enough force to knock a large man unconscious. The short woman, especially, fought like a demon. I found out later that she had doubled for the heroines in the fight scenes of several movies. But she was not to be the main attraction this morning. After the women finished up, Dr. Nie led me into the room. The men looked at me curiously. The women all giggled and shifted to the far corner of the room, taking turns looking quickly at me and then at the ground.

The assistant trainer came over to greet us. Dr. Nie introduced her as Little Liu, and me as the American Professor Mr. Sima Ming (my Chinese name). I had to go through this ritual at least once a day in China, where "distinguished Foreign Guests" must be introduced politely, meaning that their credentials are blown well out of proportion. I explained to her that I was not a professor, but an English teacher, and that since she was older than me, she should refer to me as Little Sima, but she and Dr. Nie agreed that since I had been educated in America, I should be a professor, and that since I had traveled far my experience was great so I should at least be Mr. Sima Ming.

Little Liu pointed to the athletes. "These are the members of the Hunan Provincial Wushu Troupe. Today you are our guest. Please feel free to ask any questions you like, and voice your criticisms to help us improve." "Where is he?" Dr. Nie asked her. "He'll come soon," she assured him, "but he didn't want to get here first. He wanted the professor to wait a while." Liu invited me to sit down on one of the long wooden benches that lined the walls of the room. "Now they'll practice their solo routines."

The solo routines of wushu are something like floor exercises in gymnastics; each routine is a prearranged series of moves, created by the master and student together, that best displays the student's versatility and special strengths, but within the aesthetic boundaries of that particular style of wushu. For example, a double-edged sword routine must not contain moves characteristic of sabre. Each style has its own repertoire and personality, and mixing them is considered a sign of poor taste or careless training. First, one of the young men who had been fighting earlier with a long pole performed the "Drunken Sword." In this style the fighter must stumble, weave, leap and bob as if drunk, at the same time whipping his sword around him at full speed, all the while maintaining perfect control. Then a woman with a single braid reaching to her waist performed the double sabre. The two blades flashed around her but never touched, and she finished by leaping into the air, crossing the sabres and landing in a full split. One after the other, the athletes performed routines with spears, halberds, hooks, knives and their bare hands. My stomach hurt by now just from the excitement of watching them; I'd never seen martial arts of this quality before, nor sat so close to such tremendous athletes as they worked. Just as the last man finished a routine with the nine-section steel whip, someone clapped once, and all the athletes rushed into a line and stood at perfect attention. I turned toward the wooden doors to see who had clapped and for the first time saw Pan.

I recognized him immediately as one of the evil characters in Shaolin Temple, and I knew from magazine articles about the movie that he had choreographed and directed the martial arts scenes. This movie, shot partly on location at the real Shaolin temple where Chinese boxing has been practiced for more than fifteen hundred years, featured China's most famous boxers and was produced and distributed by studios in Hong Kong. It became an immediate success in East Asia when it was released in 1981, and remains China's only block-buster film to date. Not long after my arrival in Changsha, several people had mentioned to me that someone connected with this movie was in Hunan, but no one had actually seen him or could agree upon who he was. They did agree, however, that one would need a significant "back door" to gain an introduction, if he was really in Hunan at all. Pan had a massive reputation as a fighter from the days when scores were settled with blows rather than points. His nickname, "Iron Fist," was said to describe both his personality and his right hand, which he had developed by punching a fifty-pound iron plate nailed to a concrete wall one thousand to ten thousand times a day.

Pan walked over to where the athletes stood, looked them over, and told them to relax. They formed a half-circle around him; some leaned on one leg or crossed their arms, but most remained at stiff attention. He gave them his morn-ing address in a voice too low for me to hear, but it was clear from the expressions on his face that he was exhorting them to push harder, always harder, otherwise where will you get?

He stood about five foot eight, with a medium to slight build, a deep receding hairline, a broad, scarred nose and upper front teeth so badly arranged that it looked as if he had two rows of them, so that if he bit you and wrecked the first set, the second would grow in to replace them. Most noticeable, though, were his eyebrows. They swept up toward his temples making him look permanently angry, as if he were wearing some sort of Peking Opera mask. At one point he gestured to one of the athletes with his right hand, and I saw that it was strangely disfigured. Dr. Nie, who must have known what I was thinking, leaned over and said, "That is the iron fist."

Pan looked fearsome, but what most distinguished him was that, when he talked, his face moved and changed ex-pression. I had been in China for eight months, but thought this was the first time I had seen a Chinese person whose face moved. Sometimes his eyes opened wide with surprise, then narrowed with anger, or his mouth trembled with fear and everyone laughed, then he ground his teeth and looked ready to avenge a murder. His eyebrows, especially, were so mobile that I wondered if they had been knocked loose in one of his brawls. He commanded such presence that, for the duration of his address, no one seemed to breathe. At last he finished. He clapped his hands once again and the Athletes jumped back to their positions in the room, ready to continue their morning workout. He started to walk toward the far side of the room, where all the weapons lay on a wooden rack, then pretended to notice us for the first time. He looked surprised, spread his palms in a welcoming gesture, then said to Dr. Nie, "Why didn't you tell me we had a guest?"

Dr. Nie introduced me once again as Professor Mr. Sima Ming, this time adding that I was a wushu expert and had performed several times in China with great success. "The professor practiced Chinese martial arts for nine years before coming to China and has performed not only for our college, but for the governor of Hunan as well." While this was true, it was not true that I was an expert, or that the success of my performances was due to the quality of my wushu. Anything a foreigner did in front of a Chinese audience received thunderous applause. "He is especially good at 'Drunken Fist'." In fact, I knew very little Drunken Fist, but since all my performances occurred after huge banquets, where drink-ing contests with baijiu were required, my thrashing about was usually identified as "Drunken Fist." I would typically jump over a table, trip over a chair and throw it around, fall down a few times, punch an imaginary opponent and leave to be sick. Before I could explain all this, though, Dr. Nie turned to our host and said, "And this is Master Pan Qingfu. There is no need to introduce him further."

Pan extended his hand for me to shake. It was not deformed, but simply decorated with several large calluses on his knuckles and finger joints that had turned black as if scorched. I put my hand in his, and to my great surprise and relief, he shook it gently. We sat down and he asked how it happened that I spoke Chinese and lived in China.

As we spoke the troupe continued to practice, even more furiously than before, now that Pan had arrived. Every few minutes he pointed to his stopwatch, shook his head and asked some poor athlete if he was napping or practicing. He criticized one of the women so fiercely that it looked as if she were on the verge of tears. He made her repeat a move, a complicated leap ending in a crouched position, until she collapsed in a heap on the floor. "Who's next?" he shouted, and another athlete came forward, taking care not to step on the woman as she dragged herself off to the side. None of the athletes even twitched an eyebrow when receiving in-structions or criticism. He ordered, and instantly they obeyed, until they could no longer stand.

After two hours or so morning practice came to an end. Pan reminded them to be on time for afternoon practice and seemed about to dismiss them when a smile came over his face. He pointed at me. "Please welcome our American friend." The athletes burst into applause, smiling with what energy they had left. "He has practiced wushu for nine years—don't you think he should do something for us?" The applause turned to cheers of delight. I felt all the blood drain from my face and thought I would faint if I stood up. As soon as I could speak I refused, but this only brought louder cheering. Dr. Nie, ever the friend in need, announced that I was just being modest, and that I was as strong as a lion and fast as a swooping pigeon, or something like that, and began to pull me from the bench. I looked at Pan; he was smiling at me the way a wolf might smile at a lame deer.

Then the blood rushed back into my face, and I nearly saw double with anger. Humiliating unwitting foreigners is something of a popular sport in China, and it occurred to me that my little spectacle would soon be legendary. But he had me. If I accepted, I would go down in local history as the foreigner who made a fool of himself in front of Pan Qingfu and the Hunan Wushu Troupe; if I refused, I would be remembered as the foreigner who left the Hunan Sports Unit with his tail between his legs.

I stood up, and the applause died down. Pan sat down, continuing to smile. I explained that my wushu couldn't be compared to theirs and added, truthfully, that I had never imagined I would see such expertise as they possessed. I then said that for me to perform a Chinese routine would be a waste of time, since they did wushu so much better. I had come to learn. Better for me to do something they might not otherwise have a chance to see. I told them that in America, fighters have been exposed to a variety of Asian martial arts, Western boxing, and African dancing rhythms. Making it up as I went along, I explained that a distinctly American style has come out of all this, and is called "On the Street Boxing." I started clapping out a syncopated beat, began moving in a modified hustle, and let loose, trying to make up for what I lacked in gymnastic skill with unrestrained violence. At the time I was not in good condition, so after a few minutes, when I started to taste blood in my throat, I stopped. The athletes exploded into cheers, and Dr. Nie slapped Pan's shoulders in excitement, but Pan sat dead still, with the same smile on his face. I started to see black around the edges of my field of vision and no longer heard all the noise, but only saw Pan at the end of a darkening tunnel. He stood up and walked, toward me, stopping when his face was very near my own. His smile had disappeared. In a very low voice he said, "That's not gong fu." We stared at each other for a long time, then he raised one eyebrow. "I could fix it, if you wanted." I must have nodded, because then he asked me if I could chi ku, eat bitter, the Chinese expression meaning to endure suffering. Lying, I said yes. Then he asked me if I was afraid of pain. Lying again, I said no. "You want?" he asked. "I want," I said, and became his student.

I was to meet Pan at the training hall four nights a week, to receive private instruction after the athletes finished their evening work out. Waving and wishing me good night, they politely filed out and closed the wooden doors, leaving Pan and me alone in the room. First he explained that I must start from scratch. He meant it, too, for beginning that night, and for many nights thereafter, I learned how to stand at attention. He stood inches away from me and screamed, "Stand straight!" then bored into me with his terrifying gaze. He insisted that I maintain eye contact for as long as he stood in front of me, and that I meet his gaze with one of equal intensity. After as long as a minute of this silent torture, he would shout "At ease!," and I could relax a bit, but not smile or take my eyes away from his. We repeated this exercise countless times, and I was expected to practice it four to six hours a day. At the time, I wondered what those staring contests had to do with wushu, but I came to realize that everything he was to teach me later was really contained in those first few weeks when we stared at each other. His art drew strength from his eyes; this was his way of passing it on.

After several weeks I came to enjoy staring at him. I would break into a sweat and feel a kind of heat rushing up through the floor into my legs and up into my brain. He told me that when standing like that, I must at all times be prepared to duel, that at any moment he might attack, and I should be ready to defend myself. It exhilarated me to face off with him, to feel his power and taste the fear and anticipation of the blow. Days and weeks passed, but the blow did not come.

One night he broke the lesson off early, telling me that tonight was special. I followed him out of the training hall, and we bicycled a short distance to his apartment. He lived with his wife and two sons on the fifth floor of a large, anonymous cement building. Like all the urban housing going up in China today, the building was indistinguishable from its neighbors, mercilessly practical and depressing in appearance. Pan's apartment had three rooms and a small kitchen. A private bathroom and painted, as opposed to raw, cement walls in all the rooms identified it as the home of an important family. The only decoration in the apartment consisted of some silk banners, awards and photographs from Pan's years as the national wushu champion and from the set of Shaolin Temple. Pan's wife, a doctor, greeted me with all sorts of homemade snacks and sat me down at a table set for two. Pan sat across from me and poured two glasses of baijiu. He called to his sons, both in their teens, and they appeared from the bedroom instantly. They stood in com-plete silence until Pan asked them to greet me, which they did, very politely, but so softly I could barely hear them. They were handsome boys, and the elder, at about fourteen, was taller than me and had a moustache. I tried asking them questions to put them at ease, but they answered only by nodding. They apparently had no idea how to behave toward something like me and did not want to make any mistakes in front of their father. Pan told them to say good night, and they, along with his wife, disappeared into the bedroom. Pan raised his glass and proposed that the evening begin.

He told me stories that made my hair stand on end, with such gusto that I though the building would shake apart. When he came to the parts where he vanquished his enemies, he brought his terrible hand down on the table or against the wall with a crash, sending our snacks jumping out of their serving bowls. His imitations of cowards and bullies were so funny I could hardly breathe for laughing. He had me spellbound for three solid hours; then his wife came in to see if we needed any more food or baijiu. I took the opportunity to ask her if she had ever been afraid for her husband's safety when, for example, he went off alone to bust up a gang of hoodlums in Shenyang. She laughed and touched his right hand. "Sometimes I figured he'd be late for dinner." A look of tremendous satisfaction came over Pan's face, and he got up to use the bathroom. She sat down in his chair and looked at me. "Every day he receives tens of letters from all over China, all from people asking to become his student. Since he made the movie, its been almost im-possible for him to go out during the day." She refilled our cups, then looked at me again. "He has trained professionals for more than twenty-five years now, but in all that time he has accepted only one private student." After a long pause, she gestured at me with her chin. "You." Just then Pan came back into the room, returned to his seat and started a new story. This one was about a spear:

While still a young man training for the national wushu competition, Pan overheard a debate among some of his fellow athletes about the credibility of an old story. The story described a famous warrior as being able to execute a thousand spear-thrusts without stopping to rest. Some of the athletes felt this to be impossible: after fifty, one's shoulders ache, and by one hundred the skin on the left hand, which guides the spear as the right hand thrusts, twists and returns it, begins to blister. Pan had argued that surely this particular warrior would not have been intimidated by aching shoulders and blisters, and soon a challenge was raised. The next day Pan went out into a field with a spear, and as the other athletes watched, executed one thousand and seven thrusts without stopping to rest. Certain details of the story as Pan told it—that the bones of his left hand were exposed, and so forth—might be called into question, but the number of thrusts I am sure is accurate, and the scar tissue on his left palm indicates that it was not easy for him.

One evening later in the year, when I felt discouraged with my progress in a form of Northern Shaolin boxing called "Changquan," or "Long Fist," I asked Pan if he thought I should discontinue the training. He frowned, the only time he ever seemed genuinely angry with me, and said quietly, "When I say I will do something, I do it, exactly. as I said I would. In my whole life, I have never started something without finishing it. I said that in the time we have, I would make your wushu better than you could imagine, and I will. Your only responsibility to me is to practice and to learn. My responsibility to you is much greater! Every time you think your task is great, think how much greater mine is. just keep this in mind: if you fail—here he paused to make sure I understood—"I will lose face."

Though my responsibility to him was merely to practice and to learn, he had one request that he vigorously en-couraged me to fulfill—to teach him English. I felt relieved to have something to offer him, so I quickly prepared some beginning materials and rode over to his house for the first lesson. When I got there, he had a tape recorder set up on a small table, along with a pile of oversized paper and a few felt-tip pens from a coloring set. He showed no interest at all in my books, but sat me down next to the recorder and pointed at the pile of paper. On each sheet he had written out in Chinese dozens of phrases, such as "We'll need a spotlight over there," "These mats aren't springy enough," and "Don't worry—it's just a shoulder dislocation." He asked me to write down the English translation next to each phrase, which took a little over two and a half hours. When I was finished, I asked him if he could read my handwriting, and he smiled, saying that he was sure my handwriting was fine. After a series of delicate questions, I determined that he was as yet unfamiliar with the alphabet, so I encouraged him to have a look at my beginning materials. "That's too slow for me," he said. He asked me to repeat each of the phrases I'd written down five times into the recorder, leaving enough time after each repetition for him to say it aloud after me. "The first time should be very slow—one word at a time, with a pause after each word so I can repeat it. The second time should be the same. The third time you should pause after every other word. The fourth time read it through slowly. The fifth time you can read it fast." I looked at the pile of phrase sheets, calculated how much time this would take, and asked if we could do half today and half tomorrow, as dinner was only three hours away. "Don't worry!" he said, beaming. "I've prepared some food for you here. just tell me when you get hungry." He sat next to me, turned on the machine, then turned it off again. "How do you say, 'And now, Mark will teach me English'?" I told him how and he repeated it, at first slowly, then more quickly, twenty or twenty-one times. He turned the machine on. "And now, Mark will teach me English." I read the first phrase, five times as he had requested, and he pushed a little note across the table. "Better read it six times," it read, "and a little slower."

After several weeks during which we nearly exhausted the phrasal possibilities of our two languages, Pan announced that the time had come to do something new. "Now I want to learn routines." I didn't understand. "Routines?" "Yes. Everything, including language, is like wushu. First you learn the basic moves, or words, then you string them together into routines." He produced from his bedroom a huge sheet of paper made up of smaller pieces taped together. He wanted me to write a story on it. The story he had in mind was a famous Chinese folk tale, "How Yu Gong Moved the Mountain." The story tells of an old man who realized that, if he only had fields where a mountain stood instead, he would have enough arable land to support his family comfortably. So he went out to the mountain with a shovel and a bucket and started to take the mountain down. All his neighbors made fun of him, calling it an impossible task, but Yu Gong disagreed: it would just take a long time, and after several tens of generations had passed, the mountain would at last become a field and his family would live comfortably. Pan had me write this story in big letters, so that he could paste it up on his bedroom wall, listen to the tape I was to make and read along as he lay in bed.

Not only did I repeat this story into the tape recorder several dozen times—at first one word at a time, and so on—but Pan invited Bill, Bob and Marcy over for dinner one night and had them read it a few times for variety. After they had finished, Pan said that he would like to recite a few phrases for them to evaluate and correct. He chose some of his favorite sentences and repeated each seven or eight times without a pause. He belted them out with such fierce concentration we were all afraid to move lest it disturb him. At last he finished and looked at me, asking quietly if it was all right. I nodded and he seemed overcome with relief. He smiled, pointed at me and said to my friends, "I was very nervous just then. I didn't want him to lose face."

While Pan struggled to recite English routines from memory, he began teaching me how to use traditional weapons. He would teach me a single move, then have me practice it in front of him until I could do it ten times in a row without a mistake. He always stood about five feet away from me, with his arms folded, grinding his teeth, and the only time he took his eyes off me was to blink. One night in the late spring I was having a particularly hard time learning a move with the staff. I was sweating heavily and my right hand was bleeding, so the staff had become slippery and hard to control. Several of the athletes stayed on after their workout to watch and to enjoy the breeze that sometimes passed through the training hall. Pan stopped me and indicated that I wasn't working hard enough. "Imagine," he said, "that you are participating in the national competition, and those athletes are your competitors. Look as if you know what you are doing! Frighten them with your strength and confidence." I mustered all the confidence I could, under the circumstances, and flung myself into the move. I lost control of the staff, and it whirled straight into my forehead. As if in a dream, the floor raised up several feet to support my behind, and I sat staring up at Pan while blood ran down across my nose and a fleshy knob grew between my eyebrows. The athletes sprang forward to help me up. They seemed nervous, never having had a foreigner knock himself out in their training hall before, but Pan, after asking if I felt all right, seemed positively inspired. "Sweating and bleeding. Good."

Every once in a while, Pan felt it necessary to give his students something to think about, to spur them on to greater efforts. During one morning workout two women practiced a combat routine, one armed with a spear, the other with a dadao, or halberd. The dadao stands about six feet high and consists of a broadsword attached to a thick wooden pole, with an angry-looking spike at the far end. It is heavy and difficult to wield even for a strong man, so it surprised me to see this young woman, who could not weigh more than one hundred pounds, using it so effectively. At one point in their battle the woman with the dadao swept it toward the other woman's feet, as if to cut them off, but the other woman jumped up in time to avoid the blow. The first woman, without letting the blade of the dadao stop, brought it around in another sweep, as if to cut the other woman in half at the waist. The other woman, without an instant to spare, bent straight from the hips so that the dadao slashed over her back and head, barely three times in rapid succession before moving on to the next exchange. The women practiced this move several times, none of which satisfied Pan. "Too slow, and the weapon is too far away from her. It should graze her back as it goes by." They tried again, but still Pan growled angrily. Suddenly he got up and took the dadao from the first woman. The entire training hall went silent and still. Without warming up at all, Pan ordered the woman with the spear to get ready, and to move fast when the time came. His body looked as though electricity had suddenly passed through it, and the huge blade flashed toward her. Once, twice the dadao flew beneath her feet, then swung around in a terrible arc and rode her back with flawless precision. The third time he added a little twist at the end, so that the blade grazed up her neck and sent a little decoration stuck in her pigtails flying across the room.

I had to sit down for a moment to ponder the difficulty of sending an object roughly the shape of an oversized shovel, only heavier, across a girl's back and through her pigtails, without guide ropes or even a safety helmet. Not long before, I had spoken with a former troupe member who, when practicing with this instrument, had suddenly found himself on his knees. The blade, unsharpened, had twirled a bit too close to him and passed through his Achilles' tendon without a sound. Pan handed the dadao, back to the woman and walked over to me. "What if you had made a mistake?" I asked. "I never make mistakes," he said, without looking at me.

Learning the long sword proved more demanding than any of the other wushu Pan had taught me. The morning after he agreed to teach it to me, Pan arrived very early with two broom handles, led me up to the bathhouse and began the training without a word. In the past, he had always told stories and imitated me with great humor to illustrate his points and to make me relax. Now, he rarely spoke and made no effort to be humorous, insisting that I simply drill until he taught me the next move.

My last month in China was a busy one, as I had to complete my teaching duties, prepare my belongings for the move back to the States, attend farewell meetings and banquets and begin saying goodbye to my friends, students, colleagues and teachers. Still, I practiced as much as I could with my broom-stick, never knowing when Pan would come next, and always wondering what would happen if I "made him sad." With two weeks to go, he stopped coming.

I tried frantically to get word to him, so that I could at least see him once more before I left, but no one could reach him. Rumor had it that he was in North China, but why, and for how long, no one knew.

The night before my departure, I was in my room packing the bag I had made for my swords and other weapons. I remember debating whether or not to pack my broomstick along with the swords when I suddenly jumped with fright. Pan stood not three feet behind me, with a rolled-up carpet under his arm. He smiled and told me to follow him. We would finish tonight, no matter how long it took. I reached for my broomstick, and he shook his head. "You won't need that anymore," he whispered, and we went outside. We made our way up to the bathhouse, and when we got there Pan put the carpet down and looked around at the night scene. "You leave tomorrow, don't you?" "Yes." "I will miss you." I stood dumb for a moment. "I will miss you, too." One of the coal trains blew its whistle, and Pan smiled. "I will leave tomorrow, too. By the time you reach America, I will be home as well. We are both going home." He told me that after years of waiting, his request for a transfer back to North China had been accepted. He paused for a few minutes, taking in the view, then said in English, "Let's begin."

He unrolled the carpet and took out two long swords. He handed me one, and we set to work. I felt light as a feather, and time had no meaning at all. We were both soaked with sweat, and he laughed and told stories the whole time. At last we did a routine together, then he told me to do it alone.

"This is the end of your training. The last move of this routine will be your own, and after that, as far as wushu is concerned, you will proceed alone." At that moment, everything was magnificent—the night, the heat, the sword, Pan and I—we were all magnificent. I flew through the routine, and when it was done, I thought I had never known such exhilaration before. Pan nod-ded, put the sword he was hold-ing back on the carpet, rolled it up and faced me. He stood straight and looked right into my eyes, and suddenly I was back in the training hall, standing at attention during our first lesson. I waited for it, for the critical moment of our duel. Then, very slowly, he spoke: "I brought two swords tonight. I am taking only one back with me."

14. Fists of Fantasy: Martial Arts Fiction

James Grady has published more than a dozen novels, including Six Days of the Condor *(the basis for the Robert Redford movie). Grady's work has been honored with the Grand Prix Du Roman Noir (France) and the Raymond Chandler Medal (Italy). He's written film scripts for TV and major studios and directors. His short stories have won national awards in America, and he spent four years as an investigative reporter for syndicated columnist Jack Anderson. Grady is a longtime student of taiji, and has also studied judo, tae kwon do, karate,* bagua *and* xingyi.

From *Fists of Fantasy* by James Grady

> *"Literature's only excuses (are) exploring the questions of innocence and experience, good and evil."*
> —Stephen King

> *"Action is character."* —F. Scott Fitzgerald

Our lives breathe fiction.

Stories tell us how we lived and how to live, then let us escape life's daily grind. Stories shape our psyches as dreams or fantasies for Freud and Jung to quarrel over like critics at a Soho art gallery. The stories/lies we tell are our armor as Tracy Chapman sings: *"There is fiction in the space between you and me . . . fiction in the space between you and reality."* Sages from Joseph Campbell to Bruce Springsteen record how myths/stories drive cultures and consciousness.

Stories—fictions—pack potent punches for martial artists.

Most martial artists—certainly most Americans—first learn about martial arts through fictional mediums. While most of such contemporary educational initiation comes through motion pictures and television, many living American martial artists had their first exposure to systematic Asian combat systems through literature like Ian Fleming's 1959 novel *Goldfinger*. Until tale-tellers jack in to some cyber/holographic creative medium *à la The Matrix* or late 20th Century cyberpunk novels to develop fictional experiences directly from their cerebrum, *written tales*, be they screen plays (the blueprints for the film medium's creative teams), poems, short stories, or novels, will constitute the basis of fiction.

Additionally, much of how we learn and train as martial artists comes from fictional construction. The activities we engage in with titles like karate, *gung fu*, and *aikido* are learning systems set against the hypothetical story of battling an attacker. Indeed, the katas, poomse, and forms we use in training are dramatizations of such encounters. Whether it is the Yang style T'ai Chi form or Tae Kwon Do's *Kwang-Gae*, we act out our responses to an imagined foe, and spend years training in this fictional construction to hone our spirits, minds and bodies for an ambush of such reality.

Perhaps our koan is: *To survive the truth, master a lie*.

Exploring the nexus between martial arts and prose fiction requires a disclosure. For a working author to critique others' prose efforts veers close to a conflict of interest; for a feeble student of martial arts to pontificate about them borders on the absurd. These are truths I admit and *still* have the gall to proceed.

Our nexus of martial arts and fiction shimmers with both process and product.

Writing fiction feels like Western boxing's sparring, karate's *kumite*, Judo's *randori*, T'ai Ch'i's pushing hands: a dance of co-operation and opposition with a muse whose face is much like yours, where your next move is not so much "thought out" as it is "sensed" or "intuited," where years spent learning, practicing and experiencing the success and failure of skills like paragraphing and verb-noun configuration come together in a reaction that dictates a keystroke on a computer screen or pen scratch on a virgin page. Just as senseis and sifus caution their well-trained students about "over-thinking" a fight, I argue that for a writer, too much building-block linear thought inhibits fruitful reaction to a fictional moment, just as too little concept of literary strategy and consciousness creates a second rate sentence.

Time and place fall away when you are at your best in sparring. You become one with your opponent, engage in a violent dance akin to love-making. The more you release/focus into "there," the "better" you will do and that "there" will become. Zen mind, no mind, *wu wei*: these are not esoteric terms, they are physical/spiritual/mental realities martial artists approach in our best moments even as some other person in the "there" attempts to slam his non-esoteric fist into our forehead.

Writers like ball players talk of being *in the zone*, of slipping into an altered state of reality where "it" just happens, and what results is their best fiction. Just as Yang Cheng-fu might spontaneously burst into laughter while holding a T'ai Chi posture, writers can be overwhelmed by emotions they experience because of the "there" they create out of ether. Tears rain on keyboards. When you are *there*, kicks and punches blasting in, a push attacking your slamming heart, electricity crackling up your spine, your whole being flowing with the moment, zero borders between you and the "there," ask: *"Are you writing or fighting?"* and the answer is *"Yes."*

Perhaps the preceding paragraph makes you feel like you've been sucked into insanity. Possibly that's true, but probably that journey is necessary to understand the process of fiction writing. Not coincidentally, whether it's a 49-year-old man whispering to an 10-year-old boy as they agonize through an eight hour

Tae Kwon Do black belt exam, or an otherwise practical woman trembling as she sinks all her weight through one screaming leg for a Squatting Single Whip T'ai Chi posture in a windowless concrete basement classroom that's vibrating from the blaring speakers in the rock 'n' roll CD store upstairs, martial arts students routinely doubt their own sanity: "We gotta be crazy to do this."

Art is rebellion against pure sanity.

That wink of light on the process of fiction writing leaves us back alone in the darkness if we do not consider the product of the process: the fictions themselves.

Fiction loves martial arts—at least, in theory.

Fiction is drama, the blood of drama is conflict, and martial arts are rooted in conflict. Add to that Fitzgerald's observation about action defining character, and fiction's attraction to martial arts screams louder than any *kia*.

However, as martial arts proves daily, theory and reality are two different things.

Fictionally writing about martial arts is a challenge where failure creates the deadliest criticism a writer can hear: *"Boring!"*

"John clobbered Paul." *Who cares?* And really, who cares much how John did it? Written on the page as opposed to depicted on the silver screen, martial actions are flat and uninteresting *unless* they occur in a context that the reader cares about and involves characters he likes in a setting that has aroused his curiosity or concern. Making a reader care about the overall story doesn't mean finding a tonnage of words to describe a razzle-dazzle combat technique that might (or might not) succeed in a Detroit alley. In fact, the more time spent on such details, the greater the danger that the reader's attention will drift off the whole of the story, thus diluting the work's *raison d'etre* and power, and glazing the reader's eyes. Consider our three word tale: "John clobbered Paul." Does it make the story more interesting to say: "John back-kicked Paul"? Perhaps a little. But compare those two stories with: "Mary clobbered Paul." The drama of story 3 hooks more readers more deeply than either of the other two, and the "hooking" element is not the depiction of martial acrobatics, but an enhancement of the classic elements of fiction.

Fiction works because of magic beyond the sum of its parts. An overemphasis on any one part dilutes that magic. That's one reason why "male adventure novels" or "blood and guts" bombasts barely climb to the popcorn level on the literary food chain. Most of them are just-for-the-money charades written with Junior High locker room smugness, shotgunned with cliches, choked with overly technical description of semi-possible action, crippled by a lack of any profound ethical stance, poorly plotted with cardboard characters, and implanted with a heart that is absurd.

All of which leads to a central premise: The concept of a "martial arts story" is doomed at birth. Considering whether or not such an effort is "good" is like searching for phrases to praise a corpse. Dead is dead.

Which leaves us with the concept of good fiction that uses martial arts well. Luckily, such fiction exists.

Critiquing fiction to find examples for our concern is an overwhelming task. There are too many books and stories to consider. Moreover, criticism is in large part a question of taste: what I find worthy may horrify you.

Following wiser minds than mine, my "critical criteria" for praising stories using martial arts avoided "getting stuck in structural analysis," and strove to keep in mind Henry James's dictum: "Be one on whom nothing is lost." I sought stories and writers who caught the magic that makes good fiction— and who portrayed martial arts within that magic. For martial arts, I stuck to Asian systems, though there are wonderful fictions involving Western boxing. I avoided stories propelled by weapons or empowered by surr/supra/magic realism (thus *a priori* eliminating some fine novels like Carolyn See's *Golden Days*), sought only work worthy of praise: savaging anyone's efforts from the safety of the critic's seat is too easy and gains readers nothing.

What I offer is a fist of fiction, five writers and their works worthy of your time to read.

Fiction abounds with cartoon characters proclaimed to be "the world's greatest martial artist" or "the deadliest man alive." Such absurd hyperbole too often sets the tone for the rest of the story, and thus dooms the tale from word one. Consider the realities of luck, timing, and circumstance that shape every combative encounter. A heavyweight hero with stellar black belt rankings in a dozen martial arts (who somehow is still vibrantly young despite the expenditure of time necessary to have attained all that education) only has the fighting ability of a 7-year-old if he's in the fevered grip of Hong Kong flu. Even on his best day, our stellar fighter can be flattened by a banana peel or a sucker punch from a little old lady.

Centering fiction on "the best" character means the drama of his encounters with other characters is nonexistent. If he is "the best," then he can not lose in any encounter, and therefore no drama exist. At most, his adventures portray as mayhem manuals, a prose creation that probably only satisfies the Marquis de Sade.

That leaves our fictional superstar with only two possible dramas: the existential battle against (or for) himself, or the surprise opponent who will 'best the best.' The existential battle exists for all characters in good fiction, but is especially true in warrior fiction, where the character must convince himself (and thus the reader) that risking one's life in painful encounters is somehow better than staying home with a sweetheart and/or a cold six pack and a warm TV. The surprise opponent plot runs the risk of begging the question, of merely creating a successor to "the best" and thus leaving us in the same old dull swamp of superlatives.

But fiction loves irony, and our irony is that one of the five fingers of our martial arts & fiction fist involves the cartoonish character of "the greatest martial artist alive" opposing a heroic creation brought to life not only in novels, but also in movies, TV shows—and newspaper strip cartoons. While the magic for this work comes in part from its creator's fertile imagination and solid talent, fantastic though this story and character are, its real power comes from its inspiration of experienced truth.

Northern Persia (Iran) near the Caucasus in 1942 was a blood-soaked geography. A young British army sergeant named Peter O'Donnell commanded a mobile radio detachment battling the Third Reich's death-head minions for the oil fields. As they had for thousands of years in hundreds of wars, shattered refugees staggered through that wasteland. O'Donnell's unit camped by a stream. As the soldiers cooked their evening stew, the young sergeant looked up.

A lone barefoot girl of about 12 appeared nearby wearing a rag of a dress, all her belongings wrapped in a blanket she balanced on her head. From a thong around her neck dangled a piece of wood: lashed to it with a wire was a long nail. This was her weapon, her existential statement to the world that she would not accept victimhood.

"She had been on her own for some time, because she wasn't phased, she was her own person, this little kid," remembers O'Donnell. He had one of his men take a mess tin of stew and a mug of tea to her. As she ate, O'Donnell put tins of food with a can opener near her so she could get them without coming too close to the foreign male soldiers. She spoke in a language none of the Brits understood, though they knew it wasn't Arabic. She washed the utensils in the stream and brought them back to the tins of food. Her gestures asked if the supplies were for her. After the Brits nodded yes, she put the food in her bundle.

"She stood there for a few seconds," says O'Donnell, "then she gave us a smile (that) could have lit up a small village. . . . She said something and walked off into the desert going south . . . She was on her own (but) she walked like a little princess."

Gone. Vanished into the chaos of war and history. But seared into O'Donnell's heart.

Twenty years later, as 'Bond, James Bond' heroes swelled through entertainment fiction, writer O'Donnell "thought it was about time someone came up with a female who could do all the things the males had been doing. But for me she had to be plausible, so I had to give her the kind of background that would make her plausible."

With plausibility in mind and the gutsy refugee girl scarred on his heart, O'Donnell created Modesty Blaise.

In the fad and product tie-in driven entertainment blitz of our 21st Century, it's difficult to recognize how "big" Modesty Blaise was in the last third of the 20th Century. O'Donnell's creation lived in a dozen internationally successful books, a movie, a TV series, and a London newspaper cartoon strip. Now 40 years after her creation, she has fan-driven Web sites. Though "politically correct" and refined cultural mavens will not give her this due, Modesty represents a feminist literary milestone: never before had a series female protagonist received such global acceptance for living a fictional violently adventurous life in which gender was merely a facet of her existence. Modesty bested competent men on the fictive battlefields males had ruled since Adam and Eve fled the snake-poisoned garden. And she did so with brains, athleticism, courage, honor—all without losing her heterosexual femininity. She had a male who was her best friend and lieutenant, not her lover or boss. Though vulnerable (a rape survivor), she was victorious.

O'Donnell made her a refugee child/reformed thief, a rogue who stumbles onto the side of the angels largely through alliances with British intelligence. While his novels usually pit her against bizarre villains in outlandish plots (thus avoiding formulaic Cold War confrontations prevalent in that era) and utilize a now-dated British prose cadence/style, Modesty's stories are powered by that strain of "plausible" action and vibrant character.

Extensive research helped O'Donnell shape Modesty, whether it's the 30 years of *National Geographic* Magazines in his office bookcase or consultations with the British Amateur Fencing Association—or his work in creating her martial arts skills.

During a trip to Haifa in 1962, when he was developing Modesty, O'Donnell stumbled across a paperback edition of *Zen Combat* by Jay Gluck (Ballantine Books, 1962). Subtitled: "A Complete Guide to the Oriental Arts of Attack and Defense—Karate, Kendo, Zen Archery, Aiki", the book also discusses Chinese Kempo, Judo, *bushido*, fire walking, *ki*, and weapons—especially the kongo, a six-inch long dumbbell shaped weapon favored by Modesty, who also studied numerous unarmed combat styles.

"I've had no martial arts training (other than his WWII army schooling)," says O'Donnell, "but have quite often watched workouts in the dojo. A girl called Christine Child, who was British Judo Champion and also a film stunt girl, wrote to me as a fan, and later introduced me to Brian Jacks, British Middleweight Champion. My greatest need was to have shots of combat moves that I could send to (his artist/illustrator) Romero . . . Christine and Brian put on an hour-long performance in the dojo for me, and I had a photographer who took scores of pix. Apart from this, my research has been in books and magazines such as "Combat"—the latter mainly for further pix. . . ."

O'Donnell's talent and imagination bow in at top form in *The Silver Mistress*, the seventh Modesty Blaise book (1973) and the one most germane to this essay. To rescue her kidnapped friend and mentor Tarrant, the head of the British Secret Service, Modesty must face Sexton, the self-proclaimed world's greatest martial artist, our cartoon character if ever one existed. Except O'Donnell brings Sexton to life—and has Modesty use the very cartoon nature of Sexton's character to defeat him.

Escaping from captivity, Modesty and Tarrant flee pursuing villains through an underground cavern. She pauses, strips, and hands him a can of scavenged machine oil:

She stood up naked, holding her shirt and wrapping it about both her hands, then said sharply, "Grease me. I can't do it myself. I've got to keep my hands dry. Grease me all over. Hurry."

Tarrant complies. In the half-light of the cavern, the grease gives Modesty a silver sheen (hence the title). Sexton had given the captives a martial arts demonstration in his gym to intimidate them, but all the while, Modesty was thinking. As she sets her ambush in the rocky cavern, she tells Tarrant: "This isn't a surface for fancy kicks and chops, so he'll want to get hold of me, and I need an edge there."

Her Sherlock Holmes analysis of Sexton's character have given her another slim but credible edge. She uses that edge to set-up Sexton, and in the ensuing one-on-one unarmed challenge combat, she kills him. Modesty tells Tarrant: "He was the best I've ever seen. I could never have taken him on his own ground."

"On his own ground," Tarrant repeated slowly. She was no doubt right about that. But the ground and the situation were all part of the battle, any battle. A point Sexton had missed and she had not.

And that's a point hundreds of authors miss with their "greatest martial artist" creations.

Women in fiction have been empowered by martial arts just as have been women in life. Modesty Blaise has `fictional sisters' who share her study of martial arts, some dating back to Chinese legends of the woman warrior Mulan (whether in the Disney movie of the same name or as revised in Maxine Hong Kingston's *The Woman Warrior*). But the degree to which martial arts figures in those stories tends to be minimal, whether the characters are serial figures in several books or not. For example, notch-below-black-belt-herself author S.J. Rozan's well written fictional private eye character Lydia Chen has a Tae Kwon Do black belt, but is more inclined to fill her hand with a pistol than a fist, and her martial arts background is more important as a cultural/family issue than a character point (Lydia's girlhood New York City neighborhood kung fu school wouldn't take females as students, even Chinese girls like her).

Using martial arts to develop a character and doing so over multiple books is a technique exemplified by author David Hunt (a pseudonym) in his two Kay Farrow novels. Unlike Modesty Blaise or numerous other fictional martial artists male and female, Kay's life and profession are not geared toward confrontation: she's a photographer—not portraits, commercial work or journalism, but art. That core of work defines her life, making her more a recording witness than an activist. Her stories reflect how she is drawn into adventure and confrontation as much as what happens when she gets there. Kay is also defined by a medical condition startling for a photographer: she's an achromat—completely color blind, and suffers from photophobia (an aversion to bright light). From the moment she opens her eyes, her world is radically different from the rest of us—a perceptive reality that is reflected in her photographs, her attitudes, her adventures.

Hunt writes in what *Publishers Weekly* called: "a vibrant, melancholy narrative voice" that *The New York Times* says creates an ambiance for the reader that's "strange, seductive . . . as eerie as a midnight walk in the fog." Hunt also chose to define Kay by making her an aikido student—emphasis on 'student.'

"I felt that it was important that Kay's aikido skills not be a constant," Hunt told JAMA,[1] "rather that she should develop them through the two books. In other words, I didn't want her to just be an aikidoist who goes to class, but a person training to improve and working toward the black belt exam. This required a lot of commitment on her part, and reflected the kind of self discipline and striving that was essential to her character."

And that choice by the author is a key to the quality of Hunt's work: his character's aikido is not just an add-on or an empowering device, not just a party trick for our heroine, but is instead an integral, integrated and living part of her being. Using martial arts in that fashion reflects its best use in real life—and makes for better fiction.

Author Hunt has no martial arts training, yet his authorial vision compelled him to do more than chose a combative art at random.

"I decided to make Kay an Aikidoist after reading a book "Women in Aikido" by Andrea Siegel," says Hunt. "It just seemed the "right" martial art for the character. I was especially intrigued by the concept of blending as opposed to punching or kicking. . . . Since Kay is very petite, 106 lbs., but feisty and puts herself in dangerous situations photographing the hustler scene at night, I wanted her to have defensive skills. . . . She is gentle and vulnerable and also doesn't take any shit. All this worked well with a character seriously committed to aikido training. I also enjoyed creating the character of her sensei (Rita), a black woman, a former kick-ass Marine, not one of those metaphysical Northern California Zen-utterance sensei types, but a real direct type person who likes Kay a lot and with whom Kay identifies."

Hunt attended classes by Sensei Robert Nadeau in San Francisco, and classes on Martha's Vineyard.

"And then," says Hunt, "to get the black belt exam right, I attended an Aikido summer retreat at Colgate College."

Many non-practicing martial arts writers would have stopped their research after reading one book and perhaps watching a few Bruce Lee or Steven Seagal movies. But not Hunt, and his extra effort shows. His thoughtful approach to blending martial arts into Kay Farrow flowers in the second novel, *Trick Of Light* (1998), a story whose through-line is an intertwining of her personal crises, the plot's driving evil force, and Kay's final preparations for her black belt exam. After Kay's horrible experiences, that exam blossoms to end the book:

> Everything feels "right" this afternoon. I have found my center. I own the

---

1. The *Journal of Asian Martial Arts.*

place where I stand, and a good-sized area around me. Rita has counseled me many times: "When you step onto the mat, take possession, make it your own."

Kay comes to the multiple attacker portion of her test.

I stand ready to take them on, claiming my space, drilling my legs down into the mat, preparing to blend. And then, just as they come at me, I enter a trance state. Even the bright sunlight that floods the field house doesn't distract or blind me now.

I don't think about anything, don't calculate, don't prepare, simply take them on as they come . . . I float. . . . No gesture is wasted. . . .

I am the at the center of a whirlpool of energy, aware of everything around me yet fazed by nothing. Time is warped. Actions that appear to others as sudden are for me orderly and slow....I am at the center of it all, she-who-harmonizes, she-who-*is*-the music, blending effortlessly, cleanly, in tune with the cosmic process, every breath clearly drawn, every move structured as in a dance.

The exam serves as an epiphany for Kay:

I did it, and now I have regained my life. My time of mourning and anger is over. Once again my life belongs wholly to me.

What more could any character expect?

The "serial" approach to literature—the same character appearing in successive novels—leads us to our third author/example, another pseudonym: Adam Hall, one of nine pen names used by the amazingly prolific British writer Elleston Trevor, slain by cancer in 1995.

The British born and educated Hall pictured himself as a writer from age 5. A drop-out from sadistic British schools, Hall wanted to be a Spitfire pilot in World War II, but vision problems made him only a Royal Air Force mechanic. He began seriously writing at 19, while still battling the Nazis. One of his best known "Trevor" works is the book adapted to a movie of the same name, *The Flight Of The Phoenix*, but what we praise here is Adam Hall's decades long series of book about a British spy named Quiller.

Influenced in part by John le Carré (another British writer working under a pseudonym), in 1965 Hall published *The Quiller Memorandum*, the story of a British agent—"shadow executive"—employed by a heartless covert government organization called The Bureau, a bureaucracy with its own language, mores and arrogance of mission, the classic never-admitted-to-exist secret agency that populated both the fiction and fact of the Cold War. Quiller is a paradox, an organization man who operates as a lone wolf, a falcon launched into one crises after another, a man who thinks in terms of nerve synapses and tactical esoteria, a troubleshooter who refuses to carry a gun, because guns create a false sense of confidence. Better, thinks Quiller, to rely on instincts, intelligence—and unarmed combat skills.

Yet when Hall began writing the Quiller series, his only martial arts training was whatever rough-trade tricks he'd learned in the RAF.

"The early books, when they mentioned any kind of karate, were cheats," said Hall in 1982.

He invented Asian sounding terms for techniques and action segments and wrote best sellers. *The Quiller Memorandum* became a George Segal, Alec Guinness, Max Von Sydow movie written by Harold Pinter that disappointed Hall, but did not deter him from continuing the Quiller series. Nor did a short-lived BBC TV series.

Hall was a fanatic for accuracy and research: he wrote the Hong Kong police to get a copy of a parking ticket so the few words he'd use to describe it would not be false. That drive for precision, plus a lifetime of adventure (race car driving, among other pursuits), led him—at age 58—to begin studying martial arts, an educational journey so profound that when a reporter asked him to list the most important events that had a lasting effect on his life, besides moving from one country to another (Britain, Spain, France and finally to the United States), Hall mentioned only studying karate.

A longtime student of yoga, Hall's first formal martial arts training was in "Chinese kenpo" (*ch'uan fa*), but then scheduling conflicts led him to Shotokan karate, an art he practiced with his son, Jean-Pierre Trevor. In 1984, at age 64, Hall received a black belt under Sensei Shojiro Koyama. Hall dedicated a Quiller novel to his sensei, and once noted that "karate fines down the environment to this one, personal attack on one's own limitations. . . . I know myself better. I know other people better. There's nothing quite like karate to reveal character."

Evolution in Hall's personal life and martial arts study reflected in Quiller. Like many classic serial heroes, on one level Quiller never changed, never aged from the veteran operative in his 1965 debut through the 17 books that ended in 1995 with a novel finished three days before Hall's death. On other levels, Quiller grew. He became more compassionate, and his cynicism adopted a modest world-embracing rather than condescending world-weary view. And martial arts became a deeper, more realistic force in Quiller's life. His battle scenes and tactics were not pure Shotokan, but as Hall progressed in his own studies, the fictions began to feel more real.

One of the central ironies of the Quiller oeuvre is Hall's prose style. Most so-called "action/espionage/thriller genre" novels are written in straight-ahead, traditional linear prose. Hall defied such popular stylistic simplicity. At times the Quiller books spew out in a maddening, almost James Joycean first person stream-of-consciousness machinegun prose, with run-on sentences shotgunned by undefined terms. Chapters and scenes often begin with the after-effects of the action that defines the plot, then unfold on a serpentine time line that forces the reader to pay strict attention—and propels him deeper into the book. A lesser writer couldn't ape Hall's style; most who tried would inspire readers to hunt them down and beat them to their knees with the book. But Hall was not a lesser writer. A winner of a Mystery Writers of America Edgar Award and the French *Grand Prix de Literature Policiere*, his powerful talent of adrenalized style, character and ethic caught the magic that is great prose, attracting legions of fans who cherish his work beyond the author's mortal time.

For sheer totality of elegance, my personal Quiller favorite is 1994's morally complex, vividly written *Quiller Salamander*, but to illustrate Hall's use of martial arts, consider this opening segment of 1971's *The Warsaw Document*:

> There would be no warning, I knew that.
>
> In the total darkness I thought I could see things: the glint of his eyes, his bared teeth; and in the silence I thought I could hear his breath and the soft tentative padding of his feet as he looked for me, but all I saw and heard was in my imagination and I knew that soon my nerves were going to start playing up because of the worry; the worry that there'd be no warning when he came at me. He'd come the instant he found me.
>
> Breathing was difficult because this place wasn't very big and we were so close that one drawn breath would be a giveaway; also, it would have to be expelled before the next inhalation and I was afraid of being caught with empty lungs. I breathed tidally, right near the top, part of my conscious mind registering the smell of hemp and coconut.
>
> It was worse than I'd thought, the waiting. There was nothing to go on: no means of orientation. He was only a man but he was invisible and inaudible and these were the attributes of a phantom and my scalp was raised. It needn't be true that he was where I thought he was: somewhere in front of me where my hands could get at him. Even in the dark there's comfort if an enemy can be faced: the real dread is of being taken from behind.
>
> That was where he came for me: from behind. We hadn't touched; we had simply come so close that the instincts were triggered and the nerves galvanized and I was already in a throat lock with my knees buckling to a flat kick before I could hook at him, but my hands were free and I caught him and reached his thumb as we pitched down, breaking the hold while he used his foot again and missed and tried again and connected a fraction too late, his breath grunting as I forced him over. We fought close, neither wanting to lose the other in the unnerving dark. My shoulder hit the wall and I used the chance, going down low and recoiling against him, but the momentum wasn't enough, and he deadened the spring and forced me into a spine-bending *yoshida* that paralyzed the arms. Then some fool came in and switched the light on.

Radical prose style, controversial subject matter, and discipline learned from martial arts propelled our fourth author into prominence. Jay McInerney debuted in 1984 with a huge commercial and cultural hit novel: *Bright Lights, Big City*, a stream of consciousness saga/satire about oh-so-cool, self-absorbed young Manhattan hipsters who turbo charge their lives snorting lines of cocaine as they taxi down neon streets they call success. Written in a frenzied, immediate second person style —"You are not the kind of guy who would be at a place like this at this time of the morning. But here you are, and you cannot say that the terrain is entirely unfamiliar, although the details are fuzzy. . . ."—the book chronicled a time and place before basketball star Len Bias's overdose death alerted Sixties-jaded America that cocaine—as writer George Pelecanos puts it—"was the drug that always drove the car and never gave up the keys."

But *Bright Lights* was not McInerney's first attempt at fiction—nor is it either his work of focus here or in my view his best book of that era in his career. That credit belongs to his novel *Ransom* (1985).

"I lived in Japan from 1977 to 1979," said McInerney. "I started writing a novel about Japan when I returned to the States and worked on it for two years in grad school studying creative writing and English at Syracuse University. Whether or not it was *Ransom*, I'm not sure—but parts of it survived. Finally, out of frustration at my inability to make a novel about Japan, I turned to more recent experience and wrote *Bright Lights, Big City* . . . quickly; it was done in six months. Finally, while waiting for its publication, I returned to the idea of a Japan novel and started almost from scratch *Ransom*—"exactly the kind of book I expected to write all along . . . *Bright Lights* came out of nowhere, in a way"—is an ex-pat novel in the tradition of Ernest Hemingway, a crime novel in the tradition of James Cain, and a martial arts novel in the tradition of. . . .Well, in the tradition of the other four writers in our fantasy fist.

While living in Japan, McInerney studied Shotokan karate in Tokyo for six months, then Go Ju Ryu in Kyoto for a year and a half. Though that education was crucial to his novel, it is perhaps more important to McInerney realizing his life as an author:

"I absolutely believe that it was the discipline of karate which got me disciplined about fiction. The lesson was very simple really—if I didn't practice every day, I lost ground. I finally realized writing fiction was as fierce a discipline as karate."

Reading *Ransom* feels like riding in a jetliner as it plummets towards earth, an odd kind of exhilaration and fascination in which you *wonder* whether your marvelous flying machine will pull up safe at the last moment.

The novel recounts the life of American ex-pat Christopher Ransom, who came to Asia to escape a domineering, manipulative father and "looking for freedom in the homeland of fatalism, looking for he didn't know what—but something more vital than the pallid choice of career."

His story begins and ends in Japan, but with a slipstream time line that reveals Ransom's early days in Asia, a time zone of love and horror near the Khyber Pass in Pakistan, when he becomes mesmerized by fellow ex-pats Annette and Ian. The gravity of their narcissism sucks the troubled, questing Ransom into their intertwined orbits as he mistakes their hollow self-assurance for the kind of self-empowerment he craves. Convinced of their own supreme self-importance, Annette and Ian graciously allow Ransom to pledge them his soul and survival, a classic act of a passionate young man who's pure of heart but fogged of mind. Such characters in such a place face an inevitability that McInerney builds with exacting, keenly spaced suspense.

With those scars etched on his already-battered heart and suffering from "Asia burn," the novel begins as Ransom opens his eyes after having been knocked out sparring in his karate class that meets outdoors on an asphalt courtyard. His sensei tells him he was dropped by a reverse roundhouse kick from Ito, "the monk," the sublime karateka who Ransom yearns to equal.

Upon arriving in Japan, Ransom by chance happened upon the class:

> Every night for a week Ransom watched them practice. He had not noticed the fighting so much as the grace of movement. . . . They conveyed an extraordinary sense of self-possession. For months Ransom had drifted across landscapes in a fevered daze, oblivious to almost everything but his own pain and guilt. The dojo with its strange incantations and white uniforms seemed to him a sacramental place, an intersection of body and spirit, where power and danger were ritualized in such a way that a man could learn to understand them. Ransom had lost his bearings spiritually, and he wanted to reclaim himself.
>
> His first lessons are in bowing and sweeping the courtyard.
>
> The school was Goju Ryu: hard-soft, based on a notion of alternating tension and relaxation, systole and diastole. The style combined the hard Okinawan techniques with the more flexible Chinese Kempo.

Ransom's school and his self-effacing attempts to find his center make him a target for Frank DeVito, an ex-Marine bully, "current Bruce Lee clone," who studies with a teacher known for his brutality and thugish movies he made starring himself. DeVito is another narcissist, a martial arts practitioner who's drawn half the circle. He realizes that training to fight and face death conveys a type of freedom, but fails to grasp that the point of freedom is to celebrate life. DeVito worships the glorious power of death—receiving it is ultimately unimaginable for him, but delivering it to someone else. . . . That is his obsession.

And looming in his eyes is Ransom, a quiet, refusing-to-engage/fight fellow American who studies with a sensei who thinks the grand award of a black belt is of little importance.

Conflict within conflict, crisis within crisis, Ransom moves through his fate.

McInerney takes us on that journey with karate/martial arts as our pilot. The novel is filled with a score of fight scenes—far more, in fact, than most "blood & guts" prose atrocities or quality "genre thrillers." He writes such action moments in flat, factual, non-dramatic language, and therefore conveys such moments with engaging, empathetic accuracy:

> Now it was Ransom's turn (to spar) . . . fixing his eyes on the Monk's, holding the gaze through the bow. The Monk settled back, way down in cat stance, all of his weight back on the rear leg, folded nearly double, while the lead foot

barely touched the pavement. He made an L with his forearms in front of his chest, the left vertical, the right horizontal. It seemed to Ransom that Ito's eyes were like pools in which no fish were showing; he would have to throw out some bait. He kicked. The Monk swept the kick away with his forearm. Ransom threw another kick, two jabs, and got knocked sideways by a kick in the ribs.

His breath was short and there was a dull pain in his ribs. The sensei told him to straighten up and fight. The ache in his ribs was either going to slow him down or serve as his weapon. He straightened up, then lowered himself into a crouch facing the Monk. When he inhaled, he drew the ache into a fine, hot wire extending from his side up into his right arm. He aimed it at the Monk's chest. When the Monk came at him he drove it home, feeling the impact of his knuckles against the Monk's sternum travel back to its point of origin in his ribs. The pain dissipated and then it was gone, as if it had traveled from his own body into the Monk's.

The sensei called the point, the first time Ransom had ever scored on the Monk. He was trying to remember how he had done it as they squared off, when the Monk kicked him in the chest for the match.

The kick in your chest from *Ransom* is worth it. The novel should be shelved with timeless period literature catalyzed by the Vietnam-to-Ronald-Reagan era, along with such gems as Kent Anderson's *Sympathy For The Devil*, Joan Didion's *Play It As It Lays*, Richard Farnia's *I've Been Down So Long It Looks Like Up To Me*, Ken Kesey's *One Flew Over The Cuckoo's Nest*, Greg Mcdonald's *Running Scared*, Tim O'Brien's *The Things They Carried*, Richard Price's *The Wanderers*, and Robert Stone's *Dog Soldiers*. And for any martial artist searching for an entertaining way to explain *this thing of ours* to a friend, *Ransom* offers some good—and disturbing—insights to share.

Sharing our last writer with readers is a privilege to relish. Charles Johnson is one of America's major writers, a serious martial artist—and a wonderful human being.

Consider the following true story. Former *Chicago Tribune* reporter Johnson rose through the ranks of American literature and academia to win the National Book Award for his work *Middle Passage*. If ever there was a justifiable moment for a writer to put modesty aside and bask in the spotlight as the audience and world cheered, that awards dinner night in 1989 was it for Charles Johnson. But instead of self-congratulation, Johnson walked to the podium and delivered an awe-struck tribute to 76-year-old writer Ralph Ellison as that icon sat in the audience listening.

"Like the day of my marriage, the days my children were born, and that night of my first martial-arts promotion," says Johnson, "I count the experience of reading that tribute (to Ellison) as one of the finest moments of my life."

That first martial arts exam Johnson took was in the late 1960's came after he found a martial arts school in Chicago called Chi Tao Chuan of the Monastery. College boy Johnson had "long wanted to systematically study a fighting art, partly because what I'd seen of Japanese karate impressed me . . . and partly because the Chicago area in the late 1960's was a pretty dangerous place for Blacks (like Johnson) and 'longhairs.'"

Johnson's sifu eventually steered him to the Tiger animal style of the school's version of gung fu. The training was arduous: "Often I wondered if I'd exit the studio alive."

And that promotion?

"I'm at a loss to explain how I felt," says Johnson, "at 19, as we received our membership cards and congratulations. The room was aglow. Though tired in every cell, my body felt transparent; my mind, clear as spring water. I couldn't have cared less if I missed my train and spent all night roaming downtown Chicago—I just wanted someone to jump me—before the next train at 8:00 A.M. I count this as one of the best nights of my life, a rare kind of rite-of- passage that showed me, as a young man, something about my capacity for discipline, enduring pain, and pushing myself beyond my expectations."

Martial arts is a powerful influence on Johnson. He met the Buddhist path he now walks in that Chicago kwoon. And call him *artist*: besides writing and martial arts, MacArthur "genius award" winner Johnson is an accomplished visual artist who's worked in mediums ranging from pen and ink sketches to television's PBS.

For Johnson, the linkages between martial arts and writing are clear:

"I've always been intrigued by Yukio Mishima's devotion to 'bunburyodo,' what he saw as the dual way of the martial and literary arts. I do think . . . there is a connection, first and perhaps foremost in the sense of the discipline martial art practice demands—that discipline of total physical and mental engagement in the here and now serves well to strengthen the discipline any writer (or artist) must have. My friend (screenwriter) Steven Barnes . . . begins his day with weights and martial arts practice BEFORE writing. I guess I do much the same, working out before I write (which is usually late evening and the wee hours of the morning) because after practice both mind and body are relaxed, clear, and I can approach the page with something like 'beginner's mind,' unconcerned about my performance the day before or even with past literary performances. . . .

"When I was a young philosophy student, it occurred to me life was, of course, a whole, but one could speak of it as flowing in three streams that come together. The streams were Mind, Body and Spirit. . . . And one could—or should—develop each stream to its full (Aristotelian) potential. For the Mind's development I chose philosophy. For the Body's, martial arts. And for the Spirit, literary and visual arts (later I added Buddhism to this). To separate any of these is (to me) engaging in a kind of existential apartheid, for one stream feeds the other, and all together enrich human life."

Like many martial artists, Johnson's education was in part dictated by geography: the college he attended was far from any gung fu kwoon, so he took the available path and studied karate. He's currently rated as an instructor in Choy Li Fut—"I haven't had the time to become a sifu". His Seattle kwoon is called "Blue Phoenix," and also teaches both long and short form Yang T'ai Chi—which Johnson also practices. Beyond his own writing, he holds a Professorship for Excellence in English at the University of Washington.

But there is no need to go beyond Johnson's writing to appreciate his artistry. Consider two short stories (available in various collections), two fists of excellence that (in what I humbly think is the proper and best pattern of literary conception) "forced" themselves upon Johnson rather than being products of a purely intellectual literary decision.

Consider *Kwoon*—first published in 1991.

"One afternoon when I was working out at home," says Johnson, "right in the middle of a heavy sweat, the story's premise came to me—what if tomorrow a truly talented, devastating killer dropped into a martial arts school and beat the stuffings out of a good teacher in front of his students, and suppose that teacher is a good transmitter of his school's tradition, and not a bad fighter but simply not as good as (the visiting challenger)?"

Johnson wanted to examine what it means to be a teacher, what it means to be a student, what it means to be a person—and how life can force one to change. In that martial arts setting, with a traditional straight-ahead prose style, he succeeds admirably.

Not to take anything from the wonderfulness of *Kwoon* or disparage that fist of Johnson's of any of its power, but Johnson's other fist is so electrifying it must be our focus.

Consider *China*—first published in 1980.

And consider it one of the finest short stories in American literature.

China began as an attempt by Johnson to get his mentor the novelist John Gardner—who was "VERY Western, Protestant, etc."—to understand, to "see . . . where (Johnson) lived" in regards to Buddhism and Eastern thought, a process triggered after Gardner read Johnson's novel *Oxherding Tale*. Gardner and Johnson exchanged a series of letters until Johnson realized that Gardner "much preferred reading stories to reading arguments. . . .

"This is how *China* came into being —a first draft in about 12 hours, which Gardner loved, even decided to add two (minor) sentences to, and which he published in his literary magazine. . . . I'd not planned on doing *China*."

The story *happened*. And *happens* for every reader:

Evelyn's problems with her husband, Rudolph, began one evening in early March—a dreary winter evening in Seattle—when he complained after a heavy meal of pig's feet and mashed potatoes of shortness of breath, an allergy to something she put in his food perhaps, or brought on by the first signs of wild flowers around them. She suggested they get out of the house for the evening, go to a movie. He was fifty-four, a postman for thirty-three years now, with high blood pressure, emphysema, flat feet, and, as Evelyn told her friend Shelberdine Lewis, the lingering fear that he had cancer. Getting old, he was also getting hard to live with. He told her never to salt his dinners, to keep their Lincoln Continental at a crawl, and never run her fingers along his inner thigh when they sat in Reverend William Merrill's church, because anything, even sex, or laughing too loud— Rudolph was serious—might bring on heart failure.

That opening paragraph serves as a textbook for fiction writers. The first sentence creates suspense—"problems . . . began," establishes specific time and place in a tactile fashion—"March . . . dreary winter evening in Seattle" contrasted with "first signs of wild flowers," creates and defines characters and sets them in opposition to each other, tantalizes the reader's all-important visceral senses of taste and smell with food and flowers, taps into readers' primal emotions—fear of aging and cancer—and does so with humor—contrasting the primal sexual sensation (again, shown tactually with a finger stroked along the inner thigh) of liberation with the stuffy inhibiting setting of restrictive church. The whipsawing of common images and outlandish truths— *sexual desire can truly lead to lethal heart attacks/do you want to give up all sexual possibilities/do you want to die*—exhilarates readers with tension but without them sensing an author's heavy hand. The scene is so intensely *ordinary*, so *common*, the reader immediately identifies with it and with both characters—yet the suspense created *by the second word* sucks the reader into hungering to know what uncommon drama these characters will face. The portrayal of characters contains empathetic "mini" scenes—Evelyn commiserating with her friend Shelberdine, Rudolph and Evelyn "crawling" along in traffic in their Lincoln Continental (no doubt in the street ahead of you as you're late for work).

All that is accomplished without a wasted or superfluous word, like an aikido or T'ai Chi adept letting the eyes/push of a reader flow into the writer's space and then with a feather touch rocketing him out through the story. Try accomplishing that in twelve hours. Or twelve years. Thus is defined the word "artist."

Johnson blends the techniques of *omniscient author* and *unreliable narrator* to unfold his story. Poor Evelyn chooses "a peaceful movie for their Saturday night outing," a low-key satire that puts Rudolph to sleep.

Until the previews of coming attractions that feature

. . . some sort of gladiator movie, Evelyn thought . . . pretty trashy stuff at that. The plot's revenge theme was a poor excuse for Chinese actors or Japanese (she couldn't tell those people apart) to flail the air with their hands and feet, take on fifty costumed extras at once, and leap twenty feet through the air in perfect defiance of gravity. Rudolph's mouth hung open.

When that movie comes to town, Rudolph sneaks off to see it, stays for the martial arts demonstration afterwards, then races home to a frantic, worried wife.

"Wonderful." Evelyn screwed up her lips. "I'm calling hospitals and you're at a Hong Kong double feature."

"Listen," said Rudolph. "You don't understand." He seemed at that moment as if he did not understand either.

Rudolph horrifies her when he announces he has signed up for martial arts lessons.

"You're fifty-*four* years old, Rudolph."

"I know that."

"You're no Muhammad Ali."

"I know that," he said.

"You're no Bruce Lee. Do you want to be Bruce Lee? Do you know where he is now, Rudolph? He's dead—dead here in a Seattle cemetery and buried up on Capital Hill."

But Rudolph has moved beyond thoughts of the cemetery to thoughts of life, visions of what he can do, what he *might* do. He is a character choosing change and transformation, a character seeking to define—redefine—himself. Such is the essence of drama.

Drama it is, especially for poor Evelyn, through whose horrified eyes we witness the transformation, as her Rudolph who can't do a push-up spends their money for equipment and lessons in an activity that for her is as comprehensible as Martian opera. Her friend Shelberdine comforts Evelyn with the wisdom that Rudolph's obsession is merely a mid-life crisis. But Evelyn senses . . .

. . . a dark vision . . . a dangerous vision, and in it she whiffed something that might destroy her. What that was, she couldn't say, but she knew her Rudolph better than he knew himself. He would see the error—the waste of time—in his new hobby, and she was sure he would mend his ways.

In the weeks, then months that followed, Evelyn waited, watching her husband for a flag of surrender. There was no such sign. He became worse than before.

That "worse" of course is irony: he improves his diet, his health, his mind, even his soul and spirit through mediation and study. What one person does effects all others; a choice of change by Rudolph forces that unsettling process on his wife, who reacts to it by targeting the agent of change, Rudolph, rather than facing herself. She insists that he return to 'being himself.'

"I can only be what I've been?" This he asked softly, but his voice trembled. . . . "I only want to be what I *can* be, which isn't the greatest fighter in the world, only the fighter *I* can be. . . ."

Reviewers and critics always face an ethical and practical dilemma. The best goal of critical reviewing is to lead people to fiction they will read, challenge and absorb into their own lives. Doing that usually means obeying the obvious marketing rule: *Don't Give Away The Ending, Dummy!* But this is not an usual author/story by any measure, nor would this conversation do the author/story justice to package an analysis of *China* with a cliff-hanger synopsis. While the goal here is to seduce every one of you to rush to acquire a copy of Johnson's story so you can experience *the whole process* of his enlightening prose, teasing you by following the obvious marketing rule undercuts the worth of that story and this article's heart: the examination of the nexus between martial arts and prose fiction. The conclusion of *China* at the Saturday tournament in Seattle's Kingdome where a frantic, panicked, yet dutifully loving Evelyn watches her husband spar in the far ring represents the apogee of that nexus:

> Yet it was not truly him that Evelyn, sitting down, saw. . . . She caught her breath when, miscalculating his distance from his opponent, her husband stepped sideways into a roundhouse kick with lots of snap—she heard the cloth of his opponent's *gi* crack like a gunshot when he threw the technique. She leaned forward, gripping the huge purse on her lap when Rudolph recovered and retreated from the killing to the neutral zone, and then, in a wide stance, rethought strategy. This was not the man she'd slept with for twenty years.... She did not know him, perhaps had never known him, and she never would, for the man on the floor, the man splashed with sweat, rising on the ball of his rear foot for a flying kick—was he so foolish he still thought he could fly?—would outlive her. . . . And then Evelyn was on her feet, unsure why, but the crowd had stood suddenly to clap, and Evelyn clapped, too, though for an instant she pounded her gloved hands together instinctively until her vision cleared, the momentary flash of retinal blindness giving way to a frame of her husband, the postman, twenty feet off the ground in a perfect flying kick that floored his opponent and made a Japanese judge who looked like Oddjob shout "ippon"—one point—and the fighting in the farthest ring, in herself, perhaps in all the world, was over.

What better apogee, what better climax could we reach?

15. AN OLD LEGACY IN A NEW WORLD

In this selection from the critically acclaimed novel Snow Falling on Cedars *by David Guterson, we come to learn something of the uses that martial training can be put to. For many Japanese who emigrated to other countries, martial arts training served as a mechanism to link younger generations with older cultural traditions that were fast eroding in new surroundings. But such training can also serve as much more than a way of preserving ethnic identity. Assiduously pursued, these arts can help us come to a deeper understanding of ourselves, with all the benefits and drawbacks that such insight brings with it.*

From *Snow Falling on Cedars* BY DAVID GUTERSON

It had been, he saw now, a war marriage, hurried into because there was no choice and because both of them felt the rightness of it. They had not known each other more than a few months, though he had always admired her from a distance, and it seemed to him, when he thought about it, that their marriage had been meant to happen. His parents approved, and hers approved, and he was happy to leave for the war in the knowledge that she was waiting for him and would be there when he returned. And then he had returned, a murderer, and her fear that he would no longer be himself was realized.

He remembered, too, his father's face, and the sword his father kept inside a wooden chest in the days before Pearl Harbor. A katana made by the swordsmith Masamune, it had been in the Miyamoto family, it was said, for six centuries. His father kept it sheathed and rolled in cloth, an undecorated and highly useful weapon. Its beauty lay in its simplicity, the plainness of its curve; even its wooden scabbard was spare and plain. His father had taken it, along with other things—his wooden *kendo* practice swords, his *sageo*, his *obi*, his *hakama* pants, his bokken—and buried them one night in a strawberry field, laid them carefully wrapped in a hole along with the dynamite he'd used to clear stumps, a ease full of books and scrolls written in Japanese, and a photograph taken of Kabuo at the San Piedro Japanese Community Center dressed in the feudal costume of a *bugeisha* and wielding a kendo stick.

Kabuo's training at kendo had begun when he was seven. His father had taken him one Saturday to the community center hall, where a dojo had been established in a corner of the gym. They knelt before an alcove at the back of the room and contemplated a shelf on which small bowls of uncooked rice had been neatly arranged. Kabuo learned to bow from a seated position.

While he sat on his heels his father explained softly the meaning of *zenshin*, which the boy understood to mean a constant awareness of potential danger. His father finished by repeating the word twice—"zenshin! zenshin!"—then took down a wooden pole from the wall and, before Kabuo knew what had happened, slammed him with it in the solar plexus.

"Zenshin!" said Zenhichi, while the boy caught his breath. "Didn't you say you understood?"

His father said that if he was to learn kendo more would be expected of him than of the average person. Did he wish to learn anyway? The choice was his. He should take some time to consider it.

When Kabuo was eight his father put a weapon in his hands for the first time—a *bokken*. They stood in the strawberry fields early one July morning just after picking season was finished. The bokken, a curved piece of cherry wood three feet long, had been Kabuo's great-grandfather's, a man who had been a samurai before the Meiji Restoration and later—after the wearing of swords was outlawed—a farmer of government rice lands on Kyushu for ten days before he joined two hundred other rebellious samurai in Kumamoto. They formed themselves into the League of the Divine Tempest and attacked an imperial garrison with swords aloft, having fasted for three clays. Its defenders, wielding rifles, killed all but twenty-nine with their opening volley; the survivors committed suicide on the battlefield, including Kabuo's great-grandfather.

"You come from a family of samurai," Kabuo's father said to him in Japanese. "Your great-grandfather died because he could not stop being one. It was his bad fortune to live at a time when the samurai were no longer necessary. He could not adapt to this, and his anger at the world overwhelmed him. I remember what an angry man he was, Kabuo. He lived for revenge against the Meiji. When they told him he could no longer wear his sword in public he conspired to kill men he hardly knew—government officials, men with families who lived near us, who were kind to us, whose children we played with. He became irrational in his behavior and spoke of purifying himself in such a manner that he would afterward be invulnerable to the Meiji rifles. He was always gone at night. We didn't know where he went. My grandmother bit her nails. She argued with him when he came home in the mornings, but he wouldn't change his ways or explain. His eyes were red, his face rigid. He sat eating from his bowl in silence, wearing his sword in the house. It was said that he had joined other samurai who had been displaced by the Meiji. They roamed the roads disguised, swords in hand, killing government officials. They were bandits, thieves, and renegades. My grandfather—I remember this—was happy to hear of Okubo Toshimichi's assassination, the man who had been responsible for the confiscation of his master's castle and the destruction of his master's army. He smiled, showed his teeth, and drank.

"My grandfather was an expert swordsman," Zenhichi had explained, "but his anger overwhelmed him in the end. It is ironic, because how often did he tell me, when I was your age and he was a contented and peaceful man, of the kind of sword a man should wield? *'The sword that gives life, not the sword that takes life, is the goal* of *the samurai,'* my grandfather said then. The goal of the sword is to give life, not to take it.

"You can be very good with the bokken if you concentrate," said Kabuo's father. "You have it in you. You have only to decide to learn—now, when you are eight."

"I want to," replied Kabuo.

"I know you do," his father said. "But look, your hands."

Kabuo adjusted them.

"Your feet,' said his father. "The front turned in more. Too much weight on the back."

They began to work on the vertical stroke, moving along between the strawberries, the boy advancing, the man retreating, the two of them together in it. "The bokken strikes," Kabuo's father said. "The hips and stomach cut. You must tighten the stomach muscles as the stroke advances. No, you're locking your knees—they must give when you strike. Elbow soft, too, or there is no follow-through, the bokken is cut off from the power of the body. Hips sink, knees and elbows go soft, stomach is hard, cut, turn, again, strike . . ."

Kabuo's father showed him how to hold the wooden sword so that the wrists were flexible and liberated. An hour went by, and then it was time for field work and they put the bokken away. Thereafter, each morning, Kabuo practiced his kendo strokes—the vertical slash that would split a man's head down the bridge of the nose, leaving one eye on each side, the skull cleaved into two parts; the four diagonal strokes—from left and right, upward and downward—that would cleave a man beneath a rib or disjoin an arm deftly; the horizontal stroke swinging in from the left that could sever a man just above the hips; and, finally, the most common of kendo strokes, a horizontal thrust a right-handed man could propel with great force against the left side of his enemy's head.

He practiced these until they were natural to him, part of who he was, the bokken an extension of his hands. By the time he was sixteen there was no one any longer at the community center who could defeat him, not even the half-dozen grown men on the island for whom kendo was a serious hobby, not even his father, who acknowledged his son's triumph without shame. It was said by many in the Kendo Club that Zenhichi, despite his years, remained the superior practitioner, the more pure between father and son, but that the boy, Kabuo, had the stronger fighting spirit and a greater willingness to draw on his dark side in order to achieve a final victory.

It was only after he'd killed four Germans that Kabuo saw how right they were, how they had seen deeply into his heart with the clarity of older people. He was a warrior, and this dark ferocity had been passed down in the blood of the Miyamoto family and he himself was fated to carry it into the next generation. The story of his great-grandfather, the samurai madman, was his own story, too, he saw now. Sometimes, when he felt his anger rising because he had lost his family's strawberry land, he gathered it up into the pit of his gut and stood in the yard with his kendo stick rehearsing the black choreography of his art. He saw only darkness after the war, in the world and in his own soul, everywhere but in the smell of strawberries, in the good scent of his wife and of his three children, a boy and two girls, three gifts. He felt he did not deserve for a moment the happiness his family brought to him, so that late at night, when he couldn't sleep, he imagined that he would write them a note explicating his sin completely. He would leave them and go to suffer alone, and his unhappiness would overwhelm his anger. The violence might at last die out of him and set him free to contemplate his destiny and his next life on the Great Wheel.

Sitting where he sat now, accused of the murder of Carl Heine, it seemed to him he'd found the suffering place he'd fantasized and desired. For Kabuo Miyamoto was suffering in his cell from the fear of his imminent judgment. Perhaps it was now his fate to pay for the lives he had taken in anger. Such was the nature of cause and effect, such was the impermanence of all things. What a mystery life was! Everything was conjoined by mystery and fate, and in his darkened cell he meditated on this and it became increasingly clear to him. Impermanence, cause and effect, suffering, desire, the precious nature of life. Every sentient being straining and pushing at the shell of identity and distinctness. He had the time and the clarity about suffering to embark on the upward path of liberation, which would take him many lives to follow. He would have to gain as much ground as possible and accept that the mountain of his violent sins was too large to climb in this lifetime. He would still be climbing it in the next and the next, and his suffering inevitably would multiply.

16. A WOMAN WARRIOR

Maxine Hong Kingston's tale draws on the rich traditions of Chinese folklore to outline an imaginative experience of martial training. Elements of religious Daoism and magic are incorporated into the story, and the fabulous nature of the action clearly shows one way that the martial arts have been interpreted in the popular imagination—as a domain of activity leading to almost superhuman and magical powers. While best suited for fables (or cinematic tales such as Crouching Tiger, Hidden Dragon) *we once again see the way in which the martial arts engage people's imagination and can serve as a metaphor for personal discovery.*

From *The Woman Warrior* BY MAXINE HONG KINGSTON

When we Chinese girls listened to the adults talk-story, we learned that we failed if we grew up to be but wives or slaves. We could be heroines, swordswomen. Even if she had to rage across all China, a swordswoman got even with anybody who hurt her family. Perhaps women were once so dangerous that they had to have their feet bound. It was a woman who invented white crane boxing only two hundred years ago. She was already an expert pole fighter, daughter of a teacher trained at the Shao-lin temple, where there lived an order of fighting monks. She was combing her hair one morning when a white crane alighted outside her window. She teased it with her pole, which it pushed aside with a soft brush of its wing. Amazed, she dashed outside and tried to knock the crane off its perch. It snapped her pole in two. Recognizing the presence of great power, she asked the spirit of the white crane if it would teach her to fight. It answered with a cry that white crane boxers imitate today. Later the bird returned as an old man, and he guided her boxing for many years. Thus she gave the world a new martial art.

This was one of the tamer, more modern stories, mere introduction. My mother told others that followed swordswomen through woods and palaces for years. Night after night my mother would talk-story until we fell asleep. I couldn't tell where the stories left off and the dreams began, her voice the voice of the heroines in my sleep. And on Sundays, from noon to midnight, we went to the movies at the Confucius Church. We saw swordswomen jump over houses from a standstill; they didn't even need a running start.

At last I saw that I too had been in the presence of great power, my mother talking-story. After I grew up, I heard the chant of Fa Mu Lan, the girl who took her father's place in battle. Instantly I remembered that as a child I had followed my mother about the house, the two of us singing about how Fa Mu Lan fought gloriously and returned alive from war to settle in the village. I had forgotten this chant that was once mine, given me by my mother, who may not have known its power to remind. She said I would grow up a wife and a slave, but she taught me the song of the warrior woman, Fa Mu Lan. I would have to grow up a warrior woman.

The call would come from a bird that flew over our roof. In the brush drawings it looks like the ideograph for "human," two black wings. The bird would cross the sun and lift into the mountains (which look like the ideograph "mountain"), there parting the mist briefly that swirled opaque again. I would be a little girl of seven the day I followed the bird away into the mountains. The brambles would tear off my shoes and the rocks cut my feet and fingers, but I would keep climbing, eyes upward to follow the bird. We would go around and around the tallest mountain, climbing ever upward. I would drink from the river, which I would meet again and again. We would go so high the plants would change, and the river that flows past the village would become a waterfall. At the height where the bird used to disappear, the clouds would gray the world like an ink wash.

Even when I got used to that gray, I would only see peaks as if shaded in pencil, rocks like charcoal rubbings, everything so murky. There would be just two black strokes—the bird. Inside the clouds—inside the dragon's breath—I would not know how many hours or days passed. Suddenly, without noise, I would break clear into a yellow, warm world. New trees would lean toward me at mountain angles, but when I looked for the village, it would have vanished under the clouds.

The bird, now gold so close to the sun, would come to rest on the thatch of a hut, which, until the bird's two feet touched it, was camouflaged as part of the mountainside.

The door opened, and an old man and an old woman came out carrying bowls of rice and soup and a leafy branch of peaches.

"Have you eaten rice today, little girl ?" they greeted me.

"Yes, I have," I said out of politeness. "Thank you."

("No, I haven't," I would have said in real life, mad at the Chinese for lying so much. "I'm starved. Do you have any cookies? I like chocolate chip cookies.")

"We were about to sit down to another meal," the old woman said. "Why don't you eat with us ?"

They just happened to be bringing three rice bowls and three pairs of silver chopsticks out to the plank table under the pines. They gave me an egg, as if it were my birthday, and tea, though they were older than I, but I poured for them. The teapot and the rice pot seemed bottomless, but perhaps not; the old couple ate very little except for peaches.

When the mountains and the pines turned into blue oxen, blue dogs, and blue people standing, the old couple asked me to spend the night in the hut. I thought about the long way down in the ghostly dark and decided yes. The inside of the hut seemed as large as the outdoors. Pine needles covered the floor in thick patterns; someone had carefully arranged the yellow, green, and brown pine needles according to age, When I stepped carelessly and mussed a line, my feet kicked up new blends of earth colors, but the old man and old woman walked so lightly that their feet never stirred the designs by a needle.

A rock grew in the middle of the house, and that was their table. The benches were fallen trees. Ferns and shade flowers grew out of one wall, the mountainside itself. The old couple tucked me into a bed just my width. "Breathe evenly, or you'll lose your balance and fall out," said the woman, covering me with a silk bag stuffed with feathers and herbs. "Opera singers, who begin their training at age five, sleep in beds like this." Then the two of them went outside, and through the window I could see them pull on a rope looped over a branch. The rope was tied to the roof, and the roof opened up like a basket lid. I would sleep with the moon and the stars. I did not see whether the old people slept, so quickly did I drop off, but they would be there waking me with food in the morning.

"Little girl, you have now spent almost a day and a night with us," the old woman said. In the morning light I could see her earlobes pierced with gold. "Do you think you can bear to stay with us for fifteen years? We can train you to become a warrior."

"What about my mother and father ?" I asked.

The old man untied the drinking gourd slung across his back. He lifted the lid by its stem and looked for something in the water. "Ah, there," he said.

At first I saw only water so clear it magnified the fibers in the walls of the gourd. On the surface, I saw only my own round reflection. The old man encircled the neck of the gourd with his thumb and index finger and gave it a shake. As the water shook, then settled, the colors and lights shimmered into a picture, not reflecting anything I could see around me. There at the bottom of the gourd were my mother and father scanning the sky, which was where I was. "It has happened already, then," I could hear my mother say. "I didn't expect it so soon." "You knew from her birth that she would be taken," my father answered. "We'll have to harvest potatoes without her help this year," my mother said, and they turned away toward the fields, straw baskets in their arms. The water shook and became just water again. "Mama. Papa," I called, but they were in the valley and could not hear me.

"What do you want to do?" the old man asked. "You can go back right now if you like. You can go pull sweet potatoes, or you can stay with us and learn how to fight barbarians and bandits."

"You can avenge your village," said the old woman. "You can recapture the harvests the thieves have taken. You can be remembered by the Han people for your dutifulness."

"I'll stay with you," I said.

So the hut became my home, and I found out that the old woman did not arrange the pine needles by hand. She opened the roof; an autumn wind would come up, and the needles fell in braids—brown strands, green strands, yellow strands. The old woman waved her arms in conducting motions; she blew softly with her mouth. I thought, nature certainly works differently on mountains than in valleys.

"The first thing you have to learn," the old woman told me, "is how to be quiet." They left me by streams to watch for animals. "If you're noisy, you'll make the deer go without water."

When I could kneel all day without my legs cramping and my breathing became even, the squirrels would bury their hoardings at the hem of my shirt and then bend their tails in a celebration dance. At night, the mice and toads looked at me, their eyes quick stars and slow stars. Not once would I see a three-legged toad, though; you need strings of cash to bait them.

The two old people led me in exercises that began at dawn and ended at sunset so that I could watch our shadows grow and shrink and grow again, rooted to the earth. I learned to move my fingers, hands, feet, head, and entire body in circles. I walked putting heel down first, toes pointing outward thirty to forty degrees, making the ideograph "eight," making the ideograph "human." Knees bent, I would swing into the slow, measured "square step," the powerful walk into battle. After five years my body became so strong that I could control even the dilations of the pupils inside my irises. I could copy owls and bats, the words for "bat" and "blessing" homonyms. After six years the deer let me run beside them. I could jump twenty feet into the air from a standstill, leaping like a monkey over the hut. Every creature has a hiding skill and a fighting skill a warrior can use. When birds alighted on my palm, I could yield my muscles under their feet and give them no base from which to fly away.

But I could not fly like the bird that led me here, except in large, free dreams.

During the seventh year (I would be fourteen), the two old people led me blindfolded to the mountains of the white tigers. They held me by either elbow and shouted into my ears, "Run. Run. Run." I ran and, not stepping off a cliff at the edge of my toes and not hitting my forehead against a wall, ran faster. A wind buoyed me up over the roots, the rocks, the little hills. We reached the tiger place in no time—a mountain peak three feet three from the sky. We had to bend over.

The old people waved once, slid down the mountain, and disappeared around a tree. The old woman, good with the bow and arrow, took them with her; the old man took the water gourd. I would have to survive barehanded. Snow lay on the ground, and snow fell in loose gusts—another way the dragon breathes. I walked in the direction from which we had come, and when I reached the timberline, I collected wood broken from the cherry tree, the peony, and the walnut, which is the tree of life. Fire, the old people had taught me, is stored in trees that grow red flowers or red berries in the spring or whose leaves turn red in the fall. I took the wood from the protected spots beneath the trees and wrapped it in my scarf to keep dry. I dug where squirrels might have come, stealing one or two nuts at each place. These I also wrapped in my scarf. It is possible, the old people said, for a human being to live for fifty days on water. I would save the roots and nuts for hard climbs, the places where nothing grew, the emergency should I not find the hut. This time there would be no bird to follow.

The first night I burned half of the wood and slept curled against the mountain. I heard the white tigers prowling on the other side of the fire, but I could not distinguish them from the snow patches. The morning rose perfectly. I hurried along, again collecting wood and edibles. I ate nothing and only drank the snow my fires made run.

The first two days were gifts, the fasting so easy to do, I so smug in my strength that on the third day, the hardest, I caught myself sitting on the ground, opening the scarf and staring at the nuts and dry roots. Instead of walking steadily on or even eating, I faded into dreams about the meat meals my mother used to cook, my monk's food forgotten. That night I burned up most of the wood I had collected, unable to sleep for facing my death—if not death here, then death someday. The moon animals that did not hibernate came out to hunt, but I had given up the habits of a carnivore since living with the old people. I would not trap the mice that danced so close or the owls that plunged just outside the fire.

On the fourth and fifth days, my eyesight sharp with hunger, I saw deer and used their trails when our ways coincided. Where the deer nibbled, I gathered the fungus, the fungus of immortality.

At noon on the tenth day I packed snow, white as rice, into the worn center of a rock pointed out to me by a finger of ice, and around the rock I built a fire. In the warming water I put roots, nuts, and the fungus of immortality. For variety I ate a quarter of the nuts and roots raw. Oh, green joyous rush inside my mouth, my head, my stomach, my toes, my soul—the best meal of my life.

One day I found that I was striding long distances without hindrance, my bundle light. Food had become so scarce that I was no longer stopping to collect it. I had walked into dead land. Here even the snow stopped. I did not go back to the richer areas, where I could not stay anyway, but, resolving to fast until I got halfway to the next woods, I started across the dry rocks. Heavily weighed down by the wood on my back, branches poking maddeningly, I had burned almost all of the fuel not to waste strength lugging it.

Somewhere in the dead land I lost count of the days. It seemed as if I had been walking forever; life had never been different from this. An old man and an old woman were help I had only wished for. I was fourteen years old and lost from my village. I was walking in circles. Hadn't I been already found by the old people? Or was that yet to come? I wanted my mother and father. The old man and old woman were only a part of this lostness and this hunger.

One nightfall I ate the last of my food but had enough sticks for a good fire. I stared into the flames, which reminded me about helping my mother with the cooking and made me cry. It was very strange looking through water into fire and seeing my mother again. I nodded, orange and warm.

A white rabbit hopped beside me, and for a moment I thought it was a blob of snow that had fallen out of the sky. The rabbit and I studied each other. Rabbits taste like chickens. My mother and father had taught me how to hit rabbits over the head with wine jugs, then skin them cleanly for fur vests. "It's a cold night to be an animal," I said. "So you want some fire too, do you? Let me put on another branch, then." I would not hit it with the branch. I had learned from rabbits to kick backward. Perhaps this one was sick because normally the animals did not like fire. The rabbit seemed alert enough, however, looking at me so acutely, bounding up to the fire. But it did not stop when it got to the edge. It turned its face once toward me, then jumped into the fire. The fire went down for a moment, as if crouching in surprise, then the flames shot up taller than before. When the fire became calm again, I saw the rabbit had turned into meat, browned just right. I ate it, knowing the rabbit had sacrificed itself for me. It had made me a gift of meat.

When you have been walking through trees hour after hour—and I finally reached trees after the dead land—branches cross out everything, no relief whichever way your head turns until your eyes start to invent new sights. Hunger also changes the world—when eating can't be a habit, then neither can seeing. I saw two people made of gold dancing the earth's dances. They turned so perfectly that together they were the axis of the earth's turning. They were light; they were molten, changing gold—Chinese lion dancers, African lion dancers in midstep. I heard high Javanese bells deepen in midring to Indian bells, Hindu Indian, American Indian. Before my eyes, gold bells shredded into gold tassles that fanned into two royal capes that softened into lions' fur. Manes grew tall into feathers that shone—became light rays. Then the dancers danced the future—a machine-future—in clothes I had never seen before. I am watching the centuries pass in moments because suddenly I understand time, which is spinning and fixed like the North Star. And I understand how working and hoeing are dancing; how peasant clothes are golden, as king's clothes are golden; how one of the dancers is always a man and the other a woman.

The man and the woman grow bigger and bigger, so bright. All light. They are tall angels in two rows. They have high white wings on their backs. Perhaps there are infinite ·angels; perhaps I see two angels in their consecutive moments. I cannot bear their brightness and cover my eyes, which hurt from opening so wide without a blink. When I put my hands down to look again, I recognize the old brown man and the old gray woman walking toward me out of the pine forest.

It would seem that this small crack in the mystery was opened, not so much by the old people's magic, as by hunger. Afterward, whenever I did not eat for long, as during famine or battle, I could stare at ordinary people and see their light and gold. I could see their dance. When I get hungry enough, then killing and falling are dancing too.

The old people fed me hot vegetable soup. Then they asked me to talk-story about what happened in the mountains of the white tigers. I told them that the white tigers had stalked me through the snow but that I had fought them off with burning branches, and my great-grandparents had come to lead me safely through the forests. I had met a rabbit who taught me about self-immolation and how to speed up transmigration: one does not have to become worms first but can change directly into a human being—as in our own humaneness we had just changed bowls of vegetable soup into people too. That made them laugh. "You tell good stories," they said. "Now go to sleep, and tomorrow we will begin your dragon lessons."

"One more thing," I wanted to say. "I saw you and how old you really are." But I was already asleep; it came out only a murmur. I would want to tell them about that last moment of my journey; but it was only one moment out of the weeks that I had been gone, and its telling would keep till morning. Besides, the two people must already know. In the next years, when I suddenly came upon them or when I caught them out of the corners of my eyes, he appeared as a handsome young man, tall with long black hair, and she, as a beautiful young woman who ran bare-legged through the trees. In the spring she dressed like a bride; she wore juniper leaves in her hair and a black embroidered jacket. I learned to shoot accurately because my teachers held the targets. Often when sighting along an arrow, there to the side I would glimpse the young man or young woman, but when I looked directly, he or she would be old again. By this time I had guessed from their manner that the old woman was to the old man a sister or a friend rather than a wife.

After I returned from my survival test, the two old people trained me in dragon ways, which took another eight years. Copying the tigers, their stalking kill and their anger, had been a wild, bloodthirsty joy. Tigers are easy to find, but I needed adult wisdom to know dragons. "You have to infer the whole dragon from the parts you can see and touch," the old people would say. Unlike tigers, dragons are so immense, I would never see one in its entirety. But I could explore the mountains, which are the top of its head. "These mountains are also like the tops of other dragons' heads," the old people would tell me. When climbing the slopes, I could understand that I was a bug riding on a dragon's forehead as it roams through space, its speed so different from my speed that I feel the dragon solid and immobile. In quarries I could see its strata, the dragon's veins and muscles; the minerals, its teeth and bones. I could touch the stones the old woman wore—its bone marrow. I had worked the soil, which is its flesh, and harvested the plants and climbed the trees, which are its hairs. I could listen to its voice in the thunder and feel its breathing in the winds, see its breathing in the clouds. Its tongue is the lightning. And the red that the lightning gives to the world is strong and lucky—in blood, poppies, roses, rubies, the red feathers of birds, the red carp, the cherry tree, the peony, the line alongside the turtle's eyes and the mallard's. In the spring when the dragon awakes, I watched its turnings in the rivers.

The closest I came to seeing a dragon whole was when the old people cut away a small strip of bark on a pine that was over three thousand years old. The resin underneath flows in the swirling shapes of dragons. "If you should decide during your old age that you would like to live another five hundred years, come here and drink ten pounds of this sap," they told me. "But don't do it now. You're too young to decide to live forever." The old people sent me out into thunderstorms to pick the red-cloud herb, which grows only then, a product of dragon's fire and dragon's rain. I brought the leaves to the old man and old woman, and they ate them for immortality.

I learned to make my mind large, as the universe is large, so that there is room for paradoxes. Pearls are bone marrow; pearls come from oysters. The dragon lives in the sky, ocean, marshes, and mountains; and the mountains are also its cranium. Its voice thunders and jingles like copper pans. It breathes fire and water; and sometimes the dragon is one, sometimes many.

I worked every day. When it rained, I exercised in the downpour, grateful not to be pulling sweet potatoes. I moved like the trees in the wind. I was grateful not to be squishing in chicken mud, which I did not have nightmares about so frequently now.

On New Year's mornings, the old man let me look in his water gourd to see my family. They were eating the biggest meal of the year, and I missed them very much. I had felt loved, love pouring from their fingers when the adults tucked red money in our pockets. My two old people did not give me money, but, each year for fifteen years, a bead. After I unwrapped the red paper and rolled the bead about between thumb and fingers, they took it back for safekeeping. We ate monk's food as usual.

By looking into the water gourd I was able to follow the men I would have to execute. Not knowing that I watched, fat men ate meat; fat men drank wine made from the rice; fat men sat on naked little girls. I watched powerful men count their money, and starving men count theirs. When bandits brought their share of raids home, I waited until they took off their masks so I would know the villagers who stole from their neighbors. I studied the generals' faces, their rank-stalks quivering at the backs of their heads. I learned rebels' faces, too, their foreheads tied with wild oaths.

The old man pointed out strengths and weaknesses whenever heroes met in classical battles, but warfare makes a scramble of the beautiful, slow old fights. I saw one young fighter salute his opponent—and five peasants hit him from behind with scythes and hammers. His opponent did not warn him.

"Cheaters!" I yelled. "How am I going to win against cheaters ?"

"Don't worry," the old man said. "You'll never be trapped like that poor amateur. You can see behind you like a bat. Hold the peasants back with one hand and kill the warrior with the other."

17. AN AMERICAN SAMURAI

Dave Lowry, a gifted writer on many topics related to the martial arts and Japanese culture, has written a delightful book on an American youth coming of age and studying the techniques and philosophy of the Yagyu Shinkage Ryu. In the process, he memorably describes the hold that the martial arts come to have on the individual. In the linkage between East and West, tradition and modernity, and the search for self that is a commonality in all places and times, it provides a fitting conclusion for the reader.

From *Autumn Lightning* BY DAVE LOWRY

AUTUMN AND OTHER THINGS JAPANESE

On a nameless sand spit in the swift straits of Kanmon, which separates Kyushu from Honshu, Miyamoto Musashi, Japan's most famous *samurai* folk hero, won the duel that was to secure him a place of honor in stories, romantic novels, and eventually on the movie screen. Musashi's opponent in the match was Sasaki Kojiro, whose phenomenal talent in swordsmanship was accentuated by the distinctive weapon he used, a blade nearly two feet longer than those carried by most swordsmen of the era. Given the reach of his sword and his fearsome reputation—according to one legend he proved his expertise to fellow passengers on a ferry crossing of Lake Biwa by shearing the topknot off a samurai who had gotten into an argument with him, drawing and cutting before the samurai had time to duck—the odds were stacked heavily against Musashi, who, at that time, was still relatively unknown, a shabbily dressed country bumpkin from Mimasaka Province.

Not only did Musashi kill Sasaki, however, he did it with a wooden sword he carved from a spare oar while being rowed out to the site of the duel. Musashi knew, as did many other of Japan's best swordfighters, that the *bokken*, far from being a supplemental training aid in *kenjutsu*, was every bit as lethal as a sharp steel blade.

The bokken in my hands was a curved piece of oak, three feet long and polished to a warm smoothness. Kotaro Sensei was drilling me in the simplest movement of the Yagyu ryu's curriculum: raising the sword above my head and bringing it down along the same path in an uninterrupted motion. He had to stop and correct me constantly. At first I held the bokken the same way one would grip a baseball bat or a golf club, with my hands as close together as possible. Sensei showed me that by separating them, right hand on top near where the guard would be on a *katana*, or real sword, and my left hand almost on the knob at the end of the hilt, I could move my wrists more freely and give the sword a wider range of play. Then he transformed my jerky chopping into a more natural swing, all the while adjusting the parts of my body that refused to cooperate.

"Feet turned so. Legs bent for springing to take shock like shock absorbers for car. Elbows same way. Both feet slide same time forward. Sword up"—not up, but exactly parallel to the floor—"cut now, cut, cut, cut."

Even though I was only slashing at the air in front of me, if my knees and elbows didn't remain flexible my body would wrench against the force of the bokken as it came down. As it was, my wrists were already aching with the unaccustomed weight of the weapon and instead of looking as if I was tugging on a bell rope like Sensei wanted, my cuts resembled those of an arthritic and inebriated woodchopper.

The details—as well as the repetition required to learn them—were endless. Kotaro Sensei's warning to me that more was expected from a *bugeisha* caused me to think he meant I would be forced to endure the tedium of training and to devote myself to the study of the sword or spear or whatever. As my education in the *bujutsu* progressed, I found the expectations were far wider.

In a variety of subtle ways, began to conform to a Japanese manner, of doing certain things; this manner was further refined by Kotaro Sensei and his wife into the samurai way of doing them. They were the sort of lessons that turned a quiet evening meal into an obstacle course of mental alertness and manual dexterity.

I learned how to eat with *hashi* (chopsticks) at the Kotaros table, chasing wriggly pieces of vegetables across plates and picking rice grains from my bowl. When I had achieved a presentable level of skill with hashi, I was instructed in how a bugeisha must use them. Normally, hashi are pushed straight into the mouth along with the piece of food held between them. After a couple of times of observing me eat in that fashion, Sensei casually reached over and popped the chopsticks on the ends with his palm, jamming them against the back of my throat like the tongue depressor of a maniac physician. Not looking forward to another impromptu tonsillectomy, I straightaway mastered the knack of turning the sticks sideways as they approached my mouth—not as a precaution against a dinnertime assailant, but to conduct myself with a samurai bearing.

The rice bowl became the object of the next lesson. A Japanese with normal eating habits grasps his bowl on its underside with his fingertips and lifts it to the level of his mouth. When I did it that way, Sensei calmly tipped the bowl into my face. Then he showed me how to hook my thumb and forefinger over the bowl's rim, just as samurai in Japan had done centuries before to eliminate the danger of being attacked while eating.

Ordinarily, martial artists don't have to spend a lot of time studying knots. The belt worn in judo or karate is wrapped twice around the waist and tied in a simple square knot. For the bugeisha, though, knotcraft was one more art to be practiced and my expertise at it was soon elevated to that of an Eagle Scout's. Instead of the narrow sash of judo or karate, my jacket was kept closed by a wide band of cloth like a kimono's *obi* that was twisted around my middle several times and then fastened in a complicated "figure ten" knot. (The name comes from the Japanese character for ten, which resembles a cross or a "plus" sign.) Over the obi I wore a *hakama* like Sensei's, with four cords of differing lengths that had to be knotted and wrapped in exactly the right way to prevent the skirt from loosening and falling down during practice. There were specific knots used for tying shut the bag where swords are stored, knots for attaching the silk cord *sageo* to a sword's scabbard, and knots for fastening the sageo to the obi once the scabbard is placed there.

Not all the details heaped upon me during those first few months with Sensei were so technical Some involved the etiquette of the dojo, manners and courtesies that had little application in the twentieth century but were a function of the *bushi's* society and therefore important to the continuance of his martial arts. Still, for a boy raised with the informality of jeans and junk food, the rigid conventions of feudal Japan were often hard to fathom.

Besides his left and right foot, for instance, a bugeisha in the dojo must also bear in mind that he has a *shimo ashi* and a *kami ashi*. The foot nearest the left side of the dojo is the shimo ashi; the one on the right side, the kami ashi. *(Kami* means "upper.")The little house I saw on the wall of the dojo before my first lesson was the home of the spirits of Sensei's ancestors and so was called the *kamiza,* or "seat of the upper deities.") In entering or leaving the dojo or approaching the kamiza, I had to be careful about having the correct foot in the correct place. After being reprimanded for forgetting to keep my steps in proper order, I once suggested to Sensei that he put down the footprints like those on dance studio floors. The flippancy failed to make the transition between our cultures. Perhaps, for my sake, it was just as well.

After Sensei's bokken had taught me the folly of bowing without remaining alert, I went on to learn Oriental etiquette in its diverse forms. From a fractional lowering of the eyes with a nod to a forehead on the floor prostration, the wide range of bowing methods was a way of establishing rank or social position for the bushi and everyone else in Japan. One family, the Ogasawara, became the Emily Posts of the fifteenth century, codifying and providing instructions for bowing in a huge volume of etiquette procedures. Every movement of the bows was intended to convey meaning and every meaning was full of subtlety.

Not all the details of an education in the bugei were as minor as leaving the dojo with the appropriate foot or inkling my head at the right angle when bowing. Language was very important, for Kotaro Sensei and his wife spoke little English at home. Even when spoken slowly and with deliberate emphasis, the simplest of words in Japanese can be terribly difficult to understand, and, unlike many European tongues that share a common ancestry in Latin, there are no dependable clues available for translating meaning. To hear a conversation between husband and wife carried on with rapid-fire staccato and imperious brusqueness and be unable to detect even the general intent of the exchange was stunning and frustrating—and frequently led me to the wrong conclusions.

"Uchi no hito!" Mrs. Kotaro would snap briskly from upstairs.

Sensei, puttering in the kitchen, would fire back, "Nan dai?"

"Ima nanji des'ka?"

"Sanji-han!"

"So'ka."

Alone in the dojo, I would be rolling my eyes in acute embarrassment at overhearing what I took to be the opening volleys of a wicked fight, but what sounded to me to be the onset of a bickering quarrel was only Mrs. Kotaro asking the time and Sensei telling her it was half past three. And it could be worse. Listening to them making up a shopping list was enough to make one want to suggest a marriage counselor.

Some of the details of my education in the bugei were equally prosaic, though they were perhaps even more important to my growing up than training itself. Little, for instance, prepared me for life around a middle-aged Japanese woman. And even had there been, Kaoru Kotaro was not always the typical woman of her generation.

Kaoru's great grandfather, Masao Yoshioka, had been one of Kyoto's most renowned painters and calligraphers, a direct descendant of a warrior clan and a samurai himself. His marriage to a daughter of a prosperous Kyoto sake merchant secured the financial position of the Yoshioka family, and so Kaoru was born and raised in wealth. As a young girl, she took for granted everything from her spacious home in Kyoto's garden district to her elegant silk *furisode* kimono. Her days were filled with the preoccupations of the offspring of

Kyoto's privileged; lessons in flower arranging and in learning to pluck with a polished bone plectrum, the long twanging cords of that most Japanese of musical instruments, the *koto*. She was carefully shielded from the harsher realities of the world outside Kyoto, shielded from the atrocities her countrymen committed against China in the twenties and thirties and shielded from all the other events that brought Japan into a world war in the forties.

Kyoto was spared virtually all of the terrible bombing that ravaged most of the rest of Japan during that war, and so through Bataan and Guadalcanal and the Battle of Okinawa, life continued on with some measure of normalcy for Kaoru. But while Kyoto survived, the Yoshioka's sake-brewing facilities in Osaka were reduced, along with the rest of that port city, to a burned-out skeleton. For her family, the Occupation and the emergence of a new Japan meant a desolate period of privation and near bankruptcy until they could reestablish their business. Kaoru remembered that time for me one afternoon, recounting the day the antiques buyer from down the street came to visit the Yoshioka home.

"That first time, he didn't take so much, just some lacquer-ware. But then he came back, and then again, maybe twice a month, and he left with more and more." Her eyes softened in recollection of furniture, and kimono, and finally her great-grandfather's paintings, all carried away to raise money to pay growing debts.

"Mother and Father sold much of what they owned," she told me, "but never the belongings of their children. So even though I was old enough to understand what was happening, and I should have, I was very selfish. I tried just not to think about it." Then one day Kaoru's older brother brought her face-to-face with the desperation of their situation. After demanding a promise of secrecy from her, he told her that he was going to sell the Cherry Tree Sword to the antiques buyer to contribute to the family's meager finances.

The Yoshika's Cherry Tree Sword was a family secret and a private joke among them. It was a beautiful weapon, six generations old, and had been given to Kaoru's brother on his fifth birthday. After the war's end, rumors began circulating that the American authorities would soon be around to confiscate weapons in private homes, to insure the safety of the Occupation Forces. Like other fine swords all over Japan, the Yoshioka blade was wrapped in cloth, sealed in a wooden box, and hidden in the hollow of an old cherry tree in the back yard. It was from there that her brother retrieved it, while Kaoru stood lookout for parents who they both knew would never have allowed so important an heirloom to have been sold. She went with him to hand the sword over to the dealer, who paid for it a price slightly less than what amounted to fifty cents for every year of the weapon's age

"Then I knew what losing the war was all about," she told me simply. Two days later, she made her own trip to the dealer, carrying her most precious possession, a Yuzen kimono, its delicate pattern of maple leaves dyed in the Ebanui process.

The privations and hardships of the Occupation left their mark on Kaoru. While she never lost the gentility of her upbringing, deep inside she was somehow tempered by the experiences of the postwar poverty, I think, resulting in a woman who was an enigma to me. Often Japanese women of Kaoru's age tend to be gregarious, gathering at one another's houses for the flimsiest of reasons to talk. Kaoru, though, kept to herself; other than her husband, she had few people who could have been called friends. She had learned to live within herself, it seemed, to endure and to experience life's pleasures and pains, never showing any more feeling about either of them than she wanted to. On occasion, we would go for hikes along an Ozark stream bed together and there she would explain to me, with the most perceptive sensitivity, why this rock had qualities of shape and hue that would add to the beauty of a Japanese-style garden, and that one did not. Yet I approached subjects like loneliness or love with trepidation, for she was rarely willing to talk about them. As she told me once, "It isn't that we are without feelings, it is only that we prefer to cultivate them in private."

Mrs. Kotaro went on cultivating her feelings in a private, hidden way, with the same care in which she cultivated her iris in the yard. Even though she would never be openly affectionate toward me in public, she gradually developed a kind of signal aimed at me when she was proud of me or happy with what I'd done. Looking at me without a word, she would slowly close both eyes, then open them, with the faintest trace of a smile on her face. It was barely noticeable and always silent, but in her own way, I came to know that Kaoru was speaking volumes to me.

Mrs. Kotaro was forced to speak volumes to me in another area of our relationship, though, when she undertook the task of teaching me to speak Japanese.

As hard as Sensei pushed me in training with the bokken, his wife was even more relentless in teaching me *Nihongo*—Japanese—once I expressed an interest. Her method was to sit across from me at the dining room table and pronounce a word, getting me to repeat it exactly. I mean *exactly*.

"Sake," she said with labored emphasis.

"Sake," I replied for the fifth time.

"No, no. *Sake* is word for alcohol drink. Word for salmon fish is sake. Try to say sake, make 'ke' part come out lower, like you are sad."

"Sake. Sake. Sake," I repeated, though my "ke" was never once mournful enough to please her.

Strangely, while Mrs. Kotaro demanded that my Japanese be painfully correct, she rarely made any attempt to improve her marginal English and, in fact, became miffed at the mildest hint that her accent was irregular. We were at a MacDonald's restaurant one evening and it was her turn to place her order with the girl at the counter.

"May I help you?" the girl bubbled.

"Please," replied Mrs. Kotaro. "Duburo hamabuguru an' a miriku shaku."

"I beg your pardon. Could you repeat that?" She looked at Mrs. Kotaro as if reading her lips would be an aid. Irritated at MacDonald's practice of hiring workers who didn't understand perfectly good English, Mrs. Kotaro repeated the order with the same results. I interrupted.

"She'll have a double hamburger and a milk shake."

"Oh . . . . What flavor is that shake?"

Without the slightest hesitation Mrs. Kotaro answered confidently.

"Banirra."

Following a stubbornly resisted bout with compulsory Spanish in primary school, my opinion had been pretty much that if anyone had anything worthwhile to say, they would say it in English. Sensei, though, had a knack that I would later come to realize he shared with all gifted teachers. He didn't order me to study Japanese with his wife, didn't suggest I get one of the university's Japanese students who visited at the Kotaro household to tutor me. He just made it clear he considered fluency in the language a necessary requirement for training in the bujutsu and that I wouldn't be taken seriously until I did as well. He *expected* it.

The pressures Kotaro Sensei exerted in this indirect way were very traditionally Japanese and they were successful because I wanted so badly to be accepted as a bugeisha of the Yagyu Shin-kage ryu. Sensei had only to note that most Westerners, due to diets high in fatty meats, have an unpleasantly rancid odor detectable at once to the Japanese nose and I immediately diverted my afterschool route to the university gym to shower before going on to the dojo. I scoured myself to a chafed pink with the gym's industrial soap to avoid the *bata kusai*, "butter stinker," pejorative I had heard him and other Japanese use sometimes in describing Westerners. Unconsciously, I adopted the same kinds of conforming behavior the bushi were subjected to in their feudalism. It was the same kind of conforming that would lead them to slit open their bellies rather than risk disappointing their masters,

My daily practice remained centered around the bokken. I attacked invisible enemies, splitting them in half with the vertical stroke that began with the sword raised above my head. When I could execute that cut with some accuracy, I moved on to the diagonal strokes and the more powerful horizontal slashes of the Yagyu style that started at waist level and were driven like a home run hitter's swing with the force of the hips. Through thousands of repetitions, I progressed slowly in the basics of kenjutsu: foot-work, rhythm, and timing. Cut, step forward, cut. Turn, cut, cut. Turn, cut, turn. Whatever Sensei's directions, I could move, my arms and legs starting and stopping at the same instant as my sword. I grew more efficient at clenching my abdominal muscles to let them do the work. According to Yagyu teaching, the arms would make a sword *hit*, while the mass of the hips and abdominal muscles would *cut*, all the way through the target. In every lesson, the emphasis was on delivering a clean blow capable of killing instantly. I was learning to do it and I soon came to fancy myself quite a swordsman.

Then Sensei took me into the backyard where he had set up an old automobile tire fixed to a wooden frame, with the top of the tire about waist level. Sensei explained that swinging a sword in the air was fine for practicing correct motion, but without the actual contact of the sword striking a resilient object, a bugeisha could never develop the strength to make a cut that would be able to cleave an opponent at one stroke. When I first struck down at the tire, I had the sensation that an electrical current was running through it, traveling up the length of my bokken and into me. My wrists had once ached with the effort of learning the cut, but now, when I applied it against the hard rubber, I flinched as a reverberating shock stung from my fingertips to the deepest muscles of my shoulders. I had to be tutored all over again in making the correct body actions: sinking my hips and keeping knees and elbows flexible in order to take the concussive lash that came back when I chopped against the tire.

Under the pewter skies of November, starlings wheeled from the wind, searching for the flock with which they would roost at night and paying no attention to the whacking sounds of the worn tire absorbing my blows. The splashy oranges and scarlets of autumn faded to a resigned brown. Leaves fell around me, gathering in heaps in Mrs. Kotaro's iris beds, defying her attempts to keep them out. At last, she gave in and even helped, mounding them against the sides of the beds as protection from the coming cold.

Sensei's insistence on a thorough understanding of the basics of swordsmanship was well-founded. My legs were toughened by the hours of churning up and down the dojo floor, and when practicing outside I could feel my feet gripping the cold ground underneath them, melding muscle and bone into an extension of the earth when the sword cut. My body hardened.

My mind, too, underwent a change. It wasn't anything like arrogance. If ever I showed the slightest inclination toward becoming, as the Japanese adage goes, "a nail sticking up from the roof," Kotaro Sensei was there to pound me back into place. The change in my attitude came as an inkling sense of meaning I found in the monotonous movements of the Yagyu style of fencing that germinated in me a little at a time under Sensei's watchful guidance. My bujutsu skills were to be an added attraction to me, as I had it figured—another of my prized things, like my French running shoes and my plastic inflatable chair. They weren't, of course. The practice was boring (even more so, in retrospect, than those damnable Spanish lessons in fifth grade), Sensei was frequently harsh and distant, and neither girls nor happiness seemed threatening to smother me just because I was spending each afternoon smacking the hell out of a four-ply radial. Yet increasingly, I was compelled to continue.

My involvement in the bugei in no small way set me apart from many of my friends who were caught up in the social maelstrom of the sixties, flung from protests at the war in Vietnam to the alluring refuge of drug experimentation to the dizzying euphoria of dances and drinking parties—all of which were features of high school life then. For others, those years might have been reddened with the hate for an unjust war or blurred by the vertigo of a pharmacopoeia of recreational chemistry, but for my generation, too young to be drafted, too old to be shielded from all that was deliciously new, the sixties were a crazy kaleidoscope of image and sensation. It was the mad modness of Carnaby Street fashions, the far-outness of Woodstock ("and there were guys and girls right on the news, swimming in a pond, *naked");* it was frayed jeans, incense, beads and headbands, and hair. It was the burnt rope pungency of marijuana, pizza's biting spice, the metal clash of rock music.

Although a marvelously exciting time to be squeezing out of childhood's shell into the dangerous freedom of the unknown, it was not idyllic. Along with the glamour and glitter of the new, there was that which was threatened merely for being old. In the opinions of my classmates, the meaningful and worthwhile could often be sacrificed wholesale for the chic. Being "with it" was regarded as vital, though "it" was largely undefinable. Nothing was so passé as yesterday's items. Last season was nostalgia; last year, ancient history.

The classical swordsmanship of the Yagyu ryu was hardly modern, and having to conform to ways considered obsolete a century before I was born couldn't very well complement the popular dictum of doing one's own thing. Yet perhaps because of my family roots, sunk into the granite bordered fields of Massachusetts with all their staid and enduring neatness, I felt no hard tugging toward unconvention. A New England identification with the past steered me away from that and into the realm of the bugei of old Japan. The inherited Puritan sense of discipline kept me there despite every shift of fad and fashion the sixties had to offer.

Like most of my adolescent peers, I devoted much of my high school years to finding out what I wanted for myself. I wasn't sure what that was going to be, but between November's frosts and December's snows, somewhere around the one hundred thousandth crack I took at the furrowed tread of the Firestone, I decided the place to look for it was going to be in the dojo of Kotaro Ryokichi of the Yagyu Shinkage ryu.

PERMISSIONS

The following pages constitute an extension of the copyright page.